THE MORAL PHILOSOPHY OF GANDHI

If man is to survive, if civilization is to survive and flower in freedom, truth, and decency, the remainder of the twentieth century and what lies beyond must belong not to Lenin or Trotsky, not to Marx or Mao or Ho or Che, but to Mahatma Gandhi.

Louis Fischer

THE MORAL PHILOSOPHY OF GANDHI

JALADHAR PAL

GYAN PUBLISHING HOUSE
New Delhi-110002

The Moral Philosophy of Gandhi

(Philosophy, Religion, Gandhian Study, History, Politics)

ISBN: 81-212-0524-7

Published in 2015 by
Gyan Publishing House,
23 Ansari Road, Darya Ganj
New Delhi-110002

Laser Typesetting at A.S. Printers, Delhi.

Printed at Mehra Offset Works, Delhi.

To

Ujjwla Pal

my mother

who always inspires me.

CONTENTS

ACKNOWLEDGEMENTS

Acknowledgement of debt or gratitude is formal without any real warmth or feeling of thankfulness behind it, so much so that it sometimes seems to be mechanical. Because the gratitude that we pay to somebody is a human, and the motto behind it is purely a psychical phenomenon which is strictly individualistic and personal. The outward manifestation of our mental life especially of feeling often falls short; and the gulf between the inner life and the outer expression through signs and symbols, i.e., language, remains unbridgeable owing to inadequacy of our media of expression. So acknowledgement of gratitude implies more than it appears to be. Still we do not yield.

The present study is a modified version of a dissertation for which the university of Calcutta had conferred the degree of Ph.D on me in 1984.

The prevailing conditions of eighties of India are the stimuli that have inspired me in this strenuous work. I ardently expected the emergence of another *naked fakir* for the redemption of the integrity of India.

Naturally, the books that I have read during this period and in the past have immensely helped me in writing this volume. Wherever a definite idea has been borrowed, I have acknowledged it in the proper context. I am indebted to some distinguished Western and Indian thinkers for the help I have received from their works. I convey my heartfelt gratitude to all of them.

My gratitude to Dr. Buddhadeva Bhattacharyya, the supervisor of this dissertation, knows no bounds. During the composition his sagacious guidance has enriched my meagre knowledge immensely. His affectionate treatment and tolerance to me go far off the relation that is usually found between the teacher and the taught. Here expression falls short of my feeling of gratitude.

I cannot help acknowledging debt to Anjali, my wife, who has virtually steered our household life during this hardship and faced all troubles. The troubles on this strenuous journey seemed worthwhile in her happy company. Her love and forbearance have been a constant stimuli to me during this period. And Babu and Bappa, my two sons, were deprived partially of my affection and care for a cause dimly known to them. Here also expression falls short of my heart.

I intend to extend my thanks to the librarian and the courteous staff of my college library for their enthusiastic assistance in making available to me many of the books referred in this volume. I pay hearty thanks to M/s. Gyan Publishing House without the active co-operation of which, I think, this book would not have been published.

JALADHAR PAL

2 October, 1997

1

INTRODUCTION

Generations to come, it may be, will scarce believe that such a one as this ever in flesh and blood, walked upon this earth.[1]

Mohandas Karamchand Gandhi alias Mahatma Gandhi is a household name in India. He has become, so to say, a part and parcel of our national life. "His name is familiar to such a degree that there is scarcely a peasant or a factory worker who does not consider him to be a friend of human kind."[2] In one way or another Gandhi has figured as a constant irritant in our way of life, mode of thought and action. To put it otherwise, his immense influence on the speech, thought and action of Indian life is beyond question. But this response to Gandhi is often emotional and sentimental leading to reverential dogmatism and blind adoration. Some worship him as a prophet standing beyond space and time. E.M. Forster observes, that Gandhi "had his roots outside time, and drew strength thence."[3] Rene Fulop Miller opines, "A man who will live in history and in Heaven with Buddha, Socrates, and Jesus!"[4] The view of Albert Einstein cited in the beginning of this section also contributes to this end. To look into the sky and receive aerial message in response to earthly queries may fulfil the cravings of a devotee. But it fails to quench the thirst of an analytical mind which demands objective assessment of a phenomenon in spatio-temporal relations. The historicity of it is indispensable and hence should be taken into account. That is to say, an accurate and precise appraisal of Gandhi is to be made in the objective context and historical perspective. The passage from the awkward youth from Kathiawad to the uncrowned emperor of the first half of the twentieth century India has no magic, or anything supersensuous about it. The ascent of Moniya of a 'Bania' (grocer) family to the eminence of the *mahatma* (great soul) of the world is a story of an uphill journey of the spirit which involves facing severe ordeals and coming out the more purified from each such experience. In Nietzschean terms, this is 'human, all too human.' The aim of this treatise is an objective and analytical study of the aforesaid 'passage' and 'ascent' of Gandhi in a humanistic perspective. For "if he is a Mahatma or Great Soul, he is also a man of the people amongst the people."[5] This is an important and noteworthy fact.

This enquiry proposes to fulfil a historical necessity too. During the freedom struggle of the early forties the mass populace from Kashmir to Cape Comorin, from Assam to Ahmedabad, irrespective of caste and creed, race and religion, almost instantaneously responded to the call of Gandhi. Now, in these years of the nineties he has become a mere statue to be garlanded on some occasions; an idol or a fetish to render lip-service for political careerists. People are cynical, sarcastic, and sometimes allergic to his name, fame and thought. As a renowned scholar of Gandhian thought observes, "In India today, the wearing of a 'Gandhi Cap' evokes suspicion rather than respect."[6] This hears harsh but is well said. The young generation, especially those who were born after independence, regard him as a 'charismatic' leader, a utopian, 'an ineffectual angel beating his wings in the void.' That is to say, the rich legacy that he left to us has suffered a deplorable devaluation in our national life during the last forty odd years. Of course, his so-called disciples, except very few, are no less responsible than the irreverent scoffers of today for this. Correspondence of preaching and practice, the *elan vital* of Gandhian thought, is utterly disregarded or forgotten. And who does not know that mere preaching without practical demonstration sinks in the quicksand of life? The lack of proper cultivation and implementation of Gandhian concepts that stood some years ago as a symbol of national harmony for which Gandhi sacrificed his life is nowadays a far cry. The heart-pricking communal disturbances of Moradabad, Meerut, Allahabad, Lucknow, Jamshedpur, Mumbai; and butchery of innocent civilians by the so-called rebels in eastern India, etc., remind us of the Mahatma who fearlessly moved about amidst communal frenzy for the promotion of brotherhood amongst humanity. As Earl Mountbatten says, "In the Punjab we have 55,000 soldiers and large scale rioting on our hands. In Bengal our forces consist of one man, and there is no rioting. As a serving officer, as well as an administrator, may I be allowed to pay my tribute to the One-Man Boundary Force....."[7] And bonafide citizens of India are declared alien and *persona non grata* in some parts of the country. To put it briefly, our country is passing through a very critical period of her history. Perhaps, preaching and practice, revival and reorientation of Gandhian concepts may, as it did in the recent past, restore our national harmony and place it on a solid foundation. One may or may not accept this prescription. Differences of opinion are inevitable in scholastic study. Further, this prescription may provoke a sceptical query as to its political relevance, since Gandhi's image conjured up till now before the public is more of a political leader than of one with a many-sided personality. But, as mentioned above, this treatise is solely concerned with an analytical and objective study of Gandhi: his life and works with special reference to moral concepts. Accordingly, merits and demerits of his thought have been herein appreciated or censured, purely from an objective standpoint. This is purely an objective study of Gandhi in an objective context without any bias on the part of the present researcher.

Here, at the outset, it would be judicious to sound a note of caution regarding the nature of Gandhi's method and subject-matter which are, so to say, in a jumbled state. This has led some scholars to utter confusion. Joan V. Bondurant, for example, observes, "It is the unsystematized and often inconsistent jungle of Gandhi's writings that makes it difficult but tempting to others to formulate a 'Gandhian Philosophy'."[8] T.K. Mahadevan comments, "In the main, however, our misperception of the Gandhian teaching arises from one single connected factor—the diffuse character of Gandhi's writings and their relative inaccessibility. For an inveterate activist, Gandhi's literary output is breathtaking. On a rough count, during the fifty years of his public life, he ground out some ten million words, now patiently put together in his *Collected Works*."[9] Indeed, his sensitive mind responded to the call of mass-populace under various circumstances without any reservation. This gave birth to an incoherent, unsystematic mess of thought that passes for Gandhism. Of course, his synthetic outlook or viewpoint of looking at the world and life in its totality is to a great extent responsible for this. Moreover, he had not the intention to be taken as a seer. He was neither a theorist nor an arm-chair philosopher who peeped into the problems of life from an ivory tower. He was an actionist par excellence. During his public life for about fifty years he dedicated himself heart and soul to the service of humanity. In that long strenuous journey he cared little for dry syllogistic rules; injunctions or formalities to be observed in an intellectual and academic discipline. The inconsistencies and discrepancies that we come across in his thought are to be considered in that perspective. We shall deal with it elaborately at a suitable place later on.

One more word and with this we intend to initiate the central idea of this treatise. It requires no special mention that a considerable research work has already been done on Gandhi's thought; and consequently a vast number of literature on it has been fast accumulating day by day. But most of it is primarily concerned with Gandhi, the political leader and Gandhi, the social reformer. That is to say, Gandhi's politics and sociology were mostly the pivotal point of those works. And hence scant justice has been done to Gandhi, the moral scientist. The books that generally pass for moral treatise on Gandhian thought are superficial and shallow studies so far. They fail to present the Gandhian moral concepts in a systematic, coherent and scientific way. This is the reason why Gandhian moral concepts till today indispensably need to be properly arranged, categorized and schematized into a moral science. It is to this end that this treatise has been dedicated. His fundamental postulates, the modes of application together with their culmination have been arranged to show the development and evolution of Gandhian moral concepts. Of course, we have interpreted them in the wide context of his other ideas and ideals with a relevant comparison and contrast with other pioneers of thought of the world. It is with this end in view that his philosophical outlook (metaphysical, epistemological, religious views, etc.), sociological and economic views (sarvodaya, education, etc., satyagraha, his moral mode of fighting evils, etc.) has been elucidated, though briefly, to present Gandhi's moral concepts more plausibly to the mass populace, especially to the young generation, who are facing a grave moral crisis in a blind, confused and angry way not only in India but throughout the world.

References

1. Albert Einstein, in D.G. Tendulkar et al. (ed.), *Gandhi, His Life and Work*, p. xi.
2. S. Radhakrishnan, 'Gandhi's Religion and Politics', in S. Radhakrishnan (ed.), *Mahatma Gandhi: Essays & Reflections on His Life and Work*, p. 37.
3. E.M. Forster, 'Mahatma Gandhi', in S. Radhakrishnan (ed.), *op. cit.*, p. 349.

4. Rene Fulop Miller, *Gandhi: The Holy Man*, trans. F.S. Flint & D.F. Tait, p. 44.
5. Carl Heath, 'M.K. Gandhi: 'Apostle of Light and Truth-Force', in S. Radhakrishnan (ed.), *op. cit.*, p. 84.
6. Raghavan N. Iyer, *The Moral and Political Thought of Mahatma Gandhi*, pp. 378-79.
7. Lord Mountbatten, cited in Pyarelal, *Mahatma Gandhi : The Last Phase*, vol. II, p. 382; also Shaheed Suhrawardy, "Look at the miracle that Mahatmaji has wrought in a single day", *ibid.*, p. 369.
8. Joan V. Bondurant, *Conquest of Violence*, p. vii.
9. T.K. Mahadevan (ed.), *Truth and Non-Violence*, p. 2.

relations, from the tradition of human civilization, both Oriental and Occidental, and above all, from his ceaseless and varied experiments with truth in the course of his life. He acknowledges debt to the forerunners in the same way of thinking without any reservation. His writings, especially the *Autobiography*, brilliantly expose this which brings into our views the roots, the influences which gave shape and form to his thought. This acknowledgement enriches his greatness immeasurably. In this chapter we shall briefly deal with the hereditary and environmental factors that primarily contributed to the development and evolution of Gandhi's mind and ideas.

Influence of Father: Truth and non-violence for which Mohandas stood was inherited to a considerable degree from his father Karamchand alias 'Kaba'. Kaba Gandhi's encounter with the assistant political agent of the British empire contributed to this end. Once the political agent put Kaba Gandhi who protested vehemently against his ill-behaviour under detention. But Kaba was adamant and did not demean himself by abject capitulation. The agent could not but help release him.[3] Later in his life, Mohandas, as Mahatma, recollects this valorous exploit of his father; and was perhaps, inspired by it. On another occasion Kaba Gandhi refused a huge monetary offer from the ruler on the plea that it was not in the original terms. This anticipates the Gandhian style of saying no to all graft, and untruth. Indeed, Mohandas inherited from his father a mature moral sense and a firm determination to follow truth which manifested itself, bit by bit, in his life.

Mahatma Gandhi, an apostle of non-violence, got first lesson in it, perhaps, from his father. In his teens, in a sudden fit of juvenile delinquency, Gandhi stole a piece of gold to pay his debtor. Conscience pricked him, the mental agony become unbearable. He confessed the guilt in black and white to his ailing father from whose eyes pearl-drops trickled down. These pearl-drops of love cleansed his heart and washed his sin away. Thus father's life and ideas cast a considerable influence on Gandhi's works and ideas.

Influence of Mother: Putlibai, the mother of Mohan, had strong commonsense and sharp intelligence. The outstanding impression which she left on the memory of Gandhi was that of saintliness. She was deeply religious and never took meals without saying and offering daily prayers. The practice of self-restraint that Gandhiji observed through fasting and daily prayers had undoubtedly its roots in that of his mother. An analytical study of his life reveals that the basic tenets of Hinduism, Jainism and Buddhism were first infused into the mind of Moniya by his mother. The virtue of non-violence was also instilled into his mind by his saintly mother. Once a scorpion was about to bite Putlibai of which young Moniya grew alarmed instantaneously. She gently said to her son, "Now it will neither harm me, nor I it." F.B. Fisher comments on this incident, "Lessons like this, coming from no printed page, but from the book of life, influenced the future life of a discerning boy. This gentle puritan mother was one of the biggest factors in making Gandhi what he is today, a prophet of self-mastery, of rational control through control of self."[4] This is marvellously said, and requires no elaboration.

Regarding disciplinary observances he was deeply influenced by his mother. While staying in London, in the face of so many temptations he boldly declares, "A vow is a vow ... my mother's definition was the definition binding on me."[5] Here a mark of caution is noteworthy. While Putlibai's fasting had a private end, i.e., of self-abnegation and self-realization, Gandhiji, on the other hand, apart from the above private ends, had some public, i.e., political and social ends behind the facade of fasting.

She was one of the factors contributing towards the formation of Gandhi's concept of ideal womanhood and housewife. She was "the first one to rise and the last to go to bed," eating only "when she could manage it." As the pivotal point of a huge joint family she kindled the spirit of altruism in her children. During the closing days Gandhi recollects, "I owe them [Gandhi's disciplinary resolutions] first of all to my saintly mother and to my good nurse. These were noble women. They taught me to tell the truth and not to fear."[6] Thus it is evident that the twin basic tenets of Gandhian thought, Truth and Non-violence, were initiated into young Gandhi's mind by his saintly mother.

Influence of Wife: In the scriptures of Hinduism the wife is described variously as *Jaya* (*Jayate asyam eti*, i.e., the husband takes new birth in the wife); *ardhangini* (the better half); *sahadharmacharini* (partner in the performance of duty); *sahakamarthacharini* (partner in enjoyment of pleasures); *sakha-sachib* (friend and secretary), etc.[7] All these above adjectives got their best manifestation in Kasturba, the wife of Gandhi.

Since their marriage in 1882 till her death in 1944—a long conjugal life for about sixty-two years—they went hand in hand without any break. They started as 'playing the husband and wife;' attained maturity together both mentally and physically; struggled jointly along with others in South Africa and India, in the family and later in community life, inside and outside the prison. She followed Gandhi's footsteps day and night like the shadow at his back. She cooked his food, cleansed his clothing, nursed him in ailment; and served him till her last breath. His becoming a Mahatma from a prey to lust and carnal desire owes much to her. By dint of her tireless service, immeasurable restraint, infinite patience and boundless love she won the heart of Gandhi and brought out the highest potentials latent in his personality. She became an indivisible part of his being, and was woven into him like warf and woof. In the words of Gandhi, "Kasturba has been my mother, friend, nurse, cook, bottle-washer and all these things .... We have come to a reasonable understanding that I should have all the honours and she should have all the drudgery."[8] M. Kalarthi aptly observes, "Bapu without Ba would not have been the Bapu as we know him."[9]

Gandhi directly or indirectly learnt the lesson of humility from Kasturba. While staying in Durban one day Gandhi forced her to clean the pots of a Christian clerk. As she did not perform it voluntarily, he "caught her by the hand, dragged the helpless woman to the gate." But when she entreated him in the name of Heaven to behave himself he felt ashamed and shut the gate. He recollects, "The wife, with her matchless powers of endurance, has always been the victor."[10] Indeed, Kasturba was the soul of humility.

Gandhi's vow of *brahmacarya* (celibacy) was successful only due to natural response from Kasturba. Gandhi resolved to observe celibacy in order to render more service to mankind; and in its observance Kasturba surpassed him at the first stage. Kasturba ceased to be his wife, and he looked upon her hereafter as mother. Thus the Shastric description of wife as *Jaya*, is fulfilled here in toto. Their contended couple life is a noble instance of monogamous family in modern society.

Kasturba's personality was a curious mixture of submission and assertion at the same time. Although Gandhi described her as the acme of modesty still he had to yield on some occasion to her. When none could attain success in pursuing Gandhi to take milk, it was Kasturba who with her sublime love could win over him. In his words, "I can no more describe my feeling for Hinduism than for my own wife. She moves me as no other woman in the world can...."[11]

On another occasion Gandhi himself entertained some guests without disturbing Kasturba who was then taking rest. When she enquired of him about the matter Gandhi replied in a tone of apology, "As you know, and to tell you the truth, I am at such times, afraid of you." "You? afraid of me?"[12] was the response with a loud laugh. From the above two incidents we should not brand Gandhi as a henpecked personality. In course of our discussion we shall find that Gandhi feared none except God. His so-called obedience to Kasturba was inspired by an unlimited sublime love for her. They interacted and made each other.

Influence of Rambha: Here a few lines regarding the influence of Rambha, the housemaid, would not be irrelevant. Gandhi's contact with her, although short-lived and trifling, had a deep-rooted influence on his mind. In his youth he lost interest in temples on account of 'glitter and pomp,' and rumours of immorality. Rambha suggested the repetition of *Ramanama* as a remedy for the fear of ghosts and evil spirits. This suggestion acted as an armour in moments of crisis throughout his life. To quote Gandhi, "I think it is due to the seed sown by that good woman Rambha that today *Ramanama* is an infallible remedy for me."[13] Thus two of the cardinal virtues, Truth and Fearlessness, that he preached at a later period of his life, owes, directly or indirectly, to Rambha, the housemaid.

Influence of Raychand Bhai: Gandhi writes, "Three moderns have left a deep impress on my life, and captivated me: Raychandbhai by his living contact; Tolstoy by his book, *The Kingdom of God is within you*; and Ruskin by his *Unto This Last.*"[14] "I have said elsewhere that in moulding my inner life Tolstoy and Ruskin vied with Kavi. But Kavi's influence was undoubtedly deeper if only because I had come in closest personal touch with him."[15] Rajchandra Ravjibhai Mehta alias Raychand (Raichand) Bhai was a jeweller, a poet. He was spotless in character; had a vast knowledge of the scriptures and a burning passion for self-realization. He was also known as *Shatavadhani* that is, one who can remember or attend to a hundred things simultaneously. Born of a Vaishnava father and Jaina mother Raychand dedicated himself towards Jainism and showed a deep leaning to Vaishnavaism towards the end of his life. To him God is self and self is God. God has no abode outside the self which is a conscious substance. It is permanent and eternal. In its contact with the earthly things it gets polluted in *Karmic* veils. But a sound knowledge of its true nature leads to Nirvana. Perfection, Non-attachment, Truth, Non-violence, Universal benevolence, etc., are cardinal virtues which deemed universal observance.[16]

A critical analysis will reveal that the 'living contact' between the two was very short since they first met in 1891 and Kavi died in 1900. During this short period they had a scanty correspondence and very few meetings. Gandhi describes his relationship with Raychand in Gujarati as *gaadha parichay* (deep acquaintance), and not *angata mitrata* (intimate friendship).

The influence of Raychandbhai on Gandhi was not so deep as he claimed. Both of them understood it clearly that their paths were different. D.K. Bedekar observes, "... Raichand came to have a tremendous influence on Gandhi, though the two youths were so dissimilar in their life-styles and urges."[17] Here the mental disposition of Gandhi when he first met Raychand is noteworthy. On the same day his elder brother disclosed the news of his mother's death which caused 'severe shock'; and his 'cherished hopes were shattered'. He was also then physically exhausted due to seasickness. So Raychand cast a mystical spell over Gandhi who was exhausted both mentally and physically. Later correspondence of Gandhi from South Africa was urged by a spiritual crisis that he suffered due to scant knowledge of Hinduism amongst people of other faiths. After that correspondence Gandhi came to India in 1896. So far as it is recorded in Raychand's biography, the two friends did not meet again. Hence the 'living contact' between the two was a dim and bloodless one. The fact is that the 'Mahatma' was then sprouting in Gandhi of flesh and blood who fervently looked for a guideline; and found it in Raychand for the moment. Raychandbhai initiated Gandhi in a zealous quest to know the inherent potentiality of human beings. He acted as a midwife of Gandhi to deliver his own being. In this sense Kavi's influence on Gandhi is remarkable which should not, however, be stretched too far.

Here a few lines regarding Gokhale is necessary. Gandhi says, "I have declared myself a disciple in the political field of one whose portrait you have asked me to unveil this morning and I have him as my *Rajaguru*. It was in 1896 that I made this declaration, and I do not regret having made the choice."[18] G.K. Gokhale was one of the pioneers of our freedom struggle. He was a spiritualist, a 'saintly politician' who had freedom of India as the ultimate goal of life. His was not a lip-service but an ardent move to spiritualize the political institutions and political life of India. We shall see in this treatise that Gandhi tried to follow this trend throughout his life.

Influence of Western Thinkers

(a) *Socrates:* Socrates (470-399 B.C.) was the wisest and most controversial person of his time. He adopted the dialectical method to know the truth which was also synonymous with good. According to Socrates, there are two kinds of knowledge, the apparent and insecure one; and the real and permanent one. Moral and virtuous life is elemental to human beings; and hence there is no holiday from it. It is this moral fervour of Socrates that attracted, we shall see shortly, Gandhi most.

Gandhi's acquaintance with Socratic teachings may be traced out in the formative period of his mind during which he was infusing *satyagrahi* spirit into the Indians of South Africa against British imperialism. In 1907 Gandhi appraised Socrates as an eternal moral preacher. To quote him, "Many men were opposed to the morality which Socrates observed in this day."[19] He was so impressed by Socrates that he hailed him as a hero. Gandhi recommended 'Defence and Death of Socrates' as a follow up study to *Hind Swaraj*.[20] So Socratic influence on Gandhi appears to have been deep and remarkable.

Both these thinkers were spiritualists and idealists. Both of them were misunderstood and misrepresented by their followers and critics. In this sense they were tragic figures amongst their contemporaries. Still the history of mankind records their transcendence of spatio-temporal limitation. And the influence of Socratic teachings on Gandhian thought, is not negligible. Socrates is one of the pioneers whom Gandhi held in the highest esteem and followed.

(b) *Emerson:* Ralph Waldo Emerson (1803-82), an American, a radical transcendentalist was dissatisfied with the contemporary trend of philosophy—the mechanistic conception of the universe and the psychology of sensation. He fervently prayed for divine existence within him that would enhance his self-reliance, and promote individualism and moral regeneration.

Gandhi's first acquaintance with the Emersonian thought occurred during his stay in London as a student. In a letter to his son Manilal, Gandhi writes in 1909, "...I have been reading Emerson, Ruskin and Mazzini... please tell Maganlalbhai that I would advise him to read Emerson's essays"...[21] Thus Gandhi was so much influenced by Emersonian philosophy that he could not help propagating it. The sweet note of this influence lasted for years, and the writings of this western teacher were his favourite reading both in South Africa and afterwards in India. Gandhi's association with the Emerson Club in South Africa and later admission into London Emerson Club as a member in 1914 prove his hearty and ardent respect for Emerson. The impression that Emersonian philosophy engraved on young Gandhi's mind found maturity, and manifold expression on different occasions in his middle age, and continued to inspire him till the last days of his life. But in spite of his hearty appreciation of Emersonian thought he did not follow him in toto.

(c) *Carlyle* : Thomas Carlyle (1795-1881) : Carlyle was an essayist and historian of eminence. In *The French Revolution* he preached the idea of history as a 'divine scripture' and concluded that the French Revolution was a just and inevitable judgement upon the folly and selfishness of the monarchy and nobility. The terror of God's glory and the immortality of the soul are the two predominating features of his thought. He stirred the conscience of his time, and helped people to enjoy 'the dignity of their work'.

During his stay in London as a student Gandhi read Carlyle's monumental work *on Heroes, Heroworship, and the Heroic in History.* While in Jail he read Carlyle's *French Revolution* and that book confirmed the glory of non-violence in his mind.

Gandhi's antipathy for utilitarianism which preaches 'greatest happiness of the greatest number' is well known. Gandhian theory of sarvodaya and utilitarianism are opposed to each other though the distinction seems to be trifling in practice. Utilitarianism got its materialistic and hedonistic tone in the writings of Carlyle. As W.L. Davidson comments, "One wonders how far Thomas Carlyle, with his vehement rhetoric, is responsible for this."[22] In this context Buddhadeva Bhattacharyya observes, "It may be just a guess—for we are not sure—that Gandhi who read Carlyle might have formed his opinion from that source."[23] Indeed, it would not be unsound to think that Gandhi who read Carlyle avidly, and heard much of him in London, was consciously or unconsciously influenced by him regarding his antipathy for utilitarianism.

Fearlessness is one of the cardinal virtues prescribed by Gandhi. Here also he quotes one of Carlyle's maxims, "There is practically nothing impossible for those who would persevere in the face of the heaviest odds. Nothing is possible for those who would brag, bluster and merely make a brave show.... Every noble work is at first impossible."[24] Thus Gandhi's virtues of courage and fearlessness had, perhaps, their roots, directly or indirectly, in Carlyle's preachings.

(d) *Tolstoy:* Count Leo Tolstoy (1828-1910), the Russian writer and thinker was dissatisfied with Christianity and the then Russian society. In the later period of his life he renounced the 'intolerable luxury' of inheritance and lived till death the simple and natural life of a rustic. In his *Autobiography* Gandhi remembers Tolstoy as one of the 'three moderns' who influenced him by his books, especially *The Kingdom of God is within You* "the profound morality, truthfulness and independent thinking of which overwhelmed him and left an abiding impression on his mind."[25] Commenting on his 'satyagraha movement in South Africa', Gandhi appreciates the spiritual patronage of Tolstoy who blessed the movement 'in its infancy' as a ray of hope to the downtrodden people of the earth. Not only this, in his last letter to Gandhi, Tolstoy congratulates him heartily on his yeomen's service to the cause of the downtrodden in Transvaal by saying, "your activity in the Transvaal, as it seems to us, at this end of the world, is the most essential work, the most important of all the work now being done in the world, wherein... all the world, will unavoidably take part."[26] Great men think alike. Gandhi and Tolstoy, though separated by geographical barriers, had much in common.

Tolstoy prescribed as well as practised non-violence, non-killing, manual or bread labour, non-possession and minimum needs. Condemnation of landlordism, military enterprises, praising and helping the pacifists and non-resistants are few of his innumerable performances.

Eclecticism is one of the salient features of Gandhian thought. All was grist that came to his mill. His originality was composed of many simples. He derived mental nourishment from different eastern and western sources. But the uniqueness of his personality is that he did not get lost in them. He seized the essential and noble ideas from them and assimilated all into a system which is undoubtedly his own. Although he revered and followed Tolstoy he was not a thoroughgoing Tolstoyan.

(e) *Ruskin:* John Ruskin (1819-1900), in the last half of nineteenth century author, social reformer, and art critic, was a shining star in the world of thought. Ruskin's mother, a strict disciplinarian, moulded his character, and steered the future course of his thought to some extent. The Bible became the backbone of his thought and works in a sense.

While making a train journey from Johannesburg to Durban Ghandhi read Ruskin's *Unto This Last* the 'magic spell' of which shook his whole being and inspired him to live an ideal life as prescribed in it. "The book was impossible to lay aside, once I had begun it. It gripped me... I believe that I discovered some of my deepest convictions reflected in this great book of Ruskin, and that is why it so captured me and made me transform my life."[27] This book acted as a midwife to bring to light the philanthropic convictions that were hidden with all potentialities in Gandhi.

Both Gandhi and Ruskin proclaimed the approach of a new era. They dominated the world of thought of their times and created a tremendous commotion in their surroundings, near and far. Ruskin had undoubtedly an influence on Gandhi. But in transmuting the Ruskinnian lesson into action Gandhi was original. Herein lies the uniqueness of Gandhian thought.

(f) *Thoreau:* Henry David Thoreau (1817-62), the American writer, poet and philosopher naturalist and iconoclast also impressed Gandhi. He advised people to "I live free and uncommitted," as far as possible. The unwanted complexity of modern civilization is the root cause of all sorts of wretchedness. Another characteristic of Thoreauvian thought is the glorification of manual labour. In 'Civil Disobedience' he proclaims the supremacy of an individual conscience, and condemns the state as a machinery of oppression. Thoreau preached best possible cooperation with all people and establishments when they led towards good, and maximum possible non-cooperation including violent resistance when they promoted evil. He believed in the inherent purity of every individual; emphasized the supremacy of conscience under all circumstances, and had the vision of a future society without any government.

Here it is noteworthy that Thoreau himself was much benefitted by the thoughts of ancient India. He was an ardent admirer of Buddha whom he often named beside Christ. The *Gita*, the *Upanisadas* and the *Puranas* (particularly *Vishnu Purana*) were his favourite readings. The sacred scriptures of ancient India acted as a common platform between these two great thinkers.

Oscar Cargill comments, "Thoreau's idea... attracted the attention of Mohandas Gandhi while he was a student of Cambridge."[28] This piece of information does not tally with the facts as given in Gandhi's *Autobiography*. Again, Henry S. Canby tells us that Gandhi came to know of 'Civil Disobedience' during his stay in London in 1907 as a student of law.[29] Moreover, a cursory glance at a chronology of Gandhi's life will reveal that in 1907 he was struggling with British imperialism in South Africa. So the above two views are, undoubtedly, unsound. E.H. Erikson views the eventful life of Gandhi from a psychoanalyst's angle of vision. On 11 September 1906, Gandhi delivered a fiery speech against 'Black Act' to Indian delegates from all parts of Transvaal. At the gathering Gandhi proclaimed, "... I can boldly declare, and with certainty that so long as there is even a handful of men true to their pledge, there can only be one end to the struggle and that is victory."[30] E. Erikson comments on this, "Gandhi would often repeat this faith, and it is hard to believe that at that time he was not familiar with Thoreau's statement that 'I know this well, that if one thousand... is done for ever.' (*supra*).[31]

In a letter to Henry S. Salt, Gandhi admits the deep influence of 'Civil Disobedience' on him by saying, "The essay seemed to be so convincing and truthful that I felt the need of knowing more of Thoreau, and I came across your life of him, his *Walden,* and other essays, all of which I read with great pleasure, and equal profit."[32] In 1909, after his return from Pretoria jail where he had been detained for refusing to produce certificates of registration and fingerprints he tells us that he had an opportunity there to study about thirty books, Thoreau was one of them. In 1910 he published *Hind Swaraj* in the preface of which he reverentially acknowledges his debt to Thoreau and others. In 1913 Gandhi launched a movement, passive resistance, against the Immigrant's Regulation Bill and quotes Thoreau, "We share the belief, with Thoreau, that one true passive resister is enough to win a victory for right."[33] In the month of April 1919 Gandhi conducted a movement throughout India against *The Rowlatt Act;* and in that movement a satyagraha leaflet containing extensive extracts from 'The Duty of Civil Disobedience' by one Henry Thoreau, 'school master of Massachusetts' was distributed amongst the mass along with many other publications.[34] While explaining the meaning and mode of non-cooperation in 1920 Gandhi quotes Thoreau, "Possession of power and riches is a crime under an unjust government; poverty in that case is a virtue only to strengthen his position."[35] In the month of April 1930, the British Government promulgated an ordinance imposing restrictions on the press. Gandhi gave a clarion call to the people to oppose it vehemently and quoted Thoreau, "Let us realize the wise dictum of Thoreau, that it is difficult, under tyrannical rule, for honest men to be wealthy. If we have decided to hand over our bodies without murmur to the authorities, let us also equally be ready to hand over our property to them and not sell our souls."[36] Here also we find Gandhi to be in agreement with Thoreau.

Thoreauvian influence on Gandhi was so deep that whenever he faced any difficulty he took refuge in Thoreau's ideals and quoted his preachings without any hesitation. To a question put by Baldwin, Gandhi replied, "[Thoreau's Civil Disobedience] contained the essence of his political philosophy, not only as India's struggle related to the British, but as to his own views of the relation of citizens to Government."[37] On 1 July 1942 he wrote a letter to President Roosevelt in which he again acknowledges gratitude by saying, "I have profited greatly by the writings of Thoreau and Emerson."[38] In the same year he made an appeal to American friends, "You have given me a teacher in Thoreau, who furnished me through his essay 'On the Duty of Civil Disobedience' scientific confirmation of what I was doing in South Africa."[39] Thus Thoreauvian influence is explicit both in speeches and activities of Gandhi.

A relevant question may be asked: Did Gandhi borrow satyagraha from Thoreau? Gandhi denies it outright. In a letter to P.K. Rao of the Servants of Indian Society, Gandhi writes, "The statement that I had derived my idea of 'Civil Disobedience' from the writings of Thoreau is wrong."[40] Indeed, satyagraha, Gandhi's mode of fighting evils, is a dynamic principle which derived nourishment and enriched itself only through experience. The ideal of *satyagraha*, not the title, was working in the form of a hypothesis in his mind long before he read Thoreau in jail in 1906. Thus the assumption that Gandhi borrowed his idea of satyagraha from Thoreau, in spite of the fact that he enriched it, in his words, "scientific confirmation,—by Thoreauvian ideal of 'Civil Disobedience', does not appear to be chronologically sound".

Nevertheless, Thoreau's influence on Gandhi is beyond doubt. Gandhi personally appraises the Thoreauvian essay 'Civil Disobedience' as a 'masterly treatise' which has 'left a deep impression on him.' B.N. Ganguli observes, "Gandhi's spiritual kinship with the American recluse Thoreau has become almost apocryphal and has passed into legend."[41] From the formative period till the last phase of his public life we find him often quoting Thoreau to strengthen his position. To quote Gandhi, "From Thoreau and Ruskin I could find out arguments in favour of our fight."[42] Thus Thoreau's influence on Gandhi is immense and immeasurable.

Influence of Different Religions

(a) *Hinduism*: Gandhi was out and out theist, a Vaisnava of the Ramananda cult. He often called himself a *sanatan* Hindu, a *vedantist.* He finds solace, a *kamdhenu* in the *Gita*. To quote him "My notions were an outcome of a study of the *Gita, Ramayana, Mahabharata, Upanishads,* etc."[43] Vincent Sheean observes, "Centuries of Hinduism produced him.... he was profoundly Hindu."[44] Ranjee Shahani comments, "Gandhi could only have been a Hindu. His qualities and defects were peculiar to his race. In India alone could he have been born."[45] It is in Hinduism that he lived and breathed and derived mental nourishment. Although a staunch Hindu, Gandhi reorientated and innovated the traditional concepts in his own way at the demand of circumstances. In this light he was both a traditionalist and a reformist at the same time.[46]

(b) *Islam:* Gandhi's *Autobiography* narrates that he inherited from his father a firm sense of 'toleration for all faiths.' While staying in England as a student he read Carlyle's *Heroes and Heroworship* from which Gandhi "learnt of the Prophet's greatness and bravery and austere living."[47] The puritian in Gandhi was impressed, and spontaneously responded to it. His reading of Washington Irving's *Life of Mahomet and His Successors* raised Muhammad in his estimation.[48] This regard for Islam possessed his mind throughout life. During the last phase of his life Gandhi declares, "I certainly regard Islam as one of the inspired religions, and therefore the Holy Quran as an inspired book and Muhammad as one of the prophets."[49] Hence comes his emphatic "conclusion that the teaching of the Quran is essentially in favour of non-violence. Non-violence is better than violence, it is said in the Quran."[50] Although the concept of non-violence had already become firmly entrusted in his mind at that period it would not be unwise to surmise that the *Koran* was one of the fountains from which he quenched the thirst for non-violence. It had a pragmatic, prudential and far-going impact on those days of communal disturbances. Furthermore, Gandhi remembers with reverence the distinctive contribution of Islam to the cultural heritage of India. "Its unadulterated belief in the oneness of God and a practical application of the truth of the brotherhood of man for those who are nominally within its fold"[51] impressed Gandhi deeply. His concept of oneness of mankind as a whole got confirmation, and perhaps inspiration from that source.

Both Muhammad and Gandhi were men of action. They practised what they preached. The Prophet's supreme, practical instinct as a Reformer, combined with his intense faith in God as the sole Creator and Director of the Universe, has been a constant strength and support to Mahatma Gandhi himself in his own struggle.[52]

(c) *Christianity:* During his student days in London he read the Bible. The Old Testament did not attract the attention of young Gandhi. "But the New Testament produced a different impression, especially the Sermon on the Mount which went straight to my heart. I compared it with the *Gita.*"[53] The Sermon on the Mount, seemed to him contain the nucleus of Christianity; and endeared Jesus to him. In this light he was ready to call himself a Christian. He found practically no "difference between the Sermon on the Mount and the Bhagavad Gita...."[54] On many occasions Gandhi found consolation and derived inspiration and strength from the Bible, particularly from the New Testament.[55] 'During his first sojourn in South Africa it was Christian influence that had kept alive in him the religious sense'.[56] The influence was so strong that, he confesses, "there was a time when his mind was wavering between Hinduism and Christianity'[57] Here further explanation regarding the influence of Christianity on him is unnecessary. Gandhi often quotes Jesus and acknowledges his indebtedness to Christianity. Gandhi's concept of non-violence got nourishment and confirmation in Christianity. In Gandhi's eyes, Jesus Christ represented the purest form of passive resistance or soul force; and Jesus was the king of satyagrahis. Gandhi openly declares, "Christ died on the cross with a crown of thorns on his head defying the might of a whole empire. And if I raise resistance of a non-violent character, I simply and humbly follow in the footsteps of the great teachers..."[58] "The virtues of mercy, non-violence, love and truth in any man can be truly tested only when they are pitted against ruthlessness, violence, hate and untruth... History relates this of Jesus Christ. With his dying breath on the Cross, he is reported to have said: "Father, forgive them for they know not what they do."[59] Western scholars like Rev. J.J. Doke and Horace Alexander claim Christianity to be Gandhi's primary source of non-violence. To a question put by Rev. Doke, Gandhi replies, "It was the New Testament which really awakened me to the rightness and value of passive Resistance...."[60] The truth is that Gandhi learnt the first lesson of non-violence from his father. And this concept was already active in his young mind. The reading of the Bible only kindled this noble trait of his personality. Thus the Bible was not the primary source although the Gandhian concept of non-violence derived nourishment from it.

Gandhian economics was immensely influenced by Christian thought. Renunciation and non-possession are the pivotal points of Gandhian economic thought. Gandhi preached and practised the life of simplicity and poverty. This he owes, directly or indirectly, to Christianity to some extent.

In political life Gandhi endeavoured to innovate political institutions spiritually. Here also he acknowledges debt to Christ. To quote Gandhi, "Jesus, in my humble opinion, was a prince among politicians. He did render unto Caesar that which was Caesar's. He gave the devil his due. He ever shunned him and is reported never once to have yielded to his incantations...."[61]

Gandhi's concept of *brahmacharyya* too was enriched by his intimate relation to Christianity. Buddhadeva Bhattacharyya comments, "His intimate Christian association, it may be presumed, cast a permanent influence on his concept of sin, purity and sexual morality."[62]

Sarvodaya is a key concept of Gandhian sociology. He derived the concept from Ruskin's *Unto This Last* which again had its roots in the Bible. *Sarvodaya* or the welfare of all at all levels, spiritual and material, is the concern of both Christianity and Gandhian thought.

Fasting as a means of self-purification plays a significant role in Gandhi's life. Although the influences of his mother and cultural heritage both are primary still, the influence of Jesus is admitted by Gandhi as one of the contributing factors. In his words, "Buddha, Jesus and Mohamed fasted so as to see God face to face.... In my fasts I have but followed these great examples no doubt for ends much less noble than theirs."[63]

Gandhi's concept of conscience or 'the inner voice' was, perhaps, an outcome of the Christian influence. The *Sanatan* Hinduism does not believe in each individual following his or her own conscience to work out his or her liberation.

In spite of other contributing factors the Christian influence on Gandhian concept of bread-labour is most evident. Gandhi says, "Thou shalt earn thy bread by the sweat of thy brow"— This is a *mahavakya* of Jesus Christ. The *Gita* also seems to say the same.[64] Gandhi was a vegetarian by birth. And his liking for vegetarianism was strengthened by Christian and Western contact. He quotes from Genesis 1-29-32 and Isaiah (XI. 6-9) of the Bible in favour of vegetarianism. Gandhi declares, that "before the Fall we were vegetarians and we shall be vegetarians again in times of restitution."[65] Whenever he faces a problem he searches for inspiration and strength in the Bible. Although he had enough arguments in favour of vegetarianism in Hindu scriptures, he quotes the Bible only to render it a universal appeal.

Gandhi's utmost emphasis on individuality, and his clarion call to an individual to struggle, if nobody helps, alone was directly or indirectly influenced, to some extent, by Christianity. Gandhi's favourite Christian hymn was that of Newman, "Lead Kindly Light", and he often repeated the phrase "one step enough for me."

The Cross symbolized the law of suffering to Gandhi, and inspired him to go through the ordeals that he faced during the struggle for independence. In his words, "Jesus's death on calvary was his crowning achievement.... Harishchandra is remembered for his endless sufferings. India cannot attain freedom until lakhs upon lakhs have become fearless and are ready to seek imprisonment in their innocence."[66] Thus in those hard days of freedom struggle Jesus was a fountain of strength and inspiration to Gandhi.

Gandhi dedicated his whole life towards the service of humanity which he owed much to Christian influence. He often appraised Jesus as a great teacher, as a saviour of humanity. It would not be inept if we say that Gandhi was, to a great extent, influenced by Christianity in his service towards humanity.

Gandhi's entire life may be summed up as a ceaseless quest for truth which, a close scrutiny would reveal, is not different from that of Christianity. His close Christian associates (Andrews, Doke, Holmes, Horace, etc.,) felt, in his quest for truth, the true spirit of Christ in action. On the other hand, his intimate relationship with them would not have been possible without a genuine understanding, on his part, of Christianity. Indeed, his views are so closely allied to Christianity, and its influence on him is so deep that the claim to call him a Christian is difficult to put aside.

(d) *Jainism:* "Jainism was, perhaps, the most logical of all faiths, and its most remarkable characteristic was its scrupulous regard for all things that lived."[67]

Kathiawad is the home and heartland of Jainism. It has produced a galaxy of Jaina thinkers like King Kumarpala, the spiritual leader Hiravijaya Suri, the littérateur Hemachandra; the great Mahavira; the legendary *tirthankaras*; Vijaya Dharma Suri, the Jaina *Acharyya* contemporary to Gandhi, and Raichand Bhai, etc. Gandhi's technique of *padayatra* (walking tour) reminds us that of Vijaya Dharma Suri. Gandhi being born and brought up in Kathiawad might have been influenced, consciously or unconsciously, by the technique of walking tour of Jaina teachers.

The influence of Jainism is also evident in the political and economic concepts of Gandhi. The Jaina *Acharyyas*, although holding an exalted and revered position, looked after the welfare of all sections of people. The Banias (merchants) owing to their weaknesses, both physical and political, solicited the favour of rulers through the intervention of *Acharyyas*. In this way the ancient Banias of Kathiawad adopted non-violence against rulers and sought the good graces of *Acharyyas* in order to foster their mercantile interest. Gandhi, a saintly personality like the *Acharyyas*, launched *Swadeshi* movement to make the Indians self-sufficient in every walk of life. But unconsciously helped the mercantile interest of swadeshi enterprises by boycotting foreign goods. His dauntless Salt March to Dandi in 1930 formed an important phase in this regard. The theory of Trusteeship of wealth can be traced in germinal form in the fable and history of ancient Kathiawad. Kumarpala, the great Jaina king of Kathiawad, renounced his right to the property of those who left no male heirs after their death. Customarily, such properties used to vest in the King.[68]

Jainism also cast a deep impression on the ethico-religious life of Gandhi. The virtue of *ahimsa* (non-violence) was preached by Buddhism, Jainism and Hinduism in India long ago. Buddhism emphasized the non-killing of animal life and non-injury to men. Jainism proceeds a step further and prescribes non-killing of animal life, even of the smallest insect. Gandhi revives this ethics of non-violence of ancient India and applies it to every sphere of life. He drew inspiration from Jain ethics of the cultivation of friendship for all creatures, compassion for the wretched, delight in the virtuous and indifference to the vicious. Further, Gandhi's observance of vows was also a direct or indirect impact of his Jain contact. C. Devanesen comments, "Gandhi's faith in the efficacy of vows is traced to the influence of his mother, Putlibai. It is not unlikely, however, that she herself was unconsciously influenced by old Jain traditions."[69]

In the formulation of his epistemological theories also the impact of Jainism is evident. He called himself an *anekantavadi* and a *syadvadi*. He says, "I have therefore no objection to calling it real and unreal, and thus being called an *anekantavadi* or a *syadvadi*. But my *syadvada* is not the *syadvada* of the learned, it is peculiarly my own."[70]

(e) *Parsis:* The Parsis, Zorathustrians, migrated from Persia into Western India in the eighth century. The hardship of life blessed them with foresight which inspired them to receive European contact enthusiastically. And consequently, they attained progress and prosperity in every walk of life while other Indians were lagging behind due to their conservative outlook. They were pioneers of every movement, explorers of new avenues, beginners of new enterprises. In a word, they initiated almost all social changes that came about in Western India, especially in Gujarat. Gandhi was influenced by many Parsi people of his time, he chose the Parsi dress for his wife and children on the eve of his first voyage with them to South Africa. Thus in his youth Gandhi imitated the 'most civilized' Parsis and arranged the family provisions after their fashion.

In his political life he came in contact with many Parsi leaders to whom he paid tribute in later life. Of them, the names of Dadabhai Naoroji, Dinshaw E. Wacha, Sir Pherozeshah Mehta, Parsi Rustomji, etc. are noteworthy. During his stay in London as a student he was much impressed by the speech and personality of Naoroji. The lectures delivered by Naoroji were of immense benefit to him. Gandhi writes, "Whenever an address by him was announced, I would attend it, listen to him from a corner of the hall and go away after having feasted my eyes and ears."[71]

Sir Pherozeshah Mehta acted as friend, philosopher, and guide in the social and political life of Gandhi as Raichand Bhai helped him in religious crisis. Sir Mehta helped him to address a public meeting in Bombay the speech of which was approved and liked by Sir Mehta. Various types of help on several occasions from Sir Mehta inspired Gandhi to respect this outstanding personality of the early phase of freedom movement as the unscaleable Himalaya.

In 1897 Rustomji, at the risk of his life, sheltered Gandhi along with his wife and children when a rioting white mob surrounded his house. Their regard for each other was so deep that in 1899 Gandhi appointed him the head of Trustees to look after the gifts bestowed on him before his return to India. Rustomji responded immediately to Gandhi's call of financial assistance with which a small charitable hospital was established there. Furthermore, the generosity of R.J. Tata, a Parsi business magnate, helped Gandhi immensely to launch *satyagraha* movement in South Africa.

During the period of prohibition movement in Bombay in 1939 Gandhi pays tribute to the Parsi community as a whole for their yeoman's service to humanity. Thus the Parsis were 'Godsend' to the Gujarati, to Gandhi himself. "The Parsis, so to say, were sent by Khuda from Iran exclusively for the service of Gujarati."[72] He enthusiastically read the Zorathustrian literature; and very highly regarded Zoroaster like Jesus and Mohammed.

None can deny the impact of the surroundings upon him. The environmental factors, both natural and man-made, contribute towards the growth of human personality. During his stay in England as a student the social, political, economic, cultural, religious trends, mores and customs, etc., of the West contributed to a great extent to the development and formation of the mental aptitude of Gandhi. Kipling's reactionary attitude "Oh, East is East, and West is West and never the twin shall meet"[73] had no appeal to Gandhi. In him the traditional concepts like truth, non-violence, tolerance, celibacy, etc., got blended with activism, boldness, energy, cleanliness, etc., of the West. His 'discovery of India' was performed through the study of invaluable books like *Song Celestial* and *Light of Asia* by Western writers. There he read, as stated above, the *Holy Bible* which greatly influenced him. Apart from this spiritual illumination, his exclusive love for vegetarianism was enhanced during this period. The preaching and practice of the dictum: 'cleanliness is next to godliness' in the West taught him much. He also learnt activism of the West which he introduced into the life of semi-comatic people who awakened from a slumber of past centuries and joined hands with him to build up a new brave India. His political consciousness was enriched and polished at that time. The intellectual trend, emergence of new ideas and new values, individualistic liberalist movement, romantic reaction against industrial civilization, left deep impression on the mind of young Gandhi. This impact is most evident in Gandhi's political movements and programmes. He aimed at, after the Western pattern, a sovereign independent parliamentary state along with its functional organs such as conference, resolutions, votes, newspapers, etc. Hence we may call him, after Albert Schweitzer, 'a Modern European' or more specifically an Euro-Indian.

To sum up: With Tennyson's Ulysses Gandhi could boldly declare, "I am a part of all that I have met."[74] Of the thousand roots we have taken into account only a few, the salient ones. He shared the views, Oriental and Occidental, in his own way. As he was an ardent and ceaseless experimenter in truth, his eclectic yet sceptic mind tested all views which he came across the hard grindstone of his own experience; and modified, changed, enriched, sometimes abandoned, ideas in the light of experience and surroundings. Modern scientific and technological advancement has achieved its goal to a great extent. The world has shrunk into a home and geographical barriers among peoples no longer exist. Nowadays, nobody is astonished at the influence that an American exerts on an Indian or an Indian exercises on a Russian. What interests us is the effect of that influence. In the absorption of ideas of the aforesaid personalities Gandhi was as original as a common man.

One point more, and this is regarding his religious ideas. We have discussed the influence of Islam, Christianity, Buddhism, Jainism, Zoroastrianism the impact of political personalities was stronger than their religion, i.e., Zoroastrianism, not to speak of Hinduism, on him. He regarded all these faiths as 'inspired religions.' They are not exclusive, but complementary to one another. Their true spirit, true meaning lies in their interdependence and interrelation.[75] The Hinduism of his faith is not sectarian. It includes all that is best of Islam, Hinduism, Christianity, Buddhism, Jainism, Zoroastrianism, etc.[76] "It harmonises them and gives them reality."[77] Hence the formulae of sectarianism here is meaningless. What he calls universal religion is nothing but humanism. In the bosom of his humanism all faiths of the world were immersed. It is in humanism that Gandhi lived and breathed; and that is the keynote of Gandhian thought.

References

1. M.K. Gandhi, *An Autobiography, op. cit.*, p. 230.
2. William Shakespeare, *The Merchant of Venice*, Act I, sc. I, *op. cit.*, p. 224.
3. *An Autobiography*, p. 3.
4. F.B. Fisher, *That Strange Little Brown Man*, p. 9.

5. *An Autobiography*, pp. 34-41.
6. Vincent Sheean, *Lead, Kindly Light*, p. 187.
7. Kalidas, the ancient Sanskrit poet, describes a wife, "*Grihini sachib sakhimitha/ priyasishya lalite Kalabidho* (wife, counsellor, companion in solitude and beloved pupil in fine arts), (*Raghuvansam* 8/67). Also Shakespeare, "Thy husband is thy lord, thy life, thy keeper/Thy head, thy sovereign... When they (wife) are bound to serve, love, and obey." (*The Taming of the Shrew*, 5/2; *op. cit.*, p. 314).
8. Tendulkar, *Mahatma*, vol. II, p. 298.
9. M. Kalarthi, *Ba and Bapu*, p. x.
10. *An Autobiography*, p. 205; also F.B. Fisher, *op. cit.*, p. 153.
11. Cited in M. Kalarthi, *op. cit.*, p. iii.
12. *Ibid.*, p. 49.
13. *An Autobiography*, pp. 23, 34.
14. *Ibid.*, p. 65.
15. *Modern Review*, vol. XLVII, no. 6, June 1930, p. 681.
16. For his views and works see J.N. Farquhar, *Modern Religious Movements in India*, pp. 327-28; Goverdhandas S. Brahmachari, *Mahatma Gandhi and Kavi Rajchandraji, Questions-Answers*; D.K. Bedekar, *Towards Understanding Gandhi*, pp. 77-95.
17. D.K. Bedekar, *op. cit.*, p. 87.
18. *Speeches and Writings of Mahatma Gandhi*, G.A. Natesan & Co. (4th ed.), p. 1009; *also An Autobiography*, pp. 169-74.
19. *Ethical Religion*, p. 16.
20. *CWMG*, vol. X, p. 65; also Tendulkar, *op. cit.*, vol. I, p. 242.
21. *Ibid.*, vol. IX, pp. 208-9.
22. William L. Davidson, *Political Thought in England—The Utilitarians from Benthan to Mill*, p. 5.
23. Buddhadeva Bhattacharyya, *Evolution of the Political Philosophy of Gandhi*, p. 140.
24. *Young India* (8 March 1928), p. 75.
25. *An Autobiography*, pp. 65, 99, 115.
26. Tendulkar, *op. cit.*, vol. I, p. 123; also *CWMG*, vol. X, p. 370.
27. *An Autobiography*, p. 220.
28. Oscar Cargill (ed.), *op. cit.*, pp. xiii-iv.
29. Henry Seidel Canby, 'Thoreau and the Machine Age' in *Yale Review*, (March 1931), vol. XX, p. 517.
30. M.K. Gandhi, *Satyagraha in South Africa*, p. 106.
31. E.H. Erikson, *Gandhi's Truth*, p. 200.
32. Henry S. Salt, *Company I have Kept*, London, 1930, pp. 100-1, in George Hendrick's article cited above, p. 167.
33. *CWMG*, vol. XII, p. 58.
34. *Ibid.*, vol. XV, p. 497.
35. *Ibid.*, vol. XVII, p. 490.
36. Tendulkar, *op. cit.*, vol. III, p. 36.
37. *Thoreau Society Bulletin*, April 1945, cited in George Hendrick's article, *op. cit.*,

p. 165. Elsewhere Gandhi concludes, "Hence the classical statement of Thoreau, that government is best which governs the least." *Young India*, 2 July 1931, p. 162.

38. Tendulkar, *op. cit.*, vol. VI, p. 116.
39. *Ibid.*, p. 143.
40. Letter to P. Kodananda Rao dated 10 September 1935, quoted in *Incidents in Gandhi's Life*, edited by Chandrashankar Shukla, 1949, pp. 114-15.
41. B.N. Ganguli, *op. cit.*, p. 49.
42. M.K. Gandhi, *Speeches and Writings of Mahatma Gandhi*, p. 226.
43. *Harijan*, 3 October 1936, p. 266.
44. Vincent Sheean, *op. cit.*, pp. 6, 19.
45. Ranjee Shahani, *Mr. Gandhi*, p. 1.
46. See chapter VII (sec. Non-Violence), chapters VIII-IX Nine (sec. Gandhi's Humanism).
47. *An Autobiography*, p. 49.
48. *Ibid.*, p. 115.
49. *Harijan*, 13 July 1940, p. 207.
50. *Ibid.*, p. 193.
51. *Young India*, 21 March 1929, p. 95; also *Young India*, 30 April 1931, p. 88.
52. C.F. Andrews, *Mahatma Gandhi's Ideas*, pp. 62-64.
53. *An Autobiography*, p. 49.
54. *Young India*, 22 December 1927, p. 426; also 31 December 1931, p. 429.
55. *Ibid.*, 25 February 1920, in *Ibid., 1919-22, op. cit.*, p. 50.
56. *An Autobiography*, p. 194.
57. *CWMG*, vol. XIX, p. 571.
58. *Ibid.*, vol. XVIII, p. 408.
59. *Harijan*, 28 April 1946, p. 106.
60. J.J. Doke, *M.K. Gandhi: An Indian Patriot in South Africa*, p. 84.
61. *CWMG*, vol. XVIII, p. 196.
62. Buddhadeva Bhattacharyya, *op. cit.*, p. 384.
63. *Harijan*, 18 March 1939, p. 56.
64. *CWMG*, vol. XIV, p. 135.
65. The spirit of *The Moral Basis of Vegetarianism*, pp. 23-28.
66. *CWMG*, vol. XX, p. 284.
67. *Ibid.*, vol. IV, p. 370.
68. *Ras Mala*, I, p. 188, cited in C. Devanesen, *op. cit.*, p. 31.
69. *Ibid.*, p. 30.
70. *Young India*, 21 January 1926, p. 30.
71. *An Autobiography*, p. 58.
72. *CWMG*, vol. IX, p. 460.
73. Rudyard Kipling, 'The Ballad of East and West', in *Barrack-Room Ballads and Other Verses*, p. 75.
74. A.L. Tennyson, *Poems of Alfred Lord Tennyson*, p. 155.
75. *CWMG*, vol. XXIX, 1968, p. 326.
76. *Harijan*, 30 April 1938, p. 99.
77. *Ibid.*, 10 February 1940, p. 445.

3

PHILOSOPHICAL OUTLOOK (I)

Gandhi was not a philosopher in the academic sense of the term. He had neither training in this line nor any knack to form a philosophical discipline. His primary concern was alleviation of all sorts of human suffering. Hence he says, "There is no such thing as 'Gandhism', and I do not want to leave any sect after me. I do not claim to have originated any new principle or doctrine. I have simply tried in my own way to apply the eternal truths to our daily life and problems.... Well, all my philosophy, if it may be called by that pretentious name, is contained in what I have said. You will not call it 'Gandhism': there is no *ism* about it."[1] The system that we strive to frame out of his writings is merely a scholastic viewpoint. His antipathy for any sort of 'ism' or system left his thinking unchained. Here lies the secret of his continuous evolution of thought and personality.

Since he had no training in philosophical discipline he plodded through the problems of life, paying little attention to academician's subtle distinctions. He was a self-styled philosopher, a philosopher of life, so to say. He says, "Philosophy without life corresponding is like a body without life...."[2] The traditional philosophy was primarily speculative in nature, and hence the problems of life were to a great extent neglected there. Consequently, Gandhi, the humanist, reluctant to be an ivory tower thinker, paid attention to the problems arising out of harsh realities of life. The 'eternal truths' of the great teachers of the world appealed to him for their practical values. He followed, and transmuted, and applied them to life in his own way. P.T. Raju aptly observes, "Mahatma Gandhi infused life into some of them [Indian philosophical concepts] by coming across them in the very course of his life, which is a struggle for the discovery of truth."[3] In this voyage of life he brought to bear a new philosophical outlook that formed an integral part of his thought and was interwoven into it. As an ardent social thinker he viewed life in its totality; the problems of life as a whole. He made no watertight compartments of the various fields of life. To him the problems of life—ethical, economic, religious, social, political, etc.—formed an organic whole. So he treated it, not piecemeal, but in its entirety. Here perhaps, he was, directly or indirectly, influenced by traditional philosophical systems of India. Acharya Brajendra Nath Seal calls it the synthetic outlook of Indian philosophy.[4] It can fairly be said of Gandhi too. From the standpoint of philosophy as a discipline we can arrange his thought as follows:

His Epistemology

(a) *Empiricism:* Gandhi's thought was deeply rooted to earth, in the hard realities of life. Mere speculation or knowledge devoid of any practical applicability of life bore no meaning to him. His sole aim was alleviation of sufferings. With this objective in mind he conducted experiments in truth throughout life. Accordingly his method of dealing with the problems of life was positive, empirical and inductive. Gandhi declares, "The body might be destroyed, the spirit will proclaim its freedom. This to me is not a theory; it is *a fact of experience.*"[5], "My method is empiric", he told Rolland.[6] Any reader of his life and works will not fail to observe this empirical element of his thought. Buddhadeva Bhattacharyya aptly comments, "From the standpoint of methodology, Gandhi's approach was deductive, empirical and pragmatic.... He developed a keen empirical outlook towards life in general and political and social events in particular. He observed, experienced and suggested the way out. His plea for the removal of untouchability, his crusading mission for communal amity, his solutions for the economic regeneration of poverty-stricken India, bear testimony to his rich experience of life based upon empirical investigation. As was his wont he looked at things empirically and pragmatically."[7] P. Spratt holds a similar opinion, "His thinking is of an empirical character...."[8] The empirical element of Gandhian thought will become clear in course of our discussion.

(b) *Syadvad:* It is a key concept of Jaina philosophy. It tells us that an existent is possessed of an infinite number of attributes, which may be contrary, even contradictory in nature. And since the knowledge of infinite attributes is not attainable, the affirmation or negation of a predicate is not untrue although finality or absoluteness cannot be claimed of it. Every proposition is true, but only under certain conditions, i.e., hypothetically.

Gandhi says, "I have therefore no objection to calling it real and unreal, and thus being called an *anekantavadi* or a *syadvadi.* But my *syadvada* is not the *syadvada* of the learned, it is peculiarly my own. I cannot engage in a debate with them."[9] Gandhi tells us that every individual, due to imperfection, is liable to error. And since he can at a time grasp only a fragmentary truth of an object, he cannot claim finality of his knowledge. A corollary necessarily follows from it that an individual should readily admit the truth of other's views from their standpoints. This spontaneously leads to tolerance for the views of other persons, and this is one of the salient features of non-violence. Thus this *syadvad* or relativity of knowledge had a far-reaching effect in the movements led by Gandhi. Here a mark of caution is called for. Gandhi's humanitarian outlook urged him to interpret the traditional concepts in his own way through which he tried to redress the suffering of the dumb millions.

(c) *Rationalism:* Rationalism treats every self as essentially active and rational. It relies on inner-self, not on extraneous conditions of the senses, in the acquisition of knowledge. In India the rationalistic trend is found even in the epic period. In the *Yoga-Vasistha Ramayana* we are told: "Never neglect the intellectual approach (*vicara*), never minimize its value" (*Mumukshu-Vyavahara-Prakarana*, 12/12). For one who is fallen into the dark abyss of ignorance, there is no means of rescue except *vicara*, the analytical-intellectual approach. (*ibid.*, 14/48). Buddha preaches, "On the way to truth never take the help of others, rely on your own *vicara* or reason" (*Dighanikaya*, vol. I, *Mahapari nirvana sutta*). Gandhi was deeply influenced by the rationalism of Ramayana from which he quotes, "A *Shastra*, though man-made should be accepted, if it appeals to reason; and the contrary one rejected, though claiming to be inspired. We should be guided by our sense of the just alone. A saying sound in reason should be accepted, though it proceed from a child; and the contrary one rejected as a straw, though it purport to proceed from the God Brahma."[10] Thus Gandhi was aware of the rationalistic trend of Indian thought.

Gandhi followed the rationalistic tradition in his own way, and condemned blind dogmatism as an obstruction to truth. In his words, "Blind adoration, in the age of action, is perfectly valueless, is often embarrassing and equally often painful."[11] Gandhi's eclectic mind was an open one in the sense that it fought against age-old prejudices and customs that hindered free thinking. Active opposition to blind dogmatism for the exercise of intellectual discourse is a feature of rationalism. Another characteristic of Gandhi's rationalism is his belief in the essential rationality of human nature. To him, each and every man is a spark of divinity of Truth. Every individual is spiritual and hence rational by nature. It is our objective to manifest the supremacy of reason through a proper control of our sentient life. Gandhi writes, "... there are chords in every human heart. If we only know how to strike the right chord, we bring out the music."[12] The rationality of human nature is a postulate of Gandhian thought. The third feature of Gandhi's rationalism is the declaration of reason as the standard of universal assent. To quote him, "Every formula of every religion has in this age of reason, to submit to the acid test of reason and universal justice if it is to ask for universal assent."[13] "... I reject any religious doctrine that does not appeal to reason and is in conflict with morality."[14] Gandhi was primarily an ethico-religious person. Although it was a hard task still Gandhi sought the subjugation of religious doctrines to reason only to find out truth and thereby establish the supremacy of reason over sentient life. Gandhi prefers irrationality if it serves a moral purpose. He allows heart precedence to reasons. Reason is often subjugated by other mental faculties. On this N.A. Nikam observes that Gandhi was not a rationalist in the accepted sense of the terms. Critical inquiry was not his path.[15] Indeed, strict adherence to any discipline or rules was not in keeping with his nature. His humanism supplemented by an ethico-religious outlook did not inspire him to conduct a critical inquiry, especially in the domain of theology.

Reason undoubtedly plays an important role in Gandhian thought. He wanted to render upto Caesar that which is Caesar's. To quote Gandhi, "Reason has its place, only it must not usurp the heart."[16] "Experience has humbled me enough to let me realize the specific limitations of reason. Just as matter misplaced becomes dirt, reason misused becomes lunacy.... Rationalists are admirable beings, rationalism is a hideous monster when it claims for itself omnipotence. Attribution of omnipotence to reason is as bad a piece of idolatry as is worship of stock and stone believing it to be God.... I plead not for the suppression of reason, but for a due recognition of that in us which sanctifies reason itself."[17] He knew "the specific limitations of reason" and hence recognized its due role, and its limited efficacy. To know the source, scope and limitation of a mental faculty, here reason, is certainly a feature of rationalism. But reason is not the only source of knowledge. It has merits as well as demerits. Attribution of 'omnipotence' to it is unscientific and unjust. In this light although Gandhi cannot be called a rationalist in the strict sense of the term, his treatment of it, as a golden mean which neither underestimates nor overemphasized its role, seems to be a sound one.

(d) *Pragmatism:* Pragmatism preaches to take into account our personal ends and interests in every walk of life. Although this movement is connected with the names of some modern western thinkers (William James, F.C. Schiller, John Dewey, etc.) a noted scholar traces its origin in the ancient philosophy of the Hindus.[18] In this light Gandhi's inheritance of pragmatism seems to be an obvious one. His humanistic outlook urged him to treat the problems of life from the practical standpoint. Hence an analysis will reveal the pragmatic elements latent in his thought. (1) In epistemology he follows the pragmatic trend. To quote him, "... as long as I have not realized this Absolute Truth, so long must I hold by the relative truth as I have conceived it. That relative truth must, meanwhile, be my beacon, my shield and buckler."[19] In spite of his firm conviction in Absolute Truth Gandhi admitted relative truth at the demand of the situation. (2) In his religious ideas too pragmatic elements are evident. Gandhi tells us that a "religion which takes no account of practical affairs, and does not help to solve them, is no religion."[20] This champion of humanism was seriously moved and aggrieved at the outbreak of a communal riot in Bombay. He then wished the rioting communities, the Hindus and the Muslims, to espouse atheism if that "served to stop communal hatred and riot."[21] This shows that he could relinquish his belief in God in which he lived, moved and had his being only to serve a practical purpose, i.e., communal harmony. The pragmatic trend is so deep in him that apart from the traditional moves, he offers also a pragmatic argument for the existence of God. He persuades us to believe in God, at least, for its practical utility. To him service to humanity is equivalent to the service of God whom he found amongst the dumb and starving millions. K. Ramakrishna Rao observes, "Gandhi derived a lot of comfort from his belief in

God as he moved from crisis to crisis fighting bitter battles against adversaries vastly superior to him in terms of physical power with a very remote possibility of success...."[22]

In his moral ideas too pragmatism is a predominating note. Like religion, ethics also has no meaning without practical demonstration. It is this pragmatism that urged him to rearrange traditional virtues, and increase their number in keeping with the temper of the age and the demand of the situation. Because of this pragmatic bearing moral laws are, to him, neither subjective nor objective but subjective-objective in nature. Like an architect's plan the value of moral principles depends on its bearing in practical life. Like truth, absolute and relative, moral ideals also are relative, neither eternal nor immutable. They are experimental and environmental, depending upon the situation with which they are related. Gandhi brings out the relative character of good and evil by saying, "If I wish to be an agriculturist and stay in a jungle, I will have to use the minimum unavoidable violence, in order to protect my fields..."[23] Here the pragmatic nature of the concept of good and evil needs no more elucidation.

Let us now turn to his political views. As he made no division of different fields of life he treated the problems concerning politics from the pragmatic standpoint. Gandhi writes, "For me, I say with Cardinal Newman: 'I do not ask to see the distant scene; One step enough for me'."[24] This interest in the present, in the next step, makes Gandhi a pragmatic in his political thought. This pragmatic outlook is evident in his correspondence with the Government where he writes, "I am prepared to advise the Working Committee to declare that in view of changed conditions mass civil disobedience envisaged by the resolution of August 1942 cannot be offered and that *full co-operation in the war effort* should be given by the Congress, *if* a declaration of immediate Indian independence is made...."[25] No more citation is necessary. A votary of pacifism and non-violence like him intends to extend full cooperation in the war to the British Government only for the sake of independence of India. He could not help being a pragmatist in this regard. And, perhaps, no practical leader can.

In his plan for social and political uplift also pragmatism plays a prominent role. Gandhi's *Swadeshi* programme was also directed to some pragmatic end. The concept of *Swadeshi* implies political, moral and economical significance. Politically, it aimed at *Swaraj* or self-rule; morally it had the cardinal virtue, bread-labour as its end; and economically its purpose was to make people self-sufficient from the pecuniary standpoint. Similar implications may be sought in his campaigns for the removal of untouchability, liberation of women, etc. In short, his programmes for social and political uplift (namely, *Swadeshi*, *Panchayat*, *Ramarajya,* etc.) were launched after a critical survey of their practical consequences, more specifically, earthly usefulness.

In his aesthetics too pragmatic outlook predominates. He wanted the musicians to propagate communal harmony. He laid emphasis on village industries the productions of which were, to him, beautiful and lively in spite of their roughness simply on the ground that they fed the hungry millions.

To sum up: his pragmatic outlook pervades every aspect of his life. This is one of the salient features of Gandhian thought.

(e) *Eclecticism:* Eclecticism is an age-old characteristic of Indian thought. In the *Rg-Veda* we are told, "Let noble thoughts come to us from every side." (*Rg-Veda*, 1.89.i). Gandhi inherits this trend urged by an ardent humanism and pragmatic outlook. He says, "I hope I am as great a believer in free air as the great Poet. I do not want my house to be walled in on all sides and my windows to be stuffed. I want the cultures of all the lands to be blown about my house as freely as possible. But I refuse to be blown off my feet by any."[26] As discussed above Gandhi admitted this frankly that he only interpreted and tried to apply the 'eternal truths' of old to life in the present day.

In his religious ideas too, this eclecticism is evident. It is in Hinduism that he lived, moved and had his being. But he seized the essence of Christianity, Jainism, Buddhism, Zoroastrianism and Islam, and turned it in his own way into a universal religion. Gandhi was conscious of the charge of eclecticism and says, "... my Hinduism seems to some to be a conglomeration and some have even dubbed me an eclectic. Well, to call a man eclectic is to say that he has no faith, but mine is a broad faith... based on the broadest possible toleration."[27] F.H. Bradley observes, "Eclecticism I have found preach that 'Every truth is so true that any truth must be false'."[28] But Gandhian eclecticism is not nihilistic. It opens an avenue to universal assent. Herein lie the uniqueness and originality of Gandhi as a thinker and philosopher.

(f) *Conscientiousness:* There is a galaxy of conscientious thinkers both in the West and in the East. Although its roots can be traced in the teachings of Sophocles, Euripedes, the Stoics and Socrates, the notion was fully developed in the eighteenth century only by William Penn, Bishop Butler, Kant, Vinet, etc.; and was variously called as the voice of "Delphic God," the doctrine of "Inner Light," "Pure Reason," "Logos", etc. A similar idea appears in the concept of *vidhi* of the Prabhakara; and in the *niyoga* of the Jain, Buddha and Charvaka school.[29] But in spite of its rich and colourful tradition no thinker before Gandhi did lay so much emphasis on conscience as the "final arbiter" in every walk of life. To Gandhi, "the etymological meaning of conscience is 'true knowledge.' The dictionary meaning is 'faculty distinguishing between right and wrong and influencing conduct accordingly'."[30] At the outset we can say that, although he applied it to every field of life, conscience was primarily a moral concept to him.

A sympathetic reviewer will observe, perhaps with surprise, Gandhi's sensitiveness to conscience even in his early life. He never told a lie either to his teachers or to his school mates. Here also he took refuge in conscience as the most authentic means of knowing truth. In this light Gandhi was a thoroughly conscientious person.

(g) *Mysticism:* The word 'mysticism' comes from a Greek root which means 'to close'. It meant occult knowledge, secret knowledge, sacred knowledge. William James points out four chief marks of mysticism, namely, ineffability; transiency; and passivity.[31] Evelyn Underhill, however, calls it "transcendental and spiritual"; otherworldly "ecstasy but is better named the Unitive State."[32] E.V. Hartmann brings forth the following characteristics, namely, 'quietistic contemplation'; practical and worldly; charms, theurgy, magic and practical medicines; physical and mental symptoms such as bodily fits, convulsion, ecstasies, etc., asceticism; religionism; revelation or spiritual promptings; contrary even contradictory features leading to obscurity; etc.[33]

Some renowned writers treat mysticism from the positivistic standpoint and decline to call Gandhi a mystic. G. Ramachandran opines, "He was a common man who pulled himself up to the most uncommon height. He was no God but became a God-man."[34] An almost similar idea forms the nucleus of C.D.S. Devanesen's book *The Making of the Mahatma*. Benoy Gopal Ray tells us that Gandhi's inner voice is nothing but the voice of the subconscious. "He was not a mystic since he never led the mystical life."[35]

On the other hand, a galaxy of scholars branded Gandhi a

mystic. Romain Rolland called Gandhi a mystic.[36] Madan G. Gandhi comments, "Like all mystics who possess a power beyond themselves, he draws his life from God."[37] V.M. Bedekar observes, "Gandhi's aim was the realization of God or the highest self and he was in this religious sense a direct descendant in the line of the devotional mystics of old."[38] I.C. Sharma opines, "... he was more a mystic in the practical sense...."[39] Gopinath Dhawan, F.M. Bar, Verrier Elwin and other famous writers opine the same view.

Gandhi was out and out a religious person who strove ceaselessly to realize God throughout life. His transcendental and spiritual outlook, other-worldliness, sense of entire dependence on God, liking for devotional songs, etc., turned him into a mystic. V.M. Bedekar observes, "Gandhi was essentially a man of religion. The roots of his mystic personality lay in other-worldliness and he had a transcendental faith in God."[40] Further, Gandhi's firm conviction in the essential divinity of man contributes to that end. Humility which is a feeling of lowliness before God is necessary for mystical experience. Humility is one of the essential qualities of a satyagrahi. Gandhi preached and practised it throughout life. J.A. Picton observes, "Mysticism consists in the spiritual realization of a grandeur and a boundless unity that humbles all self-assertion by dissolving it in a wider glory."[41] Undoubtedly, Gandhi was an incarnation of humility. A student of Gandhi's life knows well the role of prayer in his everyday life. Evening prayer was a must to him. Thus Gandhi's heart-searching prayer to divinity certainly constitutes one of the elements of his mystical personality.

Righteousness is a salient feature of mysticism. It is the nucleus of Gandhian thought. It is in it that Gandhi lived and breathed. And Gandhi's inner voice or 'the still small voice' is unwittingly a feature of his mysticism. Mysticism often turns into asceticism. Gandhi's ascetic mode of living and thinking gave him a mystic identity.

Transiency is another feature of Gandhian mysticism. The mystical experience of Gandhi came upon him suddenly and occasionally. In his words, "The hearing of the Voice was preceded by a terrific struggle within me. Suddenly the Voice came upon me. I listened, made certain that it was the Voice, and the struggle ceased. I was calm."[42]

Following the argument of Hermann Lotze, we can claim Gandhi to be a mystic. According to Lotze, one of the characteristics of a mystic is that he conceives natural calamities as the outburst of human sin. To quote him, "Neither experience nor *a priori* theory... lend any colour to the assumption that the sin of man produced physical evil in the order of Nature. The view attracts man on account of its mystic and unintelligible character, but has no other recommendations."[43] Gandhi firmly believed in the natural calamities as physical evils, as just consequences of human sin.[44]

Mystics are often guided by heart, and not by reason. Gandhi preferred heart to reason. In a sense heart is the ultimate arbiter of Gandhi's life. Gandhi says, "My reason follows my heart."[45] Hence, faith, the function of heart, is one of the constituents of Gandhi's mysticism.

In most cases, mysticism is manifested through some physical and mental symptoms, such as bodily fits, convulsions, epilepsies, ecstasies, etc. Gandhi observed a 'day of silence' every week. As mentioned above the emergence of the inner "Voice was preceded by a terrific struggle within" him. He attained, though not fully, union with God, in Evelyn Underhill's terminology, 'Unitive State', step by step. Jawaharlal Nehru once remarked, "His calm, deep eyes would hold one and gently probe into the depths. Whether his audience consisted of one person or a thousand, the charm and magnetism of the man passed on to it... he gave the impression of tremendous inner reserves of power."[46] The above-mentioned symptoms, both mental and physical, are remarkable and hence should be taken into account.

Some mystics turn away from active life and fall back upon 'quietistic contemplation' while some participate deeply in the practical affairs of the world and become reformers in various walks of life.[47] Gandhi's public life, his ceaseless struggle for the cause of humanity requires no special elucidation.

Dictation of the spirit is another important point of mysticism. Let us take up Gandhi's experience in the above light. Gandhi writes, "I write just as the Spirit moves me at the time of writing ...."[48] Gandhi's contact with a mysterious power, Spirit, confirms our opinion that Gandhi was a mystic. Gopinath Dhawan observes, "Indeed, Gandhiji is a mystic spying, as it were, upon the twilight movements of the spirit."[49]

To conclude, we have so far brought out the various elements of mysticism in Gandhian thought. We call Gandhi a mystic in the above light, and conclude with P. Spratt, "... though he shows none of the more sensational phenomena of mysticism, the description [as a mystic] is justified."[50]

(h) *Defender of Faith:* The novelty of Gandhian epistemology lies in his admission of faith as a source of knowledge. To Gandhi the efficacy of the senses and reason is limited. It is faith, the function of the heart, that transcends reason, and opens new avenues to knowledge. To quote him, "Faith then does not contradict reason but transcends it. Faith is a kind of sixth sense which works in cases which are without the purview of reason."[51] Faith and reason are not antagonistic; rather they are complementary to one another. It is here noteworthy that the data which it supplies us is *a priori* since "faith can only grow from within; it cannot be acquired vicariously."[52] But this faith does not inhere in each and every individual equally. It is enhanced and developed through prayer, the means of self-purification. In his words, "Faith, on the other hand, cannot be developed except through prayer."[53] Thus faith, to Gandhi, stands as a sixth sense, *a priori* one, which is sharpened through prayer only. Gandhi also admits mystical experience as a way of knowing. But both faith and mystical experience contribute very little of Gandhian epistemology since they rotate in the theocentric orbit to Gandhian thought. And as they are characteristically individualistic these methods of knowing fail to attain universal assent in the realm of epistemological thought.

We have so far conducted a general survey of Gandhi's epistemological ideas, and brought out the empiric, rationalistic, pragmatic, eclectic, mystical, relativistic and conscientious elements of his thought. Gandhi's epistemology is a curious mixture of all these trends. Hence like his philosophical outlook, a synthetic one, Gandhi's epistemological approach is based on a synthetic method.

His Metaphysical Outlook

Gandhi was one of the leading creative thinkers of Indian thought during the first part of this century. His activism, both in speech and deed, made a tremendous impact upon social, religious, and especially in the political life of the people of India. His metaphysical ideas too were immensely influenced by his synthetic outlook. As Paul F. Power observes, "In Gandhi's case certainly metaphysics and political notions are intertwined."[54] That is why, a proper evaluation of Gandhi's philosophy demands a brief elucidation of his metaphysical outlook. As he was born and brought up in traditional atmosphere, he could not evade the influence of Indian philosophy on him. One of the chief characteristics of Indian philosophy is that it emphasizes a close tie with the problems of life. Gandhi was not a typical philosopher who sitting in an armchair of an ivory tower would meditate on speculative metaphysical discourse. Mere speculative knowledge which had no practical bearing upon human life could not attract him. To quote Gandhi, "Philosophy without life corresponding is like a body without life."[55] So philosophy and life are identical to him. His philosophy of humanism is deeply rooted in the life of our countrymen.

(a) *Gandhi's Critique of Materialism:* Gandhi's acquaintance with materialism was not at all a happy one. During his stay in England the romantic reaction against industrial civilization was most vocal. Economic exploitation and dehumanization, the offshoots of industrial civilization, impressed a sorry picture of materialism on his mind. As a result most of his doctrines were directed ostensibly against the vulgar materialism of the West. We shall see in the following section that Gandhi believed in an absolute Spirit, God or Truth, as the ultimate reality. The supremacy of Spirit over matter is the predominating note of his thought. Gandhi rejects materialism in its totality and thereby proclaims the supremacy of spirit over matter. The fundamental assumptions of Gandhian thought such as Truth, God, Non-violence, Celibacy, are all non-material concepts. Gopinath Dhawan aptly observes, "A living, unshakable faith in God, an insistence on the primacy of spirit, is the core of his philosophy."[56]

(b) *An Absolute Idealist:* Absolute idealism is a metaphysical doctrine that preaches reality to be an all-inclusive one which admits internal relations, degrees of truth and entities. Gandhi believed in God or Truth, a spiritual One, as the ultimate truth and reality. It is an all-inclusive reality which comprehends everything in its infinite bosom. To quote Gandhi, "We are all sparks of truth. The sum total of these sparks is indescribable, as-yet unknown Truth, which is God."[57] "We are not, He alone Is."[58] Thus from the metaphysical standpoint Gandhi's only reality is God who manifests Himself in the various existent things of the world. While all other existent entities are real only apparently, God, the only one, is real absolutely. This is one of the basic tenets of absolute idealism. Secondly, in the epistemological sphere also absolutistic note dominates. He believed in the degrees of Truth to which he sticks. For the time being since absolute Truth, the ultimate goal, is beyond our grasp due to imperfection. Gandhi says, "As I proceed in my search for truth it grows upon me that Truth comprehends everything."[59] This is clearly an absolutist standpoint. Ontologically, God or Truth is the highest entity, value or ideal. Further God or Truth as the only reality transcends all spatial and temporal relations. Gandhi like an absolutist holds that all existent entities are related internally to one another, and the fall of one individual will lead to the downfall of all human beings. This is an addition to absolutist trend of thought.

Self-realization as God-realization is the highest goal of an absolutist. This is also the viewpoint of Gandhi. Thus Gandhi's concept of Truth or God is epistemologically, metaphysically and ontologically an absolute concept. Hence comes Gandhi's open declaration, "I am an *advaitist* ...."[60] P.T. Raju opines, "There is no doubt about Mahatma Gandhi's being an absolutist and a monist."[61] Indeed, the basic concepts of Gandhian thought are metaphysical, i.e., supersensuous and idealistic, spiritual in nature. The twin concepts, truth and non-violence, around which Gandhi weaves his entire thought are absolutist in nature although they fall short of relativity at the demand of circumstances. Here a mark of caution is necessary. Gandhi derived his mental nourishment from the traditional thought of India which has remained, to a great extent, wedded to metaphysical idealism or absolutism for a long time. These metaphysical concepts, here an *advaitist*, came to him spontaneously, and he used them without knowing their implications fully. From this, as also his other concepts, namely, rationalism, *syadvad*, etc., we can call him an absolutist although not in the strict sense of the term.

(c) ***A Practical Idealist—His Realism:*** Gandhi was fond of saying, "I am a practical idealist." To a critical ear it may sound paradoxical but a sympathetic reviewer will not miss the truth hidden in the above statement. Gandhi preached as well as practised. He derived the basic tenets from the idealistic trend of traditional thought but practised them in his life; and implemented them in practical field to redress the sufferings of humanity. Buddhadeva Bhattacharyya observes, "... there were two Gandhi's—the idealist philosopher and the realist politician—who, paradoxically enough, represented a singularly unified character."[62] The truth is that Gandhi was a contemplative as well as a man of action. He tried his best to translate ideas into action, "Example is better than precept" was his slogan. He made no distinction between ideals and actions, intents and consequences, means and ends, individual ethics and corporate ethics.

In this context Morarji Desai comments, "Gandhiji was an idealist—a practical idealist—who had no use of any ideas if they were not capable of being implemented and being acted upon in life. And this is what we have to learn from him."[63] Shriman Narayan observes, "Gandhiji was a practical idealist who tried his very best to solve various difficulties and problems in a rational and scientific manner..."[64] K. Ramakrishna Rao remarks, "It is one of the most valuable of Gandhi's contributions to India that he inspired a new outlook without disturbing the social equilibrium."[65] Indeed, although Gandhi derived mental nourishment from traditional concepts, and wandered within the framework of Indian idealism, his ardent zeal to serve humanity, his pragmatic interest induced him to face the multi-faced realism of practical life. His keen sense of astute realism foresaw the need of the day. The starving millions sought bread and no ideals, wanted shelter and no poetry. Hence he infused life into lofty ideals, and gave a new orientation to them in keeping with the temper of the age. In this light non-violence, traditionally known as a passive virtue, got wide, experimental and activistic dimension in the hand of Gandhi who applied it to every sphere of life with equal vigour. Thus non-violence, to Gandhi, is an ideal as well as a mode of direct action to solve all conflicts, whatever may be its nature. Similar interpretations may be offered to other virtues prescribed by Gandhi. Throughout his works idealism and realism, the two over-conflicting doctrines, go side by side, interacting upon one another. This is the spirit of the 'practical idealism' or 'idealistic realism' in Gandhian thought.

(d) *A Monist or a Pluralist?* The monism of Gandhian thought necessarily follows from his views on absolute idealism. His view of ultimate reality as an all-inclusive spiritual one reminds us of the fundamental assumption of idealistic monism. Gandhi felt the presence of an omnipresent all-inclusive reality in the midst of a bewildering mass of phenomenal diversity. In his words, "All I say is that there is a sameness, identity or oneness behind the multiplicity and variety."

Gandhi as a practical idealist, as a firm believer in human beings as end in themselves, could not do away with this world of the senses altogether. He felt oneness in multiplicity, identity in diversity, eternity in all perishables, reality amidst the unreal. To quote him, "We need not debate whether what we see is unreal; and whether the real behind the unreality is what we do not see. Let both be equally real, if you will."[66] That is to say, in spite of his belief in spiritual or idealistic monism he believed in the manyness of reality. This unwittingly proves his monism as a concrete entity. Surendra Verma aptly observes, "It is extremely difficult to decide whether the spiritual monism of Gandhi is abstract monism or concrete...."[67]

Gandhi's belief in pluralism follows as a necessary corollary to his *syadvad* or relativity of knowledge. He says, "I am an *advaitist* and yet I can support *dwaitism* (dualism)... I have therefore no objection to calling it real and unreal, and thus being called an *anekantavadi* or a *syadvadi*. But my *syadvad* is not the *syadvad* of the learned, it is peculiarly my own ...I very much like this doctrine of the manyness of reality .... My *anekantavada* is the result of the twin doctrine of *Satya* and *Ahimsa*."[68] What does *anekantavad* mean? Etymologically, it means *na ekanta,* i.e., nothing is absolute. This doctrine of *anekantavad* or pluralism was preached by Jains of Indian philosophy to assert innumerable predicates of an object.

Gandhi believed in individuals as end in themselves; and the villages of his ideal state, *Ramrajya,* were all independent units. In religion also he accepted the autonomy of all faiths which fostered tolerance in him. A critical inquiry may explore more seeds of pluralism in his thought. But this pluralism is apparent, and not real. Gandhi was basically committed to the absolutistic and monistic trend of Indian thought. But Gandhi the humanist cannot but admit the plurality, the phenomenal diversity. He used the term *anekantavad*, like *syadvad*, *advaitism*, etc., without any precise and sound understanding of them which convey technical implications in philosophical discussions.

(e) *Substance:* The concept of substance goes with the concept of reality in the history of thought. Gandhian thought is not an exception to this. As mentioned above, since he had no scholastic training in philosophical discipline, he did not treat it separately. His synthetic outlook was also to a great extent responsible for this. However, an analytical mind will find out the following concept of substance from his thought, scattered here and there.

Gandhian substance is, and is not, in space and time simultaneously. It is immutable and changeless. Amidst the various changes of the phenomenal world it maintains identity and remains constant. In this sense, the Gandhian substance is eternal, and hence beyond temporal relations. To quote him, "I do dimly perceive that whilst everything around me is ever changing, ever dying, there is underlying all that change a living power that is changeless, that holds together, that creates, dissolves and recreates. That informing power or spirit is God. And since nothing else I see merely through the senses can or will persist, He alone is."[69] Thus, to Gandhi, substance is one, changeless and eternal.

The substance is not material but a form, an essence. Though the substance incarnates in, and manifests through the bewildering mass of phenomenal diversity, it is above and beyond them. In an enigmatic way, it is a peculiar feature of Gandhian thought that subsists amongst the material objects without any effect, nay reaction. Gandhi explains, "God is the source of Light and Life and yet He is above and beyond all these ...."[70] "... The divine essence is the sum total of all life."[71] This Gandhian concept of substance as immutable, eternal, pure essence reminds us, of course with some variations, of the Eleatic Being and Plato's Ideas.

Substance, to Gandhi, is of the nature of spirit and consciousness. It is an absolute consciousness or spirit that assumes innumerable forms in material objects. Gandhi says, "The truth is that God is the force. He is the essence of life."[72] "...God is the Force among all other forces. All other forces are material. But God is the vital force or spirit which is all-pervading, all-embracing and therefore beyond human ken."[73] In this context V.P. Varma observes, "Gandhi conceived of *Sat* or Truth not only as an ethical category but as an ontological being of the highest realm..."[74] Here perhaps, Gandhi was influenced by the Vedantic concept of reality, *Brahman* as *sachchidananda* (existence-consciousness-bliss).

According to Gandhi, the substance, is one and many, monistic and pluralistic at the same time. He says, "We are *not*, He alone *Is*."[75] "He is *one* and yet many."[76] The absolutist Gandhi preaches, like Spinoza, the monistic substance with all the attributes of God or Truth which will be explained more elaborately in a subsequent section.[77] But the humanist Gandhi spontaneously admits the plurality, the phenomenal diversity. Thus one and many, monistic and pluralistic, real and illusory nature of substance go side by side in his thought. The co-existence of contrary, sometimes contradictory, attributes is a characteristic of Gandhian thought.

To sum up: Gandhian substance is eternal, immutable, formal, an essence, a spirit, a consciousness, one yet many and material at the same time. When treated as God or Truth it becomes the lion's den into which everything enters and gets merged. But, if considered, in the earthly and humanistic context it assumes realistic and lively form. Thus Gandhian substance is immanent and transcendent at the same time.

(f) *Cause and Effect:* The concept of substance is closely connected with the concept of cause and effect. The innumerable substances or existents of the universe do stand to one another in various relations to which the relation of interaction or reciprocity of cause and effect is important. Here, before we take up the Gandhian view, a very brief sketch of the Aristotelian concept of causality is indispensable since till today this stands as the most popular and exhaustive treatment on the topic. And we intend to arrange the Gandhian concept of cause and effect after the Aristotelian table for better understanding and discussion.

According to Aristotle the causes of change are fourfold: material, formal, efficient and final. (1) The matter "out of which a thing comes to be" is the material cause. For example, a statue is carved out of a lump of bronze. Here the lump of bronze is the material cause of the statue; (2) The "form or pattern or formula" after which the statue is made is the formal cause; (3) "The immediate origin of the movement", say the muscular energy and the instruments used by the sculptor is here the efficient cause; (4) "The end or aim or purpose" say the perpetuation of the memory of a person is here the final or teleological cause.[78]

An analytical survey will reveal that all the above Aristotelian forms of cause are present, explicitly or implicitly, in Gandhian thought. Material cause underlying this phenomenal world has been a favourite topic to thinkers of eminence from Thales, Anaximenes, Anaximander down to these modern days. Gandhi accepted God as the ultimate material cause of this phenomenal world. To quote him, "We are all sparks of Truth. The sum total of these sparks is indescribable, as yet unknown Truth, which is God."[79] Here the Gandhian conviction that an absolute Spirit or Consciousness is the ultimate stuff of the universe is subject to various criticisms that have been raised by the realistic school against the idealistic thinkers. Further, Gandhi argues from the aetiological standpoint to find out the ultimate material cause in a First cause or uncaused cause, i.e., a *causasui* or God. But to tender a causal argument and stop at an uncaused cause seems to be unintelligible to a rational mind. We shall take up this point again in the next chapter. Furthermore, Gandhi continues, "We may all have different definitions for God.

If we could all give our own definitions of God there would be as many definitions as there are men and women. But behind all that variety of definitions there would be also a certain sameness which would be unmistakable. For the root is one."[80] Thus, to Gandhi, God is the ultimate stuff of the universe.

Gandhian concept of formal cause too cannot transcend the divine axis. He sees divinity and divine design in each and every existent of the universe. To him each and every member of mankind is created after the image of God, and hence in man essentially inheres a spark of Him. The ultimate goal of human life is to regain this form, this essence of divinity in man. Gandhi says, "God made man in His own image."[81] "He is the essence of life."[82] "... the divine essence is the sum total of all life."[83] Thus the formal cause of the world, according to Gandhi, incarnates in God.

Gandhi interpretes the efficient cause of the world in the above light. He explains, "God is the Supreme Alchemist. In His presence all iron and dross turn into pure gold. Similarly does all evil turn into good."[84] Gandhi, although a champion of human freedom, preaches freedom of will under the divine superintendence. That is why the ultimate credit of efficiency and creation goes to God who creates, dissolves and recreates everything. Thus, to Gandhi, God is, apparently and finally, the efficient cause of the world.

Gandhi's concept of final cause too follows the same track. He perceives a divine design in every existent of the universe. The realization of this heavenly design is the teleo or final end of the world order. Gandhi says, "He moves all and yet no one can move Him. Not a blade of grass moves without His will."[85]

To sum up: Gandhi's concept of cause and effect like that of substance rotates in the divine orbit. His religious mind can never come out of it. This divine note runs predominantly throughout his thought. This theocentric interpretation of earthly phenomena may gratify the query of a devotee but not an analytical mind which demands an objective and rational elucidation on a scientific plinth. This trend is not new in the history of human thought. A good number of great thinkers from Plato down to Spinoza, Locke, Berkeley, etc. followed the same track. But to divinize an empirical fact like cause and effect is not to explain it scientifically. It is rather turning away from fact. A scientific explanation investigates the root of the changing phenomena here, in this mundane world. It is immanent, and not transcendent of this empirical world. In this sense, Gandhi's theocentric approach to cause and effect fails to command universal assent.

(g) *Space and Time:* The influence of Indian philosophy is remarkably felt throughout the Gandhian thought. His conception of space and time is no exception. D.M. Datta observes, "Regarding Gandhi's conception of space and time we find that he was influenced by the general Indian ideas about them."[86] Thus an adequate estimation of Gandhian concept of space and time demands an elucidation of them against the background of Indian philosophy.

The long journey of Indian philosophy is steered by a moral and spiritual outlook, a training for the individual to attain liberation *(moksa)*. The contribution of vastness of the space-time concept in the development of this moral and spiritual outlook is not at all negligible.

The ancient Indians drew a picture of the vastness of space-time universe that may appear fantastic to a modern mind. In the *Visnu Purana* (Pt.II, chapter seven) we are told that the world *(Brahmanda)* contains fourteen regions *(lokas)* in it... The earth *(bhutala)* is one of them. These regions *(lokas)* fourteen in number, are floating in the vastness of the universe in a scattered manner. These regions *(lokas)* are separated from one another by tens of millions *(kotis)* of *Yojanas*. And there are thousands of millions of such worlds *(brahmandas)* in the vast bosom of this space-time universe.

The description of the vastness of time also seems to be beyond the range of mathematical calculation to an ordinary mind. In other words, an ordinary man faces great difficulty when he ventures to describe it by our common mathematical units. The unit adopted for the measurement of time is a day of Brahman, the creator of the universe. Each day of the creator, *Brahman*, is equal to one thousand *Yugas* or four hundred thirty-two million calendar years of human beings. Each day of the creator marks the period in which creation of each cosmic order is completed. The night of the creator is meant for rest. At night which has duration equal to the day, the creator, *Brahman*, ceases all his creative activities which leads to the utter destruction of each cosmic order. This process of creation and destruction *(Srsti* and *Pralaya)* occur alternately at day and night, and form a series without any beginning.[87] D.M. Datta comments, "The world is thus regarded as beginningless. Time is without beginning and without end."[88] This concept of time has influenced two eminent poets, one in Sanskrit, and the other in English. Bhavabhuti writes, "Time is without limit and the world is wide."[89] T.S. Eliot contributes, "Time present and time past."

There is another sense in which the concept of time (*Kala)* has been used in Indian philosophy as identical with the absolute or as the inexorable fate mercilessly ruling over the human beings and gods. An almost similar view is found in the Greek conception of destiny, and in *kismet* of the Muslims. As S. Radhakrishnan opines, "The Greek held that there was an inexorable destiny higher than man or God which could not be altered by effort or prayer. The same dread fate appears in the faith of the Calvinists and the *kismet* of the Muslims."[90]

According to Jainism, there are two kinds of space (*Akasa). Lokakasa* (ordinary space) in which soul, matter, etc. exist and *Alokakasa* (empty space) beyond this ordinary world. Space is imperceptible and inferential. According to Nyaya-Vaisesika schools space *(dika)* and time *(kala)* are imperceptible substances each of which is one, eternal, infinite and all pervading. The Mimamsakas mostly follow the Vaisesika conception of *padarthas* and their subclasses. According to the Yoga system of Patanjali, time, a mere creation of the mind, has no basis in reality while the exponents of the *Agama* take it as the sole cause of cosmic process, both of creation and destruction.

From the above discussion we can form a fair idea of the vastness of space-time universe as it was conceived by the ancient Indians. Gandhi shares this traditional view. To quote him, "God's time never stops...."[91] Gandhi conceives of time as continuous, not discrete, and without any beginning and end. Humanism is the pivotal point of his life and philosophy. His boundless optimism inspired him to believe in human beings who in spite of their inherent imperfection would some day fully realise the value of truth and non-violence. And for this ultimate triumph of truth and non-violence, Gandhi can wait like Bhavabhuti thousands of years, since to him, "a few thousand years are but a speck in the vast time circle."[92] Elsewhere he writes, "Our existence as embodied beings is purely momentary; what are a hundred years in eternity? ....we do not exaggerate, when we say that life on earth is mere bubble."[93] The terms 'speck', 'bubble' connote the transitoriness of human life. This transcient feature of human beings, nay of existence, fostered boundless patience in him. This is the key to his plan for taking far-reaching programmes, and his preference of eternal vast time circle to that of immediate success. But this spirit of the concept of time is contradicted by some statements made by him. In course of our discussion on Gandhian-pragmatism[94] we found him saying, "One step enough for me"; "I know only the moments' duty, I have no desire to know the distant scene. If the present is attractive enough.... ", etc. Probably, its root lies in the inherent contradiction of Gandhian thought. Compelled by the demands of the situation, the humanist Gandhi sometimes adopted pragmatic steps to solve earthly problems, and as a result occasionally betrayed Gandhian rationalism.

The infinite vastness of space and the universe has taught innumerable religious poets and Vaishnava theists to think of tininess of the human body in comparison to the universe. As an ardent Vaishnava, Gandhi was ever conscious of it. The realistic perception of our insignificant existence in this universe has taught him boundless tolerance and humility not only in political and religious spheres but also at every step in life.

To conclude, Gandhi's concept of space and time like that of cause and effect cannot come out of its theocentric axis. Though the vastness of space and time is confirmed by modern science Gandhian treatment of it, owing to its divinistic trends faces the same fate as that of cause and effect.

(h) *Self: Its Immortality:* There are four main views of the self in Indian philosophy. The Nyaya-Vaisesikas' treatment of the self is from the realistic standpoint. To them, self is many, eternal, indestructible and infinite. Consciousness belongs to self, a unique substance, as an accidental attribute. The Advaita Vedanta and the Visistaadvaita Vedanta views are to some extent idealistic. According to Advaita Vedanta, the self is one, unchanging and self-shining consciousness. It is consciousness as such. On the other hand, the Visistaadvaita Vedanta maintains an almost similar view with slight variation. The qualified monism of Visistaadvaita Vedanta holds that the self is not pure consciousness as such but a conscious subject called the ego or the 'I'. To the Buddhists, the self is not a permanent entity as other Indian systems think. Like Hume, they hold that the self is a stream of consciousness with a mere empirical reality. The Charvakas adopt a materialistic outlook and tell us that the living body with the attribute of consciousness, an epiphenomenon, is called the self which is destroyed along with the destruction of this material body. The Samkhya realism admits besides *prakriti* another ultimate principle, namely, *purusa* or the self. According to Jainism, the self or *jiva* is a conscious substance which is eternal but undergoes change. The *jivas* differ from one another according to the degrees of consciousness that inhere in them. Though formless, they extend like light. To sum up: the general trend of Indian philosophy treats the self as eternal and pure in itself.

Gandhi writes, "Soul *is* apart from life. The latter is conditioned by the body, the former is not."[95] Gandhi's "it is self-acting... not conditioned by the body" resembles partially the Jaina texts (Nyayavatara, verse 31) which tell us that the soul performs its activities and is different from the body. Gandhi's view that "it persists even after death" reminds us of the famous verse of the *Gita* that 'it (soul) does not undergo any change even if the body is destroyed' : *(no hanyate hanymane sarire)* (2/20). "The soul is Godhead within man" clearly brings out his idea of identification of the soul with God. Indeed, this kind of concept that human beings are divine in nature; that God or Absolute is of the nature of the soul *("Ayam atma Brahma"—Brhadaranyaka Upanisad*, 2-5-19) is one of the chief metaphysical characteristics of Indian philosophy. Most of the systems of Indian philosophy emphasize on purity or divinity of human nature and the soul apparently gets infected with earthly impurities but is not so in itself. Gandhi followed this trend of divinity and oneness of soul in different bodies. Let us take into account his statement "it is matter rarefied to the utmost limit." Here the term *matter* should not be interpreted in the literal sense. Gandhi often used the terms God, Truth, Reality as synonymous. These are not of the nature of physical matter. And the self being of the nature of God cannot be a physical matter. Hence like other philosophical concepts he used the term *matter* not in the technical sense. His "rarefied to the utmost limit" reminds us of the ancient Greek philosopher, Anaximenes, who preached for the first time the theory of condensation and rarefaction of matter. According to Anaximenes, the subtle things like fire, soul, etc. could be found by rarefication of air, the ultimate reality.[96] What Gandhi intends to say is that the self is subtle, spiritual, and transcendent of and immanent in the body at the same time. Gandhi does not make any sharp distinction between the empirical and the metaphysical self although the Vedanta and Samkhya used it in both empirical *(vyabaharika)* and metaphysical *(paramarthika)* senses.

Gandhi's belief in the immortality of the soul is a necessary corollary of his concept of the soul. He openly declares "I believe in the immortality of the soul."[97] "The ultimate goal of our life is the realization of self, God or Truth.... The soul survives after the destruction of the body like a Phoenix, and merges in the infinite bosom of God or Truth. This concept is well expressed in the immortal lines of Wordsworth, Our birth is but a sleep and a forgetting;/The Soul that rises with us, our life's Star,/Hath had elsewhere its setting/ And cometh from afar/... do we come/From God, who is our home."[98] It is here noteworthy that the concept of immortality of the soul plays a subtle yet important role in Gandhian thought. It kindles a burning inspiration in the mind of satyagrahis to sacrifice this body and life, and thereby realize the virtues like truth, non-violence, etc., hereafter.

(i) *Law of Karma and Rebirth:* Gandhi's belief in the law of *karma* and rebirth follows as a corollary of his belief in the immortality of the soul. Gandhi's family background, religious and social surroundings, living contact with tradition-loving people of India were, to a great extent, responsible for his firm belief in the law of *karma* and rebirth. For a comprehensive understanding of the Gandhian concept a brief explanation of the traditional concept is necessary. All the systems of Indian philosophy except the Charvakas, believe in an eternal moral order which governs not only the activities of all creatures but also of the heavenly bodies and gods. This eternal, inexorable moral law has been variously described by different systems. In *Rg Veda* it is *Rta* (*Rg-veda*, 1.1.8, 1.23.5, 1.123.13, *passim*), in the Mimamsa it is *Apurva*, in the Nyaya-vaisesika it is the theory of *Adrsta*, in Buddhism it assumes the form of *Samskara;* and a general concept of *karma* is accepted by all—Vedic and non-Vedic, theistic and atheistic—systems of Indian philosophy. In spite of differences they preach almost the same law of the conservation of moral values, merits and demerits of actions.

Gandhi says, "I firmly believe in the Law of *karma*, but I believe too in human endeavour, I regard as the *summum bonum* of life the attainment of salvation through *karma* by annihilating its effects by detachment."[99] "The law of *karma* is inexorable and impossible of evasion."[100] As regards the concept of rebirth Gandhi declares, "I am a believer in previous births and rebirths."[101] "... believing as I do in the theory of rebirth, I live in the hope that if not in this birth, in some other birth I shall be able to hug all humanity in friendly embrace."[102] Gandhi's concept of the soul and its immortality, *karma* and rebirth are interwoven into his basic metaphysical outlook fostered by the general trend of Indian idealism. It was immensely conducive to the development of the morale of *satyagrahis* during the freedom struggle. To quote him, "Re-incarnation or transmigration is a cherished belief with millions in India...."[103] Thus it had not only a religious but also a political and social utility. It is to be mentioned here that Gandhi's belief in the law of *karma* did not stand as an obstruction to, or an excuse for abandonment of human endeavour *(purusakar)*. His indomitable search for truth, the burning desire to serve humanity converted his preachings into action. That is to say, his belief in the law of *karma,* was quite compatible with the freedom of the human will.[104]

Gandhi drew heavily upon the metaphysical concepts of ancient India. The rich metaphysical heritage that accumulated through centuries is reflected in his thought. But he was not a traditionalist. He infused life into the ancient concepts and invested them with new meanings. Since preaching and practice were identical; and no watertight division was admissible amongst the various fields of life Gandhi planted these highflown metaphysical ideals, considered only theoretical so far, into the very soil from which he derived them. The ideals of traditional metaphysical idealism got deeply rooted into his being and were manifested objectively in the service of humanity. Apart from the questions whether Gandhi's contribution to metaphysical thought is worthwhile or whether it stands logical and scientific scrutiny, it is undeniable that in him socialization of metaphysical concepts occurs, perhaps, for the first time in the history of human thought. Ideation and practice go side by side in his metaphysical venture. Accordingly he calls his idealism a practical one. The humanist Gandhi here supersedes Gandhi, the metaphysician. He infuses life into the metaphysical concepts in terms of human needs and the demands of the age. Hence his metaphysical concepts are both theoretical and practical, immanent and transcendent at the same time. Here lies the novelty and significance of metaphysical concepts in Gandhian thought.

References

1. *Harijan*, 28 March 1936, p. 49; also Tendulkar, *Mahatma*, vol. IV, pp. 54-55; *Harijan*, 2 March 1940, p. 23.
2. *CWMG*, vol. XXXIII, p. 234.

3. P.T. Raju, *Idealistic Thought of India*, pp. 292-93.
4. S.C. Chatterjee and D.M. Datta, *An Introduction to Indian Philosophy*, p. 3; S. Radhakrishnan calls it 'synthetic vision'. See his *Indian Philosophy*, vol. I, p. 81.
5. Pyarelal, *Mahatma Gandhi: The Last Phase*, vol. II, p. 137.
6. Tendulkar, *op. cit.*, vol. III, p. 143.
7. Buddhadeva Bhattacharyya, *Evolution of the Political Philosophy of Gandhi*, p. 348.
8. P. Spratt, *Gandhism: An Analysis*, p. 130.
9. *CWMG*, vol. XXIX, p. 411.
10. *Ibid.*, vol. XXXVI, p. 87.
11. *Ibid.*, vol. XXIV, p. 232.
12. *Harijan*, 27 May 1939, p. 136.
13. *CWMG*, vol. XXVI, p. 202.
14. *Ibid.*, vol. XVIII, p. 73.
15. Cited in Buddhadeva Bhattacharyya, *op. cit.*, p. 71.
16. *Harijan*, 12 December 1948, p. 346.
17. *CWMG*, vol. XXXI, pp. 496-98.
18. W.H. Sheldon, 'Contrast between East and West,' in C.A. Moore (ed.) *Essays in East-West Philosophy*, p. 294. Cited in Buddhadeva Bhattacharyya, *op. cit.*, p. 8.
19. *An Autobiography*, p. xv.
20. *Young India*, 7 May 1925, p. 164.
21. Cited in Buddhadeva Bhattacharyya, *op. cit.*, p. 76.
22. K. Ramakrishna Rao, *Gandhi and Pragmatism*, p. 172.
23. Tendulkar, *op. cit.*, vol. VII, p. 128.
24. *CWMG*, vol. XIX, p. 173; for similar statements, see *Young India*, 26 December 1924, p. 427; *Harijan*, 20 April 1934, p. 78; *Harijan*, 23 June 1946, pp. 189-90.
25. *Gandhiji's Correspondence with the Government 1944-47*, p. 6.
26. *CWMG*, vol. XX, p. 159; also *Harijan*, 28 March 1936, p. 49.
27. *Ibid.*, vol. XXXV, pp. 254-55; also *Young India*, 22 December 1927, p. 425.
28. F.H. Bradley, *Appearance and Reality*, p. x.
29. For details see Raghavan N. Iyer, *The Moral and Political Thought of Mahatma Gandhi*, pp. 129-33; also see A. Campbell Garnett, 'Conscience & Conscientiousness,' in W.K. Frankena and J.T. Granrose (eds.), *Introductory Readings in Ethics*, pp. 249-61.
30. *CWMG*, vol. XXXI, p. 442.
31. William James, *The Varieties of Religious Experience*, pp. 370-72.
32. Evelyn Underhill, *Mysticism*, p. 81.
33. Edward V. Hartmann, *Philosophy of the Unconscious*, pp. 354-60.
34. G. Ramachandran, 'The Core of Gandhi,' in S. Radhakrishnan (ed.) *Mahatma Gandhi: 100 Years*, pp. 313-14.
35. Benoy Gopal Ray, *Gandhian Ethics*, p. 19.
36. Romain Rolland, *Mahatma Gandhi*, p. 94.

37. Madan G. Gandhi, *Gandhian Aesthetics*, pp. 83-84.
38. V.M. Bedekar, 'The Vrata in Ancient Indian Culture and Gandhi,' in *Gandhi Marg*, vol. IV, no. 4, October 1960, p. 322.
39. I.C. Sharma, *Ethical Philosophies of India*, p. 300.
40. V.M. Bedekar, *op. cit.*, p. 322.
41. K. Ramaswami Sastri, *The Evolution of Indian Mysticism*, p. 9.
42. *Harijan*, 8 July 1933, p. 4.
43. Hermann Lotze, *Outlines of a Philosophy of Religion*, p. 143.
44. See Ch. VI (Sec. natural calamities).
45. *Harijan*, 6 April 1940, p. 79.
46. Jawaharlal Nehru, *Mahatma Gandhi*, p. 54.
47. Edward V. Hartmann, *op. cit.*, pp. 354-60; also K. Ramaswami Sastri, *op. cit.*, p. 17.
48. *An Autobiography*, pp. 206-7.
49. Gopinath Dhawan, *op. cit.*, p. 125.
50. P. Spratt, *op. cit.*, p. 127.
51. *Harijan*, 6 March 1937, p. 26.
52. *Ibid.*, 9 October 1937, p. 292.
53. *Ibid.*, 28 January 1939, p. 443; also *CWMG*, vol. XXXIII, p. 232.
54. Paul F. Power, *Gandhi on World Affairs*, p. 35.
55. *CWMG*, vol. XXXIII, p. 234.
56. Gopinath Dhawan, *op. cit.*, p. 39.
57. Answer to three questions put by S. Radhakrishnan in S. Radhakrishnan and J.H. Muirhead (eds.), *Contemporary Indian Philosophy*, p. 21.
58. *CWMG*, vol. XXVI, p. 225; also *CWMG*, vol. XLVIII, p. 405.
59. K. Kalelkar (ed.) *To a Gandhian Capitalist*, p. 49.
60. *CWMG*, vol. XXIX, p. 411.
61. P.T. Raju, *op. cit.*, p. 297.
62. Buddhadeva Bhattacharyya, *op. cit.*, p. 480.
63. Morarji Desai, inaugural address to the lectures delivered by Shriman Narayan, in Shriman Narayan, *Gandhi: The Man and his Thought*, p. x.
64. Shriman Narayan, *op. cit.*, p. 2.
65. K. Ramakrishna Rao, *op. cit.*, p. 4.
66. *CWMG*, vol. XXVIII, p. 428.
67. Surendra Verma, *Metaphysical Foundation of Mahatma Gandhi's Thought*, p. 30.
68. *CWMG*, vol. XXIX, p. 411.
69. *Ibid.*, vol. XXXVII, p. 349.
70. *Ibid.*, vol. XXVI, p. 224.
71. An answer to Will Durant, '*On the Meaning of Life*,' in V.B. Kher (ed.), *In Search of the Supreme*, vol. II, p. 262.
72. *Harijan*, 22 June 1947, p. 200.
73. *Ibid.*, 18 August 1946, p. 267.
74. V.P. Varma, *The Political Philosophy of Mahatma Gandhi and Sarvodaya*, p. 38.

75. *CWMG*, vol. XXVI, p. 225.
76. *Ibid.*, vol. XXIX, p. 412.
77. See, ch. VI (sec. Morality is the basis of all).
78. David Ross, *Aristotle*, pp. 71-75.
79. S. Radhakrishnan and J.H. Muirhead (eds.), *op. cit.*, p. 21.
80. *CWMG*, vol. XXVI, p. 224.
81. *Harijan*, 24 August 1947, p. 289. This reminds us of Biblical phrase "And God said, Let us make man in our image, after our likeness." (Genesis, I).
82. *Harijan*, 22 June 1947, p. 200; also *CWMG*, vol. XXVI, p. 224.
83. An answer to Will Durant, *op. cit.*, p. 262.
84. *Harijan*, 24 August 1947, p. 289.
85. *Ibid.*, 16 June 1946, p. 183.
86. D.M. Datta, *The Philosophy of Mahatma Gandhi*, p. 65.
87. S.C. Chatterjee & D.M. Datta, *An Introduction to Indian Philosophy*, pp. 22-24.
88. D.M. Datta, *op. cit.*, p. 66.
89. *Ibid.*
90. S. Radhakrishnan, *Indian Philosophy*, vol. I, p. 441.
91. *Harijan*, 16 June 1946, p. 183.
92. *CWMG*, vol. XXVIII, p. 148.
93. *From Yeravda Mandir*, pp. 30-31.
94. See, Ch. III, (sec. Pragmatism).
95. *CWMG*, vol. XLII, p. 474.
96. John Burnet, *Greek Philosophy*, pp. 25-27.
97. *Harijan*, 15 February 1948, p. 33, also *CWMG*, vol. XLVIII, p. 180.
98. William Wordsworth, 'Ode on Intimation of Immortality from Recollections of Early Childhood' in F.T. Palgrave (ed.), *The Golden Treasury*, pp. 347-48.
99. *Young India*, 18 October 1928, in *Young India 1927-28*, p. 878.
100. *Ibid.*, 21 April 1927, in A.T. Hingorani (ed.), *The Teaching of the Gita*, p. 70 fn.
101. *Harijan*, 18 August 1940, p. 254; also *Harijan*, 15 February 1948, p. 33.
102. *CWMG*, vol. XLV, p. 349.
103. *Ibid.*, vol. IX, p. 446.
104. See, Ch. IV, (sec. Freedom of Will).

4

PHILOSOPHICAL OUTLOOK (II)

We have earlier discussed Gandhi's epistemological and metaphysical concepts. But a comprehensive view of his philosophical outlook demands an elaboration of his ethical and religious concepts. As Gopinath Dhawan opines, "His political philosophy and political technique are only corollaries of his religious and moral principles."[1] Although stated in an exaggerated way, the above opinion contains, as our later discussion will disclose, an element of truth in it. The moral and religious concepts interact upon one another throughout Gandhian thought.

His Ethical Concepts

(a) *Asceticism:* Asceticism as a moral theory advises us to be stringently moral, to practise severe self-discipline, to extirpate desires that fetter the soul to the life of the flesh. It preaches a life of suffering, self-denial, and self-sacrifice. The flesh is antagonistic to the spirit which is essentially pure in itself. Hence the flesh, the life of desires must be tortured and crucified at the altar of the spirit. John S. Mackenzie observes, "This sometimes goes so far, as in the case of the Indian mystics and the Mediaeval monks, as to lead to the positive infliction of torture. The ostensible reason for this is frequently the idea that torture is pleasing to the gods; but the fundamental reason seems to lie in the desire of suppressing the flesh and its lusts."[2]

Now let us consider the elements of asceticism in Gandhian thought. Gandhi prescribed the vows of truth, non-violence, celibacy, control of the palate, non-thieving, non-possession, fearlessness, etc., as obligatory for the inmates of *Satyagraha Asram*. Self-purification which is the keynote of Gandhian morality can be attained only through the rigid observance of the above puritan virtues. The simple term *ahimsa* (non-violence) implies not only non-killing or harmlessness but also uttermost selflessness, forgiveness, and conquest of anger, pride, and hatred. Here it is necessary to note that Gandhi's idea of *ahimsa* was not based on the Vedic concept of it. He derived the concept of *ahimsa* virtually from the ascetic sources as preached by the Jainas, Buddhists and Yogins; and it was this ascetic or *sramanic* concept which he adopted. In this context Unto Tahtinen comments, "Gandhi's idea of *ahimsa* was not based on the Vedic concept of *ahimsa*. He ruled out all exceptions in the application of *ahimsa*. He derived his *ahimsa* from the ascetic sources, and it was this ascetic or *sramanic* concept which he applied, for the first time, to politics and economics."[3] Thus the ascetic element is evident in Gandhi's concept of non-violence.

He advised the *satyagrahis* never to assault, insult or curse his opponents. The Socratic dictum "There is no holiday from virtue" was deeply rooted in his being. He preached as well as practised the virtue of *ahimsa* in his life. Several times he resorted to fasting day after day, sometimes week after week with an ardent zeal to purify his inner self, sometimes to awaken conscience amongst the frenzied communal masses. In short, according to Gandhi, the realization of truth without any expectation of results, even if it costs life, should be our *summum bonum*. Indifference to pleasure and pain, natural and simple life should be cultivated. All desires and instincts, especially sexual instincts except for procreation, should be suppressed if extirpation is not possible. We should be non-violent in thought, word and deed. Self-torture, self-suffering, receiving others' misdeeds on oneself and suffering the consequences thereof, etc., are the salient features of Gandhi's moral thought. Thus ascetic and rigoristic features are evident in Gandhian thought. In this context, Nirmal Kumar Bose observes, "he (Gandhi) represented a hard, puritanic form of self-discipline, something which we usually associate with mediaeval Christian ascetics or Jain recluses."[4]

A relevant question may be asked: Can Gandhi be called an ascetic in the strict sense? J.B. Kripalani observes, "... in no healthy normal society can his life be considered as one of the mortification of the flesh."[5] Gandhi himself says, "It is wrong to call me an ascetic. The ideals that regulate my life are presented for acceptance by mankind in general. I have arrived at them by gradual evolution. Every step was thought out, well-considered, and taken with the greatest deliberation. Both my continence and non-violence were derived from personal experience and became necessary in response to the calls of public duty."[6] The pragmatic and humanistic note of the statement is here noteworthy. The golden thread that weaves his thought into an integrated whole is the ceaseless search for truth which can be roughly expressed in a dictum: *Freedom: from within and without.* For the emancipation of the motherland Gandhi wanted a band of workers (*satyagrahis*) like himself who would be free from all sorts of human bondage, both internal and external. He did not want them to be ascetics or recluses who would mostly seek self-liberation rather than the liberation of mankind in general. Removal of human sufferings is the keynote of his self-discipline otherwise called 'asceticism'. Our later analysis of cardinal virtues prescribed by him will show that they arose not from any rigoristic and abstract end but rather from objective ends, like social, religious, political, economic, etc. necessities of the surroundings of that time.[7] Verrier Elwin opines, "When he (Gandhi) told his followers that they mustn't marry, that they must have no sexual relations, it was not out of any absolute spiritual philosophy, it was rather a political expedient for the time being. And we must remember that for him ethics and politics were the same."[8]

To conclude, we have so far brought forth the ascetic elements of Gandhian thought. Our later analysis will show that humanism is the nucleus of it. His ardent zeal for the welfare of humanity, his dedication to the service of humanity often inspired, more strictly, compelled him to prescribe some ways of life that may appear to an ordinary mind rigorous and ascetic. But this is not the last word. This is "a temporary ethic, an ethic for an interim period."[9] Thus asceticism in Gandhian thought is apparent, an interim one, not absolute and final.

(b) *Eudaemonism:* The word eudaemonism is derived from the Greek root *'Eudaemonia'* which means well-being or welfare. The spirit of eudaemonism is that well-being or welfare of the people by dint of 'well-doing' should be the end of our lives. Service to humanity is a master passion with Gandhi. Welfare and well-being of the people were the burning questions that engaged his mind day and night. His campaign of *sarvodaya* (welfare of all) can be cited as an example. To him, human beings, irrespective of caste, creed and religion, are sparks of infinite Truth or God who is also the supreme Good, the almighty moral Governor. Human beings can realize Truth or God by social service, by single-hearted dedication to the service of humanity. To quote Gandhi, "The bearing of this religion on social life is or has to be seen in one's daily social contact. To be true to such religion one has to lose oneself in continuous and continuing service of our life.... Hence, for me, there is no escape from social service, there is no happiness on earth beyond or apart from it."[10] Moreover, *ahimsa* plays an important role in the teachings and preachings of Gandhi. Non-violence in thought, word and deed is the means towards the realization of Truth. And active service to humanity is one of the chief constituents of non-violence. In short, welfare and well-being of the people are the pivotal points of Gandhi's humanism, and thereby of his life and works. This is the eudaemonistic element of Gandhian thought.

(c) *Altruism:* The term altruism is derived from *altrui* which means somebody else, and hence the etymological meaning of altruism is regard for others as a principle of action. J.S. Mackenzie explains, "... the term *Altruism* has been used to denote devotion to the ends of others."[11] As discussed above Gandhi led almost an ascetic life, and dedicated his eventful life to the cause of others. Gandhi's way of life and practice, the code of discipline, and cardinal virtues that he prescribed for the *satyagrahis*, although criticized as rigoristic, were purposely designed towards some teleological end, the welfare of human beings in general. His first acquaintance with Marxian literature at Poona Jail seemed to reinforce the altruistic cast of his mind. The Marxian literature *A Handbook of Marxism* engraved an eternal moral in his mind. He summed up this moral in a sentence, "All for each and each for all."[12] Hence comes Gandhi's clarion call to all, "Nations are sustained neither by wealth nor by armies but by righteousness alone. It is the duty of man to bear this truth in mind and practise altruism, which is the highest form of morality."[13] Thus altruism "is the highest form of morality" towards which he dedicated the *sarvodaya* campaign, nay, the whole of his life and works.

(d) *Truth—The Ultimate Moral Standard:* The problem of a moral standard is a burning question amongst the moral scientists. In our everyday life we face so many problems of which rightness or wrongness of the happenings around us is one. This urges us to pursue an ideal or standard through which the value of actions from the ethical standpoint can be assessed. This spirit of an ethical norm or ideal or standard is well expressed by J.S. Mackenzie who says, "The study of Ethics in the stricter sense begins with the consideration of the nature of the Ideal, Standard, or End, by reference to which conduct is pronounced to be right or wrong, good or evil."[14] Gandhian moral science is no exception to this.

Truth is used in Gandhian thought in various senses. It may be variously called the highest goal, highest good, absolute existent, God, ultimate moral standard, etc. R.N. Iyer aptly observes, "From first to last, *satya*, or truth, was sacred to Gandhi—the supreme value in ethics, politics and religion, the ultimate source of authority and of appeal, the *raison d' etre* of all existence."[15] Since, to Gandhi, religion and morality are identical "there is no religion higher than Truth and Righteousness." Here Gandhi treats Truth as the highest righteousness from the religious standpoint. R.N. Iyer comments, "The Moral Law is the Law of Truth; *satya* is identical with *dharma*, and *rta* (cosmic equilibrium) is the same as *sat* (Absolute Truth)."[16] Sometimes Gandhi mentions service to mankind as the ultimate moral standard. "Thus service of the Indians in South Africa ever revealed to me new implications of truth at every stage. Truth is like a vast tree, which yields more and more fruit, the more you nurture it."[17] So, to Gandhi, truth is the highest moral standard which can be realized through service to humanity. In short, Gandhi uses the term truth in various contexts with different implications. Everywhere it is invested with the majesty of an ultimate standard to which final appeal may be made. Buddhadeva Bhattacharyya observes, "*Ethical Religion* incidentally affords an indication of the meaning of Truth.... When not used in a metaphysical sense it seems to mean the moral law, or set of laws.... The deduction is confirmed by his writings, in which Truth is made to cover very many principles."[18]

Gandhi distinguishes between truth as the *summum bonum*, i.e., an absolute, universal, infinite truth and truth as a vow or a means, i.e., relative truth. Since truth in the absolute sense is identical with God every attempt on the part of any human being to grasp the absolute or ultimate truth needs must fail owing to his inherent imperfection. To quote Gandhi, "But it is impossible for us to realize perfect Truth so long as we are imprisoned in this mortal frame. We can only visualize it in our imagination. We cannot, through the instrumentality of this ephemeral body, see face to face Truth which is eternal."[19] Thus absolute truth is unknown and unknowable to imperfect beings like us. But that does not mean that we should remain idle. Life is a continuous process, a dynamic flow. Its course is infested with good and bad, virtuous and vicious activities. Crooked is the course of life. It demands a norm, a standard, if an absolute one is not possible, by which we can determine the merits and demerits of actions of our everyday lives. This opens an avenue to casuistry, an ethics for everyday life. As mentioned above he adopts relative truth as a 'beacon, a shield and buckler' for the period during which absolute truth is not realized. Indeed, this pragmatic treatment of truth, i.e., the adoption of relative truth is the keynote of his satyagraha movement.

A similar distinction between absolute and relative morality appears in the philosophical works of Friedrich Nietzsche and Henry Bergson. To Nietzsche all moral values are related to the geographical, historical, social and other conditions of the people. Moral values like good and evil, virtue and vice are not eternal, absolute, and immutable, but relative that vary from man to man, time to time, and place to place.[20] Henry Bergson distinguishes between closed or relative morality and open or absolute morality. The former one admits concessions under special circumstances, and commands a few individuals of a particular society. Open or absolute morality, on the other hand, is inherent, implicitly or explicitly, in human beings of all times of all places.[21]

Gandhi struggled throughout his life for the oppressed and downtrodden of humanity. In every sphere of life absolute truth, the ultimate moral standard, showed him the path like the pole-star. Circumstances sometimes compelled him to take shelter in relative truth. Nevertheless, it is not at all a deviation from absolute truth. Gandhi says, "Euclid's line is one without breadth but no one has so far been able to draw it and never will. All the same it is only by keeping the ideal line in mind that we have made progress in geometry. What is true here is true of every ideal."[22] Thus ultimate truth liike the Euclidean geometrical line is his ultimate moral standard. But since it is beyond our grasp, he adopted relative truth to solve the problems of everyday life. Truth is absolute in the abstract sense while relative in the contextual sense.

(e) *Self-realization or Perfection—The Summum Bonum:* The problem of the ultimate standard of morality and the ultimate end of life are interwoven into one another. The realization of the self—the harmonious development of our whole nature—is a favourite topic of the moral scientists, both Western and Eastern. A galaxy of eminent Western thinkers from Socrates to Mackenzie—have contributed to it. In the Upanishadic ages, the saints proclaimed, *Atmanam Biddhi* or know thyself. The orthodox systems of Indian philosophy have enriched this tradition. It is here noteworthy that the self here signifies an individual self; and not any abstract or social self. William Lillie observes, perhaps aptly, "In morality, as the phrase self-realization reminds us, the perfection with which we are concerned is the perfection of the individual self, and every individual counts."[23]

An ardent desire for the realization of God or that perfect being of whom we are only sparks is present throughout Gandhian thought. It is his faith that perfect Being or God being latent in us, we can realize Him bit by bit through self-discipline. Gandhi says, "I am being daily led nearer to It by constant prayer."[24] He believed in human perfectibility, with certain limitations, from the core of his heart. It is the *summum bonum*, the ultimate goal, which we should strive our utmost to realize. Of course, Gandhi is fully conscious of our inherent imperfection. But this natural limitation would not obstruct our way to perfection. By dint of ceaseless efforts men should bring out their potentiality, more precisely perfection, in its full bloom. To quote him, "Man will ever remain imperfect, and it will always be his part to try to be perfect."[25] Buddhadeva Bhattacharyya here comments, "He knew that man at the present stage of his being was not perfect, but that did not negate the theoretical possibility of further development which amounted to his perfectibility. This idea of human perfectibility is a keypoint for the philosophy of non-violence."[26] Indeed, human perfectibility is a part and parcel of his philosophy of life. Throughout his life he was in search of it. The ever-developing nature of human beings is the *elan vital* of perfectionism. Gandhi believed, at least, in the theoretical perfectibility of every human being. Any man, however depraved, may undergo reformation and thereby attain perfection by ceaseless self-disciplinary efforts. But this optimism is shaken owing to inherent imperfection. That is why Gandhi urges us not to give up our attempts to realize it. He says, "We shall ever fail to realize it, but shall never cease to realize it."[27] It reminds us of the immortal lines of Tennyson, "...but strong in will/To strive, to seek, to find, and not to yield."[28]

(f) *Freedom of Will:* Every science aims at some definite and well-disciplined knowledge. For this purpose it brings out laws and corollaries under the category of some fundamental rules which are taken for granted without any critical inquiry. In geometry the conceptions of dot, straight line, circle; in psychology the conception of mind; in logic the fundamental rules of thought; in moral science the concept of the freedom of will are such fundamental axioms. In a sense the postulate of freedom of will is the nucleus of moral science. An individual as a moral agent, as a permanent self must act freely, i.e., act without any compulsion, because, he cannot be held responsible for actions performed under extraneous influence. The ethical terms—right and wrong, merit and demerit, reward and punishment, virtue and vice—all lose their significance without freedom of will. Thus freedom of will is a necessity, an indispensable postulate of moral life.

Gandhi's concept of freedom of will is a necessary deduction from his concept of *karma* and rebirth which we have already discussed. And we have seen that he treated all human beings as sparks of Truth or God. He perceived a celestial design throughout the universe. All human beings, because of inherent imperfection, are at every step of their lives under the superintendance of the divine power, God. Not only that even a blade of grass cannot exist without His permission. The divine unseen Power governs the course of events including the minds of men. Gandhi says, "Man can change temperament, can control it, but cannot eradicate it. God has not given him so much liberty. If the leopard can change his spots then only can man modify the peculiarities of his spiritual constitution."[29] The deterministic note of divine influence on the Gandhian concept of free will is evident from the above excerpt. He felt the heavenly rhythm in every sphere of his eventful life. B.G. Gokhale observes, "Gandhi's view is essentially ethical and spiritual and comes close to the ancient Indian view that human history is the unfolding of man's waywardness constantly checked by divine will and love."[30]

For an adequate assessment of Gandhian standpoint a few words regarding the Western trend of divine determinism would not be irrelevant. An extreme form of theo-centric determinism is found in the writings of St. Augustine who dedicated almost everything to God and denounced the role of human freedom. Calvin followed his footprint. Ambrose, the ancient man of lore, wrote, "If God knows the future beforehand, and it must come to pass, prayer is vain."[31] This note of divine determinism is fairly expressed in the composition of Geoffrey Chaucer and John Milton. To Chaucer God's foreknowledge is a necessary condition of our freedom of will.[32] In

Milton's *Paradise Lost* God foretells the success of Satan in perverting mankind. God argues, in defence of divine justice, that in spite of divine determinism man can exercise his will freely.[33]

From the above it is evident that divine determinism does not altogether annihilate human freedom. Human beings, although hedged by an infinite variety of circumstances, may steer the course of life so as to mould their destiny by dint of efficiency and endeavour. Did Gandhi view this problem from the above angle of vision? Without a doubt the answer is 'yes.' Every student of the history of Indian freedom movement knows it well that Gandhi was a tireless soldier, a champion of freedom throughout his life. In spite of his firm belief in divine determinism he actively participated in the flow of his life, and brought a revolutionary change in the social and political outlook of the people of India. Indeed, Gandhi did not take the inexorable law of *karma* and freedom of will as antithetical. He believed in the unlimited potentiality of human efforts or endeavour (*purusakara*). Here he was immensely influenced by the traditional concept of human endeavour or *purusakara*. In *Yoga-Vasistha-Ramayana* (2.4-9) we are told that karmic network may be overcome, and eradicated by earnest zeal and sufficiently strong personal endeavour (*purusakara*). In *Panchadasi* (6.158) *purusakara* is appreciated on humanitarian ground. It proclaims that divine power manifests itself in human beings as personal endeavour. Bhisma, the great hero of *The Mahabharata*, declares in *Santiparva*, "I consider personal effort to be above all; belief in fate makes man dull. (*purusam hi param manye*; *daivam nischitya muhyate*)." It is echoed also in *Yajnavalkya-Smrti* (1.351) which describes personal endeavour as the matrix of all success. It says, "Just as a chariot cannot move on one wheel, so fate (*daiva*) without personal endeavour (*purusakara*) cannot lead to success. In *The Gita*, (18.14) we are told that five factors, prescribed by both Sankhya and Vedanta, collectively lead to success of all actions. Of them *cesta* (personal endeavour) plays the pivotal role.

Gandhi seems to have formed his mind in the above light. He laid much emphasis on personal endeavour although the inexorable law of *karma* played a key role in his life. To quote him, "Although I believe in the inexorable law of *karma* I am striving to do so many things, every moment of my life is a strenuous endeavour, which is an attempt to build up more *karma* to undo the past and add to the present."[34] Thus his belief in traditional *karmic* law did not make him a cripple. His belief in the infinite potentiality of human beings showed him the way to truth. It is by dint of *purusakara* or personal endeavour that an individual can come out of the *karmic* maze, can undo the obstructions of the past, steer out future course of life, and thereby become the architect of his fate.

His Religious Ideas

(a) *An Atheist:* We have seen the influence of Hinduism, especially that of the Vallabhacarya sect, Christianity and Jainism on the mind of young Gandhi. While Gandhi was in his teens his native state Kathiawad was passing through a critical stage of history. The British administration was exerting its influence vigorously on the native rulers of Kathiawad. The vigorous campaign of the Christian missionaries and consequent conversion of natives created a tremendous impact on the mind of young Gandhi. The impact of Western culture and civilization on the people of Kathiawad was remarkable. Indians, the Young Bengal group of Bengal, and Young Bombay party who were moulded in the English educational machinery, and brought up after the fashion of the Western society, were shinning in the midst of a declining society. Gandhi passed his childhood and boyhood in the above-mentioned formative background of a fast-changing social order. A correct assessment of the mind of young Gandhi demands a critical inquiry of some delinquencies of his teenage in the above light. Otherwise, it may lead to disastrous misunderstanding. Some scholars of eminence reflect on some incidents of his teenage, and cast doubt on his belief in God. One eminent scholar whom we shall shortly discuss charges him with atheism outright. Of course, some lines of his *Autobiography* and some humanitarian statements made by him loosely at different phases of his life are to a great extent responsible for this.

Generally the term atheism points to the doctrine that preaches proofs of the non-existence of God. Here *a* means not and *theos* means God. Thus literally atheism means Godlessness. G. Ramchandra Rao alias Gora's opinion may be considered in this context. In support of his thesis he tenders the following arguments: In the draft of Congress publications Gandhi's role is well known. He prescribed solicitation of the blessings of God in the Congress pledge. But when objections were raised from some corner he readily consented to drop it without hesitation by saying, "So far as the conscientious objection is concerned the mention of God may be removed from the Congress pledge of which I am proud to think I was the author. Had such an objection been raised at the time, I would have yielded at once."[35] From this Gora feels inclined to present the Gandhi-image to a definite pattern, i.e., to his own conviction in atheism. But this standpoint cannot be founded on a rational plinth. Because Gandhi tendered a more emphatic argument for the existence of God in the same issue of *Young India*. There he moves. "One may banish the word 'God' from the Congress but one has no power to banish the Thing Itself. What is a solemn affirmation if it is not the same thing as in the name of God. And surely conscience is but a poor and laborious paraphrase of the simple combination of three letters called God."[36] Thus Gora in his eagerness to find atheistic elements in Gandhian thought ignored, perhaps consciously, this valuable point of Gandhian theism.

In 1946 Gandhi in order to accommodate Gora as a political follower dropped the term 'God'—by replacing it with another term "some power which we may or may not call divine"—from the pledge of Independence Day. In 1948, he consented to perform the marriage ceremony of Gora's daughter without any reference to God. A critical analysis will show that the replacement of the term God by the term 'some power' does not at all point to his disbelief in God. Further, in a similar instance while conversing with Nirmal Kumar Bose he was contented with the replacement of God by the term 'Truth'.[37] Thus the aforesaid replacement does not necessarily signify atheism.

Gora picks up some loose statements of Gandhi to build up castle of atheism in the air. In 1945 in the course of a conversation with Gora, Gandhi declares, "I can neither say my theism is right, nor atheism is wrong." He calls himself a 'superatheist.'[38] And during a barbarous rioting in Bombay he exclaimed with grief that since belief in God is the root cause of communal butchery man should give it up in order to maintain peace in the country.[39] From this Gora infers that "within my knowledge, there was visible change in his attitude towards atheism between 1941 and 1948."[40] Hence he concludes, "If he felt that the progress of humanity required leaving God altogether, I am sure, he was not the man to hesitate."[41] Here Gora's assessment appears to be unsound. Because he fails to see the spirit of the aforesaid statements. The apparent atheism that we observe here arose out of a practical necessity, i.e., his deep concern for the cause of humanity. The paradoxes or contradictions that we observe, here and there, in his thought are due to his boundless love for mankind. A thorough reading of his thought will prove his theism beyond doubt. Because in the above-cited paragraph he warns Gora, "Atheism is a denial of self. No one has succeeded in its propagation."[42] Gandhi saw God face to face in humanity. Hence his concern for God-man or *Naranarayan* did not always follow the logical track.

Louis Fischer also notices the same trend of thought in young Gandhi. He collects data from the narration of early life by Gandhi in his *Autobiography.*

D.G. Tendulkar calls Gandhi an atheist outright. He writes, "He broke one Hindu custom after another. He became an atheist."[43] Here it is noteworthy that Tendulkar also takes *Autobiography* as the chief source of information on Gandhi's life. In order to have a proper assessment of Tendulkar's comments, the original passages, the source of his information, need elucidation.

Gandhi narrates some incidents of his moral degradation on which Tendulkar comments: "He broke one Hindu custom after another." (*supra*) Gandhi recollects, "My friend once took me to a brothel.... I was almost struck blind and dumb in this den of vice.... She naturally lost patience with me, and showed me the door, with abuses and insults.... I have ever since given thanks to God for having saved me.... A relative and I became fond of smoking. Not that we saw any good in smoking or were enamoured of the smell of a cigarette. We simply imagined a sort of pleasure in emitting clouds of smoke from our mouth.... But we had no money.... So we began to steal coppers from the servant's pocket money in order to purchase Indian cigarettes .... But we were far from being satisfied with such things as these. Our want of independence began to smart. It was unbearable that we should be unable to do anything without the elders' permission. At last, in sheer disgust, we decided to commit suicide."[44]

Now let us examine, in the above perspective, Tendulkar's objection whether these violations of customs, or 'failing,' to quote Gandhi, "point to atheism or not." The 'failings' were not deep-rooted psychologically. These sprang from juvenile desire of an immature boy to enjoy the world as it presents itself. When adolescence, the golden period of human life, knocks at the door of later boyhood, new horizons burst upon the youngster's sight and he hears the clarion call of the brave new world. This indomitable spirit, though immature, challenges everything that stands in its way. It is from this juvenile standpoint that Gandhi's confessions are to be evaluated. Guidance and affectionate care of elders seem to him 'want of independence' and 'unbearable'. Smoking a cigarette, to him was "a sort of pleasure in emitting clouds of smoke from our mouths." It was just smoking for the sake of smoking. Other delinquencies that we have mentioned above have their origin in curiosity, and were not motivated from atheism in any way. And Tendulkar's comment that 'Mohandas went through a short spell of religious crisis' is, by no means, justified by the facts stated above.

In the *Autobiography* we find that Gandhi in his teens used to go with elders to the Haveli, the Vallabhachari places of worship run by chief priests (*Maharajas*) in the royal style. The Haveli could not attract the mind of young Gandhi because he "did not like its glitter and pomp." C.D. Devanesen observes, "Gandhi reacted, however, against the constant dressing up of Thakorji in fine clothes. He rejected the *ananda* of ecstatic aspects of Haveli worship, assisted by music and flowers, and took what was in consonance with his asceticism."[45] Again, the "rumours of immorality being practised there" is not at all baseless. The Havelis as we have seen were places for worship of the Vallabhacharjya sampradaya which was founded by Sri Vallabha, a Telugu Brahman in the fifteenth century. Sri Vallabha followed *Bhakti* (devotion) cult which worships Lord Krishna as *Ananda-swarupa*, an evershining store house of bliss, a symbol of lively sport or *lila*. They observed the religious rites with light and colour, 'glitter and pomp.' C.D. Devanesen observes, "The danger, however, in this kind of worship of Sri Krishna was that it sometimes results in eroticism attracting criticism."[46] The sexual corruptions of the Vallabhacharis were often an object of gossip amongst the people of Kathiawad. It was to these charges of immorality that Gandhi referred to in his *Autobiography*. C.D. Devanesen comments, "The young Gandhi was undoubtedly influenced by the charges of immorality aimed against his own sampradaya and his later attitude to sex certainly resembles that of the Swaminarayan sect."[47] Gandhi who made morality the nucleus of life naturally 'lost all interest' in the Havelis. But loss of interest does not mean atheism as alleged by Philip Spratt. At that time he also 'developed a sort of dislike' for Christianity on the ground that he could not endure the diet, clothes and especially the abusive campaign of Christian missionaries. Thus the terms 'lost all interest', and 'dislike' in no way amount to atheism.

Gandhi himself admits his doubts in the *Autobiography*. Gandhi writes, "There was a cousin of mine, still alive, for whose intellect

I had great regard. To him I turned with my doubts. But he could not resolve them.... 'With intellect more developed and with more reading I shall understand it better,' I said to myself."[48] This last sentence strikes the keynote of Gandhian theism. Gandhi optimistically hopes that his doubts regarding the scriptures will be removed in the course of further studies. And the term 'with intellect more developed' clearly shows that he was fully conscious of the immaturity of his intellect. Gandhi wrote his *Autobiography*, the chief source of all criticism, at an age when his intellect has attained maturity. He had then overcome the doubts, and solved the puzzles that arose in his mind in his teens. We have seen above that Gandhi used various concepts of Indian philosophy without knowing their full implications. He declared himself a *syadvadi*, an *anekantavadi*, etc., which he was not in the strict sense. Being born and brought up in the traditional order of Indian society, he coined up the notions that were frequently used by people in his surroundings. The doubt that Gandhi felt is not total absence of belief. Doubt is an intermediate stage between belief and disbelief. Gandhi confused the term atheism with doubts and 'failings', i.e., juvenile delinquencies.

(b) *A Pantheist:* From the above it is clear that in spite of his doubts, 'failings' and declaration of atheism he was a firm believer in God. The eagerness of a host of critics to brand him as an atheist was due to a misunderstanding of Gandhian thought. A relevant question may be asked: What is, according to him, the relation of God to the world? Is God a transcendent Being as in Deism preached by John Toland, Tindal and Chubb? Or, is God immanent in this world as pantheism advocated by Spinoza, Hegel, the Hegelians and Vedanta claims? Or, is God both immanent in and transcendent of the world of things and minds with which He is not completely identified? The last view is propounded by pantheism. An analysis of Gandhi's idea of God may suggest some solution to this problem.

In the realm of Western thought God is generally described as Omnipotent, Omnipresent, Omniscient, Eternal, etc. Gandhi's idea of God, although it includes Western attributes, goes far beyond it. He describes, "God is that indefinable something which we all feel but which we do not know...."[49] Elsewhere Gandhi says, "...God is nameless and since God has many forms we also consider Him formless, and since He speaks to us through many tongues we consider Him to be speechless and so on."[50]

Surendra Verma sums up the attributes of God after Gandhi as follows: "For him God has a double significance, metaphysical as well as religious. God is not only the Ultimate Reality with him. He is also a practical reality for his living response.... Gandhi conceives God to be 'One without a second'.... for all practical purposes Gandhi regards God to be a concrete person... but from the philosophical point of view God is for him impersonal.... God as he conceives Him is 'the Law and the Law-giver rolled into one'...."[51]

From the above discussion we can draw a vivid picture of Gandhian concept of God as an all-embracing spirit which in stead of absorbing the world, things and minds in its infinite bosom, allows them to enjoy relative reality and discharge their respective function. Like Deists he does not separate the world system from God which gives rise to dualism. On the other hand, he does not like pantheists reduce the dignity of human being to a mere moral agent, a dumb ethical machinery of God who as the only reality denies freedom of human beings, the mere appearances, so to say. To Gandhi, as we have seen, human beings enjoy freedom although it is limited by divine will. He conceives God as both physical and meta-physical, personal and impersonal, theoretical and practical, immanent and transcendent at the same time. The immanence and transcendence of God in this world is the pivotal point of panentheism. Thus Gandhi's conception of God leads to panentheism.

(c) *God as Truth—Truth as God:* From the early dawn of civilization man is pursuing truth. This long search after truth has given birth to various dogmas upheld by different schools of thinkers. In the metaphysical world the problem and nature of truth have been the burning questions of idealism and realism. In epistemology, it is the pivotal point of coherence, correspondence, pragmatic and other theories. Generally we use the term truth in the epistemological sense of truth or falsity which we attribute to propositions of our thinking. As he was eclectic by nature, Gandhi viewed the problem of truth from metaphysical, epistemological, ethical, religious, political—all possible angles of vision. We have discussed its metaphysical (as ultimate reality) and moral (as the ultimate moral standard) implications above. Here we shall bring out the religious implication of truth in Gandhian thought.

What is the nature of truth in Gandhian thought? Is it an object that stimulates visual sensation? Is it anything of the nature of sound that can entertain auditory sense organs? Or does it transcend the purview of our five sense-organs? So many questions may be asked in this regard. To a question, what is Truth? Gandhi answers, "A difficult question, but I have solved it for myself by saying that it is what the voice within tells one. How then, you ask different people think of different and contrary truths? Seeing that the human mind works through innumerable media and that evolution of the human mind is not the same for all, it follows that what may be truth for one may be untruth for another and hence those who have made these experiments have come to the conclusion that there are certain conditions to making experiments ... those who would make diligent search after Truth—God—must go through these vows: the vow of truth—speaking and thinking of truth, the vow of *brahmacharya*, of non-violence, poverty and non-possession. If you do not take these five vows you may not embark on the experiment."[52]

In the realm of religion Gandhi perceives truth as an all-inclusive reality which manifests itself through the diversity of this world. That is why he attributes truth, that assumes different forms in different perspectives, to God. Truth is the only suitable term, available to human beings, that can approximate to the infinite attributes of God. Of course, as a true agnostic and absolutist he believes that these attempts would give us an approximate, and never a final, idea of God. To quote Gandhi, "You have asked me why I consider that God is Truth. In my early childhood or youth, I was taught to repeat what in Hindu scriptures is one thousand names of God.... But these thousand names of God were by no means an exhaustive list. We believe—and I think it is the truth—that God has as many names as there are creatures.... But deep down in me I say God may be Love, but God is Truth. If it is possible for the human tongue to give the fullest description of God, for myself I have come to the conclusion that God is Truth."[53] We shall see later that truth and God are one and convertible terms to Gandhi. The connotation of the term Truth which appears to our minds at the first sight is epistemological in nature, namely, it is a piece of knowledge that conforms to reality. Gandhi treated 'God and Truth' as convertible terms, and viewed them from all possible viewpoints—epistemological, metaphysical, ethical, religious, etc. That is why to treat Truth from merely epistemological standpoint—as a quality of propositions or judgements—is to attain a partial, a fragmentary picture of Truth which, in fact, is a concrete and all-inclusive reality. Indeed, this epistemo-centric thought web is the main obstacle to our clear understanding of Gandhi's dictum: God is Truth. So, we should give up this narrow outlook and consider it in a wider perspective. Gandhi's view may suggest some clue in this respect. In his words, "In 'God is Truth' 'is' certainly does not mean 'equal to' nor does it merely mean 'is truthful'. Truth is not a mere attribute of God but He is That. He is nothing if He is not That. Truth in Sanskrit means *Sat*. *Sat* means 'Is'. Therefore, Truth is implied in 'Is'. God is, nothing else 'Is'. Therefore the more truthful we are, the nearer we are to God. We *are* only to the extent that we are truthful."[54] It is here clear that *Satya*, the Sanskrit substitute of the word Truth, may unlock the hidden implications of the Gandhian dictum, 'God is Truth.' *Satya* or Truth is impersonal and personal, abstract and concrete, ontological and existential at the same time. This 'God is Truth' means although God is an idea, a principle, an Impersonal Being, He is also an existence who commands truth and validity over the universe.

It is now evident that Gandhi endeavours to bridge the gulf between epistemology and metaphysics, truth and reality. He supplements it by simple conversion and says, "...for myself I have come to the conclusion that God is Truth. But two years ago I went a step further and said Truth is God...."[55] Could Gandhi treat truth as the ultimate reality, the highest being like God? Was Gandhi conscious of the distinction between truth and reality—a burning issue common to almost all philosophers of all ages? A cursory glance at the history of philosophy may conduce to a clear understanding of this topic. Plato identified truth or true knowledge with reality. Hegel identifies reality with rationality. To him whatever is rational is real and whatever is real is rational. Thus truth and reality are not different at all. An echo of this is heard in the Upanishads, and Vedanta school of Indian philosophy. God or Brahma is described as the ultimate reality, highest knowledge, infinite bliss, etc. (*Satyam, Jnanam, Anantam, Brahma*). Thus to the Upanishadic seers and Samkara truth and reality are identical entities. And long before the emergence of Gandhi thinkers, both Eastern and Western, treated truth as identical with reality or God.

Now, a query naturally comes to our mind: What makes Gandhi shift or convert the proposition 'God is Truth' into 'Truth is God'? A critical survey of his thought will reveal the following grounds for this conversion. Firstly, the word 'God' does not command universal assent. The atheists in their eagerness to realize truth have denied the very existence of God. Here the word 'atheist' is a general concept which includes materialists, naturalists, humanists, rationalists, secularists, etc. The materialists and naturalists ardently search after truth though they disbelieve in the supernatural powers like God, deity, etc. A humanist, whether a theist or an atheist, dedicates his life to the service of beings, man or animal, only to realize the essence of humanity in him. In the same way a secularist may lead the best possible moral life without paying any heed to or even barring the religious ways of society. The interesting conversation that Gandhi had with Nirmal Kumar Bose may be remembered. Gandhi explains, "In their passion for discovering Truth, they have not hesitated even to deny the very existence of God—from their own point of view rightly. And it was because of their reasoning that I saw that I was not going to say, 'God is Truth', but 'Truth is God'. Therefore I recall the name of Charles Bradlaugh—a great Englishman who lived 50 years ago. He delighted to call himself an atheist. But knowing as I do something of his life, I never considered him an atheist. I would call him a godfearing man although he would reject the claim, and I know his face would redden. I would say: No Mr. Bradlaugh, you are a truth-fearing man, not a god-fearing man, and I would disarm his criticisms by saying 'Truth is God' as I have disarmed criticisms of many a young man."[56] Gandhi was a votary of truth throughout life. His doubt regarding the existence of God, although initially controversial, his loyalty to truth is beyond any sceptical query. That is why in order to accommodate the atheists, secularists, etc. who are in some sense worshippers of truth, he converted 'God is Truth' into 'Truth is God.' The pragmatist Gandhi made this conversion only to popularize, to make it appealing universally, to attract people from all walks of life. This truth Gandhi now elevates to the status of Godhood. Godliness becomes an attribute which Gandhi confers upon truth. It is this new orientation that enables Gandhi to keep his mind open to genuine friendship with atheists like Gora. Gandhi's conversations with Gora and with Bose reveal the open-mindedness of Gandhi as a new type of theism. The traditional theist can have no genuine dialogue either with atheists or with sceptics."[57]

Secondly, it is not only that the concept of God is not accepted by all but also that the theists, believers in God in general, differ from one another as regards the exact nature of God. The idea of God has been variously interpreted by prophets, innumerable preachers from different perspectives. In Islam and Christianity, God is preached as One without any parallel while in Hinduism the plurality of God, approximately three hundred and thirty millions in number, is well accepted by the devotees. In Hinduism there are paganism, idolatary, tree and nature worshipping on the one hand, and on the other hand there are highly subtle metaphysical ideas of God or ultimate reality. To some He is immanent, to some again transcendent, to some others both transcendent and immanent at the same time, and so on. In short, the concept of God differs from religion to religion, person to person, country to country, time to time. But as regards the nature of truth Gandhi observes no disparity at all. To quote him, "...I never found a double meaning in connection with Truth and not even atheists have denied the necessity or power of Truth."[58]

Thirdly, innumerable heinous misdeeds have been committed in the name of God, under the garb of religion. Gandhi says, "Add to this the great difficulty that millions have taken the name of God and have committed nameless atrocities in the name of God."[59] He was conscious of communal riots between Hindus and Muslims of India designed to attain some abominable political and religious ends. In his youth he was disgusted with the immoral acts of *Maharajas* (chief priests) who styled themselves representatives of God. In the history of Islam and Christianity large-scale atrocities, massacres of people without any regard to sex and age are recorded. In the middle ages, the *Jihads* or religious wars of Mohammedans against unbelievers in Allah; Crusades were instigated by the Church for alleged religious ends, and the claim for partition of India on communal basis, are burning examples of atrocities committed in the name of God. During a barbarous rioting in Bombay between the Hindus and the Muslims, Gandhi wished humanity to go without any idea of God so that peace might be maintained in society. All these factors contributed to the replacement of the dictum: God is truth by the dictum: Truth is God. Gandhi optimistically holds that a worshipper of Truth in place of God can never indulge inhuman and immoral acts. Here a sceptic may raise questions: Are not people vitiating the sanctity of Truth? Are not people committing inhuman and immoral acts in the name of Truth? Gandhi was conscious of such acts. He surmised, "Not that scientists do not very often commit cruelties in the name of Truth. I know today in the name of Truth and science inhuman cruelties are perpetrated on animals when men perform vivisection. To me it is a denial of God whether you recognize Him as Truth or by any other name. So I know that there are these difficulties in one's way no matter how you describe God."[60] As a life-long votary of truth he experienced celestial flavour in it, and thought it more beneficial to humanity than the word 'God.' In short, "after a continuous, relentless search after Truth which began so many years ago" Gandhi's pragmatic outlook inspired him to conclude that Truth is God in stead of God being Truth.

Fourthly, Gandhi ponders this great argument from the metaphysical standpoint. To him God and truth are ontologically on a par. He argues, "... We have another thing in Hindu philosophy, viz., God alone is and nothing else exists. Now the same truth you find emphasized and exemplified in the *Kalama* of Islam...."[61] We have already discussed that Truth in the sense of *sat* or existence is like God an idea and being at the same time. It manifests itself, although maintaining ontological status, in and through the objects of the world. It is the phenomena of reality, of practical life, that we appreciate as true or condemn as false. It is only to attribute a realistic touch to Truth, to make it more plausible to people that Gandhi extends the original connotation of the term truth and declares Truth is God.

Fifthly, he had a political motto behind it. Of course, this argument is, to some extent, a corollary of the first argument, namely, to ascribe a universal appeal to it. Gandhi confessed that his singlehearted devotion to Truth has drawn him into the field of politics. His experience foretold him the difficulties which we have already discussed a bit earlier from the use of the terms God or Allah or Rama, etc. That is why he put a common goal of truth before his fellow workers who could serve the country without any dissonance with their own faith. In their turn the people also responded to his clarion call for freedom voluntarily, and faced the barbaric oppression of British imperialism dauntlessly.

Lastly, he preaches this dictum from the psychological standpoint. This is deeply rooted in the core of his heart. Wherever his reason failed he took shelter of faith in this topic. To quote Gandhi, "I claim to be a votary of truth from my childhood. It was the most natural thing to me...."[62] The last two sentences clearly indicate the devotional plinth on which he endeavoured to base this argument. Indeed, faith in God and Truth was so natural and spontaneous to him that he treated them as 'convertible terms' without any hesitation.

A critic, a logician, may find fault with this conversion, and declare it fallacious which, we shall see very shortly, is only apparent and not final. A very brief discussion of the rules of conversion will be conducive in this regard. H. Joseph defines, "A proposition is converted, when its subject is made the predicate, and vice versa, its quality (affirmative or negative) remaining unchanged."[63] The original proposition is known as convertend and the conclusion is called converse. The rules are: (1) The subject of the convertend becomes predicate of the converse, (2) The predicate of the convertend becomes subject of the converse, (3) The quality of both is the same. That is to say, if the convertend is affirmative, the converse would be affirmative; and if the convertend is negative, the converse would be negative, (4) No term may be distributed in the converse, which is not distributed in the convertend.

Now let us examine the conversion in question. The converse, Truth is God, is clearly a universal affirmative proposition. The original premise (God is Truth) being an *A* or universal affirmative proposition distributes the subject only and the predicate 'Truth' remains undistributed. But in the converse, being the subject of an *A* proposition, the term 'Truth' is distributed. Hence the fourth rule is violated here. But there are some exceptions to this rule. According to traditional logic simple conversion of the above type is permissible if the subject and predicate are co-extensive with one another. More elaborately, conversion is of two types, simple conversion and conversion per accidence or by limitation. In the case of simple conversion the premise and conclusion do not change their quantity. For example, by simple conversion we get from an *E* proposition, *E* and from an *I* proposition, *I*. And in the case of conversion accidence or limitation, the premise and conclusion are quantitatively different. As for example, by conversion of an *A* proposition we get *I*. Gandhi converted simply an *A* proposition 'God is Truth' into an *A* proposition 'Truth is God,' and committed a fallacy. In fact, from 'All roses are flowers' we cannot logically convert into 'All flowers are roses.' Similarly, the proposition 'All men are mortal' cannot be converted into 'All mortals are men.' But in some special cases where the predicate of an *A* proposition is co-extensive with the subject, simple conversion is permissible. The cases are: (a) In an *A* proposition where definition of a term is mentioned, simple conversion is permissible. For example, 'All men are rational animals' can be safely converted into 'All rational animals are men.' Here rational animality serves as the definition of men; (b) In an *A* proposition where the subject and predicate are definite singular terms, simple conversion is permissible. For example, 'The Himalayas is the highest mountain of the world' can be simply converted into 'The highest mountain of the world is the Himalayas'. Here 'the Himalayas' and 'the highest mountain' are definite singular terms; (c) Lastly, in an *A* proposition where the subject and the predicate are coterminous, simple conversion is permissible. In other words, if the subject and the predicate are synonymous or identical, logical conversion is possible. For example, 'All living beings are endowed with life' can be converted into 'All beings that are endowed with life are living beings.' Here 'living beings' and 'endowed with life' are identical. To Gandhi also God and Truth are convertible and co-extensive terms. Thus after a proper scrutiny Gandhi's conversion of the dictum 'God is Truth' into 'Truth is God' stands sound from the logical standpoint.

Moreover, humanism was the nucleus of Gandhian thought. He cared little for the verdict of logicians. He says, "I am not a man who sits down and thinks out problems syllogistically. I am a man of action. I react to a situation intuitively. Logic comes afterwards, it does not precede the event."[64] "In dealing with living entities, the dry syllogistic method leads not only to bad logic but sometimes to fatal logic."[65] The above two extracts clearly show Gandhi's attitude towards logic. His rationalism was productive, and not barren. Throughout his eventful life he was in living contact with the common people who were oppressed and downtrodden victims of the imperialist machinery; with whom he shared sweets and sours, joys and sorrows of life. But the rules of logic, especially of formal logic, are aften blind to the demands of life. Indeed, in formal logic, if the prescribed rules are observed strictly, whether they tally with facts of life or not, the argument will be approved by logicians. For example, 'All men are immortal,' 'Ram is a man,' therefore, 'Ram is immortal,' is a valid mood (Barbara in the First Figure) since all the rules of syllogism have been observed here strictly. But we know truth is diametrically opposed to this argument. This sort of argument of barren logic, logic devoid of truth and life, was an eye-sore to Gandhi who sought after Truth every moment of his life. Here a mark of caution is necessary. Gandhi condemned lifeless, barren and bad logic but he never underrated reason or the reasoning process, which is the source of logic. On this logical problem P.T. Raju observes, "No student of logic can fail to understand the significance of the change from 'God is Truth' to 'Truth is God' ...every significant judgement presupposes an existent subject, and the judgement is about the subject. In the judgement 'God is Truth', the existence of God is presupposed. But this existence may be questioned, when the predicate, Truth, would have to be referred to a non-existent subject; and the judgement would be without logic significance. But none questions that there is truth in the universe. When it is said that God is the same as that Truth, the judgement becomes significant and practically amounts to the proof of God."[66] Indeed, quest of truth was the dynamo that fiercely inspired Gandhi in every walk of life, in every activity of his colourful life. This concept of Truth, to him, was a concrete and not an abstract one. His ceaseless and life-long struggle was aimed at the realization of this eternal Truth in its diversified forms in our everyday lives. That is why the 'dry syllogistic method' that ignores humanity, overlooks the demands of life out of sheer intellectual vanity, was an object of aversion to him.

(d) *Rama—Historical and Eternal:* In *Ramayana*, we are told that four sons were born to King Dasaratha of Ayodhya of whom Rama, the living incarnation of Lord Vishnu or Supreme Being, was the eldest. He underwent a banishment for fourteen years with his devoted wife Sita and younger brother Lakshmana in different jungles of central and southern India only to honour the sanctity of the words of his father. He defeated and killed Ravana, the demon king of Lanka (now Sri Lanka) who stole Sita from the thatched hut at Panchabati. After his return to his motherland he established *Rama Rajya*, the best possible ideal state of the world. In his early age, Gandhi was instructed to pronounce the name of Rama by the motherly maidservant, Rambha, in order to overcome fear of ghosts. And as in other western and northern Indian families Rama was worshipped as a family deity in the Gandhi family. It would not be irrelevant if we say that the idea of Rama was infused as an ideal into his blood in early life. The impact of this infusion is evident not only in his private as well as in public life but in his moral, religious and political concepts also. Gandhi says, "Rama did justice even to a dog. By abandoning his kingdom and living in the forest for the sake of truth Rama gave to all the kings of the world an object lesson in noble conduct. By his strict monogamy he showed that a life of perfect self-restraint could be led by a royal householder. He lent splendour to his throne by his popular administration and proved that *Ramarajya* was the acme of swaraj."[67] Indeed, this was candid appraisal on the part of Gandhi. It is with the historical Rama, the son of the great king Dasaratha, on his ideal that he started his public life.

But his practical experience, his pragmatic outlook in the context of public life, inspired him to extend this tiny speck of history, Rama, into an eternal spirit, God. His concept of *Ramarajya*, his worshipping of Rama, were often an object of criticism amongst the people of other faiths. Gandhi surmised very aptly, that the Rama of history, worshipped as he is by a section of Hindus, may stand as an obstacle to our freedom movement. Hence he warns us, "I warn my Mussalman friends against misunderstanding me in my use of the word *Ramarajya*. By *Ramarajya* I do not mean Hindu Raj. I mean by *Ramarajya* Divine Raj, the kingdom of God. For me Rama and Rahim are one and the same deity. I acknowledge no other God but the one God of Truth and righteousness."[68] "My Rama is another name for khuda or God. I want the *Khudai Raj*, which is the same thing as the kingdom of God on Earth."[69] During the freedom movement *Ramdhoon*, an eulogical and devotional hymn, was in the lips of every Gandhiite, irrespective of caste and creed, race and religion. This *Ramdhoon* which he used to sing in the prayer meetings every morning and evening with fellow freedom fighters manifests Gandhi's concept of universal religion in a nutshell. It offers solace to the restive minds of communal and religious fanatics by proclaiming boldly Ishvara, Allah and Rama are synonyms of God. Hay Rama! were the last words that came from his lips at the time of his death. Gandhi explains the transition of Rama of history into the Rama of eternity as follows: "My *Rama*, the *Rama* of our prayers, is not the historical *Rama*, the son of Dasaratha, the king of Ayodhya. He is the eternal, the unborn, the one without a second."[70] In this way Gandhi, the practical idealist and the pragmatist transforms the Rama of history into an eternal being beyond spatial and temporal relations, i.e., God.

In this connection the term *Ramanama* demands an elaborate explanation for the better understanding of Gandhian standpoint. By this term Gandhi intends to glorify the necessity of divine spirit, God or Allah or Rama, etc. in every walk of life. By Rama, we have seen, he means the divine spirit universally worshipped by all theists. And by 'nama' he boldly proclaims that Rama, his object of worship, is not confined within the boundary of any state or country; not chained by temporal relations. Thus his conception of 'Ramanama' also pictures Rama as a divine spirit beyond space and time. And this 'Ramanama' went so deep into his being that whenever in necessity, he sought the solution or remedy of every problem, spiritual or mental, in it. It is his solace, saviour and shelter at the same time. It is the root cause of his being, the echo of every heartbeat. What is astonishing here is that he proceeded a step further and prescribed it as a healing art. To him, it is the unfailing remedy in every ailment and on it everybody may rely without any hesitation. "No matter what the ailment from which a man may be suffering, recitation of Ramanama from the heart is the sure cure."[71] Let the scientists, especially the medical men, conduct a thorough research on the efficacy of it in their respective fields. We are not concerned here with their condemnation or appreciation. We should grasp the central idea latent in it. The 'Ramanama' or the utterance of the spirit of God creates a psychological impact on the mind of the individual. Auto-suggestion or will-power, whatever brand a psychologist may ascribe to it, to Gandhi it is the divine power, Rama who improves our morale, both physical and mental, and infuses indomitable strength to fight the enemy, both outside and inside the organism.

(e) *Proofs for the Existence of God:* Knowledge of God is a time-honoured controversial issue amongst the thinkers. In the world of thought, both Eastern and Western, arguments have been tendered to prove or disprove the existence of God. All these attempts, as the history of religion records, turn into a chase after a black cat in a dark chamber. Some declare Him as knowable, and some emphatically assert Him as unknown and unknowable. To Gandhi, God cannot be known although an ardent seeker like him may feel Him since all the ways of knowing are inadequate in this context. Senses, through which people generally look at everything, cannot prove God who is a supersensuous reality. Again, our senses are often subject to delusion, and owing to their limited scope have been severely criticized as inadequate medium by the epistemological thinkers. Gandhi follows this trend and declares, "It transcends the senses."[72] Reason also faces the same fate. All its attempts to grasp God go in vain. "He transcends speech and reason."[73] "So must it be with the existence of God. He defies reason."[74] Intuition also cannot serve us well although, we shall see later, it throws much light on the topic. Gandhi laid much emphasis on faith through which he claims to have known God, at least he has felt Him. Sometimes he speaks like a bonafide mystic to have known God by dint of the 'still small voice' which is latent in every human being. Sometimes like an agnostic he says, "Human intellect is incapable of fully understanding

God's ways,"[75] and "God is beyond human comprehension.[76] But human beings owing to inherent nature cannot rest satisfied with this universal futility. With an eye to this insurmountable failure they are ceaselessly striving to have a coherent knowledge of God. Gandhi is not an exception to this general trend. To him although God's existence, like perfectibility, is and will be beyond human grasp still He can be proved in a sense." It is possible to reason out the existence of God to a limited extent.[77] With this end in view and to assemble people under his banner Gandhi often spoke of God, and tendered proofs of His existence. Since he had no mind to form a system of thought, the proofs, not categorized, are scattered throughout his writings and speeches. So the captions that we contemplate to offer for our convenience to the arguments professed by Gandhi in the following pages are our own. He would have been astonished if he was told of these philosophical terms. We shall take into account arguments of Gandhi as per traditional philosophical usages that are commonly known as proofs for the existence of God.

Here a word of caution is necessary. At the outset we should remember that the proofs in question are not proofs in the strict sense of the term. They are possessed of undoubted value and weight. But this weight does not amount to demonstration so that it may have no room for doubt. Kant claimed that God is incapable of proof as well as of disproof. So in the technical sense of the term the existence of God is a hypothesis which is accepted not because it is demonstrated, but because it enables us to explain the known facts. It is with this preoccupation that we can proceed to the consideration of the traditional proofs of the existence of God. Again, these proofs have hardly played any part in producing convictions of divine existence where it was not already present. William James observes, "The fact is that these arguments do but follow the combined suggestions of the facts and of our feeling. They prove nothing rigorously. They only corroborate our pre-existent partialities."[78] Their obvious function has rather been to confirm religious belief than to create it. Still it is undeniable that they have a great historic importance or that they have played a very important part in the history of theological literature. Apart from that their present importance also cannot be minimized. They express a deeprooted conviction which common sense will never cease to hold. This is the reason why they have survived in spite of repeated attacks launched against them by their adversaries with all the rational weapons at their disposal. These arguments remain up to this day as very good working hypotheses which serve to explain facts of religious consciousness. Above all, their achieved value consists in the fact that they are the steps of the process by which we rise to the knowledge of God. In the above light we shall consider the arguments tendered by Gandhi one by one under the traditional captions.

(1) *The Cosmological Arguments:* It is the argument from the contingency of the world. It starts from the word 'cosmos' as given, and from the character of the world infers the existence of God to explain it. In a nutshell this argument preaches that because the contingent world which is dependent, ever-changing and unsubstantial in character, exists, therefore, there must exist a Being who is necessary, independent, permanent, and substantial in character. Gandhi argues, "I do dimly perceive that whilst everything around me is ever changing, ever dying, there is underlying all that change a living Power that is changeless, that holds all together, that creates, dissolves and recreates. That informing Power or Spirit is God."[79] Here Gandhi views the world of our experience as a *contengentia mundi* which can be explained only in terms of a permanent, substantial and necessary Being who is God. A similar type of argument appears in the philosophical works of Aristotle who initiated this cosmological proof, of course in an embryonic stage, in his concept of the *Unmoved Mover*. But Gandhi's plea from a transitory to an eternal, from a contingent to a necessary Being fails to command universal assent. Because to negate the transitory is not to get the eternity or mere nullification of the finite does not amount to the infinite. John Caird opines, "He is not necessary: for he is related to the world as a cause to its effect; but in the relation of cause and effect, the cause is as much conditioned by the effect as the effect by the cause. Even if this argument proved necessity, it would not be a necessity of existence but merely a necessity of causation."[80] Thus Gandhi's move to prove the existence of God from the standpoint of the world as a *contengentia mundi* cannot stand logically.

Again, this cosmological argument is also called aetiological for it makes use of the principle of casualty. The series of causes and effects which constitute the world runs back step by step. But an infinite line of causes is impossible since it leads to infinite regress. Hence, in order to avoid it the human mind is compelled to stop short, and place at the head of the series a First Cause, an uncaused cause, a *cause sui,* a being who is necessary and unconditional, and in relation to which all other causes are only of secondary importance. Gandhi pleads, "If we exist, if our parent and their parents have existed, then it is proper to believe in the Parents of the whole creation. If He is not, we are nowhere."[81] A similar type of casual argument from the point of view of creation is preached by the later Nyaya school of Indian philosophy. Udayana, in his classic work *Nyaya-kusumanjali* (5.1), endeavours to prove the existence of God on the ground of combination. All composite objects of the world, from the smallest to the biggest (mountains, stars, etc.) are creations of some intelligent being (*Karta*) who has a direct knowledge of subtle atoms out of which material objects are composed. That being must be Omniscient and hence God exists. Thus before the emergence of Gandhi the Naiyayikas in India, and Western thinkers like Paul Janet, Herman Lotze, James Martineau, etc., tendered causal argument of God's existence.

Now let us examine the Gandhian argument from causal standpoint. An uncaused First Cause at the zenith of all causal series betrays the very spirit of causal principle that every effect must have a cause. If the universe is said to be unintelligible without a First Cause, is not the uncaused First Cause an unintelligible conception? And the assumption that every series must have a first term is false. In mathematics we find that the series of proper fractions has no first term (e.g., '34, '37, '47, etc.). In this context John Lewis observes, "There is no logical compulsion to accept a Cause of the system of causes, there is no necessity to seek for the first whence and the last whither of the whole cosmic process."[82] In Indian philosophy we find a parallel uncaused cause in Buddhism where *Avidya* (ignorance) is said to be the matrix of causal links which comes from nothing else. *Pratityasamutpada* or the doctrine of Dependent Origination describes the world system as a network of twelve causes (*Nidanas*) of which *Avidya* (ignorance) stands first. Thus Gandhi like other aetiologists fails to prove the existence of God from the causal standpoint.

(2) *The Teleological Argument:* This argument is variously called as the teleological, the physico-theological or the design-argument that rests on the presence of an order in the universe. The term *telos* means an end or purpose. The teleological argument conceives of God as the designer of the order that prevails in the universe. There is a general order of regularity and a special order of adoption or adjustment. Inorganic Nature reveals general order and Organic Nature manifests special order more conspicuously. Astronomy discloses

relations of number and proportion so that Nature seems to be "a living arithmetic in its development, a realized geometry in its purpose." The laws of Nature are mathematical relations. The order of the universe is perfectly designed. Apart from the postulation of a supreme intelligence, disorder, chaos and indefiniteness would prevail against order, cosmos and constancy. Pythagoras, Anaxagoras, Plato, and Aristotle in ancient Greece, and modern scientific thinkers like James Jeans, Eddington, Keith, etc., argue that this supreme intelligence is none but God.

Gandhi also feels a teleological order and design in the universe. As an idealist he cannot appreciate the blind mechanistic interpretation of the universal order. Gandhi writes, "...I do feel ...that there is orderliness in the Universe, there is an unalterable law governing everything and every being that exists or lives. It is not a blind law; for no blind law can govern the conduct of living beings and, thanks to the marvellous researches of Sir J.C. Bose, it can now be proved that even matter is life. That law then which governs all life is God."[83] Even in the natural calamities he perceives divine purpose. Not only in the external world he feels the divine design but also in the inner life. Gandhi perceives divine design everywhere—both in the inner and external world. This design leads us to the postulation of an Omniscient Perfect Being who constantly supervises it, and He is none but God.

In the Nyaya school of Indian philosophy an argument from design, support (*dhrti*) was tendered to prove the existence of God. This support (*dhrti*) signifies that this wonderful universe is supported by an infinite being or God.

But in the history of theology the teleological proof also has been criticized as inadequate and illogical. Modern science tells us that the order and system have come to this universe after a long evolutionary process. The heavenly bodies rotate on their axes driven by their intrinsic nature. And hence the guidance or superintendence of a divine designer, God, is a myth only. John Caird condemns this argument on the ground that it assumes that "the relation of God to the world is a purely arbitrary one" and it reduces the status of God to "a *deus ex machina* of arbitrary power."[84] Thus Gandhi's attempt to prove the existence of God from the teleological standpoint also fails.

(3) *The Ontological Argument:* The term ontology stands for

the study of reality as such, from *Ontos* or real thing and *logia* or discourse. By ontology, as to etymological meaning stands, we mean the science of pure being or reality as such, i.e., what only is or exists. In theology the ontological argument finds in the very idea of God the proof of His existence. The thought of God in the mind demonstrates His Being. The idea, if fully developed, becomes the object.[85] This conclusion from thought to being or the assertion that the reality of God is involved in the idea of God constitutes the gist of the argument. It is urged that there is something unique in the idea of God so that it cannot be a mere idea. The difference between the idea of existence and existence in reality, it may be argued, is quite evident and hence the two can never merge in one. But the advocates of the ontological argument maintain that the existence of God should not be considered on at par as that of other objects of the world on the ground that in the former case existence merges with the very idea of the existence of God. In short, the two, idea and existence, in the case of God cannot be separated. This argument was formulated in different forms by different thinkers of the West. St. Anselm presented the argument in its scholastic form, i.e., idea proves existence; to Descartes the idea of God is unique in the sense that it involves existence; Spinoza, like Descartes, also proves the existence of God from the idea of God as the source and sum of all perfection; Leibnitz bases his argument on the distinction between the possible and the actual, the essence and the existence.

Gandhi attempts to prove the existence of God from the idea of God. In the preceding section 'God is Truth: Truth is God' we have seen that both God and Truth are synonymous to him. Since the term truth (*sat*) etymologically conveys the necessary idea of existence in it, and Truth and God being synonymous, the concept of God, according to Gandhi, implies His existence undeniably. He says, "... *Sat* or *Satya* is the only correct and fully significant name for God" (see sec. Truth is God) or "Truth in Sanskrit means *Sat*. *Sat* means 'Is'. Therefore, Truth is implied in 'Is'. God is, nothing else Is." (see sec. Truth is God). In this way Gandhi transforms the epistemological and ontological concept Truth into an existence, a reality, God.

The above is an account of ontological proof for the existence of God in Gandhian thought. In the history of theological literature the ontological argument could not sail smoothly. It was bitterly criticized, perhaps aptly, by later theologians like Kant, John Caird, etc.[86] The ontological argument in spite of its firm basis in religious consciousness faces the same fate as that of the cosmological and teleological arguments.

(4) *The Moral Argument:* The moral argument by its very essence occupies a prominent role in theological literature. It seeks to show that the best solutions of the problems of moral life are attained in the existence of God. The moral life itself involves the existence of God, or the divine existence is an embodiment of moral law. Kant found in the pure practical reason an assurance of the divine existence. William Hamilton tells us that the only valid argument for the existence of God and immortality of the soul rests on the ground of man's moral nature. J. Martineau presents God as the Governor and source of all moral laws, the fulfilment of which presupposes the existence of God. James Seth and H. Rashdall maintain that the moral laws are revelations of a Divine Mind, God. In short, the moral argument demonstrates that the moral law is manifested with all its implications in God, and hence God exists.

We have seen above that although Gandhi's faith in God in early life was dim, he had firm conviction in Truth as 'the substance of all morality.' It is with this moral concept Truth, God and Truth being synonymous, he strove to prove the existence of God. To quote him, "All the dry ethics of the world turn to dust because apart from God they are lifeless. Coming from God, they come with life in them...."[87] "So long as the seed of morality is not watered by religion, it cannot sprout...."[88] The moot point here is that morality is primary, and hence it can stand by itself. The human beings, owing to inherent imperfection, seek moral fulfilment in God who is the acme of moral life. In other words, our moral life leads to the existence of God. Moreover, in the moment of crisis, spiritual and material, the verdict of conscience is an absolute obligation—a categorical imperative in the Kantian sense—to Gandhi because it is the voice of God or Truth. Thus the moral concepts of truth and conscience with their full bloom prove unwittingly, to Gandhi, the existence of God.

The Naiyayikas of Indian philosophy adduce a similar moral argument for the existence of God on the basis of *Adrsta,* the unseen storehouse of merit and demerit corresponding to happiness and miseries. And since all human beings are prey to this *Adrsta* which is itself unintelligent, a supremely intelligent being, "God must be its guide and supervisor." (*Kusumanjali,* 1.19.)

But the moral argument in general, whatever its merits from the point of view of morality might be, fails to achieve universal assent. The logical defect involved here is that it seeks to derive the higher from the lower, the whole from the part. Religion belongs to human nature in its totality while ethics, the science of morality, represents only one aspect of man's beinghood. Thus the moral argument, like other theistic arguments, proves itself most to those who already believe in God. But to say so is not to admit that its evidence is invalid.

(5) *The Pragmatic Argument:* Here Gandhi tenders proof of the existence of God from the pragmatic standpoint. Pragmatism insists on the necessity of taking our personal ends and interests into consideration in every sphere of our lives. And since personal ends and interests are innumerable, pragmatism without, committing itself to any definite position, contents itself with the attainment of utility or usefulness in anything we may encounter. S. Radhakrishnan humorously comments, "In the image of the Italin pragmatist Papini, pragmatism is like a corridor in a hotel which opens into numberless chambers.... "[89] The implicit point in the above citation seems aptly applicable in the case of Gandhi. In the midst of utter despair and crisis, spiritual or material, he sought solace and shelter in God. In the history of philosophy William James was, perhaps, the first to prove the existence of God on the basis of practical ends. He admitted the validity of the idea of God on account of the gainful service rendered by religious experience in "our practical lives." It is the idea of God that kindles rays of hope amidst darkness, offers solace in the mind of the wretched, "positively determines fear and hope and expectation, and is foundation for the saintly life."[90] This emotional usefulness of the idea of God acts, sustains the devotees in the struggle of life.

Like William James, Gandhi too firmly asserts the utility of the idea of God in our lives. To quote him, "... There are those who are struck with doubt and despair. For them there is the Name of God. It is God's covenant that whoever goes to Him in weakness and helplessness, him He will make strong...."[91] "I can certainly say that though everyone else may forsake you, God never forsakes people in distress...."[92] Gandhi tells us that the unflinching faith in God gives strength to a *satyagrahi* "to bear all kinds of tortures without a murmur." God is the 'ultimate mainstay' of an individual in this world ridden with hatred and conflicts. Gandhi virtually dedicated himself at the altar of God to whom he prayed for everything like an infant in the lap of his mother. This mundane utility of the idea of

God which he felt during his experiments with truth demonstrates the proof of His existence.

But a close scrutiny will reveal that the pragmatic proof also faces the same fate as that of the aforesaid ones. Pragmatic ends often vary from person to person, time to time and consequently fail to attain universality. Further the revolutionaries undergo all sorts of earthly sufferings without any belief in God. They try to realize their ends within the scope of human efforts. Thus the pragmatic argument proves the existence of God only to those who already believe in Him.

(6) *The Authoritative Argument:* Gandhi argues from authority to prove the existence of God. Authority or *Sabda* is accepted as a source of valid knowledge both in Indian and Western philosophy. Authoritarianism generally maintains that our knowledge is based on the experience of the self within and the world outside us. These experiences may be either the normal experiences of ordinary men or the intuitive experiences of saints, seers, prophets, etc. Those who have no direct experience of God or of a supersensuous reality depend on the authority of sages, seers, etc., for knowledge of God. In our everyday lives we find that the great scientists and their findings have been the source of our knowledge regarding scientific investigations. Gandhi points to the personal experiences of spiritually eminent men who have been ruling the hearts of devotees from time immemorial and are being adored till today on this ground. He says, "Precisely in that manner speak the *Rishis* and Prophets. They say anybody following the path they have trodden can realize God."[93] "Such testimony is to be found in the experiences of an unbroken line of prophets and sages in all countries and climes. To reject this evidence is to deny oneself."[94] The prophets and sages like Krishna, Christ, Mohammed, Chaitanya, Ramakrishna, etc., were infalliable to him.

Again, Gandhi put forward authoritative argument from the historical standpoint too. The idea of God and the history of mankind are rowing together on the same boat. Of course, like the human civilization the idea of God has undergone various transformations, and consequently has assumed different forms, still it is there. In his words, "...And since belief in God is co-existent with the humankind, existence of God is treated as a fact more definite than the fact that the Sun is.... There is no record in history of the failure of such search."[95] In fact, none can point out a period in the whole history of mankind when the idea of God was absent. From the early dawn of civilization it is there, and perhaps, it will be so long human beings are on the surface of earth. But this argument too faces the same fate as that of the ontological argument. The persistent reiteration of a concept from time immemorial does not demonstrate its existence in practical life.

Further, Gandhi argues from *ex consensu gentium*. "The argument *ex consensu gentium* is that the belief in God is so widespread as to be grounded in the rational nature of man, and should therefore carry authority with it."[96] Gandhi appeals to the democratic authority, the democratic criterion of majority for the existence of God. It is not only the seers and prophets but also ninety-nine per cent of human beings have believed, in some form or other, in the existence of God. To quote him, "I am one of the millions of wise men who believe in Him."[97] Although a sceptic may argue that the opinion of majority is not always right, still as a mass leader Gandhi could not overlook and undermine the faith of millions in God. He proudly declares himself as one of the wise torch-bearers of the mammoth rally of theism.

(7) *The Psychological Argument (Faith):* Apart from the authoritative move (religious, democratic and historical) Gandhi tenders argument from the psychological standpoint, i.e., faith (*sraddha*). The general trend of Indian philosophy accepts faith as firm belief in God.

In the theology of Gandhi, faith plays a vital part through which alone we can have an acquaintance of God. He distinguishes between blind faith and living faith. Blind faith is superimposed on our minds by authority and tradition without any inner urge. But living faith comes from the core of our hearts. It has a burning eagerness to attain union with God. This faith is a subtle psychic stage which is strictly personal and hence a universal scientific law in respect of it is impossible. It is self-acting, self-illuminating, and interlinked with the cardinal virtues prescribed by Gandhi. This faith is so deep in his being that if he was cut to pieces God would give him the strength to proclaim His existence and glory.[98] As mentioned above it is a subtle psychical state that transcends reason. Gandhi says, "An atheist might floor me in a debate. But my faith runs so very much faster than my reason that I can challenge the whole world and say, 'God is, was and ever shall be'."[99] A sceptic, a critic may seize upon these words and condemn Gandhi as a dogmatic, superstitious man with a blind and irrational faith in God. Gandhi was conscious of this drawback in his mental makeup and admits, "You may call this a superstition, but I confess it is a superstition that I hug."[100] It is here amusing that Gandhi who condemned blind faith and irrationality (*supra*) ardently intends to cling to a so-called superstition, i.e., uncritical and unquestioning faith in God. Is Gandhi's move on the ground of faith devoid of reason? The fact is that each and every religion shows a leaning to some source (faith, devotion, etc.) which is often off the rational track. They are not antagonistic; rather they go hand in hand, and through mutual dependence enrich their efficacy. They are complementary to one another. As Gandhi says, "faith is the function of the heart. It must be enforced by reason...."[101] Thus Gandhi's move to prove the existence of God on the basis of faith is not wholly devoid of reason. To him, faith is above reason, and never contrary to it. It is neither non-rational nor infra-rational, but supra-rational.

(8) *Mystical Experiences Argument:* Gandhi offers mystical experience as a proof for the existence of God. He knew that mere dry argument can never convince a rational mind which has no vivid or faint idea of God acquired through experience or otherwise. This experience or 'living faith' can be acquired only through prayer, penance and self-purification. It is known to all that prayer and penance were his everyday rituals. He strove heart and soul to realize God through experience, prayer and self-purification. He underwent a series of moral and spiritual ordeals through which he acquired a humble power to receive heavenly blessings or divine revelations. Of course, Gandhi is not the only recipient of rare mystical experience which has a rich tradition, and a galaxy of spiritual greats in it. He had Moses, Christ, Mohammed, Chaitanya, Ramakrishna and other mystics in his mind. He admits, "My claim to hear the voice of God is no new claim." Gandhi's faith in God is the motive power of his life, the very element of his existence.

We have discussed elaborately Gandhi's move to prove the existence of God from all possible angles of vision, i.e., cosmological, teleological, ontological, moral, pragmatic, authoritative arguments, as also those based on faith and mystical grounds. All these arguments, although firmly convincing to him, he suspected, may fail to achieve the assent of sceptics, atheists, etc. That is why he prescribes living faith for everybody. This burning and living faith turns him into an extreme catholic in his ideas about God. He admits two stages through which one has to pass in order to realize God. In his words, "There are two stages in knowing God. The first is faith and the second and the ultimate stage is experience-knowledge arising from it."[102] This post-experience faith in God is the keystone of Gandhi's theology. He appeals to the inexperienced persons to rely on those who, like him, have a bit of experience of God. This is the faith in which he lived and moved. Ramakrishna Paramhamsa, a mystic of the previous century from Bengal who taught that God-realisation is the only goal of life, advised people to rely on faith in the existence of God. His proverbial teaching is "To God, faith is the way/Through reason He is far away." Thus long before the emergence of Gandhi faith was accepted as the ultimate arbiter regarding the existence of God.[103]

According to the preference of Gandhi "experience-knowledge arising from faith is the only road to God realization." Gandhi started with belief and reached this superhuman psychical stage step by step by dint of which he could have faith in God as the zenith of all good qualities that human beings are capable of attributing to Him. In fact, we can know God only when we rise above our normal mental life of feeling, willing and thinking and transform ourselves into God-realizing souls. In his words, "If you would swim on the bosom of the ocean of Truth, you must reduce yourself to a zero."[104] In our search for God the above mentioned three empirical elements of our normal mental faculty are amalgamated into a transcendental consciousness by divine lustre which is strictly individualistic, and can be apprehended by that blessed soul only. This transcendental psychical state enriches the entire being of that blessed soul and spiritually illuminates his whole personality. All attempts to prove or demonstrate this transcendental consciousness, to universalize "experience-knowledge arising from faith" after the pattern of scientific investigation, will, as in the past also, perhaps, in future, face the same fate, reach the same goal, namely, universal futility.

References

1. Gopinath Dhawan, *The Political Philosophy of Mahatma Gandhi*, p. 41.
2. John S. Mackenzie, *A Manual of Ethics*, p. 358.
3. Unto Tahtinen, *Ahimsa (Non-Violence) in Indian Tradition*, p. 121.
4. Nirmal Kumar Bose, *My Days with Gandhi*, p. 174.
5. Benoy Gopal Ray, *Gandhian Ethics*, p. 56.
6. *Harijan*, 3 October 1936, pp. 268-69.
7. See Chapter VIII.
8. Verrier Elwin in Francis Watson and Maurice Brown (eds.), *Talking of Gandhiji*, p. 28.

9. *Ibid.*
10. S. Radhakrishnan and J.H. Muirhead (eds.), *Contemporary Indian Philosophy*, p. 21.
11. J.S. Mackenzie, *op. cit.*, p. 273; also William Lillie, *An Introduction to Ethics*, p. 249.
12. Pyarelal, *Mahatma Gandhi: The Last Phase*, vol. II, pp. 136-37.
13. *Ethical Religion*, p. 24.
14. J.S. Mackenzie, *op. cit.*, p. 27.
15. R.N. Iyer, *The Moral and Political Thought of Mahatma Gandhi*, p. 150.
16. *Ibid.*, p. 176.
17. *An Autobiography*, p. 159.
18. Buddhadeva Bhattacharyya, *op. cit.*, pp. 135-36.
19. *From Yeravda Mandir*, p. 4.
20. F. Nietzsche, *Beyond Good and Evil*, pp. 104, 123, 227-28.
21. Henry Bergson, *The Two Sources of Morality and Religion*, pp. 8-104.
22. *Harijan*, 15 September 1946, p. 309; *Harijan*, 23 December 1939, pp. 386-87, *Young India*, 17 March 1927, p. 86; J.D. Sethi, *Gandhi Today*, pp. 33-36; *Harijan*, 21 July 1940, p. 211.
23. William Lillie, *An Introduction to Ethics*, p. 196.
24. S. Radhakrishnan & J.H. Huirhead (eds.), *op. cit.*, p. 21.
25. Nirmal Kumar Bose, *Studies in Gandhism*, p. 65; an almost similar view was held by Kant and C.D. Broad. See William Lillie, *op. cit.*, p. 295.
26. Buddhadeva Bhattacharyya, *op. cit.*, p. 111.
27. *Speeches and Writings of Mahatma Gandhi*, p. 363.
28. Tennyson, 'Ulysses', in *Poems of Alfred Lord Tennyson*, p. 157.
29. *Satyagraha in South Africa*, p. 219.
30. B.G. Gokhale, *Indian Thought Through The Ages*, pp. 20-21.
31. Cited in J.R. Lucas, *The Freedom of the Will*, p. 71.
32. Chaucer writes, "... if free choys be graunted me/To do that same thyng, or do it noght/Though God forwoot it er that was wroght/Or if his wityng streyneth never a deel/But by necessitee condicioneel." (... If freedom of choice is given to me to do it or not, even though God has foreknowledge of my choice before it is made, God's knowledge does not force my choice at all, but by conditional necessity). Geoffrey Chaucer, 'The Canterbury Tales (The Nun's Priest's Tale)' in *The Complete Works of Geoffrey Chaucer*, p. 203.
33. John Milton writes, "... predestination overruled/Their will, disposed by absolute decree/ Or high foreknowledge. They themselves decreed/Their own revolt... they themselves ordained their fall." John Milton, *Paradise Lost*, Book III, p. 6.
34. *Harijan*, 19 August 1939, p. 238.
35. *CWMG*, vol. XXVI, p. 223; also Gora alias G. Ramchandra Rao, *An Atheist with Gandhi*, p. 53.
36. *Ibid.*, p. 224.
37. Nirmal Kumar Bose, *My Days with Gandhi*, pp. 49-50.

38. Gora, *op. cit.*, p. 54.
39. *Ibid.*
40. *Ibid.*
41. *Ibid.*, p. 55.
42. *Ibid.*, pp. 54-55.
43. D.G. Tendulkar, *Mahatma*, vol. I, p. 26.
44. *An Autobiography*, pp. 17-19.
45. C.D.S. Devanesen, *The Making of the Mahatma*, p. 36.
46. *Ibid.*, p. 34.
47. *Ibid.*, p. 35.
48. *An Autobiography*, p. 25.
49. *CWMG*, vol. XXVI, pp. 224-25.
50. *Ibid.*, vol. XLVIII, p. 404.
51. Surendra Verma, *Metaphysical Foundation of Gandhi's Thought*, pp. 32-34; D.M. Datta, *op. cit.*, p. 29.
52. *CWMG*, vol. XLVIII, pp. 405-6.
53. *Ibid.*, p. 404; Elsewhere he writes, "God and Truth are one," See *CWMG*, vol. XXVII, p. 204.
54. *Ibid.*, vol. L, p. 175.
55. *Ibid.*, vol. XLVIII, p. 404.
56. *Ibid.*, pp. 404-5.
57. D.K. Bedekar, *Towards Understanding Gandhi*, p. 127.
58. *CWMG*, vol. XLVIII, p. 404.
59. *Ibid.*, p. 405.
60. *Ibid.*
61. *Ibid.*
62. *Harijan*, 9 August 1942, p. 264.
63. H. Joseph, *An Introduction to Logic*, pp. 232-33.
64. Pyarelal, *Mahatma Gandhi: The Last Phase*, vol. I, p. 120.
65. *Harijan*, 14 August 1937, p. 212.
66. P.T. Raju, *Idealistic Thought of India*, p. 297.
67. *CWMG*, vol. XXV, p. 558.
68. *Ibid.*, vol, XLI, p. 374; also *Harijan*, 22 June 1947, p. 201.
69. Pyarelal, *op. cit.*, p. 549.
70. *Harijan*, 28 April 1946, p. 111.
71. *Nature Cure*, p. 115.
72. *CWMG*, vol. XXXVII, p. 348.
73. *Ibid.*, vol. XXVI, p. 224.
74. *Ibid.*, vol. XXVII, p. 347.
75. Tendulkar, *op. cit.*, vol. III, p. 313.
76. Gora, *op. cit.*, p. 25.
77. *CWMG*, vol. XXXVII, p. 349.
78. William James, *The Varieties of Religious Experience*, p. 429.
79. *CWMG*, vol. XXXVII, p. 349.

80. John Caird, *op. cit.*, pp. 129-30.
81. *CWMG*, vol. XXIX, p. 412.
82. John Lewis, *Science, Faith and Scepticism*, p. 15.
83. *CWMG*, vol. XXXVII, p. 349.
84. John Caird, *op. cit.*, pp. 141-42.
85. Brand Blanshard in his *The Nature of Thought* (vol. I.) argues that "ideas are germinal objects" (p. 501); "the idea, if fully realized, would be its object" (p. 508); "that ideas are potentialities actualised in objects" (p. 512).
86. John Caird, *op. cit.*, pp. 145-46.
87. *Harijan*, 24 August 1947, p. 289; *Harijan*, 3 October 1936, p. 268; *Young India*, 24 November 1921, p. 385.
88. *Ethical Religion*, p. 20; for details see pp. 3-21.
89. S. Radhakrishnan, *The Reign of Religion in Contemporary Philosophy*, p. 224.
90. William James, *op. cit.*, pp. 435-38.
91. *Harijan*, 1 June 1935, p. 123.
92. Tendulkar, *op. cit.*, vol. IV, p. 133; also vol. III, p. 109.
93. *Harijan*, 13 June 1936, p. 140.
94. *Ibid.*, p. 140; also *CWMG*, vol. XXXVII, p. 350.
95. *Harijan*, 21 September 1934, p. 252.
96. William James, *op. cit.*, p. 428.
97. *Young India*, 21 January 1921, p. 31.
98. Tendulkar, *op. cit.*, vol. II, p. 294; *Harijan*, 14 May 1938, p. 109.
99. *Young India*, 21 January 1926, p. 30.
100. *Harijan*, 14 May 1938, p. 109.
101. *Ibid.*, 6 April 1940, p. 79.
102. Gandhi's letter quoted in *Mahadev Desai's Diary*, vol. I, p. 135.
103. Shri Ramakrishna says, "God cannot be realized through mere scholarly reasoning." M. *The Gospel of Sri Ramakrishna*, p. 32; "God can be realized by true faith alone." *Ibid.*, p. 234.
104. *CWMG*, vol. XLVIII, p. 406.

5

FUNDAMENTAL MORAL CONCEPTS

Criteria of Moral Action

John Locke declared: "Morality is the proper science and business of mankind in general...."[1] Gandhi firmly believes in this dictum. He preached and practised the same with his characteristic stark honesty and sincerity. And in doing so he, consciously or unconsciously, took into consideration so many topics that fall within the purview of moral science. On several occasions at the demand of circumstances he gave his opinion on ethical problems that might sound naive to a well-disciplined ear. But Gandhi's primary concern was humanity. His mode of thinking did not follow the hard and fast rules of scholarly discourse. He wove the moral world around humanism, the nucleus of his thought. Let us elucidate his ethical concepts one by one.

Historically, a moral judgement passes from settled habits, customs, traditions, and mores, ceremonial and civil laws to reflective principles that form the plinth of a scientific ethical system, applicable to all times and all people. Although customs and mores, conventions and usages are not moral judgements themselves, they do contribute prominently to their historical evolution. Gandhi felt the necessity of 'conventional behaviour' in a society. The customs and usages are often observed by the inhabitants without reflective thinking. They are indispensable for day to day affairs, for the maintenance of social order. But they are not moral judgements in the strict sense of the term, because they are not voluntary products of our free will. Gandhi condemns mere conventional actions as immoral, and intends to eliminate them from ethical consideration on the ground that we do not act in these cases voluntarily. Conventional actions are often instinctive, and hence non-voluntary. Thus to Gandhi a moral action is not a blind or instinctive exercise of our minds. It is a reflective one, an outcome of our free will.

On what grounds do we base our moral judgements upon an action? What should be the criteria or conditions of a moral action in Gandhian ethics? A critical analysis will reveal the following criteria of moral actiions in Gandhian ethics.

Firstly, volition is the nucleus of moral action, and voluntary actions are performed knowingly and intelligently by self-conscious free agents with desire, prevision, and choice of ends and means. A mechanical act fails to achieve moral worth owing to the fact that the intent to which it should be referred as a consequence is absent. Unless we have control over our actions, we cannot be held responsible for them. Thus a moral action must be the product of a voluntary will.

Secondly, according to Gandhi, moral intent is another criterion of moral action. There is no conflict between preaching an ideal and practising it. There is an organic relation among thought, speech and action in Gandhian thought. He practised whatever he preached. If an action is not prompted by moral intent it loses moral worth. The consequence or result, whatever be its practical value, cannot justify itself instigated by an immoral intent. In other words, it is not enough that the action performed by us is in itself good, it should inevitably arise out of a good intention. An action is moral when done because it is morally right without any reference to any personal benefit that may accrue from it. Gandhi says, "It is not enough that an act done by us is in itself good; it should have been done with the intention to do good. That is to say, whether an act is moral or otherwise depends upon the intention of the doer."[2] Thus an action in order to have moral worth must be prompted by good intention.

Thirdly, an action is morally good if it is done in the spirit of Kantian dictum: 'Duty for duty's sake' irrespective of its consequence, happiness or misery. The actions that arise from self-interest or are initiated by hope of happiness in the next world have no moral worth because the intent is not pure, and the standpoint that an action should be done only for the sake of doing it, is absent here. Selfless action or action without attachment and aversion, and with no desire for enjoying its fruits, is heard in the *Gita* where we are advised to 'have a right to actions, but not to their fruits' (2/47). The *Gita* played, and Gandhi admitted it several times, an important role in the formation of Gandhi's moral concepts.

Fourthly, the moral action must be free from compulsion, fear and coercion which obstruct the growth of human personality, the way to truth, and hence is not moral. Gandhi says, "...an act to be moral... has to be free from fear and compulsion."[3] When an individual is compelled to perform an act or behave in a particular manner, he either acts mechanically and is not aware of the reason why he should act thus, or he does not share the intent of the oppresser. Thus the action of a man under compulsion is not free and voluntary, and hence cannot have moral worth. This criterion is, in a sense, a corollary of the first one.

Fifthly, universality is a criterion of moral action in Gandhian ethics. Gandhi says, "...the higher morality must be comprehensive; it must embrace all men. Considering our relation to mankind, every man has a claim over us, as it is our duty always to serve him."[4] Moral actions are universal in a sense that they could be performed by all men under similar circumstances, irrespective of place and time. If an action is motivated by selfish ends it becomes subjective, and lacks universality which is a prime requisite of moral science. *Sarvodaya* as Gandhi conceived, calls upon us to transcend the immediate good of an isolated individual and embrace the universal good, the good of all mankind. Because, the welfare of the individual is necessarily bound with the welfare of the whole world. Thus, to Gandhi, an action can have moral worth only when it serves a universal end, i.e., a moral action must be universalized.

Lastly, practicability is another feature, if not a criterion, of a moral action in Gandhian ethics. His pragmatic outlook urged him to introduce moral values into practical life. The moral ideals, so to speak, had value only if they could control "the practical ordering of our lives." To quote him, "...mere knowledge is not enough, it should be followed by appropriate action. An ethical idea is like an architect's plan. The plan shows how the building should be constructed; but it becomes useless if the building is not raised accordingly. Similarly, an ethical idea is useless so long as it is not followed by suitable action."[5] Mere intellectual discourse was lifeless to him. His implementation of traditional moral norms into practical life constitutes a progressive trait in his personality. He deviated from the contemplative trend of traditional Indian thought and turned the semi-comatic people into a bold nation.

To sum up: An action is moral in Gandhian ethics if it is volitional, intentional, universal, practical, selfless, and free from fear and compulsion simultaneously. If anyone of the above factors is lacking it would not be a moral action in the Gandhian sense of the term. Indeed, a moral action must be performed "consciously, deliberately with a determined will, regardless of gain or loss, of life or death, without turning to look back, ready to sacrifice themselves."[6]

Elements of Morality

A hollow preaching, an empty ethical law, cannot be of any use to humanity. It must contain some elements that will render immense benefit to mankind in general. This motto urges Gandhi to fulfil the moral law with the following data.

Firstly, a peaceful disposition of the whole personality is indispensable for moral life because tranquility, calmness and mildness of temperament is conducive towards moral development. Indeed, serenity of mind endows vastness on our moral insights. On the other hand, 'at first sight,' Gandhi argues, "it may appear that people with a violent disposition rise in life; but a little reflection will show that, when the sword of violence falls, it may be on one's own neck."[7] Violence often begets violence in practical life. Not only this, violence obstructs the path to moral progress, and obscures the moral ideal. That is why Gandhi recommends a peaceful disposition as one of the elements of morality.

Secondly, "freedom from bad habits forms another element of morality."[8] By the term 'habit' we mean the capacity and tendency resulting from frequent repetition of the same act. Habit is generally formed by repeated voluntary activities. Such repeated performance of a voluntary act makes it easier, mechanical, irresistible, automatic and almost instinctive. The habits, good or bad, exert immense influence on the character or moral development of the agent. An individual is appreciated as good if he acquires certain good or virtuous habits, and condemned as bad if he is addicted to vicious or evil habits. Gandhi warns us against the danger of bad habits. Bad habits are detrimental not only to moral uplift of an individual but also to his physical well being. History tells us that the citizens become too much addicted to bad habits (drinks and drugs) during the last days of the Roman empire. That is why Gandhi advises us to get rid of all bad habits, and cultivate virtues that are conducive to moral progress. It is here noteworthy that Aristotle laid emphasis on the formation of good habits. A virtuous individual consciously creates a world of good habits in which he lives and acts. He habitually possesses a certain kind of knowledge or insight that is truly an outcome of the cultivation of good habits. According to Aristotle, the good habits play an important role in our moral lives. This is exactly the viewpoint of Gandhi also.

Thirdly, "another element of morality is chastity." Gandhi says, "...races without morality have completely disappeared."[9] It is universally accepted that regulated sex and disciplined ways of life have a far-reaching influence upon the moral character of a race or nation. Indeed, chastity or honesty in speech, thought or deed promotes not only our moral uplifts but also our longevities, our span of lives. That is why Gandhi prescribes *brahmacharya* or continence as a cardinal virtue which is to be observed by all.

Fourthly, altruism is another element of morality. Altruism roughly expresses the view that there is something intrinsically good in self-sacrifice or doing good to others. In his words, "...it is the duty of a man to bear this truth in mind and practise altruism, which is the highest form of morality."[10] It is true that without altruistic instinct human beings would not have survived. The infants would not have survived if they were not nursed tenderly and protected carefully. Altruism is the basis of subtle human instincts like love, affection, self-sacrifice, etc. in the absence of which life would have become a dry and barren desert. That is why Gandhi prescribed altruism as an important element of morality.

Lastly, righteousness is another element of morality in Gandhian ethics. The term 'right' is derived from the Latin word *rectus*, meaning straight or according to rule. An action is appreciated as righteous if it is in conformity with the moral law or laws, at the zenith of which is, according to Gandhi, truth. Truth is an eclectic concept in Gandhian works that absorbs in its infinite bosom all the 'good' of human thought, not to speak of ethics specifically. This righteousness or conformity to truth is the pivotal point of Gandhian moral thought.

To sum up: The cultivation of calmness, mildness, and tranquility of personality; fostering of good habits; observance of chastity, altruism and righteousness, etc., are the elements of moral life in Gandhian ethics.

The Moral Law

In our everyday lives we are to pass judgements upon actions done by us or by others. Some actions are appreciated by us while some others are condemned. In this act of appreciation or condemnation we adopt, consciously or unconsciously, a norm, a standard according to which the judgement is made. This sense of value-judgement or criterion of appreciation or condemnation of right and wrong actions respectively is already inherent in us. It is *a priori* because from experience, which is often delusive and contradictory, we can never establish a moral law that would exert command universally independent of space and time and irrespective of caste and creed. Gandhi shares this opinion of the pioneers of moral science and holds, "We have in our minds certain ideas and on the basis of those we judge the acts of others... independent of and apart from men's wishes and opinions, there is something like a moral standard which we may call moral law."[11] Thus, according to Gandhi, moral law is inherent, *a priori*, universal and independent of space and time, i.e., eternal.

We notice the following characteristics in Gandhi's conception of a moral law. "...moral laws are immutable. Opinions change, but not morality." The eternal maeal laws are objective and hence our wishes, opinions and ignorance have nothing to do with them. Indeed, mistakes and superstitions arise out of our ignorance and are our personal considerations, our failure to understand the moral laws in their full bloom, the truth. But as soon as "the eye of knowledge is opened" it penetrates into the dark chamber of ignorance and manifests the vision of the moral law before us. In short, moral laws are eternal and objective.

Secondly, the moral law is the verdict of our conscience, 'the still small voice,' in the words of Gandhi. It is self-imposed and comes from within because it is the product of our pure hearts; as Kant says, "it dwells in our hearts."

Thirdly, the moral law is mainly concerned with the inner being of a man specially with his motives, intentions, etc. Indeed, it is the inner man with whom moral science deals. In the words of Gandhi, "...we find no difficulty in judging an act in so far as the intention is known."[12] Thus the moral law does not take into account any external behaviour of an individual. It rather penetrates into the depth of our personalities.

Fourthly, the moral law is intrinsically the best, the 'highest law'. The early Greek thinkers made no distinction between the moral law and the laws of the state. But the gradual dawning of moral consciousness prepared man's mind for the concept that there is a deeper basis of moral law than the rules and regulations of the state. In the sacred books of ancient India (*Shastras*) the moral basis of statutory laws is evident. The *Manusamhita* is a landmark in this regard. But on close examination we shall see that the laws of state are limited in scope. They can exercise no influence beyond the prescribed range. As for example, the laws dealing with income tax, apply only to a limited number of people whose annual income is above a certain amount. Similarly, an honest grocer may not abide by the unwritten unfair customs of the business circle and remain poor. But it is otherwise with the moral law which is a mandate of the conscience, the inner voice of our personalities. It is imperative on all of us. And since it is self-imposed it is indispensably obligatory and universal in its scope. That is why Gandhi says, "a moral law is distinct from and better than the laws of the State or those of business."[13] In this way in Gandhian ethics, the moral law is superior to all other laws and universal in its scope. Many other thinkers have opined the same.

Fifthly, "there is thus a great difference between moral laws and temporal laws."[14] Gandhi here distinguishes between moral laws and temporal laws. What does he mean by temporal laws? As against the immutable moral laws the laws of the state and business are all conditional in the sense that they differ from state to state, age to age in keeping with public opinions or customs. But this is not so with the moral law. The moral laws like 'Always speak the truth' and 'Never tell a lie' are independent of space and time, state and nation. Truthfulness will be appreciated till the end of time while liars condemned. To quote Gandhi, "It (the moral law) cares not for custom nor for public opinion. To a moral man, public opinion or custom is binding only so long as it is in harmony with the moral law.... Such a law no people or individual can violate to the end of time."[15] This Gandhian distinction between the moral and temporal laws corresponds to Kantian distinction between the categorical imperative and the hypothetical imperative. Thus the Gandhian moral law is unconditional, universal, immediate and imperative by nature. Since it is independent of consequences, the results—whatever might be their nature—have no impact upon the nature of the moral law. The moral law—the immediate verdict of the conscience and the command of truth mediately—maintains its majesty. Thus the moral law in Gandhian ethics is pregnant with its own intrinsic value.

Sixthly, "...the moral law is supreme and divine."[16] We have seen that the moral law is independent of public opinions and customs, state and nation, space and time. Its celestial lustre remains bright and ever-shining, dauntless and taintless through ages. Socrates was killed by poison on the allegation of vitiating the minds of the youth. Although the moral law or laws that Socrates observed in his day were condemned and opposed vehemently still "the world admits that the morality he observed has remained, and shall remain, morality for ever."[17] Thus the moral law is supreme, divine and everlasting.

Seventhly, the moral law is mysterious and the key to all earthly necessities. Gandhi says, "This mysterious moral law brings prosperity to the man who observes it: it sustains the family that obeys it, and the community which lives by it ever flourishes. Freedom, peace and happiness are the lot of the nation that lets itself be ruled by this highest law."[18] Gandhi's treatment here is purely pragmatic. Humanism is the nucleus of Gandhian thought. His essays on various topics of moral science, compiled under the title *Ethical Religion*, were composed to awaken moral consciousness amongst the readers. He knew it well, as all great leaders do, that flesh is weak and hence the earthly pleasures seem to the men sweeter than the rigorous moral law. This is the reason behind his preaching of the moral law enveloped with earthly necessity. The observance of this highest law showers heavenly blessings in all respects on the moral man, the family, the community and the nation while the violation is visited with utter destruction to which the fate of splendid civilizations of Assyria, Babylon, Rome, Greece, etc. bears witness.

To sum up: The moral law in Gandhian ethics is *a priori*; universal eternal; immutable; independent of space and time; objective; self-imposed; dwells in the heart and deals with the inner being of our personalities. It is the highest; the best of all laws; supreme, divine, and unconditional imperative pregnant with its intrinsic value; and although mysterious unlocks the door to earthly necessities.

Object of Moral Judgement

A relevant question naturally arises in our minds: What should be the object of our moral judgements? On what object or matter do we pass our judgements? In our everyday lives we make moral judgements on a variety of objects, namely, good will, good character, good intention, good purpose, good motive, good end, etc. In a general way, we may call voluntary actions the object of our moral judgements. These voluntary actions are our 'willed activities', i.e., activities of our free will. This assumption of 'willed activities' leads some thinkers to declare the will as the object of moral judgement. Kant also declares that the good will, a product of pure reason, is the only object of our moral judgements. This good will has 'full value in itself' and 'shines like a jewel' even if it accomplishes nothing. But this formalistic attitude to the good will is devoid of matter and senses—is a false abstraction, an absurdity. Jacobi tells us that the Kantian good will is 'a will that wills nothing.' We shall later lucidly describe this point.

On the other hand, the intuitionists claim that the motives of our actions are the object of moral judgement. Etymologically the term 'motive' means that which moves us or causes us to act in a particular way. According to intuitionists, particularly, Martineau, Green and Bishop Butler, the proper object of moral judgement is motive, the idea of the end or goal the steers our will. But this view too faces difficulties in connection with the conflict between motive and consequences. For example, an efficient surgeon performs an operation most carefully in order to cure a patient, but the patient unfortunately dies. Here the motive of the surgeon is undoubtedly good but the result is bad. On the contrary, the consequence may be accidentally good although the motive behind it is bad. A person flings a coin to a beggar with intention to hit his head while the beggar picks it up and buys food with it. Here the action is undoubtedly bad because the motive is bad. But the intuitionist attempt to establish motive as the object of moral judgement is not altogether futile. In their analysis they have brought the nature of motive to limelight and evaluated the fact that motive too plays an important role in the formation of the object of moral judgement.

Some thinkers pass moral judgement upon the character of the agent. By character we generally mean the permanent, or to some extent constant, mental constitution of the agent. To put it otherwise, through our social intercourses and everyday actions we acquire a kind of permanent disposition of our mental states which may roughly be named as character. In our practical lives we judge an individual's character by the nature of his actions. So some ethicists have claimed that character of the person should be the object of moral judgement. Gandhi followed the general moral trend of ancient India which laid much importance on the development of character. He prescribed cardinal virtues for the *satyagrahis* to promote their moral characters. But this view of character as an object of moral judgement is also not tenable. In order to judge a piece of action we are to consider the series of actions of the agent's life as a whole. The motto is that 'there is no holiday from virtue.' In order to have a complete moral estimate of an individual we are to assess the moral elements latent in his character. This is not an easy task. Further, an individual of good character may not always perform good actions while a person of bad character may sometimes perform good actions. Thus character, though an element of it, cannot be the sole or prime object of moral judgement.

Another view deserves our attentions here. It has been claimed by some and also by Gandhi that the intention of our actions should be the object of moral judgement. The term intention is a complex psychological phenomenon and hence demands an elaboration.[19] Roughly speaking, intention is the whole scheme of action planned deliberately by the agent. Its connotation includes a variety of features depending on the span of imagination, knowledge, farsight and surroundings of the agent. In the broadest sense, it means the end and the means together. It includes the motive or the idea of the end as well as the idea of the means. Let us explain it with examples. St. Crispin, we are told, used to steal leather from the rich with a view to manufacturing shoes for the poor. Here the action is immoral because of the employment of unfair means although the motive or end was quite right. On the contrary, in the above mentioned beggar-coin episode the end is good although the motive is bad. Indeed, it is the end and the means together that justify an action. This clearly points to the whole complex psychological phenomenon, intention or volition, as possessing moral quality. An intention is the end which the agent definitely aims at together with the means that the agent employs for the realization of the end. This view of intention as the object of moral judgement achieves appreciation from the utilitarian school, especially from Mill who opines, "The morality of an action depends entirely upon the intention—that is, upon what the agent *wills* to do."[20]

In the above perspective let us discuss the Gandhian view of intention, the object of moral judgement. Gandhi believed in the traditional concept of selfless action. On account of this he attached little importance to the outer manifestation or consequence of an action. It is the purity of the matrix, here mental states and processes, that evaluates the moral goodness or badness, rightness or wrongness of an action. He emphasized the mental antecedents—the mental states and processes out of which the action arose. To quote him, "One's way of life is not to be judged by one's visible outward actions but by one's inner leanings. For instance, if of two men, one gives a dollar to a poor person to rid himself of his presence and the other half a dollar but with love and out of compassion for the man, obviously, the one who gave half a dollar is truly moral, while the other who gave a dollar the sinner."[21] Thus to Gandhi the moral rightness or wrongness of an action depends on the 'inner leaning,' i.e., the mental state of our actions.

Now, which one of the mental states is the object of moral judgement? Is it motive or intention or something else? To Gandhi, it is clearly intention. Because it is not only the good motive but also the idea of a good end that contributes to the moral goodness of an action. In other words, to make an action good both the motive and the intention must be good. In his words, "This socialism is as pure as crystal. It, therefore, requires crystal-like means to achieve it. Impure means result in an impure end."[22] We have already seen above that intention includes both the end and the means in its connotation. While elucidating the nature of moral, non-moral and immoral actions Gandhi categorically asserts, "We cannot always fathom a man's motives, and may thus judge him wrongly. Nevertheless, we find no difficulty in judging an act in so far as the intention is known."[23] "It is not enough that an act done by us is in itself good; it should have been done with the intention to do good. That is to say, whether an act is moral or otherwise depends upon the intention of the doer."[24] Indeed, Gandhi was a pragmatist, a practical philosopher. He knew that people in general make judgements upon actions. If the actions normally produce good results the people call it good; otherwise, it is not so. But the majesty of moral judgement cannot wait for the whims of the people. It demands an eternal criterion applicable universally to all actions independent of space and time. So we conclude with Gandhi that intention, in the sense of the whole complex psychological phenomenon, is the proper object of moral judgement.

Ends and Means

Gandhi was primarily an ethico-religious man whose ardent humanism impelled him to enter into the political world, propose to himself a goal and devise a way of attaining it, which shook the fundamental pre-suppositions; of traditional political thought. The general trend of traditional political thought emphasized the discontinuity, separation and discreteness of ends and means of our action. Sometimes in their eagerness to prove the pragmatic superiority of ends they have underestimated the means and reduced it to a sinister mechanical device. And consequently it was followed by some disastrous results in the history of mankind. Gandhi challenged this erroneous method of the political world through *satyagraha* or non-violent movement which is based on a philosophy of action and reconciliation of ends and means.

For a fair understanding of the Gandhian position let us draw a brief historical sketch of the ends-means controversy. Most of the schools accept a sharp dichotomy between ends and means, and endeavour to implement it in every sphere of life, especially in the political field. Ends have been classified variously according to circumstances, such as, immediate and ultimate, essential and desirable, short term and long term, actual and utopian, etc. On the other hand, the problem of means also has been studied with keen attention. The theoretical and practical efficacy of the means together with their moral implications in connection with corresponding ends has been widely considered. It is well accepted by a vast majority of people that moral considerations have no bearing upon the adoption of means or that ends are morally and pragmatically preferable to means the extreme form of which is expressed in the much controversial dictum. "The end justifies the means." The historical background of this doctrine goes back to the teachings of Kautilya in India and to the pragmatic writings of Machiavelli in Italy. The name of Machiavelli is almost identical with this dictum. The corruption of the times, the weakness of the quarrelsome states and the threat of foreign aggression deeply moved the heart of Machiavelli. He sought for a 'redeemer,' a new prince who with his superhuman powers would fulfil his much cherished dream, the redemption of Italy. In this expedition the new prince would not be obstructed by any moral scruples and religious commandments. He is absolutely free to adopt means, whatever be its nature, for the tackling of situations. In short, nationalism and patriotism are the keynotes of Machiavellian thought. The redemption of Italy was the supreme goal of his life and works; and for this purpose he did not like to observe much rigidity in the selection of means for the attainment of ends. But unfortunately this purpose was ignored by his contemporaries, and consequently

Machiavellian thought was condemned for immorality. Of course, his obscure style and some blunt maxims of his works are partially responsible for his ill reputation. To quote Machiavelli, "It is far better to be feared than loved if you cannot be both."[25] "A Prince, therefore, need not necessarily have all the good qualities I mentioned above, but he should certainly appear to have them."[26] The contemporaries out of hatred coined the term 'Machiavellism' as an abbreviations of all mischief of Italy.

But a critical review of Machiavellian thought would throw a new light on the topic. With a view to creating sensation, and shocking his contemporaries Machiavelli liked to appear more wicked than he was. And his prescription of violence and trickery for the new prince is not altogether useless. Because, violence and trickery have a role to play in political affairs. A tree is known by its fruits. Likewise, the value of Machiavellian thought lies in its effectiveness. It is not a negative principle; and hence we should not sacrifice effectiveness at the altar of morality. Furthermore, misunderstanding and misinterpretation are also no less responsible for the ill reputation of Machiavellism. The bold and obscure maxims that earned ill reputation for Machiavelli were purely theoretical abstractions of an art, the political affairs, itself not always based on moral scruples.

What is the view of Marx and Marxists regarding ends and means? The rationalistic philosophy of Hegel, especially his dialectic, cast an immense influence on the Marxist philosophical system. To Hegel, the state as the embodiment of eternal, absolutely rational and substantive will is the highest end of an individual whose highest duty is to obey it. The individual realizes his freedom by carrying out the imperatives of the state which is an end in itself, an expression of the Spirit or the Absolute. Hegel ascribes little importance to the role of means in the attainment of an individual's end. An extreme emphasis on ends accompanied with utter regation of the role of means is one of the salient features of Hegelian thought. The Hegelian concept of ends and means, nourished from metaphysical sources, failed to command universal assent. History of mankind records that Hegelian prescription of spiritualized end in stead of individual-controlled one together with the neglect of the role of means for attainment of ends failed to serve human needs and thereby the purpose of political philosophy.

Both Marx and Engels write, "The Communists disdain to conceal their views and their aims. They openly declare that their ends can be attained only by the forcible overthrow of all existing social conditions."[27] Engels declares, "...any means that leads to the aim suits me as a revolutionary, whether it is the most violent or that which appears to be most peaceable."[28] From this some thinkers come to the hasty conclusion that Marxism is another form of Machiavellism, i.e., its end justifies the means.[29] But Marxism is not Machiavellism. The very spirit of the dialectical inseparability of means and ends in Marxian thought is overlooked here. C.G. Shah opines, "The crucial truth is hereby revealed, viz., that *there is no question of the end justifying or not justifying the means. There exists only the objective fact, viz., that the end determines the means, just as the means determine the end (the end and means are mutually convertible) due to the operation of the law of the dialectical unity of the end and the means.*"[30] Indeed, dialectical materialism is a dynamic process which changes as it proceeds endlessly. It forms its ideal or norm in proportion to its means for fulfilling the demands of the situation. The reciprocal influence and interaction between the ideal and the actual gives birth to means which in its turn, through a dynamic process, becomes harmonious with the end. As Trotsky says, "dialectical materialism does not know dualism between means and end. The end flows naturally from the historical movement. Organically the means are subordinated to the end."[31] In short, the relation between means and ends in Marxian thought does never imply that any end justifies any means and vice versa. The nature of the means is determined by the nature of the end in the given historical situation. Means and ends are inseparably and harmoniously connected with one another in such a manner that the nature of means, violent or non-violent, changes in accordance with the nature of ends and circumstances.

From the above discussion it is evident that the general trend of Machiavellism, authoritarian or absolute idealism, and Marxism is to safeguard the ends of their action by a means compatible with the corresponding ends. An almost similar viewpoint can be found in the preachings of anarchists and conservatives. Oscar Jaszi defines anarchism, "It can in general, however, be defined as an attempt to establish justice (that is, equality and reciprocity) in all human relations by the complete elimination of the state (or by the greatest possible minimization of its activity) and its replacement by an entirely free and spontaneous co-operation among individuals, groups, regions and nations."[32] In the history of Western political thought we come across some seven distinct schools of anarchism which were advocated by so many thinkers such as Max Stirner, Kropotkin, Proudhon, Tolstoy, Godwin, Bakunin, Hodgskin, Warren, Tucker, etc. Proudhon's concept of *mutualite* is the pivotal point of his anarchial thought. Individual rights and individual freedom are of supreme importance. By mutuality he means 'reciprocity of services,' 'a vast network of organized exchanges.' And since individual freedom is the matrix of social order, individuals should be free from all sorts of constraints. Bakunin proposed the abolition of inheritance together with the abolition of state-machinery, if necessary, through direct violent means. In the history of anarchial thought Tolstoy occupies a notable position. He expressed his anarchial thought in the form of a series of 'nos', namely, no service to a government, no military duty, no tax-payment, no oath taking, no police duty, etc. He aimed at the establishment of the Kingdom of God on earth as the end but emphasized non-violent, non-resistant efforts as the means. In this context Oscar Jaszi observes, "Similar ideas, in conscious support of Tolstoy but founded independently on genuine Hindu religious thought, are propagated by Mahatma Gandhi, the Indian leader, whose doctrine, however, is largely coloured by the national struggle of his people against British rule."[33] In short, all the schools of anarchism have 'no authority' concept as their central point or end, and the utmost freedom for the individual action without any restraining force as the means.[34]

But the anarchist schools in general have failed to solve the ends-means problem properly. The remarkable drawback of this school is that in its attempt to abolish authority it has failed to supply us a positive alternative which may lead us to the desired end of averting violence. A society without authority is a utopia, and never practicable. The supreme importance ascribed to goodness, reasonableness and freedom of an individual is owing to ignorance of human nature. None can guarantee that each individual will perform his respective function spontaneously at the critical moment of a non-authoritarian society without disciplined direction. Hence non-authoritarian society as an end and mutuality or non-violent, non-resistant efforts as means fail to solve the ends-means controversy.

Now, let us consider the viewpoint of the conservative school of thought. Roberto Michels says, "Conservatism means hostility to innovations in the social or moral order."[35] By conservatism we generally mean a doctrine which lays emphasis on, more precisely, preference for, the traditional, old and tried concepts of our lives than for the new and untried. Edmund Burke, John Adams, Benjamin Disraeli, John Marshall, T.S. Eliot, etc., are the prominent exponents of this system of thought. We should follow the ancestors from whom we have inherited a vast treasure of moral, social, and political values. So the cultural and heritage of a nation is to be preserved and conserved. In short, order and stability of society are the ends which can be achieved through historically developed established institutions as means.

But on a critical examination this view too fails to satisfy us owing to its keen sensitivity to any change and the adoption of non-violent means for the conservation of established institutions, order and stability of society as end. The concept of means as a technique of social action is not uniform amongst the conservatives. Some emphasize non-violent, non-resistance. Joseph De Maistre in his prescription for the status of 'hangman' in an ideal society suggests active suppression of individual will and reason through autocratic violence.

What is the view of the Liberal Democratic school regarding ends-means controversy? It has a galaxy of great thinkers like Hobbes, Locke, Bentham, Mill, Green, Hobhouse, etc., as its exponents. Locke's approach to this problem was psychological and it got confused with his political ideas. This theory took the shape of utilitarianism in the Benthamite principle, 'greatest good of the greatest numbers.' In J.S. Mill's *Utilitarianism*, one finds an elaboration of the problem of ends and means. Happiness or utility is the ultimate end of our lives. And the actions or means, whatever might be their nature, that promote happiness or utility are morally justified. The liberal democrats also preach liberty-equality complex which includes contract, negotiation, tolerance, compromise, etc. as modes of action. In short, the Liberal Democratic school sets up liberty-equality complex before them as the ultimate end; and adopts dynamic principles of compromise, adjustment, negotiation, etc., as the means for the solution of conflicts.

But this school too like Machiavellism, Conservatism, Anarchism, Authoritian Idealism, etc. fails to solve the ends-means problem satisfactorily. In a liberal democracy, the devices prescribed above can to some extent serve social life adequately. The pragmatic utility of compromise, accommodation, discussion, etc. is undeniable in our everyday lives. But in case of any external aggression when the very structure of society is challenged, and is in peril, the liberal democrats cannot but prescribe violent force as the only way out.

Their non-violent devices then utterly fail, and the indispensability of an efficacious mode of social action, namely, means becomes evident. Thus although the liberal democrats posit liberty-equality complex as the highest end, they fail to supply us with an efficacious means, an adequate mode of social action.

In the above perspective let us discuss the Gandhian viewpoint regarding ends-means relationship. But before we enter into the arena we should, in this context, bear in mind the warning of Joan V. Bondurant failing which a correct appreciation may suffer. To quote her, "Gandhi would have had no patience with attempts to classify him as conservative, liberal, socialist or anarchist. He was all these and none of them for he never lost his profoundly revolutionary character."[36] This is the most important for correctly understanding Gandhian thought. His eclectic mind absorbed everything noble that he came across, but digested and expressed them in his own way. In the course of the following discussion we shall see that in spite of his bitter aversion to 'Machiavellism' which overemphasizes adoption of any means, the apparent supremacy of means raises head here and there in his thought. With this caution in mind let us proceed step by step.

During Gandhi's movement for independence three distinct and different views regarding ends-means problems were mooted. One school of thought was vehemently vocal under the leadership of the nationalist leaders like Lala Lajpat Rai, Bal Gangadhar Tilak, Bipin Chandra Pal, Sri Aurobindo, Krishna K. Mitra, etc. They adopted the agitational technique of public work, and a kind of vigorous opposition towards the constitutional movement of the liberalist group led by Dadabhai Naoroji, Surendranath Banerjee, Gopal Krishna Gokhale, etc. They did not like the liberalist's infusion of moral and religious scruples into public life, in the strategy of freedom movement. The concept of means of this school is well expressed in the extremistic standpoint of Tilak's *Jaise Ko Taisa* (tit for tat), *Satey Satyam Samacaret* (be wicked with the wicked). In other words, according to this school, especially Tilak, crooked is the course of life, and the world is not filled with saints. Hence in the freedom movement 'the end justifies the means'; and the religious and moral ideals have nothing to do with politics. V.M. Bhat observes, "Tilak held that armed activities also had their place in the scheme of achieving independence. Tilak had faith in means both open and secret. He believed in accumulated efficacy of all political activities from petitions and prayers to armed revolts."[37] This is clearly a revival of Machiavellism in the Indian public affairs.

The second school of thought was led by the national revolutionaries (imperialist officials dubbed them as 'terrorists') who would not hesitate to adopt any violent means including bloodshed and terror for the achievement of their end, the independence of India. Some of them would welcome foreign military aid and alliance to attain national independence. The revolutionaries of Bengal and Punjab made some futile attempts to overthrow the British Government. And consequently, it was evident that violent means was not efficacious in the freedom movement. Gandhi appreciated the burning patriotism and sincere dedication of these revolutionaries from the core of his heart. But he was temperamentally different from them and as an apostle of non-violence he openly condemned the technique of action of this school.

The third view is that of Gandhi and others. We have already seen that Gandhi derived his mental nourishment from the traditional Indian thought with some variations. The *Gita*, especially the preachings of *Karmayoga*, exercised an immense influence on his course of action. His concepts of ends and means are, in a sense, derivatives of the law of *Karma* and the *Karmayoga* of the *Gita*. The law of *Karma* tells us that our present actions are consequences of the past life, and perhaps, will determine the course of future life. Gandhi condemns the immoral actions and means because they degrade the doer; and thereby fail to ennoble man. Gandhi prefers non-violent means for two reasons—the first is ethical and the second is pragmatic. The condemnation of violent means from the moral standpoint, according to Gandhi, is based on the following grounds. (a) Violence begets violence; it proliferates numerously. It obstructs man's way to perfection as a human being, envelops his noble qualities, and through instigation and degradation turns him into a revengeful machine. In other words, violent means degrades an individual and a nation, and gives birth to an endless series of future bloodshed and degradation. (b) The ultimate aim or end of violent means is to solve a problem by oppression of the opponent, and in some extreme cases by annihilation of the opponent. This is a contradiction of the divine design. To quote him, "he (man) must not destroy what he cannot create."[38] (c) 'Hate the sin, not the sinner' goes an immortal saying. We are to take into account the inner being of an individual, and not the outward manifestations. Because truth, the ultimate end of all means, is to be realized within and not without. But the violent means aims at evil lying outside and thereby takes the doer off the path of truth. (d) An individual being a spark of Truth or God involves infinite potentiality. To adopt a violent means for his annihilation is to put an end to his potentiality, his divinity. Hence reformation should be the aim of our means which violent means fails to offer us.

On the other hand, Gandhi's pragmatic outlook made him cautious regarding the adoption of violent means because of practical inconveniences it begets. An end achieved through violent means is often short-lived, and if the machinery of force declines the situation is often reversed. Thus in order to enforce a permanent and lasting impact on social life non-violent means is more beneficial than the violent ones. Indeed, experience tells us that the non-violent means of compromise, persuasion, etc., is more fruitful in practical life than the violent means. And violent means often loses the sympathy of neutral and right-minded persons whose transfer of sympathy, in some cases active support, strengthens the opponent.

From the above it is clear that violent means, to Gandhi, is not permissible in any sphere of life. The means should not only be non-violent, it should also be pure, clear crystal-like, just and spotless. He considers purity an essential quality of means. Purity is to a means what character is to a man. Just as a man loses everything if he loses character so also a means becomes pernicious and valueless if it is devoid of purity. An impure means can never attain Truth. It extinguishes its vitality in the vicious puzzle of untruth and violence. B.N. Ganguli comments, "...Gandhi leaned heavily on the ethical purity of the means, particularly the purity of motivation underlying non-violent action."[39]

Another significant feature of means in his thought is clearness and rightness. By clarity of means he assumed the concept to be free from ambiguity and obscurity. Generally, obscure and ambiguous statements are a trickery, a technique of hide and seek policy. This was firmly disliked by Gandhi. He prescribed the public defence and universal practice of the means for the attainment of end. Adoption of means of questionable character will raise doubts in the minds of *satyagrahis* and the cause would suffer thereby. D.G. Tendulkar observes, "...he would never be guilty of supporting anything that could not be publicly and honestly defended. That was his universal practice. He did not believe in questionable means even to secure a worthy end."[40] In short, to Gandhi, the means must be non-violent, pure, crystal-like clear, just, spotless, and conducive towards *sarvodaya*.

What about the end? In a word the end is Truth which he pursued throughout his life. In his epistemology relative and absolute truth appear as near and remote end; in religion it becomes God or Rama or Allah; in ethics it is perfection or liberation (*moksa*); in politics truth takes the shape of *Swaraj* or freedom; in sociology the same end is manifested in his concept of *Ramrajya*. In the preceding chapters we have already analysed some of these concepts, and the rest will be dealt with in the succeeding chapters. So further elaboration of the concept of end here seems to be unnecessary.

A relevant question may be asked: What is the relation between ends and means in Gandhian thought? To him ends and means are convertible terms like Truth and God. In his words, "The end we do not know. For me it is enough to know the means. Means and end are convertible terms in my philosophy of life."[41] Is this conversion of ends and means logically tenable? To Gandhi the argument stands, 'All ends are means, ∴ All means are ends' or to cite a concrete example from his writings, 'God is Love' (non-violence) ∴ Love is God." Here in the first argument the term 'means' being the predicate of an 'A' proposition is undistributed while in the converse the same term 'means' being the subject of an 'A' proposition becomes distributed. Hence this conversion is fallacious from the logical standpoint. But Gandhi seeks way-out by saying elsewhere, "...if the means and the end are not identical, they are almost so."[42] This means to him ends and means are synonymous or identical terms. And in some special cases where the subject and the predicate are co-extensive or definite singular terms, simple conversion of an 'A' proposition is permissible. In the previous chapter (see section: God is Truth: Truth is God) we have already dealt with this logical difficulty of conversion in Gandhian thought in detail. Above all, since humanism was his primary concern, he cared very little for 'the dry syllogistic method.'

Another feature of this relationship is brought out by him through a comparison of the relationship between a seed and a tree. He says, "The means may be likened to a seed, the end to a tree; and there is just the same inviolable connection between the means and the end as there is between the seed and the tree."[43] Here through the above comparison he opens a new horizon of the end-means controversy. The seed is potentially a tree and the tree is the seed, the means manifested. And consequently, this relation inheres between the potential and the actual, the latent and the manifest, the idea and the realized. This feature is unique; and has drawn the attention of a galaxy of eminent scholars due to its novelty. In the eye of Krishnalal Shridharani the means is "the end in process and the ideal in the making."[44] With this novelty, we shall see later, of continuity of means and ends, and means as end-creating, we touch the heart of Gandhian moral philosophy at its most sensitive spot.

Another feature of end-means controversy has drawn the attention of eminent thinkers. Some emphasized the discreteness of ends and means while others maintained them to be continuous. The discreteness or discontinuity of means and ends became an evident feature of Machiavellism which we have already elucidated in the beginning of this section. Perhaps, this trend reached its climax in the views of Vitfredo Pareto, and later in the highly ambitious ideologies of fascism. Pareto not only distinguished between means and ends but also disparaged the value of means, and thereby gave the 'upper hand' to ends. He prescribed the rational code for means while ends were allowed freedom without reservation. To Pareto, moral values contribute nothing to the basic foundation of society. The ruling elite force, the non-elite to carry out their value-system. He condemned the bourgeois morality and proposed to treat the non-elite as the 'common herd.' He justified violence or use of force in order to preserve the interest of the élite. In short, Pareto's assertion of absence of connection between means and ends; and prescription of a different code of discipline both of them failed to attain, with some variation, universal assent. An echo of this view is heard in the fascist doctrine which indulged, nay justified, all sorts of irrationality only to glorify the freedom of will. Mussolini declared, "By the exercise of his free will man can, and must create his own world."[45] And consequently, the history of the second world war records horror and tyranny as the outward manifestation of the free will through unlimited violence. Indeed, we can on no ground justify the adoption of means, available at hand, without a proper probe into the nature of ends for the achievement of which the means are used. Thus the discontinuity of means and ends is untenable for its disastrous effects in practical life, and also for its unethical implications.

We have seen above that Marxism is not Machiavellism. To Marxists means are given or implied in the objective situation, i.e., end itself. Dialectical materialism knows no dualism, no separability between means and ends. Continuity of means and ends is an essential feature of Marxism. Gandhi firmly asserts the continuity of means and ends. He says, "There is no wall of separation between means and ends."[46] They are continuous and dynamic in nature. The means create the ends which, again, turns into means for the attainment of a further end and so on endlessly. For example, he introduced the spinning wheel a means for economic freedom which, again, was turned into a means for political freedom from foreign domination; and political freedom was conducive towards the attainment of liberation or *Moksa* and so on *ad infinitum*. In this context, H. Horsburgh aptly comments, "Gandhi's fundamental principles, then, are hybrids, functioning partly as means and partly as ends."[47] As we have already mentioned, this dynamic principle has attracted some eminent thinkers of whom Ferdinand Lasalle is one. In his play, *Franz Von Sickingen*, one of the characters says, "...Show not the *goal*/ But show also the *path*. So closely interwoven/Are path and goal that each with other/Ever changes, and other *paths* forthwith/ Another *goal* set up."[48]

Gandhi's emphasis on the continuity of means and ends is further illustrated in his statement, "As the means so the end."[49] Indeed, we cannot expect a rose by planting a noxious weed. Here Joan V. Bondurant's remark will help us to a better understanding of the Gandhian position. She comments, "Means and ends in Gandhian satyagraha are distinguishable only temporally. Both means and ends partake of a continuous process. The means precede the end in time; but there can be no question of moral priority. Truth is inseparable from non-violence, and the method of achieving and clinging to the truth is non-violence. Non-violence becomes both the means and the end, and the terms become convertible."[50] This dynamic change of means and ends goes on simultaneously. In the eye of Gandhi, Truth, the ultimate end, is ever indeterminate in nature. It recedes like the horizon as we proceed step by step. In fact, whenever we adopt a means to achieve an end, we desire it to fulfil some environing conditions, some needs ensuing or at hand. This attention to environing needs generates and regenerates endlessly a series of ends which are subject to ceaseless development and hence continuous modification. In this way the present needs, immediate ends produce some distant and remote ends as circumstances demand. And since this constant modification of ends is engineered by means we may call them end-generating and end-begetting means. In Oswald Spengler we hear an echo of this note when he says that human beings need not only noble ends but also constructive and creative means.[51] This productivity or constructive feature of means is also emphasized by John Dewey who warns us against the danger of fixed-ends or the much celebrated concept of 'ends-in-themselves' which Kant and other thinkers held. To Dewey the "ends arise and function"[52] within the surroundings; and the means and ends are, like Gandhi's ends begetting means, "two ways of regarding the same actuality."[53] Again, Dewey likes to treat the ends as hypotheses for their variable character; and the means a phase in the process. He argues, "Only recognition in both theory and practice that ends to be attained (ends-in-view) are of the nature of hypotheses and that hypotheses have to be formed and tested in strict correlativity with existential conditions as means, can alter current habits of dealing with social issues."[54] Thus the hypothetical ends and the correlated means of Dewey have much in common with Gandhian view of the same.

Some scholars have alleged that Gandhi attached undue importance to the means superseding the ends. This allegation regarding the supremacy of means over the ends in Gandhian thought is not wholly baseless. The following excerpts from Gandhi's works will throw light on it. He says, "They say 'means are after all means'; I would say 'means are after all everything'. As the means so the end... the creator has given us control (and that too very limited) over means, none over the end. Realization of the goal is in exact proportion to that of the means. This is a proposition that admits of no exception."[55] "For me it is enough to know the means."[56] "A moral means is almost an end in itself because virtue is its own reward."[57] We can cite innumerable instances like these in this context. Above all, we have already seen in the preceding passage that the ends come out of the means. Thus the allegation of means-bias in Gandhian works is not entirely baseless.

This means-bias of Gandhi became an object of criticism both in contemporary and later period. Let us first discuss the criticisms which will be co-ordinated later on. R.N. Iyer opines, "Gandhi seems to stand almost alone amongst social and political thinkers in his firm rejection of the rigid dichotomy between ends and means, and in his extreme moral preoccupation with the means to the extent that they, rather than the ends, provide the standard of reference."[58] Louis Fischer comments, "Means were all to him. Ends never arrive, for all ends are means to further ends which are again means."[59] Jawaharlal

Nehru admits this means-bias by saying, "Gandhi was never tired of talking about means and ends and of laying stress on the importance of the means... the ends must inevitably come out of the means and are governed by those means."[60] Buddhadeva Bhattacharyya shares an almost similar view with them. He comments, "This insistence on the supreme importance of the means distinguished Gandhian ethics, and logically his other theories about man, society, etc., from what Nehru called 'the normal approach'."[61] The excerpts from Gandhi's writings in the preceding passage and the valuable comments of eminent scholars as cited above in this paragraph seem to prove conclusively the means-bias in Gandhian thought.

Is this means-bias real? Does it contradict other tenets of Gandhian thought? Are the comments of the above scholars valid? On a close scrutiny we shall see that this means-bias like his declaration of *anekantavadi vedantist* etc. is apparent, and not real due to the following reasons.

Firstly, the question of undue emphasis either on means or ends arises only if we take them as separate and discrete units. And if they are separate and discrete, they will become individual, autonomous units having no interaction or interrelation amongst them. But to Gandhi means and ends are not only convertible but also 'Almost identical' terms. That is to say, ascription of any importance to either means or ends would convey the same to the other. In the case of identical terms the question of part or discreteness does not arise.

Secondly, we have already seen that means and ends do form a means-ends concept which is continuous, dynamic, ever-changing in Gandhian thought. And since the means are end-makers, and ends in process, any importance given to means would enrich the idea of ends also. Indeed, in Gandhian thought all ends are adopted as means to attain some further ends and so on endlessly. In this sense we may say that all ends are means in embryo. Hence the criticism of means-domination in Gandhian thought is unsound.

Thirdly, means and ends are two phases of the same reality. Although this argument bears repetition as a corollary of the second one, still it demands elaboration. To Gandhi, *ahimsa* (non-violence) and *satya* (truth), means and ends are two sides of the same coin. They appear to be two temporally and spatially but in fact they belong to the same reality or entity. Gopinath Dhawan warns us against the so-called supremacy or dominance of means over ends by saying "Gandhiji's emphasis on the importance of means should not be misconstrued as implying that the end is, with him, only a secondary consideration. He believes that the means and the end are inseparably connected and is eager that the means used should in no way detract from the moral character of our end."[62]

Fourthly, the harsh realities of life and his personal experience taught that any neglect of or deviation from the proper means would push him off the path of truth and non-violence. Once Gandhi compromised the means—trying to win the favour of the British political agent, in his words, *sahib,* who was prosecuting a case against his brother on the charge of giving wrong advice to the Ranasaheb of Porbandar—and suffered a setback. To quote him, "I pocketed the insult, but also profited by it...."[63] Thus personal experience warned him to take much care of the means in future course of life.

Fifthly, he was very much conscious of human imperfection and the limitation of free will. Except Almighty God none could command ends or results to him. Man, a tiny speck, in the background of the vast universe is helpless to conduct the happenings of life. Man's cravings for desired ends often turn into a wild-goose chase. In other words, man with his limited power and efficiency can never guarantee ends or results. And consequently, to commit oneself unreservedly to an end, a probable one, is to undermine one's status as a rational being. That is why Gandhi says, "We have always control over the means and never on the end." The dominant theme here is that since means or methods are at our command while results or ends are beyond that, our primary duty is to take proper care of methods or means rather than the ends or results.

Sixthly, his emphasis on the means is in compliance with the *Gita* ideal of selfless action or action without attachment (*nishkama karma*): We can only strive but have no control over ends or results; but if the means is pure the end cannot be unfair. In other words, the *Gita* preaches: 'We have a right to actions, but not to their fruits *karmaney vadhikarastey maphaleshu kadachana*' (2/47). And renunciation of fruits of action promotes liberation or *moksa*, the ultimate end of life. To Gandhi, the *Gita* was "the key to the scriptures of the world," and the perfect expression of *ahimsa* or non-violence. Whenever sorrows overcast his mind he found comfort in the teachings of the *Gita*. In his words, "...it answers all my difficulties and has been my *Kamadhenu*, my guide, my 'open sesame', on hundreds of moments of doubt and difficulty."[64] In this context Vincent Sheean observes, "...it is extremely evident that the *Gita* had sovereign power over him."[65] Thus it was quite natural for Gandhi to follow the *Gita* ideal of selfless action and to adopt the means at hand than the far end. In short, the so-called supremacy of means over ends in Gandhian thought is apparent and not real.

Our discussion of means and ends would remain incomplete if we do not take into account the role of violence in Gandhi's concept of means and ends. Although he tried his utmost to lead a non-violent life still he, compelled by circumstances, could not stick to it in the literalist sense of the term. He writes, "I have never preferred killing a dacoit to winning him over with love. But he who is not equal to that love, who cannot master all the love that the act demands, has the right to protect his proteges and his property even by killing the dacoit."[66] Again, during communal disturbance in Noakhali in 1946 he openly advised the womenfolk to adopt violent means in order to protect their honour. To quote him, "When a woman is assaulted she may not stop to think in terms of *himsa* or *ahimsa*. Her primary duty is self-protection. She is at liberty to employ every method or means that come to her mind in order to defend her honour."[67] Once in the Ashram the monkeys were causing extensive damage to the crops. The Ashramites tried to frighten them but in vain. Gandhi held a discussion with his co-workers and decided to kill the monkeys until a suitable non-violent means was discovered to stop this nuisance.[68] Innumerable citations may be quoted here in this context. Pragmatic Gandhi knew the mind of the mass, and the demand of the age. Man is the first and foremost concern of his thought and works. The necessity of the age and circumstances, and his burning humanism inspired him to prefer bravery and fearlessness to perfect non-violence which is beyond the reach of human beings due to imperfection. That is why he prescribed fearlessness as a cardinal virtue, and called for its practice, if necessary, through violent means, rather than through indulgence in cowardice that undermines the divinity of an individual. In short, although Gandhi proclaimed non-violence to be the best method of establishing a moral cause or end still, compelled by the circumstances, he prescribed violent means or justified it in some rare cases in order to safeguard the majesty of morality and the dignity of human being.

To conclude: the pacifist thinkers, namely, Aldous Huxley,

Roland Holst, Charles Naine, etc., emphasize on the need of harmony between the end and the means. Aldous Huxley opines, "...no economic reform, however intrinsically desirable, can lead to desirable changes in individuals and the society they constitute, unless it is carried through in a desirable context and by desirable methods."[69] Perhaps, the closest approximation to the Gandhian view of means and ends is that of Jacques Maritain who maintains, "...means must be proportioned and appropriate to the end, since they are ways to the end and, so to speak, the end itself in its very process of coming into existence. So that applying intrinsically evil means to attain an intrinsically good end is simply nonsense and a blunder."[70] This bears a close resemblance to the Gandhian view that 'as the means so the end.'

The doctrine that justifies any means for the attainment of end is not tenable from the ethical standpoint because it often forms a criminal disposition in the agent. It is an established fact of human psychology that the means, good or bad, become by the principle of transference of interest as desirable as the end itself. By virtue of their nature the bad means are often short-cuts to the end than the long journey of good and pure means. This proclivity is an unwelcome disposition of the agent. Thus an end cannot justify any means. On the other hand, recognition of bare means without any regard for the end seems to be impractical because it often fails to fulfil the inner cravings of human beings. Absolute attention to means often turns into an empty promise, a magnificent void. Gandhi's dynamic and comprehensive means-ends concept seems to be flawless and effective. It harmonizes the inner conflict of means and ends on the basis of moral approximation. This equilibrium of the method and goal is undoubtedly unique in the world of thought and action.

Rights and Duty: The Views of the Gita and Kant Compared

"Life is duty, i.e., action."[71] The term 'duty' etymologically means that which is due; due to someone else. It implies something which an individual is bound to perform or under an obligation to do. A duty is, in a sense, a moral debt or a moral obligation of an individual or individuals to the surroundings. That is to say, the term 'duty', demands that of us which we ought to perform as moral beings. On the other hand, a right is a moral claim which is sanctioned by society for the enjoyment of the individual concerned. It is a just demand granted to him by the society for their common welfare. Society grants some rights to the individual because they are conducive towards social welfare. Thus an individual can exercise his rights only in social life. A Robinson Crusoe cannot enjoy them in an isolated island. In the words of Gandhi, "Man's highest duty in life is to serve mankind and take his share in bettering its condition. This is true worship—true prayer."[72] It is not only that the rights cannot be exercised without social relationship but also that the rights apart from appropriate relation to duty become a farce. Indeed, rights and duties are interrelated to each other in such a way that one becomes meaningless without the other. It is well said, "What one has a right to claim, it will be the duty of others to do." In the above perspective let us consider the Gandhian view of rights and duties.

We have seen above that Gandhi's approach towards life was primarily from the ethico-religious angle of vision. And following this trend he could not rise above this standpoint while commenting, now and then, on rights and duties. He uses the term *right* in various senses; political, ethical, social and others. In the ethico-religious field he uses the term *right* to mean freedom of actions the performance of which is conducive towards *moksa* or liberation. Elsewhere he uses it in a different sense when he says, "Everyone possesses the right to tell lies or resort to goondaism. But the exercise of such a right is harmful both to the exerciser and the society."[73] Here the term right conveys a material sense, i.e., the sense of physical power. Again, we find the social implication of this term in another statement where he says, "People who obtain rights as a result of performance of duty, exercise them only for the service of society, never for themselves."[74] Again, during the freedom movement of India he used the term 'right' in the political sense. It was this political right that drew him to politics in South Africa; and turned timid and shy Gandhi into a valiant champion of human rights.

Gandhi distinguishes between personal and public duties. By personal duty he means the obligations that we have to ourselves. Gandhi realized it from the core of his heart that unless duties were performed by the preacher in personal life, his preachings would be of no avail. That is why he attached supreme importance on the purity of personal life for the *satyagrahis*. Firstly, habit is the second nature. A precious proverb goes, "Tell me what a man's private habits are and I shall tell you what he is or will be." Indeed, we should cultivate only those habits that clean our bodies and minds; and promote self-realization, the highest duty of our lives. Gandhi had in mind the pivotal role of private habits in the formation of our characters. Secondly, control of the palate in the sense of control of all our appetites is the second important duty to ourselves. 'Too much of everything is bad.' We should give up excessive drinking and eating. Thirdly, abstention from sensual pleasure is another fundamental duty to ourselves. Like Kant, Gandhi demanded a rigorous extirpation of sensuous pleasures the gratification of which causes irreparable damage to our bodies, minds, intellects and souls, i.e., to our being in its entirety, and consequently, offers hindrance to self-realization.

Now, let us see what our duties to others are? Service to humanity was a passion for him. He adopted this service or duty to others not as a personal norm but also ardently intended others to follow the same path. As mentioned above, he regarded 'service to mankind as the true worship, true prayer and highest duty in an individual's life.' This implies an ethico-religious significance in the sense that he treats duties to others as true worship and prayer to God. And service to other members of society is nothing but an outward manifestation of the obligation or duty that an individual concerned feels for mankind as a whole. The concept of *Swaraj* in Gandhian thought implies this type of individual obligation to society. In his words, "Swaraj of a people means the sum total of the Swaraj (self rule) of individuals. And such Swaraj comes only from performance by individuals of their duty as citizens. In it no one thinks of his rights. They come, when they are needed, for better performance of duty."[75] This point, duty to others, requires some elaboration because it is one of the salient features of Gandhian social philosophy. Selfless action or principle of renunciation is the motto behind service to society. He explains, "The path of service can hardly be trodden by one, who is not prepared to renounce self-interest...."[76] Louis Fischer aptly observes, "Gandhi renounced in order to serve."[77] As discussed above Gandhi believes that selfless service to humanity is a duty that promotes self-realization, realization of Truth or God, which is the very purpose of our existence as human beings. And consequently, the prevailing relation between individuals, individual and society will be so simple and cordial that there will not remain the least possibility of any conflict amongst them. That is to say, the social life will be perfectly attuned to the individual life. This is the concept of *Ramarajya*, the perfect society in Gandhian thought. In short, we can establish our rights in the society only through the precise performance of duties towards others.

What is the exact relation between rights and duties? We may point at the outset that Gandhi wanted a harmonious relation between right and duty. This harmonious correspondence is one of correlation of mutual dependence; and never a discrete one. He wanted this relation to prevail universally amongst the employers and the employees, the landlords and tenants, the princes and their subjects, husband and wife, parents and children, the Hindus and the Muslims; etc.—people in every walk of life. To him, duties give rise to rights. Without proper performance of duties any claim to enjoyment of right is immoral. To him all rights flowed from duties duly performed. One has to earn rights through the performance of duties but not vice versa. There is no such thing as divine right or birth right. The kings refer to their divine origin and expect the subjects to carry out their orders, as though they were unconditional divine commandments without any hesitation. If the kings fail to work as true servants of the people, forget their duty to subjects and endeavour the exert despotic power, supposed to be derived from divine or hereditary source with the sword, the subjects should resist such immoral right which is not earned through the performance of duties. Similarly, parents, husbands, employers, etc. can claim obedience from children, wives and employees respectively only after doing their duties to them. More specifically, according to the prevailing social system, not to speak of divine or hereditary right, a Brahmin's duty is to know God and help others to do so. And consequently, the Brahmin earns the right to be fed and clothed honourably by society.

The idea that duty is the matrix of all rights was so firm in his mind that he could not come out of this web throughout life. His communication with some contemporary great men (e.g. H.G. Wells, Julian Huxley, etc.) on this problem, and the statements made by him in this regard on several occasions are chronologically arranged below to show the evolution of his mental attitude and for our better understanding. In his address to the Kathiawad Political Conference in 1925 he says, "The true source of rights is duty.... If we all discharge our duties, rights will not be far to seek."[78] On 9-10 November, 1934 Gandhi expressed his view on rights and duties to Nirmal Kumar Bose at Wardha, "Rights follow from a due performance of duties. It is the fashion now-a-days to ignore duties and assert or rather usurp rights."[79] In 1939 Gandhi writes, "There is no duty but creates a corresponding right, and those only are true rights which flow from a due performance of one's duty."[80] Gandhi says if honest and sincere citizens of a state perform their specific duties, the people to whom these duties are rendered will accord honour and prestige to those dutiful personalities on whom rights will descend automatically. That is to say, the dutiful citizens, through their performance of duties, will occupy a status amongst the people who will voluntarily offer rights to them. The voluntary service to the people followed by the consequent according to rights to the door of such service is the true spirit of Gandhian concept of rights and duties.

On one occasion Gandhi used the terms *rights* and *duties* as almost synonymous like the terms *ends* and *means*. He said, "Rights accrue automatically to him who duly performs his duties. In fact the rights to perform one's duties is the only right that is worth living for and dying for. It covers all legitimate rights."[81] Here he, consciously or unconsciously, treats all rights as equivalent to performance of duties, i.e., rights mean doing duties.

According to Gandhi, the true spirit of rights lies in the performance of corresponding duties. If the claimant demands fulfilment of rights without performing or ability to perform corresponding duties the very purpose of right is marred, and thereby the relation between rights and duties is distorted. In 1947 he expressed a similar view to Julian Huxley whom he wrote, "All rights to be deserved and preserved come from duty well done."[82] We can multiply similar citations from Gandhi's works. The pivotal point of his concept of rights and duties is that proper discharge of duties gives rise to rights. And an exercise of rights without performance of duties is unjust. In the words of Gandhi, "Every duty performed confers upon one certain rights, whilst the exercise of every right carries with it certain corresponding obligations. And so the never-ending cycle of duty and right goes ceaselessly on."[83] Indeed, rights are not favours conferred on the individual by any external agency like society, state, heredity, divinity, etc. Rights are earned from the surroundings by the individual himself through the degree of efficiency that he acquires in the hard pursuit of truth and non-violence. The society or surroundings only recognize the rights so that the individual may enjoy them smoothly.

It has been asserted that Gandhi overemphasized on duty, and undermined the importance of rights in social life. Joan V. Bondurant comments, "In traditional Hindu polity, emphasis upon duty is extended to the King. The King, above all others, is obliged to fulfil his Kingly duties towards his people... Gandhi, who would make every man a King, consistently emphasized duties as prior to rights...."[84] This is also the view of Gopinath Dhawan who opines, "Gandhiji, however, attaches far greater importance to duties than a rights."[85] Buddhadeva Bhattacharyya observes, "Gandhi's emphasis on duties as being prior to rights may lend the impression that his outlook was conservative. The conservative view holds that duty is of greater importance and priority than right."[86] It is evident from the above discussion that the duty-bias scattered here and there in Gandhi's writings might have led the above scholars to hold such an opinion. But on a critical examination we shall see that the so-called duty-bias is apparent, and not real in Gandhian thought.

Let us examine it. Firstly, an impartial judgement will bring out the fact that as an ardent humanist, Gandhi fought throughout his life, both in India and South Africa, for the establishment of civil, political, moral and economic rights of downtrodden. He raised his voice against any suppression or denial of human rights. His communication with Huxley, Wells, or the British Government reveals his earnest desire for the restoration of human rights. Buddhadeva Bhattacharyya aptly comments, "As a votary of freedom and dignity of the individual, Gandhi championed throughout his political life the rights of the racially humiliated, colonially subjugated, economically dispossessed and socially depressed humanity...."[87] V.P. Varma observes, "Gandhi's philosophy of right is a cardinal point in his philosophy of politics."[88] Thus the charge of negligence of human rights against Gandhi who fought throughout his life for it is unsound.

Secondly, to Gandhi rights were not given to individuals out of compassion. Rights are rather moral claims and just demands of the individuals concerned. That is why he prescribed active, non-violent revolt in the face of antagonistic surroundings, for the attainment of rights. He was so sincere in this holy mission, the establishment of human rights that the ultimate sacrifice, sacrifice of life, (Do or Die, *karo ya marro*) was trifling to him. Joan V. Bondurant here seems to be right when she comments, "Gandhi insisted that the individual look first to duty and not concern himself with rights."[89] Thus the charge of duty-bias if accepted, the movement of satyagraha which Gandhi adopted and enriched throughout his eventful life loses its significance. But in practice the opposite is true. Gandhian peaceful movement of satyagraha has earned universal assent as a powerful weapon for the acquisition and assertion of human rights.

Thirdly, the influence of the *Gita* on him was partially responsible for so-called emphasis on duty. As cited above Gandhi quoted the concept of selfless action of the *Gita* to illustrate the relation between rights and duties. His firm reliance on the *Gita* was evidently one of the factors of his over-emphasis on duty because duty (action) is within our grip, and not the rights (fruit). More on the point in the succeeding passages.

Lastly, all complicacies arise if we treat rights and duties as separate, discrete, and insoluble terms. The proper solution seems to treat them as one entity, the right-duty concept. Like the end-means concept, his right-duty concept is also continuous, ever changing and dynamic in nature. And since rights can be earned only through performance of duties; and because duties give rise to rights, duties create rights. Indeed, proper performance of duties endows upon the individual concerned honour and prestige which are themselves rights in disguise. And we have seen above that at least once Gandhi used these two terms as synonymous or identical. Therefore, the priority that he attaches to duty also equally applies to rights in the sense that they are two sides of the same entity, the right-duty concept. Hence the allegation of overemphasis on duties is not tenable.

F.H. Bradley, in his *Ethical Studies* describes the concept of right and duty in a very lovely way. He says, "what is duty? It is simply the other side of right... No right without duty; no duty without right and rights...."[90]

If we consider the Gandhian view in the above perspective, all the confusions and doubts will be automatically removed.

Here one more point merits consideration. What is the role of violence in right-duty concept? As an apostle of truth and non-violence he obviously banished violence from it. He believed firmly that violence which often begets violence and chaos cannot bring forth truth, good and beauty. To quote him, "Definition and performance of duties rules out violence altogether. Violence becomes imperative when an attempt is made to assert rights without any reference to duties."[91] The use of force or violence of any kind for the assertion of rights went against his principle of life, the pursuit of truth. That is why he condemned any adoption of violence for the attainment of rights which could be automatically earned through performance of duty only.

Is there any similarity between the *Gita* ideal and Gandhian concept of duty? It is universally known that the *Gita* is a dialogue between Lord Krishna and Arjuna. In the *Gita* Lord Krishna gives a clarion call to all people to carry out their respective works as divine duties. We are told that the Lord is the sole doer of all actions; and that man can only carry out the divine mission as a willing instrument of the Lord (2/33). This divinity of duty was well expressed by Wordsworth, "Stern Daughter of the Voice of God!/O Duty! if that name thou love/Who art a Light to guide, a Rod/To check the erring, and reprove."[92] In every sphere of life duties are to be performed in the sense of divine imperatives. This spirit of duty has been very much emphasized in the *Rajadharma* section of the *Mahabharata*. Honest and sincere endeavour to discharge duties assigned to us by the social order and divine commandment possesses intrinsic value irrespective of objective failure or success.[93] Here Surama Dasgupta observes, "(if an individual) ... does his duty from the sense of duty alone, he is not responsible for any consequences of his action even though they may affect others."[94] This imperative role of duty is emphasized also in the *Gita* where we are advised, as discussed above, to perform duties without any regard for consequences. We can attain liberation or *moksa* only through the performance of specific duties entrusted with us by the social order and divine commandment according to the status and stations of life. We are to do duty with regard to *varna* duties. Secondly, we are told, "Better is death in the discharge of one's duty; another's is fraught with danger" (3/35). "One's specific duties ill-done are better than another's specific duties well done" (1/47). "One should not waver in discharging his ordained duties" (2/31).[95] In many other verses, we are instructed to perform appointed duties in the spirit of 'duty for duty's sake' without attachment and aversion and any desire for enjoying their fruits. The *Gita* ideals of appointed duties is evident in Bradley's "My station and its duties,"[96] and in a liberal assessment in Plato's *Republic*. In short, the *Gita* advises us to perform *varna* or appointed duties for the sake of duty only without any attachment of fruit.

Let us see the influence of the *Gita* ideal of duty on Gandhian concept. We have already discussed Gandhi's fervent attempt to follow the invaluable preachings of the *Gita* at every step of his life. It was a dictionary, a code of life to him. R.S. Betai comments, "...Gandhiji was under the impression of the *Gita*, that had already occupied the central position in his life and the impression was growing firmer day by day, both unconsciously and consciously."[97] V.B. Kher observes, "Bhagavadgita was for Gandhiji a book of reference."[98] Gandhi also claims himself as "a student of the Bhagavad Gita."[99] In short, since his first acquaintance with the *Gita* in London, he ardently followed, both in theory and practice, the immortal teachings of the *Gita* for more than sixty years of his life.

A critical analysis will reveal the following influences of the *Gita* on him regarding duty. Firstly, in the verse "better is death... with danger" (3/35) the *Gita* refers to *varna* duties and advises us to cultivate an attitude of *samata*, *samatva*, *yoga* and being indifferent to, or taking as the same, happiness and sorrow, loss and gain, victory and defeat. Gandhi derives his concept of *swadeshi* outright from the *Gita* ideal of *swadharma*. To quote him, "...the *Gita* says: 'It is better to die performing one's duty or *swadharma*, but *paradharma*, or another's duty, is frought with danger...."[100] The above citation is self-explanatory. The *Gita* ideal of *swadharma* is transformed into *swadeshi* of Gandhian thought.

Secondly, the verse: "one should not waver in discharging his ordained duties" (2/31) tells us that we should do our duty dauntlessly; and face and remove off all hindrances that stand in the way of proper performance of appointed duties. Though the *Gita* is the best book on non-violence, according to Gandhi, yet Lord Krishna instructs Arjuna to do his appointed duty for the sake of duty; and as a Kshatriya, fight and protect the right, the good and *dharma* from the wrong, the evil and *adharma*. Gandhi similarly gives a clarion call to all co-fighters to unchain mother-India, to fight the right and just battle of independence at the cost of everything, even of their lives. Do or die was his slogan which reminds us of Tennyson's widely-known poem glorifying the majesty of duty. Tennyson's immortal lines are: "Forward, the Light Brigade!'/Was there a man dismay'd ?/ Not tho' the soldier knew/Some one had blunder'd :/Their's not to make reply./ Their's not to reason why/Their's but to do or die :/Into the Valley of Death/Rode the six hundred."[101]

Thirdly, his famous *anasaktiyoga* also follows directly from the *Gita* ideal of selfless action. The verses of the *Gita*, we have already mentioned in the preceding passages, emphasize without variation non-attachment, and renunciation of fruits of action. Indeed, the doctrine of *niskama karma* is a salient feature of the *Gita*. Gandhi also preached and practised the ideal of selfless action and acknowledged his debt to the *Gita*, the mother *Kamdhenu*, without reservation. His emphasis on duty and not on right (fruit) has its basis in *anasaktiyoga* which he enthusiastically put down in his translation of the *Gita*.[102]

Fourthly, his overemphasis on duty (action) is undoubtedly an outcome of his deep study of the *Gita*. Although this is a corollary of the preceding one still it requires further elaboration. Gandhi admits his debt by saying, "The true source of rights is duty.... The same teaching has been embodied by Krishna in the immortal words: 'Action alone is thine—Leave thou the fruit severely alone.' Action is duty: fruit is the right." (note 78 above). Thus the apparent priority that he attaches to duty is undoubtedly due to the influence of the *Gita* on him.

Now let us compare the views of Kant and Gandhi regarding rights and duties. Here a short sketch of the salient features of Kantian ethics is essential for better understanding of the problem. According to Kant, reason should be the predominating element of human nature and hence sensibility that obstructs the life of pure reason ought to be completely suppressed if not extirpated. This non-sensuous pure life gradually gives rise to pure practical reason popularly known as conscience which wills through a rational will, in the Kantian phrase 'the good will.' This good will is pure practical reason in action. It is self-legislative because it imposes the Moral Law upon itself. It is an imperative or command, of course, a self-imposed commandment. And this imperative is categorical or unconditional which ought to be obeyed for its own sake without any consideration of any end or consequence. On the other hand, other imperatives are hypothetical, and empirical or *a posteriori* because they are dependent upon variable ends of experience. The moral law is rational in the sense that it is apprehended intuitively by our moral reason and hence not derived from experience, i.e., it is *a priori*. The moral law is not only *a priori*, self-legislative, autonomous, categorical imperative, rational but also universal, objective and an end in itself. It is universal in the sense that it applies to all persons the reverse of which involves self-contradiction. It is objectively necessary for all and hence conducive towards the establishment of an ideal society, in the Kantian phrase, 'the Kingdom of ends.'

Let us point out the similarities and dissimilarities between these two great thinkers, of course in the perspective of the moral science. The similarities are:

(1) The ethical theories of both involve elements of rationalism and intuitionism. The life of pure reason or non-sensuous strict disciplined mode of livelihood is their goal. The verdict of practical

reason in Kantian doctrine and the voice of conscience, 'The still small voice' of Gandhi is apprehended through intuition, from within.

(2) To both of them moral insight is innate and *a priori* and not derived from experience of our everyday lives. It is free from all contingent and empirical factors which are variable under all circumstances.

(3) Universality is another criterion of their moral law. The law of the state and business can serve only particular interests, and fails to attain universality. But this is not so with the moral law. P. Spratt finds universality an essential element of their morality and comments, "...he (Gandhi) is trying to adhere to another Kantian principle, that his example should be universally followed."[103]

(4) The Kantian distinction of categorical and hypothetical imperatives corresponds to Gandhi's distinction between moral and temporal laws. To Kant laws of economics and hygiene serve only specific ends; and hence are conditional and hypothetical in nature while the moral law is an unconditional, categorical imperative which admits of no exception. In Gandhian ethics "there is thus a great difference between moral laws and temporal laws."[104] The temporal laws are the laws of the state and business which are conditional, particular and variable from time to time. On the other hand, moral laws are immutable and independent of space and time.

(5) Kant's categorical imperative is almost akin to Gandhi's 'still small voice,' both in kind and degree. Kant's categorical imperative is the voice of pure practical reason which comes from within, independent of sensuous experience. It is attained through gradual suppression of the sensuous elements of our being. It is an imperative or command, and categorical in the sense that it needs must be carried out. Similarly, Gandhi's 'still small voice' is the voice of Truth which also comes from within. It is non-sensuous and pure in nature which can be attained through the ascetic ascendancy of our being. That is to say, the voice of Truth can be haved by anybody through the observance of eleven vows which appears, even to liberal assessment, to have rigorism and asceticism as their pivotal points. Like the Kantian categorical imperative it is one, unmistakable and irresistible.

(6) 'Duty for duty's sake' is the slogan of both. Gandhi's insistence on duty and for its sake only has been dealt with in the preceding passages of this section. Kant elucidates his concept of duty in the these three propositions: (a) "We will therefore take up

the concept of duty, which... have been done for the sake of duty;"[105] (b) "An action done from duty has its moral worth, not in the purpose to be attained by it, but in the maxim in accordance with which it is decided upon" [106] and (c) "Duty is the necessity to act out of reverence for the law."[107] That is to say, like Gandhi, Kant tells us that an action should be performed for the sake of duty only, and it would derive its moral worth not from the purpose (*Absicht*) which is meant to be attained by it, but from the maxim (*Maxime*) by which it is determined.

(7) Asceticism is common to both. David Ross comments, 'Kant's view was in essence a return to Stoicism.'[108] Indeed, Kantian ethics has often been criticized for asceticism and rigorism for the last two centuries.

(8) Naturally both of them maintained an anti-hedonistic attitude towards moral concepts and although Kantian doctrine was out and out non-utilitarian in character, that of Gandhi cannot strictly be called so.

(9) Kingdom of ends is the aim of both. Kant says, "So act as if you were through your maxims a law-making member of a Kingdom of ends."[109] Here Kant lays the utmost emphasis on the dignity and responsibility of every human being as a rational agent. All ends are subjective and means to some other ends. But human beings, endowed with rationality, have unconditioned and absolute value and hence are ends in themselves. Here the rational nature of human beings is at the core of Kant's firm belief in their absolute intrinsic value. So an individual should neither use himself as a means to anybody else nor use any other person as a means for himself. This is the nucleus of Kantian concept of end in themselves. And in a 'Kingdom of ends,' an ideal society, every individual will voluntarily act rationally, carry out the dictate of the moral law, treat himself both as a means and an end; as a sovereign and a subject, promote his welfare along with the welfare of others; be willed and obeyed by each and all. Society will have little chance to rule the people. Similarly, Gandhi was a staunch advocate of democracy. He fought throughout his life against the authoritarian and totalitarian system of Government which treated human beings as means to some other ends, and never an end in themselves. He aims at the establishment of *Ramarajya*, a perfect society of truth and righteousness on earth which will be free from all sorts of violence, inequalities, etc. It is one of voluntary interdependence; and people would formulate rules and carry them

out without any hesitation. And since all human beings are sparks of truth or God, and absolute intrinsic values inhere in them, and hence *Ramarajya* is nothing but a Kingdom of ends. H. Horsburgh aptly comments, "Gandhi was perhaps the most Kantian national leader of whom we have any record."[110]

(10) To both of them morality is the basis of religion. According to Kant, the human mind as a rational agent finds the conception of an ideal perfection better than the conception of unconditional obedience to a perfect divine will who stands as a symbol of glory and domination, might and vengeance. But the notion of an ideal perfection brings morality within the purview of reason, the essential nature of human beings. Similarly, to Gandhi "morality is the basis of things, and that truth is the substance of all morality."[111] It is from truth that he proceeds to God; and his concept, 'Truth is God', illustrates the principle that morality is the basis of religion.

To sum up: Kant did not hear of Gandhi, and Gandhi too, so far our knowledge goes, was not at all acquainted with Kant. The above similarities are product of our intellectual discourse. Still the striking resemblance that we have discussed above between these two great thinkers contributes significantly towards a better understanding of Gandhian thought. With P. Spratt we conclude, "It is perhaps Kant more than any of the other eminent ethical theorists to whom one would look for a spirit similar to Mr. Gandhi's...."[112]

References

1. John Locke, 'An Essay Concerning Human Understanding,' BK. IV, Ch. XII, prop. II in R.M. Hutchins (ed.) *Great Books of the Western World, Locke Berkeley Hume*, vol. XXXV, p. 361.
2. *Ethical Religion*, p. 10.
3. *Ibid.*, p. 11.
4. *Ibid.*, p. 26; also *Harijan*, 16 May 1936, p. 109.
5. *Ibid.*, p. 5; also pragmatism in Ch. III.
6. *Ibid.*, p. 19.
7. *Ibid.*, p. 23.
8. *Ibid.*
9. *Ibid.*
10. *Ibid.*
11. *Ibid.*, pp. 14-15.
12. *Ibid.*, p. 14.
13. *Ibid.*, p. 16.
14. *Ibid.*

15. *Ethical Religion*, pp. 16-17.
16. *Ibid.*, p. 17.
17. *Ibid.*, p. 16.
18. *Ibid.*, p. 17.
19. For details see John Mackenzie, *op. cit.*, pp. 48-50.
20. J.S. Mill, *Utilitarianism*, Ch. II, p. 27 fn.
21. *Ethical Religion*, p. 30.
22. *My Socialism*, p. 5.
23. *Ethical Religion*, p. 14.
24. *Ibid.*, p. 10; also Mahadev Desai, *The Gospel of Selfless Action or the Gita According to Gandhi*, p. 188.
25. Machiavelli, *The Prince*, p. 96.
26. *Ibid.*, p. 100.
27. Karl Marx and F. Engels, *Manifesto of the Communist Party*, p. 94.
28. Engels, a letter to Herson Trier in 1889, cited in R.N. Iyer, *op. cit.*, p. 365.
29. Gopinath Dhawan, *The Political Philosophy of Mahatma Gandhi*, p. 54; also Madan G. Gandhi, *Gandhi and Marx*, pp. 20, 75-79; Madhu Dandavate, *Marx and Gandhi*, pp. 106-10; K.G. Mashruwala, *Gandhi and Marx*, pp. 30-42; J.P. Suda, *Manu, Marx and Gandhi*, pp. 175-76.
30. C.G. Shah, *Ends and Means*, p. 141.
31. Trotsky Dewey, Novack, *Their Morals and Ours*, p. 41.
32. Oscar Jaszi, an article on 'Anarchism' in *Encyclopaedia of the Social Sciences*, Editor-in-Chief : E.R.A. Seligman, vol. II, p. 46.
33. *Ibid.*, p. 50.
34. George Woodcock, *Anarchism*, pp. 7-8, also Joan V. Bondurant, *op. cit.*, pp. 173-87.
35. Roberto Michel's article on 'Conservatism' in *Encyclopaedia of the Social Sciences*, Editor-in-Chief: E.R.A. Seligman, vol. IV, p. 230.
36. Joan V. Bondurant, *op. cit.*, p. 188.
37. Cited in T.V. Parvate, *Bal Gangadhar Tilak*, pp. 501, 516.
38. *Harijan*, 21 September 1934, p. 250.
39. B.N. Ganguli, *Gandhi's Social Philosophy*, p. 398.
40. Tendulkar, *Mahatma*, vol. VIII, p. 10.
41. *CWMG*, vol. XXV, p. 480; also Tendulkar, *op. cit.*, vol. III, p. 299; *CWMG*, vol. XLVIII, p. 405.
42. Tendulkar, *op. cit.*, vol. II, p. 309.
43. *CWMG*, vol. X, p. 43.
44. Krishnalal Shridharani, *War Without Violence*, p. 316.
45. Cited in B.N. Ganguli, *op. cit.*, p. 395.
46. *CWMG*, vol. XXIV, p. 39[illegible]
47. H. Horsburgh, *Non-violence and Aggression*, p. 4[illegible].
48. Trotsky Dewey Novack, *Their Morals and Ours*, p. 42.
49. *CWMG*, vol. XXIV, p. 396.
50. Joan V. Bondurant, *op. cit.*, p. 193.

51. *See Joan V. Bondurant, op. cit.*, p. 231.
52. John Dewey, *Human Nature and Conduct*, p. 223.
53. *Ibid.*, p. 233.
54. John Dewey, *Logic, The Theory of Inquiry*, p. 497.
55. *CWMG*, vol. XXIV, p. 396.
56. *Ibid.*, vol. XXV, p. 480.
57. *Letter to Carl Heath*, Jan. 1941; also Tendulkar, *op. cit.*, vol. VII, p. 215; *Harijan*, 11 February 1939, p. 8; *Speeches and Writings of Mahatma Gandhi*, p. 685, etc.
58. R.N. Iyer, *op. cit.*, p. 361.
59. Louis Fischer, 'Where is Gandhiji?' in S. Radhakrishnan (ed.) *Mahatma Gandhi, 100 Years*, p. 85.
60. Cited in Joan V. Bondurant, *op. cit.*, p. X.
61. Buddhadeva Bhattacharyya, *Evolution of the Political Philosophy of Gandhi*, p. 138.
62. Gopinath Dhawan, *op. cit.*, pp. 55-56.
63. *An Autobiography*, p. 72.
64. *Harijan*, 30 January 1937, p. 405.
65. Vincent Sheean, *Lead, Kindly Light*, pp. 44-45.
66. *Young India*, 14 August 1924, p. 268.
67. Nirmal Kumar Bose, *Selections from Gandhi*, p. 167.
68. *Ashram Observances in Action*, pp. 42-43; also Buddhadeva Bhattacharyya, *op. cit.*, pp. 313-16.
69. Aldous Huxley, *Ends and Means*, p. 70.
70. Jacques Maritain, *Man and the State*, p. 55.
71. *Harijan*, 12 December 1948, p. 346.
72. *Ethical Religion*, p. 29.
73. *Harijan*, 25 March 1939, p. 64.
74. *Ibid.*
75. *Ibid.*
76. *From Yeravda Mandir*, pp. 36-37.
77. Louis Fischer, *The Life of Mahatma Gandhi*, pt. I, p. 170.
78. *CWMG*, vol. XXV, p. 564.
79. Nirmal Kumar Bose, *Studies in Gandhism*, p. 68.
80. *Harijan*, 25 March 1939, p. 64.
81. *Ibid.*, 27 May 1939, p. 143.
82. *Ibid.*, 8 June 1947, p. 184.
83. *CWMG*, vol. XLI, p. 320.
84. Joan V. Bondurant, *op. cit.*, pp. 167-71.
85. Gopinath Dhawan, *op. cit.*, p. 323.
86. Buddhadeva Bhattacharyya, *op. cit.*, p. 391.
87. *Ibid.*, pp. 388-89.
88. V.P. Varma, *The Political Philosophy of Mahatma Gandhi & Sarvodaya*, p. 170.

89. Joan V. Bondurant, *op. cit.*, pp. 171-72.
90. F.H. Bradley, *Ethical Studies*, pp. 208-12.
91. Tendulkar, *op. cit.*, vol. IV, p. 13.
92. William Wordsworth, 'Ode to Duty,' in *William Wordsworth : Selected Poems*, p. 419.
93. *Rajadharma-Parva*, Ch. 24, pp. 21-24.
94. Surama Dasgupta, *Development of Moral Philosophy in India*, p. 27.
95. J.C. Wadiyar, *The Gita and Indian Culture*, p. 8; also the *Gita* verses 2/47, 51; 3/8, 19; 5/10, 12; 6/1, 2, 4; 17/25; 18/6, etc.
96. F.H. Bradley, *op. cit.*, pp. 98, 110-11.
97. R.S. Betai, *op. cit.*, p. 170.
98. V.B. Kher, Editorial note in *In Search of the Supreme*, vol. III, p. viii.
99. Manubehn Gandhi, *The Lonely Pilgrim*, p. 177.
100. *CWMG*, vol. XLVI, p. 255.
101. A.L. Tennyson, 'The Charge of the Light Brigade,' in *Poems of Alfred Lord Tennyson*, p. 455.
102. Mahadev Desai, *The Gita According to Gandhi*, pp. 125-386.
103. P. Spratt, *Gandhism: An Analysis*, pp. 152-53.
104. *Ethical Religion*, p. 16.
105. Kant, *op. cit.*, p. 65.
106. *Ibid.*, pp. 67-68.
107. *Ibid.*, p. 68.
108. David Ross, *Kant's Ethical Theory*, p. 92.
109. *Ibid.*, p. 35.
110. H. Horsburgh, *op. cit.*, p. 53.
111. *An Autobiography*, p. 25.
112. P. Spratt, *op. cit.*, pp. 152-53.

6

SOME MORAL PROBLEMS

Morality as the Basis of All Human Activities

We have seen above that Gandhi was an ethico-religious person. His moral conviction that "morality is the basis of things, and that truth is the substance of all morality" was so firm, and deeply active in his being that he felt its omnipresent influence every moment of life. Morality became the pivotal point of his ever-active and colourful life. In his words, "Truth became my sole objective. It began to grow in magnitude everyday, and my definition of it also has been ever widening."[1] This is the keynote of Gandhian view that we intend to discuss in this chapter.

Gandhi anchored his life in morality, and endeavoured fervently to implement the moral concepts in every walk of life—social, religious, political, aesthetic, etc. It is in morality and religion that he lived, moved and had his being. He may be metaphorically described as a spider who webbed a network of various spheres of life out of moral conviction, the intrinsic value that he inherited, and manifested from early childhood. We come across some Western pioneers who, like Gandhi, endeavoured to reach destination in different fields of our knowledge and lives from the same pivotal point, the moral conviction. A brief discussion of relevant thought of these great Westerners will help us to make a correct estimate of Gandhian standpoint.

In the preceding chapter we have seen that the Kantian thought, and that of Gandhi have much in common. Like Gandhi, Kant also strove to prove the existence of God from moral standpoint. Kantian ethical theory necessarily leads to a holy Head for its completion, i.e., the route is from morality to religion. In the *Critique of Practical*

Reason[2] Kant's sole aim is to show a logical connection between morality and religion. He bases religion on morality but the converse is not true. The moral law under the efficient guidance of pure reason, and absolutely independently of empirical conditions, necessarily leads to a practical problem of completion of the first element of *summum bonum* which can be perfectly solved only in eternity, i.e., through the postulation of immortality of the soul. Again this moral law necessarily leads to the second important element of the *summum bonum*, namely, happiness which in its turn as an effect inevitably leads us to assume the existence of an adequate cause for its completeness. In other words, happiness leads us to the postulation of the existence of God as a necessary condition of the *summum bonum*.

Kant mentions the following conditions which contribute to the transition of morality to religion: (1) The human being as a rational agent cannot be the cause of the world and the nature itself. The harmony between nature and human volition is possible, "only on the supposition of a Supreme Being having a causality corresponding to moral character."[3] Thus intelligence and will, the essential conditions of morality, presuppose God as its supreme cause. (2) Again, the possibility of the "highest derived good; our empirical welfare, presupposes the reality of a highest original good, that is to say, of the existence of God."[4] (3) It is our duty to promote and realize the *summum bonum* in this world. Our reason finds this task impossible without 'the supposition of a Supreme Intelligence.' That is to say, the consciousness of our duty is a requisite condition of the *summum bonum* which again, as we have seen, becomes intelligible only on the postulation of the existence of God. (4) The second element of the *summum bonum* is happiness proportionate to morality. The ideal individual happiness of our goal is a mixture of unbound personal happiness and the highest degree of perfection possible in human beings. Here we are concerned with the rational conditions (*conditio sine qua non*) of happiness not with particular selfish desires. Thus the exact harmony of happiness proportionate to morality leads to the postulation of God's existence. (5) In Kantian thought every rational being is an end in himself and hence he can never be used merely as a means by anybody else, not even by God. In this sense every individual may be called holy in himself because he is the subject of the moral law; and it is on account of this and in agreement with this alone that anything can be termed holy. Thus, according to Kant, ascription of holiness to God initiates from the holiness of moral agents as end in themselves. To conclude with Kant, "In this manner, the moral laws lead through the conception of the *summum bonum* as the object and final end of pure practical reason to religion, that is, to the recognition of all duties as divine commands."[5]

An almost similar type of argument has been tendered by eminent ethicists like Sir William Hamilton, J. Martineau, J. Seth, H. Rashdall, etc. The burden of their argument is that the moral concepts for their full-bloom manifestation necessarily leads to postulation of the existence of God. We have dealt in detail their views along with the view of Gandhi in a preceding chapter. Only F.H. Bradley's argument here demands elaboration who says, "Reflection on morality leads us beyond it. It leads us, in short, to see the necessity of a religious point of view. It certainly does not tell us that morality comes first in the world and then religion: what it tells us is that morality is imperfect, and imperfect in such a way as implies a higher, which is religion."[6] Bradley through his unique method of dialectical argument shows the inner contradictions of moral concepts, their 'inevitable failure.' Its imperfection leads to religion where moral probabilities become real, the undone is done.

The above explains the dictum: morality necessarily leads to religion. Now let us examine the view that morality leads to politics. The view that morality has no relation to politics as allegedly held by Machiavelli and followers has been discussed elsewhere. The view that moral concepts lead to politics or the science of society for their full manifestation or completion is upheld by great Western thinkers like Plato, Aristotle, Spinoza, Hegel and others. Let us consider their views one by one, of course, vis-à-vis the Gandhian perspective.

Plato laid emphasis on both the individual and social life, especially on the latter. To draw a short sketch, his ethical doctrine deals partly with the individual good, partly with the good of society or state, and partly with the relation between the two. In *The Republic* he draws a pen-picture of an ideal state where the above threefold relations are discussed elaborately while in the *Philebus* he treats chiefly the nature of individual good. From these two works mainly we can form a consistent system of Plato's moral views. He investigates the nature of moral concept, Justice, and finds it both in the individual and in the state. The social nature of man was so deeply engraved upon his mind that the individual's goodness, he thought, could be realized only by performing his duty to social goodness. R.C. Lodge emphasizes this feature of Plato's ethics by saying, "The true art of politics is thus fundamentally concerned with public good, bringing out the social unity of the citizens, their harmonious co-operation in developing the potential resources of the group... (*Meno* 99 af)....[7] Thus Plato plans an ideal society in his *Republic* where an individual can bring out the best in him. In this way individual goodness or morality leads to social goodness or politics.

Aristotle followed the general trend of Plato's ethics, and emphasized the social nature of man. He says, a man is 'a political animal' (*Politics*, I, ii, 9.). Again, "He who is unable to live in society, or who has no need because he is sufficient for himself, must be either a beast or a god." (*Politics* BK. I, Ch. 2, 1280 b. 10). Indeed, in an uninhabited land an individual's conduct cannot be properly approved of as good or condemned as bad. Robinson Crusoe's conduct in the solitude of that desert island can be declared good or bad only against the background of social environment. An adequate assessment of an individual's conduct demands a thorough investigation, from all possible angles, of the nature and the manner of his relation to the society. An ideal social environment helps the individual best to bring out his potentiality into daylight. On the other hand, contrary environmental factors obstruct both mental and physical development of his being. That is to say, moral concepts acquire meaning only against the social background. This is the spirit of Aristotle's monumental work on Ethics; and he concerned himself primarily with the virtues of a good citizen of a state. Aristotle intermingled the individual good (ethics) with social good (political science) so deeply that he proceeded a step further and said, "Ethics is a branch of politics. That is to say, it is the duty of the Statesman to create for the citizen the best possible opportunity of living the good life...."[8] In short, to Aristotle, morality leads to politics in the sense that the science of individual good, ethics, is dependent on the science of social good for its unfoldment and complete manifestation. It is in the social environment that the moral concepts of our everyday lives attain meaning and worth. In this context H.A. Wolfson comments, "Towards the end of his discussion of the superiority of the intellectual virtues and of the life of reason Aristotle says that the means of attaining these virtues and of achieving this life are supplied by the State. And thus he shows how closely the State is related to the individual or politics to Ethics."[9]

Let us now consider the view of Spinoza in this context. The most remarkable work of Spinoza is *Ethica* in which we observe an influence of Aristotle's *Nicomachean Ethics*. In the words of Wolfson, "...a topical outline of the *Nicomachean Ethics* as it must have presented itself in the mind of Spinoza"[10] is found in *Ethica*. At a glance Spinoza's theory of Ethics is primarily concerned with the equation of three concepts: perfection, reality and activity (*Ethics*, chapter 5, proposition 40). The more active a thing is, the more perfect it is and the more reality it possesses. Will and understanding are one and the same. Moral activities steered by emotions yield sensuous objects while activities springing from reason give rise to an eternal object—the knowledge of truth, the intuition of God. Virtue (*virtus*) and power (*potentia*) are synonymous. 'Virtue is power' (*Ethics*, chapter 4, proposition 20). It is reason alone that promotes power, activity, perfection and knowledge. Knowledge that springs from insight is alone true morality or virtue. Ignorance, and its offshoot—evil and vice—are found amongst men of undeveloped reason. The knowledge and love of God who is the only substance embracing all reality within His own Being, together with intellectual love towards God, is the highest good and the highest virtue (*Ethics*, chapter 4, proposition 28).

What then is the relation between individual and society in Spinoza's thought? How is individual morality (ethics) related to social morality (politics)? In his *Theory of the State* Spinoza plans the establishment of democratic government in accordance with reason. The statutory laws with its punitive measure guides the individual to control sensuous desires and emotions by reason. The society or state, removing all obstructions, promotes the development of power, activity, perfection, knowledge and reason in an individual. Indeed, it is only in an organized society or State that true morality and true freedom can be attained and enjoyed by an individual. The problem of moral virtues leads to the problem of an organized society or state where the life of virtue and power, reason and knowledge can fully flourish. In the words of Spinoza, "Indeed, so far as the mind is concerned, our intellect would be less perfect if the mind were alone, and understand nothing but itself... none more excellent can be discovered than those which exactly agree with our nature... nothing, therefore, is more useful to man than man."[11] The moot point here is that an individual, like other objects of the universe, has a role to play. His existence and actions are to a great extent conditioned by the things that he absorbs in his being; and the things which he comes across in everyday life. They continuously regenerate and reorientate our personalities. That is to say, an individual for his existence inevitably requires food, drink and other necessities. But he also necessarily needs the co-operation of other men, living in society, for complete manifestation of latent potentialities. Spinoza emphasizes the social nature of man by quoting Aristotle's dictum that man is a 'social animal' (*animal sociale*) (*Ethics*, chapter 4, proposition 35). To sum up: according to Spinoza, the moral virtues (power, activity, perfection and knowledge) lead to social science for their exposition; and hence morality leads to politics.

Hegel's contribution to this problem is undoubtedly unique. His philosophical system is out and out rational. "The rational is real and the real is rational"—he writes in the preface to *The Philosophy of Right*. According to him, the ultimate reality is the Absolute Mind or Spirit which unfolds itself through a dialectical process of thesis, antithesis and synthesis. Thesis is contradicted by antithesis. Both thesis and antithesis are reconciled by a synthesis which provides a new thesis and so on. The most general thesis, antithesis and synthesis are Pure Being, Nature and Spirit respectively. The Absolute Mind or Spirit passes through different stages of teleological evolution in history, custom, law, morality, and moral institutions like the family, civic community, and the state. In short, the Absolute through a teleological and dialectical evolutionary process culminates in man whose ultimate goal is the fullest realization of his spiritual nature. Since this teleological evolution is directed towards a moral end, the fullest realization of Spirit in man, there is a transition of moral consciousness through process. The movement is from goodness as outward submission to an external law (thesis) to goodness as inward submission to the internal law of conscience (antithesis); both being reconciled in a higher synthesis called social morality or social ethics where a never-ceasing identification of an individual with the social life is observed.

More elaborately, according to Hegel, the most general triad of evolution are Being, Nature and Spirit; and again, the Spirit has Subjective Spirit, Objective Spirit, and Absolute Spirit as its chief triad. Again, Objective Spirit passes through three phases of evolution namely, abstract right, morality and social ethics. It is with social ethics that we are concerned at present. It is to be noted that Hegel's treatment of Objective Spirit covers the topics of ethics and politics; and differing from the traditional trend of treating them separately, he developed them in the organic unity of the system. In this context,

G.R. Mure comments, "Ethics and politics in Hegel's mature system form a single branch of philosophy, as they did for Plato and Aristotle."[12] To turn to the problem, the ethical system with which we are concerned here is the synthesis of abstract right (purely objective) and morality (purely subjective), i.e., both subjective and objective. This identity of moral subjectivity and moral objectivity forms the basis of Hegelian ethical system which consists of the family, civil society and the state. These social institutions although objective are undoubtedly products of individual thought and works. In this sense they are both subjective and objective at the same time; i.e., rationality objectified. These institutions embody the true self of the individual whose constituents are universality and rationality. In this background social ethics passes through three phases: the family, civil society and the state. In the family we observe an inward unity of interests of single individual; in the society an external unity amongst a plurality of individuals and families is found by way of adjusting the self-interests; in the state they are synthesized in an inward unity amongst the interests of one and all. For Hegel the State is the true self of the individual whose rationality and universality are here objectified. It is in the state that individuality finds its perfect expression. The true life of the individuals is found in and is identical with the state. The state is the individual actualized and objectified. So, the laws of the state are not an extraneous and alien authority, rather a self-imposed autonomy. It is the supreme embodiment of freedom because the individual being governed by the state-laws is virtually obeying his true identity, the true and universal in him. In obeying unconditionally the statutory laws he obeys only himself and enjoys therein his freedom. In no sense the state is a hindrance to individual freedom rather a way to his liberation. G.R. Mure aptly observes, "...For Hegel the true individual, which the nation-state exemplifies, is a concrete whole of different and mutually determining elements. It is the fountain of all ethical value in its elements, and as a whole it is absolute and infinite."[13] In fact, the system of the state as a whole provides an individual with the best possible opportunities by which he does live and ought to live. Through social functions he finds his own welfare, his true freedom; and what he is. In short, an individual is real only because he is social, and that only through sociality he realizes himself. Thus Hegel's view of morality leading to politics; subjectivity to objectivity; individuality to concrete, universal, absolute self-conscious personality, is well-knit in the structure of the organic nation-state. In the words of W.T. Stace, "...the true life of the individual, his individuality, liberty and rights, are realized only by his being a member of the state and finding its being identical with his own."[14]

We have so far considered above the dictum, morality leads to politics, held by some Western thinkers. Let us now take into account the Gandhian view 'that morality is the basis of all.' Morality is the *elan vital* of his life. In his early years when Gandhi, nay Moniya of Kathiwada, was playing devil's mission with his companions, especially with Sheik Mehatab, his rational and real identity was safely anchored at the moral harbour. Although the gale of delinquency shook his positive identity it could not deflect him from the moral path. Moral conviction at the core of his heart acted as an armour in those restive days of later boyhood. Not only this, it was intermingled with his total personality, and went into his being so deeply that, like the Pole Star, it determined the future course of his life. It acted the pivotal role everywhere—religious, political, social, aesthetic, etc.—every walk of his life. We shall take them up one by one.

Although he treated Truth and God, morality and religion as convertible terms yet, to him, it is morality that leads to religion. Firstly, an adequate probe into the nature of all religions of the world proves that not only their sole objective is to preach moral concepts but also that they are based for the most part on ethical principles; that it is one's duty to obey the laws of ethics whether or not one professes a religion.[15] Secondly, the history of world religions confirm that without a strong basis of morality "religion cannot subsist. True morality covers religion for the most part...."[16] So it is morality that is of utmost importance to us; and it is morality that promotes religion. Thirdly, the societies which preach "ethical religion or religious ethics believe in religion through morality."[17] Gandhi appreciates personalities like Bradlaugh, Jeremy Bentham, etc., who, though they did not adhere to theism, were out and out moral. And he condemned those who "practise immorality under the guise of religion." So, to Gandhi, it is by being moral that we become religious. Fourthly, 'religion and morality are united and should be so united' that one is imperfect without the other. In other words, in Gandhian thought moral imperfection, i.e., imperfection of moral concepts, leads to religion for their manifestation. It may be mentioned here that in Kantian thought also morality due to imperfection leads to religion. Fifthly, to Gandhi, morality is the basis of all, and hence on it religion is based.

In his words, "The founders of the religions have also explained that morality is the basis of religion...."[18] "As soon as we lose the moral basis, we cease to be religious. There is no such thing as religion overriding morality. Man for instance cannot be untruthful, cruel and incontinent and claim to have God on his side."[19] That is to say, morality can stand alone and in itself while religion cannot. A moral man is always religious in Gandhi's eye but a religious, nay a theist, may not always be moral. Sixthly, he says, "God is omnipotent, He is perfect. There are no limits to His mercy, to His goodness and to His justice."[20] The moral concepts like mercy, goodness, justice, etc., reach their zenith in God who without them become dim, lifeless and imperfect. It is morality, that yields life and colour to religion. To sum up: morality leads to religion owing to its imperfection while religion is dependent on morality for its subsistence, manifestation and vitality. A further elaboration in this respect is not called for as we have already dealt with it in detail in a preceding chapter of this dissertation.

In his aesthetic thought too morality predominates. He condemns anything and everyting as non-beauteous that goes against moral principles; against the interest of dumb and hungry millions. A piece of beauty must promote the purity and elevation of the inner self. Without this any human creation would turn into a hollow myth. To Gandhi, a statuette of a woman, half-naked and struggling with the folds of her cloth, appeared as a symbol of purity and chastity; and the scorpion, an incarnation of hellish lust or cupid. He translated the implicit meaning of the statuette into an eternal moral teaching of the victory of morality over immorality. He appreciated this piece of art as beauty because it conformed to his deep-rooted moral conviction—morality as the basis of all.

Regarding the form of an artistic object he prefers the inner being to the outward form. In his *Autobiography* (p. 228) we find him appreciating Mrs. West for "her moral beauty", her "purity of heart." Socrates, in spite of his ugly appearance, was beautiful to him because of his life-long search after truth. So were Mohammed and Jesus. To quote him, "Truth is the first thing to be sought for, and beauty and goodness will then be added upto you."[21] "...Purity of life is the highest and truest art."[22] An analysis reveals that the purity of character, a harmonious elevated life of moral excellence predominates in Gandhian aesthetics. He appreciates Pandit Khare's vocal recital as pure art because it arose from the harmony of pure life. He is moved by the devotional songs of Mirabai, and Suradas for their beauty, sincerity and ardent desire for self-surrender without which self-realization is impossible. His moral conviction is also evident in the prescription of books. He condemns the immoral literature, the *Shilling-Shockers* for their harmful inhibition to self-realization. In short, his aesthetics is firmly based on the moral plinth, and is viewed from the moral standpoint at every step.

Gandhi's political ideas too have morality as their basic foundation. He explains in no uncertain terms the reason for his active participation in politics. He says, "To see the universal and all-pervading Spirit of Truth face to face one must be able to love the meanest of creation as oneself. And a man who aspires after that cannot afford to keep out of any field of life. That is why my devotion to Truth has drawn me into the field of politics; and I can say without the slightest hesitation, and yet in all humility, that those who say that religion has nothing to do with politics do not know what religion means."[23] It is clear from the above that Gandhi participated actively in politics not for its own sake but to fulfil some moral mission, i.e., realization of Truth or God through service to the people. V.M. Bedekar comments, "...it was his deep religiosity which made him take an active part in politics."[24] This synthetic note was interwoven into his basic thought in such a pattern that a very brief discussion of it is necessary for better understanding of Gandhian position. Gandhi, like other Indian pioneers, held a metaphysical outlook which interpreted every physical existent as manifestation of one reality, Truth or God. To Gandhi God is not an abstract entity. He is the only being who inheres in all the living beings and non-living objects of the universe. But God is manifested in living beings, especially in human beings, more clearly and perfectly than in the non-livings. So drawing nearer to one's own real identity and to humanity leads an individual nearer to Truth. That is why he prescribes for complete identification of ourselves with the boundless varieties of life through social service. Indeed, life and reality, God and human beings (the exact term is *Naranarayan*) are indivisible and inseparable in Gandhian thought. The various spheres of life—political, moral, economic, social and aesthetic, etc.—are so intimately interwoven into an organic whole that on a critical observation they seem to be manifestations of the same reality, Truth or God. D.M. Datta brings out Gandhi's motive behind participation in politics as follows: "Though Gandhi became a world figure in politics, the roots of his existence lay in his moral and religious life. Political work for him was the service of God in men, without which he could not emancipate himself from the bonds of selfishness nor realize God."[25] G. Stephens Spinks comments, "...as soon as one looks at Gandhi as the innovator, the man whose morality was progressive, we can see the truth of the statement that morality and politics are identical only in the life of a living person."[26]

The above discussion clearly illustrates Gandhi's motive behind political activities, i.e., the dynamo that steered him from morality to politics. A relevant question may be asked: Did he like political activities from the core of his heart? Did he prefer political activities to moral and religious activities? In a word, the answer is, 'no'. He writes, "...I must... confess that work of social reform or self-purification of this nature is a hundred times dearer to me than what is called purely political work."[27] A critical analysis will reveal the following points implicit in the above statement. Firstly, it seemed to him that complete realization of God or Truth would be impossible without participation in politics. Because realization of truth or God demands an equal progress of all aspects of human life—social, political, moral, economic and religious, etc.—in its entirety. Political activities were immediate ends which again, according to Gandhian style, were means to God or Truth realization. In this context Shriman Narayan observes, "He regarded participation in politics as an unavoidable evil, and tried his very best to introduce religion into politics."[28] Secondly, he engaged in politics only to the extent that would be conducive to God-realization neither more nor less. This reminds us of Shakespeare's heroine Cordelia who replies to her father by saying, "Unhappy that I am, I cannot heave/My heart into my mouth. I love your/Majesty/According to my bond; no more nor less."[29] Thirdly, he preferred the ultimate goal, God-realization hundred times to "what is called purely political work." Why this apparent antipathy towards political work? Perhaps, it arose from the traditional and contemporary political happenings around him. Political life is often a conflict between the highest known moral law and the demands of expediency. The 'Machiavellian' principle of 'end justifying the means' however criticized, has been and still now is one of the basic tenets of international politics. Since the political activities generally went against the fundamental principles of morality, he felt an aversion to politics, although circumstances compelled him to participate in it actively.

A complete account of Gandhi's political ideas is not the objective of this treatise. Here our purpose is to show that like other great thinkers (Plato, Aristotle, Hegel, Spinoza, etc.) he started with moral convictions and viewed the world in that light. *Satyagraha*, the political weapon forged by him, is an example which was based purely on moral principles. It is a non-violent method of winning one's opponent through soul-force or love-force. A *satyagrahi* has to undergo a series of ordeals which he describes as virtues. These are based on strict moral principles. Above all, he did not believe in the division of life into watertight compartments. There was for him no dichotomy between private and public life. He practised in private life whatever he preached publicly. That is to say, he introduced a new trend in political field, and endeavoured to spiritualize and moralize life as a whole. This moral basis of politics gave him a unique place in the contemporary world. Struck by his spiritualization and moralization of life in its entirety, a professor from Oxford observes, "The conviction came to me, that not since Socrates has the world seen his equal for absolute self-control and composure."[30] J.B. Kripalani comments, "Political life, internal and international, must be guided by truth and non-violence. There must be no armaments and secret diplomacy.... His (Gandhi's) practical programme based on truth and non-violence is aimed at providing the moral man with a moral society."[31] We may conclude this discussion with a passage from D.M. Datta who says, "Gandhi's great mission in life was to revolutionize politics by ethics...."[32]

Now let us turn to the moral basis of his social philosophy. Firstly, his antipathy towards modern civilization had its roots in his moral conviction. The pomp and glitter of modern civilization appeared to him to be 'Satanic,' a relic of the 'black age.' Aggressive mechanization of every natural object and the ruthless dehumanization of men and women went against his principle of natural and simple life. He declared, "This civilization is irreligion...."[33] Here Buddhadeva Bhattacharyya comments, "...The civilization which did not take into account morality, had no appeal for Gandhi as it had no place in India."[34] Secondly, his movement against untouchability has a moral and humanitarian background. We have already seen that he felt the omnipresence of One, Truth or God, in all human beings. To him though we seem to be many, ultimately we are one. We are different branches of the same tree. To dishonour one as 'untouchable' is to dishonour the Truth or God in him. To quote him, "The fact that we addressed God as the 'purifier of the polluted' and by similar appellations, shows that it is a sin, to regard any one born in Hinduism as polluted or 'untouchable'—that it is Satanic to do so...."[35] He often described it as 'the monster of untouchability,' 'the ulcer of untouchability.' Thirdly, let us take up his theory of Trusteeship of Wealth. Gandhi tells us that we should take only that which we indispensably require for immediate use; and act as moral guardian of the rest of wealth for the use of the public. But if we take something that is not necessary for immediate use, we thieve it from somebody else. To quote him, "My theory of 'trusteeship' is no makeshift, certainly no camouflage.... It has the sanction of philosophy and religion behind it."[36] In this context Gunnar Myrdal comments, "...Gandhi realized this, for he demanded a moral revolution, a change of heart among the rich."[37] Here Gandhi appealed to the moral sense of equality of the rich, and attempted to spiritualize them. Fourthly, bread labour is one of the cardinal virtues prescribed for the *satyagrahis*. It means that every individual should perform an amount of physical labour which somehow or other will produce the equivalent of what he enjoys for his being. Here the influence of the *Gita* ideal that if anybody eats without offering sacrifice eats stolen food is evident. Buddhadeva Bhattacharyya aptly comments, "Bread labour, as conceived by Gandhi, is a training in moral discipline as well ass an economic answer to the enforced idleness of the millions of people."[38] Fifthly, his educational scheme has moral uplift as its goal. In that scheme he laid emphasis on the three R's (*Naitalim*) and 'learning by doing'. He says, "By education I mean an all-round drawing out of the best in child and man—body, mind and spirit."[39] Good character, development of both physical and mental strength, courage, virtue, sanitation, dedication towards social service, etc., filled in the curriculum. D.M. Datta comments on Gandhian educational system, "Gandhi's whole theory of education was fundamentally based on his deep conviction that truth and love are the most abiding bases of human society and the individual's progress. Every person should be physically, mentally, and spiritually educated to realize truth and love in every sphere of life...."[40] Lastly, Gandhi's economic policy is also a corollary of the moral conviction inherent in him. He condemned and raised voice against the immoral economic policy and commercial regulations. "True economics never militates against the highest ethical standard, just as all true ethics to be worth its name must at the same time be also good economics."[41] The moral note of Gandhian economic policy is evident here. Extracts can be multiplied to show the predominance of morality in various aspects of his social philosophy.

To sum up: We have discussed above Gandhi's moral conviction in different aspects of his thought. It is in morality, indeed, that he lived and breathed every moment of his life. God whom he worshipped in ethical religion; Truth which he pursued to realize through political activities; the One whom he endeavoured to serve through service to society; the sublimity that he enjoyed in Nature, and in human creations are mere synonyms of Truth: the supreme goal of Gandhian moral science. To put it in other words, he made religion ethical, moralized politics, spiritualized social values, and founded aesthetics, economics, etc., on a moral basis.

Concept of Evil

Human life, roughly speaking, is a curious mixture of good and evil, happiness and sorrow. Good and evil are correlative, realistic and facts of experience. The concept of good and evil changes along with the change of our experience, with the evolution of our consciousness. These concepts, as some thinkers hold, are not illusions rather real factors contributing remarkably to the scheme of life. The term 'good' etymologically means 'conducive to the end.' In this light an action or object is good if it is conducive or useful to some end while it is condemned as evil if it is subversive to the end. To put it in another way, the facts of life that carry positive value are appreciated as good, and those which appear to have negative value are condemned as evil. In this connection freedom of will, a cardinal point, draws our attention. Evil in the ethical sense, and with it we are concerned here, is solely dependent upon human volition. It presupposes freedom of will as a necessary postulate. An individual commits evil in the ethical sense if he gratifies own interest at the cost of the existing order of the surrounding. The Biblical story of Adam, the first man, losing paradise reveals the same truth that evil in the ethical sense is always a resultant of the exercise of free will in opposition to the existing order. Gandhi, it will be evident in course of discussion, treated this problem of evil in the light of freedom of will and the theory of Karma of Indian philosophy. In this context D.M. Datta observes, "He tries to understand, like Christian theists, moral evils, sins and vices, as being due to the acts of man who has the freedom of will. To this he sometimes adds the Indian theory of Karma according to which actions of man are responsible not only for virtues and vices, but also for the physical conditions into which he is born."[42]

We have seen above that Gandhi came of a staunch Vaishnava family. His family tradition and religious surrounding taught him of an almighty, omnipresent, omniscient God who is also the acme of goodness, truth and beauty. But burning humanism urged him to pay active attention to the harsh realities, i.e., evils, sins and vices of life. That is why he endeavoured to reconcile reason with faith; the reality of evils with the theological perfection and benevolence of God. More elaborately, the traditional system of metaphysical ethics (Vedanta of Indian system, and Spinoza, Hegel and Hegelians in the West) explains God as the only and all-inclusive reality. The problem of good and evil is a phenomenal experience from this point of view. Gandhi was deeply influenced by this trend of thought, and strove to harmonize the all-inclusive goodness of God with evils and vices of our lives. To him, reality is *Sat-Cit-Ananda*, Truth (good), consciousness and bliss. The reality or God is the conserver of all values—truth, goodness and beauty (*satyam, sivam, sundaram*). The question arises: If God is the creator of the universe, the evils of all kinds that persist are also His creations, and hence He is a designer of evils. In other words, the goodness (*sivam*) of God can never be reconciled with evil. Here Gandhi faces a dilemma. As a theist he ascribes all noble qualities, in this case perfect goodness, to God while his burning humanism cannot explain away the problem of evil. D.M. Datta brings out Gandhi's mind very nicely by saying, "As a man is very unwilling to attribute bad motives to a tried friend and interprets even his apparently undesirable actions, of unknown motives, in the most charitable way and vaguely trusts that there must have been some good intention behind his curious behaviour, similarly a person who has enjoyed repeatedly the benefits of the belief in God tries to understand the evils of the world as being inspired by some unknown good motive... Gandhi could not find it in his heart to believe that the evils that we find in the world are due to any evil intention of God who has been his unfailing friend throughout his life, in personal and public struggles."[43] Gandhi's faith here supersedes his reason. He thinks that faith is the never-failing key to unlock the mystery of theological problems. "I cannot account for the existence of evils by any rational method. To want to do so is to be co-equal with God. I am therefore humble enough to recognize evil as such. And I call God long-suffering and patient precisely because He permits evil in the world...."[44] The central idea is that God as the creator of the universe is certainly aware of evils, and in a sense creator of them. But these evils cannot pollute his divinity. Because He as the moral governor of the universe imposes evil as punishment on evil-doers and showers blessings on honest people as reward. Sometimes he speaks of severe tests of sufferings that a devotee has to undergo in order to merit divine blessings. Perhaps, the Vaishnavite trend of thought in Gandhi inspired him to treat the problem of evil as *lila* or sport of divine whim. And the spurious contact of evils with God, as narrated in different scriptures, is limited within this world. It never disturbs or vitiates the purity of divine benevolence.

But Gandhi's theological and metaphysical treatment of the problems of evils as analysed above faces some difficulties. To say that evils, moral and physical, are punishments or warnings of God for the violation of divine order is not to explain it satisfactorily. In the name of explaining it, he explains it away. This curious blending of moral ideals with sluggishness of theological faith has been generally condemned in Western thought also. Hermann Lotze, for example, condemns this theological approach of moral ideals by saying, "We are thus constrained to seek the origin of evil in God Himself and in such a way as not to conflict with His holiness...."[45] An almost similar type of objection has been raised by B.G. Ray against Gandhian theological approach to moral evils.[46]

Ray's observation on the topic seems to be sound from the strictly logical standpoint. But Gandhi, as we have seen, cared very little for logician's verdict. Though he admitted the role of reason in our lives still he declined predominance to it on the ground that life is above 'dry syllogistic rules.' To do justice to 'Godly' affairs, and for precise and adequate appreciation of it he requests us to become 'God-knowing' men. Indeed, strictly rationalistic and critical outlook, although indispensable for scholastic pursuits, often mar the spirit of theological discussion. That is why Gandhi accepts faith as the ultimate arbiter in this context. Above all, he confesses his naive outlook in this treatment of the problem of evils. The terms 'a villager's answer'; 'poor villagers language is not God's' convey his naive way of thinking. Gopinath Dhawan's observation in this context seems to be justified when he comments, "Gandhiji is, however, concerned not so much with philosophical explanation of evil as with the specific kinds of evil, political, social and economic."[47] B.G. Ray also admits this common-sense characteristic of Gandhian approach to the problem of evils. He observes "In this respect, his philosophy is the same as the naive philosophy of a common man."[48] Buddhadeva Bhattacharyya also shares the above opinion by saying, "...the fact should not be ignored that as Gandhi was not an academically trained philosopher, it was not expected of him to tackle these subtle philosophical questions satisfactorily."[49] The inherent truth is that humanism is the pivotal point of Gandhian thought; and this burning humanism urged him to blend the problem of evils with the benevolence of divinity. It may or may not satisfy a scholar's quest for knowledge but this is the way how his naive mind viewed problems, both phenomenal and noumenal.

The above is a short account of the theological and metaphysical implication of the problem of evil. Let us consider the nature of evil in Gandhian thought. In dealing with this problem we should remember that the distinction between good and evil is our viewpoint since God, the creator, is untouched, unhurt by it. And in a loose sense, it is phenomenal and not noumenal. Gandhi explains the nature of evil by saying, "Good and evil are, for human purposes, from each other distinct and incompatible, being symbolic of light and darkness."[50] As light shows the path of life so good brings immense benefit to mankind. And evil like darkness leads us to inertia and relevant vices. But this evil cannot exist by itself unless offset by good. Just as darkness acquires significance only because of the existence of light so also evil attains meaning and importance due to its contrast with good. Gandhi continues "...Good was self-existent, evil was not. It was like a parasite living on and around good. It would die of itself when the support that good gave was withdrawn."[51] Thus evil is sterile, self-destructive, and parasitic in nature. It is, because good exists in our lives.

As to the function of good and evil Gandhi says, "Often does good come out of evil. But that is God's, not man's plan. Man knows that only evil can come out of evil, as good out of good."[52] On 30 June 1946, he made the above remark on 'Atom Bomb and Ahiṃsa'. He foresaw the unseen peril of Atom Bomb that confronts the world today. In this phenomenal world evil often begets evil. It is only God's benevolence that can deliver good out of evil. As to the reciprocal relation of good and evil Gandhi's view seems to be paradoxical, if not contradictory. At the end of May 1946 he prescribed 'minimum unavoidable violence' to protect agricultural products from monkeys, birds, insects, etc., although *ahimsa* was his only weapon to face such problems. He says, "There is not much difference between the two. To allow crops to be eaten up by animals in the name of *ahimsa* while there is a famine in the land is certainly a sin. Evil and good are relative terms. What is good under certain conditions can become an evil or a sin under a different set of conditions."[53] This contradicts his earlier statements: "It is sinful to conquest with evil. There is no meeting ground between good and evil—good and Satan."[54] This quotation proves that his concept of good and evil passed through a long process of evolution, and underwent a radical change. Gandhi, who ruled out any communication or reciprocal relation between good and evil in his early twenties, was found advocating the relativity of good and evil under varying circumstances during the last days of his life. Crooked is the course of life. Gandhi as the votary of truth and non-violence remained faithful to absolute truth and good but his burning humanism, his practical idealism, i.e., pragmatism compelled him to admit relative truth and good in order to face the complex problems of life. This is no deviation from principle; it is rather a strengthening of life, the *elan vital* of principle.

This problem of evil has social significance for him. He fought throughout his life against all kinds of evils, i.e., political, social, economic, religious, etc. His primary concern is the moral regeneration of the individual and the nation, and for this his whole life was a ceaseless crusade against evil in general. The social order requires abolition of evils, and a victory of good over them. It is undeniable that evildoers are not few in number, and sometimes they overpower the spirit threatening to cut it off from good. But a critical analysis of the history of mankind unfolds the truth that the victory of evil is highly temporary, and never permanent. The social order overthrows it by dint of inherent power. To quote Gandhi, "Although evil seemed at times to rule the world, the eternal truth was that the world lived so long as goodness resided even in one person. Evil was nought."[55] Moreover, evildoers are cursed while good people are blessed by divine power. In order to smoothly maintain the order of society he adds an elixir, an incentive for the good people by saying, "It is enough for our spiritual growth to know that God is always with the doer of good."[56] Thus abolition of evils and performance of good actions are necessities of social life.

As discussed above good and evil are relative terms and hence, according to Gandhi, both are intermingled with the problems of our everyday lives. We often face evils as per abilities. But Gandhi warns us not to hate the evildoers but evil. In his words, "Real non-co-operation is non-co-operation with evil and not with the evildoer."[57] Gandhi often recollected the precious saying, 'Hate the sin, not the sinner.' This conviction is a resultant of his belief in the spiritual unity of all beings. All beings are sparks of the Supreme One. So to punish an evildoer is to undermine the divine in him. Moreover, as a votary of truth and non-violence he can never advise others to hate the evildoers. Gandhi gets inspiration of condemnation of evils from the scriptures of different faiths. The Hindu scriptures are full of condemnation of evildoers. The central idea of the great epics, the *Mahabharata* and the *Ramayana*, is the victory of good over evil. Jesus called down divine wrath upon 'a generation of vipers, hypocrites, whited sepulchres! Buddha condemned men who killed innocent goats in the name of religion. In the *Koran* and the *Zend-Avesta* similar instances are mentioned. The point to be noted here is that these seers and prophets had no evil intention behind these condemnations.[58] Thus by condemning evils, Gandhi was only keeping up with the tradition, both Eastern and Western.

A question arises: How can we get rid of evils without undermining the Supreme in the evildoers? To put it in other words: How can we reconcile respect to evil-doer with the abolition of evils? In spite of His Omniscience, Omnipresence and Almightiness, God's interference in this regard seems unnecessary because His intention is inscrutable for us. And God allows evils to persist, we are told, only to glorify the role of good in our lives. Moreover, Gandhi himself rules out any possibility of God freeing us from evil. Having examined that divine interference for the removal of evils is impossible. Gandhi suggests to us three ways to free ourselves from evils. Firstly, good and evil are relative terms. Evil exists only in the shadow of good. So we can abolish evils either by boycotting or purifying evil through good. Gandhi suggests, how we can boycott evil, if we withdraw our support, our toleration, from sterile, parasitic evil, it will automatically vanish away. On the positive side, we can purify evil through good. It is the divine touch of good that can mould an evil into good. Thus in its negative aspect, good boycotts evil, and in its positive side, good purifies evil.

Secondly, good means in its universal application becomes non-violence with infinite potentiality. Without *ahimsa* or evildoer we can never abolish evil. Application of violence against an evildoer leads to the denial of the Supreme in him, and consequently causes moral degradation to the user of violence. Any attempt to abolish evil through violence, in the above pattern, gets lost in a vicious circle. To quote Gandhi, "In my humble opinion, non-co-operation with evil is as much a duty as is co-operation with good...."[59] Thus violence begets violence and evil. Gandhi believed in the essential goodness of human nature, the manifestation of which demands sincere cultivation of *ahimsa*. In fine, abolition of evil is impossible without non-violent means that Gandhi preached and observed under all circumstances.

Thirdly, non-co-operation in the Gandhian style is an offshoot of Gandhian concept of non-violence. Gandhi tells us, to abolish evil by boycotting, purifying, doing good to the evildoer, of course, non-violently. But in no sense he tells us to help or tolerate evil. Indeed, doing good through non-violent means never conveys helping, tolerating, or indulging in evil. On the contrary, he tells us to non-co-operate with evil in all possible ways. Gandhi clearly says, "...if my son lives a life of shame, I may not help him to do so by continuing to support him although it may mean even his death."[60] The world knows how prophetic it was regarding his treatment of his demoralized son, Hiralal.

To conclude, Gandhi treats the problem of evil primarily from the religio-metaphysical standpoint, and consequently faces the difficulties that are generally raised against metaphysical ethics. A rational and scientific treatment of the problem of evil demands a critical probe into the socio-economic conditions of the surroundings in the historical background. This is sadly absent in Gandhian treatment of it. The attempts that he made to apply it to concrete life, although urged by his deep concern for humanity, cannot come out of the metaphysico-theological orbit. In his attempt to explain the earthly problem like evil he ignores the essentials; and in a strict sense, explains it away. In short, Gandhi's reconciliation of the problem of evil with the benevolence of divinity, in spite of its humanistic root, has no scientific basis.

Natural Calamities as Human Sin

We have seen above Gandhi's unbounded love and reverence for Nature. The beauties of Nature, the accurate rotation of heavenly bodies, the warbling of rivers, the murmuring of seas are all, to him, manifestations of the glory of God. God is the creator, preserver and destroyer of the universe. If anything goes wrong with the system, He mends and ractifies it. According to Gandhi, "He and His Law are one. The law is God."[61] This firm conviction in the identity of God with Nature is the matrix of his belief in spiritual unity of all existents. Any breach or chaos or calamity in the universe cannot be caused by the divine system which is perfect and precise at every step. Hence Gandhi comes to the conclusion that cosmic disorder and natural calamities are due to sins of human beings. His interpretation of the earthquakes of Bihar and Quetta as divine chastisement of human sins gave birth to a controversy amongst the intellectuals in contemporary India.

This idea of divine chastisement got deeply rooted in his mind in early childhood. Influenced by the religious surroundings, his childish mind got acquainted with the theory of *Karma* which tells us to be ready for just returns for our actions. Gandhi believed in the enjoyment or sufference of the consequences of our actions; and sometimes these consequences come in the guise of natural calamities. Environmental conditions cast an immense influence on the development of an individual's mind. Gandhi is no exception. His birthplace, Kathiawada, faced a lot of earthquakes and famines. People accepted these natural calamities as 'heaven-sent calamities.' He was born and brought up under the shadows of calamities. The history and traditional ideas and ideals of his surroundings, without his knowing it, contributed to the evolution of his thought and works. This is the historical context which can explain Gandhi's outlook on natural calamities.

Let us now elucidate his views in this context. Gandhi says, "It is easy enough to say, 'I do not believe in God.' For God permit all things to be said of Him with impunity. He looks at our acts. And any breach of His law carried with it, not its vindictive, but its purifying, compelling, punishment."[62] "I have long believed that physical phenomena produce results both physical and spiritual. The converse I hold to be equally true.... Visitations like droughts, floods, earthquakes and the like, though they seem to have only physical origins, are, for me, somehow connected with man's morals. Therefore, I instinctively felt that the earthquake was a visitation for the sin of untouchability."[63] We can cite numerous similar passages from his speeches and writings. But investigations and experiments conducted by physical scientists to unlock the mystery of the universe unfold the fact that natural calamities (visitations like droughts, floods, earthquakes, etc.) have only physical origins, i.e., are a resultant of mere blind, mechanical and physical forces. Earthquakes, for example, are caused by volcanic erruptions, landslides, atomic explosions, commotion in the inner part of the earth, etc. Scientists contend that accumulation of these physical factors will cause a similar calamity in future as in the past. Human efforts, though capable of, to a little extent, of checking them, have nothing to do with them. Indeed, natural laws are neutral, and hence have no connection with moral or religious defaults of human beings. Scientific explanation unfolds the truth that natural calamities, more specifically, happenings, used to take place in their own course even before the human species came into existence on earth. So the ascription of divinity to natural calamities is purely a human creation. F. Nietzsche aptly writes, "...an honest scientist believes in the unconditional rule of natural laws in the world, without, however, taking up any position in regard to the ethical or intellectual value of these laws. Wherever, neutrality is abandoned in this respect, it is owing to an anthropomorphic attitude of mind which allows reason to exceed its proper sounds."[64]

But Gandhi, essentially a religious man thinks that "there is an indissoluble marriage between matter and spirit."[65] All existents in space and all events in time are creations of God who is also the acme of goodness. He is Truth, Love, Law and everything that human ingenuity can name. Since all are sparks of the same reality, God or Truth, all existents and events are interwoven into an unseen nexus in such a manner that the degradation or uplift of one causes degradation or uplift to the other. Further, it is impossible on the part on an individual being who is imperfect, and the tiniest speck in the vast cosmic order, to know the laws and ways of God in detail. The greatest men of letters, scientists and spiritualists known to history, could disclose only a particle of divine dispensation. Sir Isaac Newton who made a remarkable contribution to the advancement of scientific discoveries, at the end of his life exclaimed that he had found only a few pebbles on the vast shore of the sea knowledge. Thus catastrophes that are the resultant of physical forces seem so to us due to our ignorance of the divine Laws. In his words, "...God is the Law. But I submit that we do not know the Law or the laws fully, and what appear to us as catastrophes are so only because we do not know the universal laws sufficiently."[66] Here Gandhi admits two things, namely, human imperfection and infinite potentiality of human knowledge. One day science may be able to predict the occurrence of natural calamities beforehand but it can never bring about the purification of self or explain the unseen nexus between the natural calamities and the human morals.

A sceptic and a Sanatanist may ask: How can Gandhi know this unseen link? Is there any relation between natural calamity and human sin? Is the earthquake of Bihar, a divine chastisement of the sin of untouchability? Here also Gandhi takes not reason but faith and instinct as the ultimate arbiter.

The belief in divine superintendence was felt by him every moment of his life. The leaves of a tree cannot move without His permission. Some Sanatanists may argue that the earthquake of Bihar was due to Gandhi's crime of preaching against untouchability. To put it in other words, the upper-caste Hindus believe that the custom of untouchability is a part of Hinduism; and the abolition of it, as advocated by Gandhi, is a breach of divine commandment. Hence the earthquake, a divine chastisement, was due to the sin of Gandhi and his follower, Rabindranath Tagore observes, "What is truly tragic about it is the fact that the kind of argument that Mahatmaji used by exploiting an event of cosmic disturbance far better suits the psychology of his opponents than his own, and it would not have surprised me at all if they had taken his opportunity of holding him and his followers responsible for the visitation of Divine anger."[67] We have seen that Gandhi treats untouchability not as an integral part but as a blot of Hinduism. That is why he tells us that the natural calamities are not vindication but purifying chastisement for our sin. So prayer which is a sign of repentance, a desire to become better and purer, should be made by each and everybody. It makes us purer, better; and through purification leads us to Him. Hermann Lotze puts question mark on this Gandhian concept.

Our discussion would remain incomplete if the reaction of Rabindranath Tagore to Gandhi's treatment of natural calamities is not mentioned here. Tagore writes, "It has caused me painful surprise to find Mahatma Gandhi accusing those who blindly follow their own social custom of untouchability of having brought down God's vengeance upon certain parts of Bihar...."[68] In reply to the above criticism Gandhi draws our attention to the differences of outlook between them. In his words, "...Gurudev and I early discovered certain differences of outlook between us ...I have the faith that our own sins have more force to ruin that structure than any mere physical phenomenon."[69] The poet Tagore request Gandhi to view the world from rational and scientific outlook because it creates tremendous impact on the masses. On the contrary, Gandhi views the world from the viewpoint of religion and morality. As discussed above, he prefers faith as the ultimate arbiter to reason; and advises us to become 'God-knowing man' in order to do justice to godly affairs.

To sum up: Our ways of knowing, often imperfect and delusive, decidedly fall short of unveiling the mystery of the universe. And no amount of human knowledge, although it may sound like agnosticism, shall, perhaps, be able to know the universe accurately. The more we know the more the horizon of knowledge recedes. This leads us to accept Gandhi's view that we do not know the works and laws of God sufficiently. That is to say our imperfection of knowledge leaves room for the possible relation between natural calamities as divine chastisements and human sin. Gandhi's treatment of natural calamities as the result of human sin may sound naive, superstitious, and hence unscientific, as discussed above, to a scholastic ear. One may or may not accept Gandhi's viewpoint. But this is how he viewed the problem. Here we should bear in mind the epistemological truth that scientific explanation based on observation, experiment, induction, the principle of the uniformity of nature, etc., is not the final and only way of knowing truth. It has its errors and limitations. And there are other ways too.

Nature of Punishment

The problem of evil, especially moral evil, leads to the problem of crime and punishment. Since the dawn of civilization the curious social thinker has asked some questions: What is crime? Why do men commit crimes? What is the relation between crime and punishment? What are the nature and justification of punishment? The term crime generally denotes those actions that violate the social order, and are liable to punishment. It generates evil consequences which often react upon the perpetrator. From the early dawn of civilization till today religion has, directly or indirectly, moulded human thought. And during this long course of evolution the idea of moral evil got intermingled with the religious idea of sin. Our inherent sense of justice demands punishment for the commission of crimes. Generally a man performing a good action is appreciated, and an individual committing a bad action is condemned. From the psychological standpoint our feelings of gratitude for good actions and revenge for bad actions justify the execution of punishment. Sociologically, the ultimate aim of punishment is to maintain law and order in society; and ethically it strives to establish the majesty of moral law. Above all, a crime is an evil committed against humanity, and hence the justification of punishment.

In the western world of thought three principal theories as regards the nature and inherent motive of punishment have been put forward. (1) The preventive or deterrent theory of punishment tells us that the aim of punishment is to deter or prevent others from committing similar offences. It is well-expressed in the famous dictum of the judge, "you are not punished for stealing sheep but in order that sheep may not be stolen." This theory treats a criminal as a thing, as a mere means, not an end in himself because it inflicts punishment on an individual not for his welfare but for the benefit of others. (2) The educative or reformative theory tells us that the aim of punishment is to educate or reform the criminal himself. A criminal is punished for his own good, and hence is not a means but an end in himself. The criminal anthropologists regard crime as a pathological phenomenon, a physiological peculiarity, a kind of insanity, an innate or acquired physiological defect. The criminal sociologists too support this view by saying that crimes are due to unfavourable social circumstances, i.e., social inequalities, maladjustments and corruptions. So the economic and social conditions of the criminals have to be improved. Freud and his followers hold that crimes are due to repressed complexes or suppressed wishes, and hence call for medical or educational treatment rather than punitive precautions. This theory, in spite of its drawbacks, has been widely appreciated and commonly accepted at the present time for its humanitarian appeal. (3) The last one, the retribution theory, tells us that the primary aim of punishment is retribution and by it the supremacy and authority of the law is defended. Punishment is inflicted on the criminal neither for his good nor for that of society but for the sake of dignity, authority and majesty of the law.[70]

An almost similar type of theories regarding the nature and justification of punishment was preached by social leaders in ancient India. An accurate and just reading of Gandhian views of the same demands elaboration of the traditional views because he was immensely influenced by tradition. (1) The aim of punishment, according to the deterrent theory, is to deter people from committing evil actions simply out of fear of severe punishment. In the *Gautma-Dharma-Sutra* we are told of punishment as an instrument of suppression (*damana*) of the uncontrolled (*adanta*).[71] Punishment is inflicted on the wicked persons to control other criminally-minded people who out of fear (*bhaya*) keep themselves from committing crimes.[72] Manu, the renowned law-composer, tells us that the whole world is kept in order by punishment. Honest and pure men are rare. The people of the world yield their due only out of fear.[73] (2) The reformatory or educative theory of punishment also formed a part of ancient Indian criminology. It aimed at the social rehabilitation of the punished person so that he may observe his own *dharma* or duty. The offenders or evilmongers may get reformed either by punishment or by instruction of a *guru* (preceptor). Those who cannot be reformed and hence purified through the effective guidance of a teacher must be corrected by punishment.[74] In the *Sukra-Niti* we are told of the efficacy of punishment meted out by the kind. It is out of fear of punishment that the evildoers get reformed and follow their own *dharma*.[75] In the *Puranic* mythology we are told of Kaliyadamana, a nice story on reformation brought forth by punishment. The wives of the snake Kaliya appraises Lord Krishna by saying that the punishment inflicted by Him on the wicked (*asat*) purges them of their sin (*Kalmasa*).[76] In the Buddhist scriptures non-violent treatment and reformation of the criminal is prescribed. We are told that the great king Vessantara conquered the angry person (*kodha*) by non-anger (*akkodha*); the wicked person (*asadhu*) by goodness (*sadhuta*); a miser by gifts; the speaker of falsehood by truthfulness; and all evil by moral goodness.[77] (3) The ideal of retribution or paying one back in one's own coin has also been prescribed by the composers of Hindu scriptures. It is a universal belief among the Hindus that an individual committing violence (*himsa*) and untruth (*anrta*) out of attachment (*sneha*) goes to a most horrible hell for his faults (*atmadosa*).[78] A sinful killer (*khala-himsra*) is killed (*vihimsita*) by his own sin (*svapapa*).[79] It is an obligation on the part of the people to kill those who deserve to be killed (*vadhya*), as per instructions and orders of the scriptures and the King respectively.[80] The above is a brief account of the nature of punishment practised in ancient India.[81]

Gandhi who was born and brought up in Indian tradition, and claimed to have an acquaintance with Hindu scriptures, might have been influenced, directly or indirectly, by the tradition in holding the views regarding crime and punishment. The blending of Indian and Western ideas in his own way is a prominent characteristic of Gandhian thought. His eclectic mind absorbs everything noble that comes to the mill of his mind but interprets them in his own way.

Here two points are to be noted. Firstly, Gandhi's views on crime and punishment is an integral part of his thought. Here his views on the spiritual unity of all human beings, and relativity and imperfection of human knowledge play an iimportant role. Human knowledge always falls short of perfection, and hence can claim no infallibility. This means that human verdict is by nature liable to error. That is why Gandhi is a bit reluctant to impose any sort of punishment on any offender. To quote him, "Punishment is God's who alone is the infallible Judge. It does not belong to man 'with judgement weak'."[82] This is the spirit with which he treated the problem and usually preferred the reformatory theory to other traditional theories of crime and punishment.

Secondly, another feature of Gandhian theory of punishment is the paradoxical obedience to cosmic law or moral law and disobedience to foreign rulers. We have already dealt with Gandhi's unbounded reverence for the law of Karma and cosmic order, and for the majesty of moral law. Gandhi's obedience to moral law and disobedience to immoral laws of an oppressive government have their matrix in the inner voice or the voice of conscience. He gave a clarion call to the nation, especially to *satyagrahis*, to violate the immoral laws that offend our moral sense, and accept the consequences of violation, i.e., punishment obediently and quietly. Even in this acceptance of punishment he preached and practised a stoical attitude towards rules. Here Thoreauvian influence on Gandhi is evident. While suffering imprisonment in South Africa in 1909 he recollects the jail-experience of Thoreau who declared, "...I did not feel for a moment confined, and the walls seemed a great waste of stone and mortar."[83] To Gandhi spirit dominates over matter. The punishment that cannot touch the soul, and inflicts torture only on the body, is useless. The spirit of punishment is that the mind of the offender should be transformed and purified so that his bodily actions may not violate moral laws.

Though Gandhi did not mention the name of traditional theories of punishment, still for our convenience, for the easy understanding of Gandhian viewpoint let us arrange them under the traditional caption one by one. (1) The preventive or deterrent element in Gandhian theory of punishment. In 1938 a group of communists met Gandhi at Segaon and asked him his views on the deterrent or preventive effect of punishment. They asked, "We feel puzzled. You have said that coercive measures should be used to put down incitement to violence. Is it right to use government violence to check the so-called incitement to violence by Congressmen?" "The question is badly put," argued Gandhi, "but my answer is there. There should be no Government violence. But if a man kills a little child and robs it of its ornaments and if I deprive him of the liberty to repeat the performance, I would not call my act violence. It would be violence, if my act was meant to be a punishment."[84] It is clear that Gandhi conceded the deterrent efficacy of punishment, of course, in a non-violent technique. His advice is to deprive the offender of liberty to repeat offences in future. The difference with the traditional view is that deterrent or preventive punishment is prescribed for its immediate magical effect on the offenders and others living in a society. It creates terror and fear owing to which the people keep themselves from committing offences. And it treats, as discussed above, a criminal as a means for the welfare of others. On the contrary, to Gandhi in every individual inheres Truth or God, and hence he is an end in himself. And his prescription for non-violent deterrence is ultimately aimed at, neither punishment nor terror, but cessation of offences in future.

(2) On Gandhi's views on the reformative or educative nature of punishment Gene Sharp comments, "In recent years this weapon of moral power was refined and given new expression and increased strength by Mohandas K. Gandhi. This resulted from his efforts at spiritual development and his experiments in new ways of combating social evils and building a just world. In his hands moral influence was combined with active, dynamic and militant action against social evils."[85] "One of Gandhi's greatest contributions is the development of an active, dynamic way of combating social evils without the use of violence."[86] What was the contribution? Gandhi explains, "The word criminal should be taboo from our dictionary. Or we are criminals ...in secret."[87] Here Gandhi uses the word 'criminal' in a wider perspective. As discussed above, strict observance of vows is the only way to realization of Truth or God. And it is universally admitted that this observance of vows with highest precision in work, thought and deed is impossible on the part of an individual. In this sense we are all criminals differing from one another in degree only. In his words, "The rich, moneyed man who made his riches by exploitation or other questionable means, was no less guilty of robbery than the thief who picked a pocket or broke into a house and committed theft."[88] If in this light we treat everybody as a criminal and thereby inflict punishment on him, the order of the society will stand still. And none would remain outside the prison to move freely. Moreover, the principle of spiritual unity amongst all human beings offers moral hindrance against the infliction of punishment on criminals on the ground that it causes moral degradation to the punisher too. That is why Gandhi prescribed measures to reform the criminals in such a non-violent

way that the society may run smoothly without hurting the truth in them.

The non-violent method of eradication of crimes as outlined above leads Gandhi to hold a view that is largely shared by criminal sociologists and anthropologists of the age. To quote him, "...we should regard even thieves and criminals as our brothers and sisters, and crime as a disease of which the latter were the victims and needed to be cured."[89] The crime committed by a criminal is an example of social malady; and the criminal is a victim of the existing social system. The proper treatment of the criminal should be from all possible quarters—social, mental, physical, etc., in stead of punishing him, teaching him a vocation so that he may reform himself and lead an honest life. And in case of physiological peculiarities we should not only cure his physical ailment but also heal up his mind and soul. In 1947 he delivered a speech at Delhi central jail where he appealed, "...all criminals should be treated as patients and the jails should be hospitals admitting this class of patients for treatment and cure...."[90] Gandhi knew that tender, soft, affectionate care could reform and purify the heart of the worst possible criminal, and the adoption of honest livelihood would rehabilitate him in society. With this end in view he suggested the adoption of some constructive programme so that the so-called criminals might become self-supporting and self-confident in every walk of life. In 1922 he planned, "All industries that were not paying should be stopped. All the jails should be turned into hand-spinning and hand-weaving institutions...."[91] In 1937 the Congress Party assumed office in different provinces of India, and Gandhi called for his colleagues to effect a radical change in jail-systems and turn jails into reformatories, workshops and educational institutions so that the ill name of prisons as appendage of a punitive system may be abolished altogether, and the prisoners, when released, may become ideal citizens of the state. Elsewhere he expresses a similar view, "I am not sure that it is right to put lunatics or criminals, dangerous or otherwise, in prisons, i.e. for punishment. Lunatics are not so put even now. And we are reaching a time when even criminals will be put under restraint for their ultimate reform, not for their punishment."[92] In an ideal state based on non-violence there shall be no crime. It is an ideal and hence may not be possible to realize in its entirety. The world is a mixture of good and bad elements. It is not filled with Buddhas, Jesus, Chaitanya and other godly persons...."[93] Gandhi suggests that all possible non-violent steps should be taken to minimize these crimes, if complete elimination is not possible. "There will be crime but no criminals."[94] The function of the police force and prison will be different from the prevailing system. It will be based on non-violence as far as practicable.

But the individual man is the pivotal point of Gandhian thought. Without self-conquest, all plans of men will go astray. It is the primary duty of the individual to adopt steps so that crimes may not be committed. Most of the serious crimes are often related to property or women. As regards women they should revolutionize the ways of living and thinking; acquire purity, self-control and simplicity. As regards property, if everybody observed the vows of non-possession and bread-labour, there shall be little scope for thieving. We must reduce the number of possessions as far as practicable. Secondly, we are to bring about a reformation in the citizens living around us. Thirdly, we should preach non-thieving so fervently that the bad as well as the good will learn to look upon all possessions as their own.[95] Once the ashramites caught a thief red-handed but Gandhi in order to bring about a reformation in the mind of the thief simply rebuked him for his offence and released him. Not only this, he goes a step further and advises us not even to offer resistance to the thief who robs us of our possessions before our eyes. Gandhi says it is thus the primary duty of the individual to treat the so-called thieves, the victims of social maladies, affectionately and tenderly so that they may undergo reformation, and rehabilitate themselves as ideal citizens of the society.

Regarding the most violent clans, tribes and notorious dacoits he calls for the same treatment even if it costs our lives. A violent tribe who lived in the neighbourhood of Sabarmati Ashram gave up all sorts of criminal activities and led normal life by dint of active non-violent treatment by the Ashramites.[96] In 1938, during the Frontier tour, he called upon the brave *Khudai Khidmatgars* to bring about reformation in the lives of 'thieves, dacoits and spoilers of defenceless women' through the same non-violent way.[97] The revolutionaries of Bengal and Punjab at that time strove to attain independence through violent means. In his words, "Personally, I do not believe in imprisoning, by way of punishment, even those who commit violence. I know that those who have done violence through political motives, are entitled to claim, if not the same wisdom, certainly, the same spirit of love and self-sacrifice that I would claim for myself."[98] Thus the violent criminals, tribes, revolutionaries, etc., are to be reformed and educated through the non-violent technique of love and self-sacrifice.

What is Gandhi's view on capital punishment? His ardent spirit of humanism urged him to advocate imposition of total ban on capital punishment whatever might be the nature of crime. Because "Once a man is killed, the punishment is beyond recall or reparation."[99] This quotation clearly elucidates Gandhian standpoint on capital punishment. God is the sole creator of human beings; and a man who pronounces death sentence upon a murderer, a criminal, can never create a human being with his utmost efforts. And imperfect human knowledge, as discussed above, is always liable to error. A criminal who has committed a murder out of sheer madness should not be revenged by the social system because the aforesaid murderer is beyond our reach and repair. So we should help the murderer to repent for his mischief and thereby reform himself.

It is evident that Gandhian view of reformation of the so-called criminals has its roots in the Gandhian concept of spiritual unity of all beings, especially of human beings. And crime, a social malady, can never pollute the inner being of an individual. That is why he preaches the removal of the disease without doing any harm to the offender who is an incarnation of Truth. And lastly, in this venture of non-violent reformation there should be no hide and seek policy. We should earn the confidence and trust of the so-called criminals by dint of love and selfless service to them. We should do nothing that may account for the betrayal of their trust. Because it would not reform, rather deform, them. Gandhi warns, "A satyagrahi would, therefore, neither retaliate nor would he submit to the criminal, but seek to cure him by curing himself...."[100] In short, his conviction of the spiritual unity of all human beings; infinite potentiality of the individual; inherent imperfection of human knowledge; and his burning humanism urged him to preach the educative or reformative theory of punishment. And it was in keeping with the temper of the age too.

(3) The third and last one of the traditional theories is the retributive view of punishment. Retribution or revengeful action was not in his temperament because it went against the pivotal principle of truth and non-violence; betrayed the spirit of reformation; and often turned a mild offender into an aggressive criminal. While launching movement for certificates of registration in South Africa in 1908 Gandhi was severely beaten by a group of Pathans led by Mir Alam. In accordance with his temperament he did not inform the

police, rather begged their release from imprisonment. This tender treatment brought the stonehearted Mir Alam to senses, who out of repentence, became a follower and friend of Gandhi in later life. In 1938 during his Frontier tour, the land of Pathans, he preached the utility of non-retaliation and recollected the aforesaid incident of reformation by saying, "This could not have happened if I had retaliated. My action can be fitly described as a process of conversion."[101] A similar attitude of non-retaliation also appears in the lenient treatment of the juvenile delinquents advocated by him on the ground that severity mars their subtle, fine, mental faculties and hardens them in crime. To quote him, "It was not permissible to punish the boys. Experience gained in two schools under my control, has taught me that punishment does not purify, if anything, it hardens children."[102] Thus Gandhi's antipathy towards revenge, retaliation or retribution is clear. Retribution loses itself in a vicious circle. It provokes the wild instinct in us to kill one another and consequently murders the entire humanity. In India where truth, non-violence, forgiveness, etc., have been preached as virtues from times immemorial, retaliation appears to him a total misfit, a blemish that lowers human dignity. In his code of conduct for the satyagrahis, he warns a satyagrahi against harbouring anger; never to retaliate for assaults even if it causes death; non-retaliation includes swearing and cursing under all circumstances.[103] Rajendra Prasad observes on Gandhian view of non-retaliation as follows: "Retaliation for some people do in one place against others, who, though they may belong to the same faith, have no part in the activities is not only opposed to all sense of justice and fairness but is inhuman and takes us back to the laws of the jungle. We should, therefore, do our part to give Gandhi the satisfaction that we do not believe in this law of the jungle."[104]

Here one more point demands elucidation. A critic may ask: Did Gandhi observe non-retaliation absolutely in his life? Did he not prescribe retaliation or retribution in some exceptional cases? At the first glance the apparent answer is: 'Yes.' Let us explain it. Gandhi says, "I have never preferred killing a dacoit to winning him over with love. But he who is not equal to that love, who cannot muster all the love that the act demands, has the right to protect his protégés and his property even by killing the dacoit...."[105] The above citation seems to be a deviation from his pivotal principle of truth and non-violence. But this is apparent, and not real. Although absolute truth was his ultimate value yet his pragmatism, his practical idealism, urged him to admit relative truth at the demand of circumstances. He firmly believed in peace, and fervently wanted it to be restored on earth. But he did not want it at any price. Further, his antipathy to war is well known. In spite of his absolute conviction in truth and non-violence he could not help approving the government sending troops to Kashmir and observe it perfectly on account of demands of circumstances. Gandhi confesses, "For me, non-violence is not a mere philosophical principle. It is the rule and the breath of my life. That is to say, the demands of nationalism and humanism, in spite of firm belief in non-violence and non-retaliation, sometimes obstructed his application of the principle of absolute non-violence and non-retaliation to practical life. An individual or a dacoit who has been repeatedly proved to be beyond reformation, and hence unworthy of love should be punished for the smooth maintenance of the social order. It is justified morally, socially and from the humanitarian standpoint too. And the so-called retaliation in rare and exceptional cases in Gandhian thought are mere 'failings' and hence should not be branded as deviations from the principle of truth and non-violence.

To conclude, on examination of the Gandhian views of crime and punishment categorized under the caption of traditional theories, we arrive at a point that apparently, and perhaps practically, seems to be unworldly. 'To err is human, to forgive is divine' is no doubt a good and humanitarian precept. Reformation of bad elements through non-violent love and tolerance is ancient, and acclaims high appreciation for its boundless humanitarian appeal. But the world is not filled, as mentioned earlier, with Jesuses, Buddhas and Chaitanyas only. There are miscreants and evilmongers too who commit mischief sometimes without any reason or for the reason best known to them. They threaten, in some cases, the very existence of the social order. So the social order, for its existence and smooth running, demands just retribution or retaliation to the offender who, through his misdeed, has lowered dignity of human beings as a whole. Of course the value of reformation through non-violent love and tolerance is never devalued. Its glory and glow will remain ever shinning so long as humanity is.

Disease as Punishment

This topic arrests our attention for its novelty, and hence demands separate elucidation. The Gandhian concept of disease as a form of punishment is something unique in the world of human thought. It is a common belief amongst the people of India that incurable and serious diseases are divine chastisements, i.e., just retribution for some sins committed by the diseased person. We have seen above that Gandhi shared the traditional view of natural calamities as divine chastisement inflicted on human beings for their sin. In his personal life also whenever he fell ill he suffered it as a just retribution or a well-deserved punishment for the breach of some principle known or unknown to him. In the month of August 1918 he had a severe attack of dysentery. He narrates, "Today I am too weak to get up or walk.... I feel like screaming. Though in such pain, I am very happy indeed. I am getting a vivid idea of what well-deserved, immediate punishment can be."[106] Here Gandhi welcomes the pain of dysentery and feels happy in thinking that the disease is a punishment for some sin committed by him, and the joyful suffering of it is the way to cure. Here the diagnosis is dictated by his moral instinct which prescribes a moral cure for the medical problem. The breach of the vow of *brahmacharya* is followed by infliction of diseases on him as punishment. Once at the insistence of Kasturba he ate a meal and suffered from acute dysentery. Since all these vows are integrally related to one another, and are conducive to self-realization any breach of them will be followed by a chastisement, i.e., disease. It is a scientific truth that an excess on the bodily system in any form causes its disorder, i.e., disease. But Gandhi's moral approach towards these medical problems is unique and mystical in character. Like other problems he views this medical one through ethico-religious glass. He lays the utmost stress on the purification of mind, the prime mover of our speech and action. If the mind is purged of all impure elements, the body will also become immune from external impurities, i.e., diseases. Purity of the mind strengthens the individual both physically and spiritually, in a sense his whole being; and blesses him with unlimited power. In short, Gandhi believes in the interaction between mind and body and tells us that mental impurity or disease leads to its manifestation in bodily disorder, i.e., disease. And the mind gets impure and corrupted through the violation of moral principles or vows. Hence diseases are inflictions of punishments on the diseased person for the violation of moral vows. It is also educative and reformative in the sense that it warns us to get reformed and take care for the future.

But this view of disease as punishment for the breach of moral vows, for the commission of some sin faces difficulties for its mystical and unintelligible character. With Nietzsche one may raise objection, "Poor humanity;—A single drop of blood too much or too little in the brain may render our life unspeakably miserable and difficult, and we may suffer more from this single drop of blood than Prometheus from his vulture. But the worst is when we do not know that this drop is causing our sufferings—and we think it is the devil! Or Sin!"[107] A critic, after H. Lotze may say that the attempt to find the origin of physical ailment in supernatural power has no scientific basis. H. Lotze says, "Neither experience nor *a priori* theory lend any colour to the assumption that the sin of man produced physical evil in the order of nature. The view attracts men on account of its mystic and unintelligible character, but has no other recommendations."[108] Thus a man of science, especially a man of medicine, may not accept the Gandhian approach to physical disorder (disease) from moral standpoint. This concept of disease as punishment may appear irrational and unscientific to any analytical mind. But we have seen above that Gandhi is primarily an ethico-religious person who treated each and every problem from this angle of vision. Not reason but faith is the ultimate arbiter in his life. He preached and practised what he believed. And who does not know that faith supersedes reason?

Prayer, Self-purification, Fasting, etc., as Reformative Measures of Crime

Gandhian concept of crime and punishment, its reformative or educative treatment, has corollaries too. Closely connected with the above topic are his concepts of prayer, self-purification, fasting, etc. We have seen above that Gandhi laid more importance on purity of an individual, especially his inner being, the sole aim of which is self-realization. He believed that unless the inner world of our being is reformed and purified, the infliction of mere external oppression can never transform us, and thereby help us towards self-realization. So he wanted to mould, to reform, each and every individual through vows, prayer, fasting etc. to that end. In this context D.K. Bedekar comments, "Purification through suffering is a cardinal tenet in Gandhi's concept of crime and punishment...." Here, apart from and in addition to the Hindu traditional views about purification, we have the influence of such Christian moralists as Carlyle, Emerson, and others. It is this influence that saved Gandhi from a one-sided development on the basis of Hindu Karmic thought."[109] That is to say, a sound assessment of Gandhi's concept of crime and punishment demands the elucidation of the concepts of prayer, fasting, etc., i.e., self-purification through suffering in general.

Gandhi explains prayer by saying, "*Prarthna* (Gujarati word for prayer) literally means to ask for something, that is, to ask God for something in a spirit of humility. Here it is not used in that sense, but in the sense of praising or worshipping God, meditation and self-purification.... When we speak out aloud at prayer time, our speech is addressed not to God but to ourselves, and is intended to shake off our torpor."[110] Thus from the spiritual standpoint the aim of prayer is to establish communion with God; from the social standpoint it endeavours to bring about peace, orderliness and repose in individual life so that the social system may be free from all sorts of disorders committed by human beings. In fact, the prayer, when chanted aloud, creates a symphonic effect with tremendous power on us as a result of which our world of thought and action often undergoes purgation and help us to transform ourselves purer and better bit by bit.

He draws our attention to the offences unseen and unobserved by the external agencies. Our unseen and unobserved offences often, being undetected, go unpunished. In such cases Gandhi calls for self-punishment and self-reformation through prayer, fasting, self-sufference and self-sacrifice. To quote him, "Prayer is a confession of one's unworthiness and weakness."[111] "Prayer is not an asking. It is a longing of the soul. It is a daily admission of one's weakness."[112] Here the influence of the confessional method of Christian church is evident. The free and frank confession of an individual's flaws and offences gives him a sublime insight by dint of which he rectifies and reforms himself through self-imposed disciplines, i.e., punitive measures. In his words, "To confess an error or sin as soon as it is discovered is to purge it out."[113] "For, confession of error is like a broom that sweeps away dirt and leaves the surface cleaner than before, I feel stronger for my confession."[114] He practised as he preached. In 1922 the non-violent movement of Chauri Chaura suddenly took a violent turn. Gandhi suspended the movement immediately and underwent a self-imposed punitive measure of five days' continuous fast holding himself responsible for the commission of violence by the masses. He exclaims, "I must undergo personal cleansing. I must become a fitter instrument able to register the slightest variation in the moral atmosphere about me. My prayers must have much deeper truth and humility about them than they evidence. And for me there is nothing so helpful and cleansing as a fast accompanied by the necessary mental co-operation."[115] Not only this, as discussed above, he feels and believes in the natural calamities as divine chastisement, calling for inward purification. During the communal disturbance in 1947 he undertook a fast for an indefinite time as a penance for the commission of mischiefs in the surroundings. He availed himself of the fast as a process of self-purification, and felt happy. In his words, "...the fast is undertaken. I have been brooding over it for the last three days. The final conclusion has flashed upon me and it makes me happy."[116] Gandhi tells us that in the midst of earthly affairs of our everyday lives we should strive to fill our minds with constant prayer so that our activities are conducted by spiritual urge. This spiritual outlook will mould and reform our activities in such a pattern that there shall be no scope for crime and mischiefs in social order. He brings forth the reformative and social significance of fasting by saying, "All fasting and all penance must as far as possible be secret. But my fasting is both a penance and punishment, and a punishment has to be public. It is penance for me and punishment for those whom I try to serve, for whom I love to live and would equally love to die."[117] It is here noteworthy that in Gandhian thought prayer and fasting are integrally related to one another. Fasting is 'the sincerest form of prayer'; and fasting without prayer turns into a mere torture of the flesh. That is to say, prayer is not a mere mechanical movement of our lips, a parrot-like repetition of some words or verses. It is verily "a yearning from within which expresses itself in every word, every act, nay every thought of man."[118] In other words, prayer must spring from the core of our hearts. Similarly, fasting is also not a mere starvation of the body. It means starvation of all senses in thought, word and deed. An almost similar view of self-contentment in self-sacrifice and self-sufference appears in the writing of F.H. Bradley;[119] and in Karl Jaspers,[120] Leo Kuper,[121] etc., of course with some variations, of the West. These thinkers renovate the significance of self-sacrifice, and point to a new orientation of the problem. It contributes immensely to a sound understanding of Gandhian meaning-system, of course in the present context. In the hands of Gandhi, prayer, fasting, self-sacrifice, etc., culminated in a moral disciplinary force to fight the evils that threaten to vitiate the inner self. In the individual it aims at self-conquest, i.e., liberation of the self from within. In the outer world as a moral weapon it creates a tremendous impact on the mass-populace for the liberation of motherland.

To conclude: Gandhi prescribed heart-felt prayer, fasting and self-mortification in general in the garb of religious ideals to fulfil some social end. According to him, man is the centre of all activities; and purity, both inner and outer especially the former, is the nucleus of man. The offences and crimes of the so-called criminals are reformed on being detected by the social authorities. But our undetected crimes and offences are also no less punishable. Moreover, the unseen evil thoughts which are often the roots of all misdeeds demand punishment for the sake of morality and justice. The majesty of moral law in order to maintain justice demands punishment for our unseen, unobserved, unpunished thoughts and deeds. It is a fact that these crimes, nay offences, although undetected by others are best known to men who committed them secretly. It is a moral obligation on the part of the individual who through violation of moral laws, and commission of crimes and offences, has undermined the majesty of moral law, and offended humanity in general, and himself as a spark of Truth or God, to suffer the just penalty for his actions. This is the underlying truth behind Gandhi's prescription of prayer, fasting and self-sacrifice or self-sufference in general. Indeed, heart-felt prayer, fasting and self-sufferance often make us purer and better. Since they are self-imposed disciplinary actions, more precisely punitive measures, they are the most effective reformatory influences on the persons concerned. The criminal in man, like the legendary bird, Phoenix, burns himself in the fire of purification, and rises, purged clean of the blemishes of past life, re-oriented, reborn, an incarnation of Gandhian Truth or God.

References

1. *An Autobiography*, p. 25.
2. Kant, *Critique of Practical Reason*, pp. 344-48.
3. *Ibid.*, p. 345.
4. *Ibid.*
5. Kant, *op. cit.*, p. 347.
6. F.H. Bradley, *Ethical Studies*, pp. 314, 334 and 342.
7. R.C. Lodge, *Plato's Theory of Ethics*, p. 270.
8. Aristotle, *The Nicomachean Ethics*, BK, I, Ch. II, trans. *The Ethics of Aristotle* by J. Thomson, pp. 14-15.
9. H.A. Wolfson, *The Philosophy of Spinoza*, pp. 240-41.
10. *Ibid.*, p. 235.
11. Spinoza, *Ethics*, Ch. IV, prop. 18, cited in H.A. Wolfson, *op. cit.*, pp. 241-43.
12. G.R. Mure, *The Philosophy of Hegel*, p. 51, fn.

13. *Ibid.*, p. 56.
14. W.T. Stace, *The Philosophy of Hegel*, p. 427.
15. *Ethical Religion*, p. 4.
16. *Ibid.*, p. 7.
17. *Ibid.*, p. 18.
18. *Ibid.*, p. 20.
19. *CWMG*, vol. XXI, p. 483.
20. Ethical Religion, p. 6.
21. Tendulkar, *op. cit.*, vol. II, p. 160.
22. *Harijan*, 19 February 1938, p. 10.
23. *An Autobiography*, pp. 370-71; also *Young India*, 2 March 1922, p. 131.
24. V.M. Bedekar, 'The Vrata in Ancient Indian Culture and Gandhi,' in *Gandhi Marg*, vol. IV, no. 4, Oct., 1960, p. 312.
25. D.M. Datta, *The Philosophy of Mahatma Gandhi*, p. 139.
26. G. Stephens Spinks, 'Politics and Morality,' in Kshitis Roy (ed.), *Gandhi Memorial Peace Number*, pp. 205-9.
27. *CWMG*, vol. XLVII, p. 246.
28. Shriman Narayan, *Mahatma Gandhi: The Atomic Man*, p. 77.
29. William Shakespeare, 'King Lear, Act. I: 89-92,' in *William Shakespeare: The Complete Works*, p. 1074.
30. S. Radhakrishnan (ed.), *Mahatma Gandhi*, p. 291.
31. J.B. Kripalani, *Gandhian Thought*, pp. 139-40.
32. D.M. Datta, *op. cit.*, p. 140.
33. *Hind Swaraj*, p. 27.
34. Buddhadeva Bhattacharyya, *Evolution of the Political Philosophy of Gandhi*, pp. 151-52.
35. *CWMG*, vol. XIX, p. 571; also *Young India*, 29 September 1927, p. 329.
36. *Harijan*, 16 December 1939, p. 376.
37. Gunnar Myrdal, *Asian Drama: An Inquiry into the Poverty of Nations*, vol. II, pp. 755-56.
38. Buddhadeva Bhattacharyya, *op. cit.*, p. 271.
39. *Harijan*, 31 July 1937, p. 197.
40. D.M. Datta, *op. cit.*, p. 134.
41. *Harijan*, 9 October 1937, p. 292; also *Young India*, 15 September 1927, pp. 306, 312.
42. D.M. Datta, *op. cit.*, p. 35.
43. D.M. Datta, *op. cit.*, p. 36.
44. *CWMG*, vol. XXXVII, p. 350; also Tendulkar, *op. cit.*, vol. VII, p. 189.
45. Hermann Lotze, *Outlines of a Philosophy of Religion*, p. 141.
46. B.G. Ray, *Gandhian Ethics*, pp. 22-23.
47. Gopinath Dhawan, *The Political Philosophy of Mahatma Gandhi*, p. 52.
48. B.G. Ray, *op. cit.*, p. 22.
49. Buddhadeva Bhattacharyya, *op. cit.*, p. 84.
50. *Harijan*, 20 February 1937, p. 9.

51. *Ibid.*, 14 September 1947, pp. 323-24; also Tendulkar, *op. cit.*, vol. VIII, p. 106.
52. Tendulkar, *op. cit.*, vol. VII, p. 144.
53. *Harijan*, 9 June 1946, p. 172.
54. *CWMG*, vol. XIX, p. 202.
55. Tendulkar, *op. cit.*, vol. VII, p. 377.
56. *Harijan*, 7 September 1935, p. 234.
57. Tendulkar, *op. cit.*, vol. II, p. 200.
58. *CWMG*, vol. XXI, p. 453.
59. Tendulkar, *op. cit.*, vol. II, p. 100.
60. *CWMG*, vol. XVIII, p. 195.
61. *Ibid.*, vol. LVII, p. 165.
62. *Ibid.*, vol. XXXI, p. 440.
63. *Ibid.*, vol. LVII, pp. 164-65.
64. F. Nietzsche, *David Strauss*, 7, in John T. Wilcox, *Truth and Value in Nietzsche*, p. 30.
65. *CWMG*, vol. LVII, p. 166.
66. *Ibid.*, p. 165.
67. Rabindranath Tagore, Cited in *In Search of the Supreme*, vol. I, p. 96.
68. *Ibid.*, pp. 95-96.
69. *CWMG*, vol. LVII, pp. 164-66.
70. For details regarding theories of punishment, see essays on 'Crimes and Punishments' in James Hastings (ed.), *Encyclopaedia of Religion and Ethics*, vol. IV, pp. 248-305.
71. *Gautma-Dharma-Sutra*, 2 February 1928.
72. *Matsya Purana*, 147-71.
73. *Manusmrti*, 7.22.
74. *Gautma-Dharma-Sutra*, 2-2-31.
75. *Sukra-Niti*, 1-23.
76. *Bhagavata-Purana*, 10-16-34.
77. *Milindapanho*, University of Bombay, 1940, p. 120.
78. *Varaha-Purana*, 187-98.
79. *Bhagavata-Purana*, 10-8-31.
80. *Manusmrti*, 10.56.
81. For details, see Untò Tahtinen, *Ahimsa (Non-violence) in Indian Tradition*, pp. 99-103.
82. Tendulkar, *op. cit.*, vol. IV, p. 299.
83. Tendulkar, *op. cit.*, vol. I, p. 100.
84. *Ibid.*, vol. IV, p. 316.
85. Gene Sharp, *Gandhi Wields the Weapon of Moral Power*, p. 3.
86. *Ibid.*, p. XII.
87. *Bapu's Letters to Mira*, p. 218.
88. *Harijan*, 11 August 1946, p. 255.
89. *Ibid.*

90. *Ibid.*, 2 November 1947, pp. 395-96.
91. *Ibid.*, 31 July 1937, p. 198; also pp. 180, 195.
92. *CWMG*, vol. XXVII, p. 133.
93. *Ibid.*, 31 July 1937, p. 196.
94. *Ibid.*, 5 May 1944, p. 124.
95. *Ashram Observances in Action*, p. 46.
96. F. Marry Barr, *Conversations and Correspondence with Mahatma Gandhi*, p. 38.
97. Tendulkar, *op. cit.*, vol. IV, pp. 298-9.
98. Cited in B.P. Sitaramayya, *The History of the Indian National Congress*, vol. I, p. 753.
Y99. *Young India*, II, p. 862.
100. Tendulkar, *op. cit.*, vol. VII, p. 190.
101. *Ibid.*, vol. IV, p. 298.
102. *Ibid.*, vol. II, p. 218.
103. R.R. Diwakar, *Satyagraha : The Power of Truth*, p. 99.
104. *The Times of India*, 14 January 1948, p. 5.
105. *Young India*, 14 August 1924, p. 268.
106. *CWMG*, vol. XV, p. 18.
107. F. Nietzsche, 'The Dawn, 83', in J.T. Wilcox, *Truth and Value in Nietzsche*, p. 88.
108. Hermann Lotze, *op. cit.*, p. 143.
109. D.K. Bedekar, *Towards Understanding Gandhi*, p. 156; also his essay; 'Gandhi's Concept of Crime and Punishment,' in *Gandhi Marg*, vol. II, 1958, p. 22.
110. *Ashram Observances in Action*, pp. 35-36.
111. *Young India*, 24 September 1925, p. 331; also *CWMG*, vol. XXVIII, p. 207.
112. *CWMG*, vol. XXXI, p. 440; also *Young India*, 23 September 1926, p. 333.
113. *Harijan*, 20 October 1946, p. 367.
114. *CWMG*, vol. XXII, p. 417.
115. *Ibid.*, p. 419.
116. *Harijan*, 18 January 1948, p. 523.
117. *CWMG*, vol. XXII, p. 420.
118. *Young India*, III, pp. 976-77.
119. F.H. Bradley, *Ethical Studies*, pp. 309-10.
120. Karl Jaspers, *The Future of Mankind*, pp. 42-43; also his essays 'Gandhi and the Concept of Sacrifice,' in *Gandhi Marg*, vol. VII, no. 1, 1963, pp. 17-18.
121. Leo Kuper, cited in Buddhadeva Bhattacharyya, *op. cit.*, p. 301.

7

CARDINAL VIRTUES

Traditional Virtues

The etymological meaning of the term virtue was associated with manliness or valour in ancient Greece. The Latin word *vir* means a courageous man or hero; the Greek word *ares* and the German word *tugend* also convey an almost similar meaning. Generally, the term virtue connotes a good habit, more specifically an acquired one, while the term duty indicates some action which we ought to perform. The former refers to the inner universe of an individual, and the latter points to its outer manifestation. That is to say, an individual performs his duty in the external world while a virtue is inhered or possessed by him. Aristotle defines it as "a disposition developed out of a capacity by the proper exercise of that capacity."[1] It is a permanent state of mind acquired through habitual performance of duty. It is a settled habit of willing in conformity with the moral law. It involves knowledge, wisdom or moral insight, and a habit of performing duties. Plato and Aristotle prescribed the life of reason for a virtuous man. Plato's four cardinal virtues are : wisdom (or prudence), courage (or fortitude), temperance (or self-restraint), and justice (or righteousness). Aristotle, however, differed from Plato in some respects and with a view to making a perfect list of virtues, he added some derivative virtues besides the cardinal ones. Two points are remarkable in this context. Both of them believed that the essence of virtue lies in the moderation of the senses (instinct, emotion, feeling, etc.,) or their subjection to the majesty of the moral law of reason. Secondly, to both of them, since 'man is a political animal' in the sense of an inhabitant of a society of whatever nature it might be, the virtue which the individual acquires or inheres must have a reference to the social well being. Wisdom (truthfulness in Gandhi), courage (fearlessness in Gandhian ethics), and temperance (continence in Gandhian virtues), etc., are common also amongst the cardinal virtues prescribed by the Indian ethical systems.

We have seen above that the mind of Gandhi was fed and nurtured in the *sanatani* tradition of Indian culture and heritage. He derived his inspiration and nourishment from this source, of course, in his own style. So a very brief sketch of the traditional cardinal virtues of Indian systems of thought may not be irrelevant here. Manu, the father of Hindu code, laid stress on non-appropriation (avoidance of theft, *chauryabhava*) repression of the sensibilities and sensuous appetites (*indriyanigraha*), veracity (*satya*), restraint of anger (*akrodha*), etc., amongst the *sadharan dharmas* or general virtues.[2] Prasastapada, the well-known exponent of Vaisesika philosophy prescribed along with others refraining from injury to living beings (*ahimsa*); seeking the good of the creatures (*bhutahitava*); speaking the truth (*satyavachana*); refraining from theft (*asteya*); sexual continence (*brahmacharya*); renouncing or restraining anger (*krodhavarjana*), etc., as generic or *samanya* duties to be observed by all irrespective of caste and creed.[3] Patanjali, the great Indian saint, in his *Yogasutra* prescribes eight-fold means by dint of which we can purge ourselves of all impurities of the mind; and, consequently, attain purification and enlightenment of *chitta* or the mind. The first of these eight-fold means is *yama* or restraint which consists of a group of virtues namely *ahimsa* (the spirit of non-injury to all creatures irrespective of limitation of caste, place and time); *satya* or veracity (conformity of word, thought and deed to facts of everyday life); *asteya* (the absence of desire for other's property. It includes both nonstealing and mental abstinence from hankering after another's property); *brahmacharya* or continence (control of the carnal desires and passions); *aparigraha* (non-attachment and non-acceptance of unnecessaries). These virtues, Patanjali holds, are universally applicable, i.e., there is no limitation as to their objects, place, time and scope (*jatideskalasamayanavacchinnah sarvanhauma mahavratam*).[4] These cardinal virtues of Patanjali show the necessity of complete abstention from all evil courses and tendencies of life which obstruct the path to self-realization.

Now let us take the Jaina doctrine of virtues. In the very first *sutra* of *Tattavarthadhigama-sutra*, Umasvami tells us that the way to *moksa* or liberation is through right faith, right knowledge, and right conduct (*samyagdarsana-jnana-charitrani moksa-margah*).[5] S. Radhakrishnan observes, "The way to *nirvana* lies through the three jewels (*triratna*) of faith in Jina, knowledge of his doctrine and perfect conduct. Belief in real existence or *tattavas* is right faith; knowledge of real nature without doubt or error is right knowledge. An attitude of neutrality without desire or aversion towards the objects of the external world is right conduct. The three together form one path, and are to be simultaneously pursued."[6] Knowledge, faith and conduct are inseparably bound up; and perfection of conduct goes hand in hand with the perfection of knowledge and faith. There is a great deal of controversy amongst the Jaina thinkers as regards the steps necessary for perfection of conduct. But in some way or other they accepted the five great vows (*panchamahavrata*) as the basic principles for perfection of conduct (*charitra*). These five great vows are: (1) *ahimsa* or abstinence from all injury to life, moving and non-moving; and also non-injury to everything in thought, speech and action; (2) *satyam* or *suntra* means truthfulness which consists in not speaking what is only true but speaking what is true as well as good and pleasant; (3) *asteyam* or abstinence from stealing. It forbids us not to take anything that is not given to us; (4) *brahmacharya* or renunciation of all kinds of self-indulgence (*kama*). It is not mere sexual self-continence, as traditionally interpreted, rather it includes abstinence from all actual and potential self-indulgence in speech, thought and deed; (5) *aparigraha* or abstinence from all kinds of attachment to sensuous objects, i.e., objects of sound, touch, colour, taste and smell. It is here noteworthy that the last four virtues (*suntra, asteya, brahmacarya* and *aparigraha*) may be directly derived from *ahimsa* as corollaries. One point more. "The Jaina list does not include the other-regarding virtues of Benevolence, Succour and Social Service. This shows that the Jaina virtues aim more at self-culture than at social service."[7]

Buddhism rejects both self-indulgence and self-mortification, and preaches an ethics of moderation. The eight-fold path (*astangikamarga*) recommended by Buddha for the attainment of *nirvana* or liberation contains in a nutshell the essentials of Buddhist ethics. The eight-fold path comprises: (1) *samyagdrsti* (right views) or sound knowledge of the four noble truths; (2) *samyaksamkalpa* (right resolve) means firm determination to renounce all sorts of attachment to the world, to abandon ill-feeling and doing harm to others; (3) *samyagvak* (right speech) means truthfulness and abstention from lying, slander, abuse and silly talk; (4) *samyagkarmanta* (right conduct) consists in abstention from killing, stealing, illegal and excessive self-indulgence, lying and intoxication. These virtues are collectively known as *Pancha-Sila*, the five great vows; (5) *samyagajiva* (right livelihood) is the earning of one's livelihood by honest means; (6) *samyagvyayama* (right effort) means constant vigilance to maintain moral progress alive; abandonment of evil thoughts and entertainment of good ideas; (7) *samyaksmrti* (right mindfulness) is constant remembrance and contemplation of the exact nature of body, everything mundane and four noble truths; (8) *samyagsamadhi* (right concentration) consists of four types of meditation. It is through the strict observance of these eight-fold path that an individual attains *nirvana*.[8] In Buddhism the altruistic trend—i.e., other-regarding virtues—predominates. The humanistic note of Buddhist ethics is beyond question. Surama Dasgupta aptly comments, Buddhism has contributed greatly to the psychological and moral analysis of man and his spiritual achievements...great emphasis has been laid on moral excellence of men, love and compassion for all beings....Their heart became so tender in love and compassion for others that they would rather postpone their final attainment till all living beings became liberated."[9]

In the Vedanta school also virtues of a similar type are prescribed as pre-requisites for the realization of the Brahman. The virtues of *dama* (sense control), *sama* (mind-control), *uparati* (absence of mental agitation), fearlessness, purity, non-injury, truthfulness, sacrifice, self-abnegation, want of greed, forgivingness, etc., are noteworthy.[10] In the beginning of the sixteenth chapter of the *Gita* quite a good number of virtues are enumerated as godly qualities (*daivi sampadam*). The cardinal virtues amongst them are: *avayam* (fearlessness), *sattvasamsuddhi* (purity of mind), *danam* (charity), *damah* (sense-control), *tapah* (austerities), *arjjabam* (simplicity), *ahimsa* (non-injury in thought, word and deed), *satyam* (truthfulness), *akrodha* (absence of anger), *adroha* (absence of enmity), etc., (16.1-2). These godly virtues are to be observed by everybody for the attainment of *moksa* or liberation.

To sum up: The prescription of the five cardinal virtues (non-injury, truthfulness, non-stealing, continence and non-attachment) is common to almost all Indian schools of thought. And knowledge and morality are thought to be inseparable because perfection of knowledge is regarded impossible without moral uplift. Two eminent scholars observe, "The value of the five great vows is recognized by the Upanisadic thinkers as well as the Buddhas (who teach the *Pancha sila*). The principles of most of these are recognized also in the commandments of the Bible."[11] The influence of these cardinal virtues is remarkable in Gandhian ethics.

Concept of Vow (Vrata)

Before we take into account the Gandhian view of cardinal virtues, one point demands special elaboration for a better understanding of Gandhian standpoint. The term *vrata* or vow, as the history of ancient literary works reveals, was originally associated with divine will or divine regulation. The oldest meaning of *vrata* is found in the *Rg Veda* where it is interpreted as "divine will or command."[12] All existents of the universe, natural and non-natural, through their spontaneous actions observe the inviolable and inexorable command or *vrata* of God. The order of nature and human society, the well-disciplined movements of the heavenly bodies, and natural forces were treated as the observance of the *vrata* of God. In the *Upanisad* we are told, "That the organ of speech speaks, the eye sees, the fire burns, and the breath breaths is explained by the fact that they observe the *vrata*."[13] But this concept of the observance of divine *varata* got intermingled with mundane affairs in course of time and acquired social, economic, moral and other implications of our everyday lives.

Virtues or *vratas* in spite of divinity as their characteristic cannot reside in a vacuum. It is the individual who as a social being observes and orients them. Naturally the religious aspect of *vrata* got blended with socio-economic demands. Still today, the *vrata* observed in different parts of India, especially in West Bengal, although enveloped in ritual performances are aimed to achieve some social purpose. This social significance of virtues is aptly described by John Mackenzie who says, "Now the virtues that are current among a people at a given time are the expression in particular forms of the Ethos of that people; and their significance can be appreciated only in relation to the general life of the times...."[14] This social significance of virtues is clearly evident in Gandhian ethics. Gandhi inherited this tendency for observing *vrata* or vow, from his pious mother; and from the Jaina tradition of his native state. He did not like any watertight division in different walks of life. So his ethico-religious mind spontaneously accepted ethical religion. Self-realization or liberation of the self was impossible without political freedom which in its turn, he felt, was impossible without social and economic uplift. So it was ardent humanism which urged him to interpret vow, a ritual one, in its diverse forms according to the conditions of society, time and space.

A relevant question arises here: What is the nature of vow that Gandhi had in his mind? We can bring out the following characteristics of vow or *vrata* from the statements made by Gandhi on different occasions.

Firstly, "A vow means unflinching determination, and helps us against temptations...The universal experience of humanity supports the view that progress is impossible without inflexible determination."[15] Inflexible determination is the sole, nay predominating, characteristic of vow or *vrata*. If a determination becomes unstable and admits of concession under the compulsion of unavoidable circumstances, it loses its status and value.

Secondly, "To shirk taking of vows betrays indecision and want of resolution. One never can achieve anything lasting in this world by being irresolute."[16] This is practically a corollary of the first one. A general or a soldier can never win without absolute vow or firm determination. A watchman who thinks that he would keep vigilance as long as he can, can never protect the property of his master. A drunkard can never give up addiction if he indulges 'an occasional cup' as nothing. This means that once a vow is taken, it is taken for ever without any concession under all circumstances. A vow nobly determined should be observed at any cost, even at the cost of life itself. To quote Gandhi, "My religion teaches me that a promise once made or a vow once taken for a worthy object may not be broken."[17]

Thirdly, vows are universal or based on universally recognized principles. That is to say, vows of 'dubious matters' and those of particular self-interest, fail to command universal assent; and hence are not vows in the truest sense of the term. Telling the truth or truthfulness is a universally accepted moral virtue. But 'telling a lie' is not so because of its inherent contradiction. Again, total abstinence from liquor is a great virtue. A *satyagrahi* will completely abstain from it even if it is required on medical grounds. It is here noteworthy that as a *vaisnava* he did not permit ailing Kasturba to take beef even when doctors insisted on it on medical grounds. Thus, to him, a vow is universal and inexorable.

Fourthly, a vow is a positive virtue, and never a negative one. It has been alleged that "vows are a sign of weakness, and may even be harmful."[18] But these allegations are based on misunderstanding and ill-digestion of the spirit of Gandhian concept of vow. Gandhi argues, "Taking vows is not a sign of weakness, but of strength. To do at any cost something that one ought to do constitutes a vow. It becomes a bulwark of strength."[19] Like *ahimsa* or non-violence, a vow is a weapon of the strongest. Its uncompromising attitude gives birth to unlimited moral courage which the statement 'as far as possible' lacks. A close scrutiny will show that the statement 'as far as possible' reveals pride, weakness; and provides 'a fatal loophole' due to its inherent contradiction.

Fifthly, a vow is a godly virtue because "God is the very image of the vow."[20] Here, to Gandhi, God appears to be the living incarnation of vow. God is God because he observes vows "even by a hair's breadth." Gandhian concept of godly nature of virtue is in conformity with scriptural concept of vow as divine command.

Sixthly, a vow is not only godly but also human, and is practically indispensable. The order of human existence is absolutely dependent upon observance of vows. The order of human society would become stagnant and dead without the observance of vows. In his words, "In fact our entire social fabric rests on the sanctity of the pledged word. The world would go to pieces if there was not this element of stability or finality in agreements arrived at."[21]

Seventhly, a vow is not only godly and human but also individualistic in the sense that an individual life without any vow would go astray. To Gandhi, a vow imparts mental stability, ballast, firmness and other qualities of valour to one's character by dint of which an individual can face, vehemently and efficiently, the harsh realities of life. It makes heroes out of clay, and infuses life to semi-comatic people. It is a touchstone that removes the barriers between the high and the low, the poor and the rich, and cleanses other odds of our lives. Just as a right angle makes "all the differences between ugliness and elegance, solidity and shakiness of a gigantic structure" so also "stability or instability, purity or otherwise of an entire career" of an individual solely depends upon the taking of a vow.

Eighthly, a vow not only infuses stability and firmness to our characters but also enriches it with moderation, sobriety, calm and quietness; and other subtle qualities of our minds. During the struggle for independence the *satyagrahis* fought with stability and sobriety, firmness and moderation, solid-rock determination and calmness against the mighty imperialist force. The amalgamation of these contrary and contradictory qualities is a resultant of vow-taking on the part of *satyagrahis*.

Ninthly, "self-restraint is the very keystone of the ethics of vow-taking. For instance, one cannot take a vow of self-indulgence, to eat, drink and be merry, in short, to do as one pleases....A vow must lead one upwards, never downwards towards perdition."[22] A critical survey of the eleven vows will disclose the fact that self-control plays a pivotal role in the life of a *satyagrahi*. Without self-restraint the vows would not be what they are. Moreover, self-restraint and vow-taking infuse impetus and stimulus into the life and thought of 'most of us.' In this sense, it opens a new horizon to our lives. To quote Gandhi, "vows are to the weak mind and soul what tonics are to a weak body."[23]

Tenthly, universal feasibility is another characteristic of a vow. Vows are easily practicable, and at the same time within the capacity of every individual. Gandhi prescribed these vows "for acceptance by mankind in general." A vow, if conditional, will not loss its efficacy or virtue. An individual may not, due to other engagements, dedicate whole of his working hours to spinning. But he may take a vow to spin for at least one hour everyday without fail except in unavoidable circumstances such as travelling, ailment, etc. Here also, the predominance of means in the means-ends controversy is noteworthy.

To sum up: A vow is an unflinching determination; absolutely resolute; universal; a bulwark of strength; godly, human and individualistic; indispensable for character-building and self-restraint; and commonly feasible.

Cardinal Virtues

Let us turn to the elaboration of cardinal virtues. On 25 May 1915, Gandhi founded *satyagrahasrama* at Kochrab, Ahmedabad, since removed to Sabarmati, a junction station near Ahmedabad. The object of this *ashram* was to render service to the country; to attain self-sufficiency and self-realization through self-purification. This self-realization through self-purification involves an intense training in moral discipline the observance of which leads to an integrated whole. These steps or vows are: (1) Truth, (2) Non-violence or love, (3) Chastity, (4) Control of the Palate; (5) Non-stealing, (6) Non-possession or poverty, (7) Physical labour, (8) *Swadeshi*, (9) Fearlessness, (10) Removal of untouchability, (11) Tolerance.[24] Of the above vows *satya* (truth), *ahimsa* (non-violence), *brahmacharya* (chastity or celibacy), *asteya* (non-stealing), *aparigraha* (non-possession) were being observed for thousands of years in India as indispensably necessary for the moral development of an individual. These five virtues or vows were prescribed by the *Upanisads*, the Buddhists, the Jainas, the *yoga* system; and in some form or other by Manu, Prasastapada and others. In early boyhood he read *Manusmriti* which was in his father's collection. In 1903 while staying in South Africa he "read Patanjali's "Yoga Sutras" along with other scriptures. And the five commandments of the Sermon on the Mount, particularly as they were illustrated by Tolstoy in the fourth chapter of his *The Kingdom of God is Within You*, influenced and strengthened to a great extent Gandhi's firm conviction in the strict observance of five vows. He confesses that although the Old Testament "invariably sent me to sleep...the Sermon on the Mount...went straight to my heart."[25] And long before the prescription of these vows in 1916 Gandhi believed and lived to a great extent up to the ideals of these great vows of ancient India. It may be noted that the spirit of these vows lies in their sincere and honest observance; in proper performance of them in thought, in speech, and in action (*manasa, vachasa, kayen*). Gandhi surmised that if mind, speech and action did not form an integrated whole, the whole programme for moral uplift would turn into a lip service, a mere show-off; and mar the whole purpose. Let us explain the eleven vows one by one.

(1) *Truth (Satya):* In every phase of his life the concepts of truth and non-violence are so intermingled with one another that it appears to be a difficult task to elucidate them with all implications. In the foregoing chapters we have dealt with the religious (Truth is God); ethical (Truth as the ultimate moral standard); epistemological (a self-styled *syadvadi*, and an absolute idealist); metaphysical (substance and casuality), etc., implications of Truth. Still this demands more elaboration for an adequate understanding of Gandhian concept of truth as a cardinal virtue.

The various systems of Indian thought in spite of their differences in other fields have one point in common: the quest of truth. In a sense it is the pivotal point of their philosophical discourse although they differ as regards approach to it. The ancient Indian philosophical literature, to put it in other words, with its dialectic, logic, etc., i.e., speculative methods of knowing point to paramount importance of truth in our lives. The common slogan is: *Satyannasti paro dharmah*: there is no religion or duty greater than truth. Truth (*satya*) and non-violence (*ahimsa*) were being observed in India for thousands of years as indispensable cardinal virtues for the moral uplift of an individual. In some form or other veracity or truthfulness was prescribed by the Upanisads, the Buddhists, the Jainas, the Yoga system, Manu, Prasastapada and others. This virtue of truthfulness or veracity of 'holding to truth' is widely popular amongst the people of India whether literate or illiterate, speculative thinker or unsophisticated villager. It forms an integral part of mass education through traditional folklore.

The moral of the traditional stories like those of Dhruva, Harishchandra, Prahlad, especially the last two, engraved a permanent mark; and had a far-reaching direct influence in his life. To quote him, "This play—Harishchandra—captured my heart. I could never be tired of seeing it...."[26] He often quoted, of course in connection with truthfulness, the story of Prahlad, a young boy who suffered inhuman torture at the hands of his father, Hiranyakasiap, for the sake of truth. Gandhi referred to Prahlad's insistence upon holding to the truth on numerous occasions to illustrate the spirit and concept of *satyagraha* to the people. The whole of his life may be summed up as a quest of truth or an experiment in truth. As discussed above, veracity or truthfulness is enlisted amongst the cardinal virtues of ancient India as an aid to the moral and spiritual uplift of an individual. It imposes no duty on the individual towards social life in the positive sense of the term. The originality of Gandhi lies in the expansion and implementation of the traditional concept of truth to a greater field of life. He released it from the ethico-spiritual bondage; and applied efficiently and to a greater extent successfully to every walk of life—social, political, aesthetic, ethical, religious, etc. In his words, "The quest for truth cannot be prosecuted in a cave. Silence makes no sense where it is necessary to speak. One may live in a cave in certain circumstances, but the common man can be tested only in society."[27] As mentioned above, Gandhi was primarily an ethico-religious man who dedicated his life to the quest of truth underlying the various interrelations amongst human beings. The whole structure of his constructive programme (e.g., handspinning, handweaving, communal amity, removal of untouchability, prohibition, etc.,) aims at the pursuit of truth and non-violence. He accepted the traditional concepts in so far as they promoted the realization of truth. He reoriented them only to achieve some revolutionary goal, to awaken the semi-comatic nation from its age-old slumber. This ascription of social values to truth, primarily an ethico-religious concept, is a remarkable feature of Gandhian thought.

Yet another characteristic of truth demands special elucidation. The relative or non-absolutistic feature of truth plays a significant role in Gandhian thought. Although we have partially dealt with it above (*supra*: truth: The ultimate moral standard) yet more elaboration is necessary for a proper and precise assessment of Gandhian position. Gandhi says, "...I am but a seeker after Truth. I claim to have found the way to it. I claim to be making a ceaseless effort to find it. But I admit that I have not yet found it. To find Truth completely is to realize oneself and one's destiny, i.e., to become perfect. I am painfully conscious of my imperfections, and therein lies all the strength I possess, because it is a rare thing for a man to know his own limitations."[28] "...You never reach the final truth, you only reach an approximation, and that too if you are extra careful in your dealings."[29] That is to say, to Gandhi the absolute truth or God is only an ideal or utopia. One can only proceed towards its realization bit by bit but never reach it. This inevitable failure on the part of mortals is due to his inherent imperfections which he can never overcome. A human being is destined to fall short of it. This failure on the part of human beings does not take from the value and dignity of absolute truth. According to him, it is like Euclid's point which, though incapable of being drawn by any human agency, has an imperishable value for mankind. Quest of truth is inherent in human nature. Man can never rest satisfied with his failure, and sit idle. Gandhi adopts relative truth as a 'beacon, a shield and buckler' for the interim period during which absolute truth is not realized. That is to say, Gandhi's belief in the relativity of truth is initial, and not final. This acceptance on the part of Gandhi is not a deviation, from the Absolute, rather it is an admission of the reality.

A critical analysis will reveal the following implications of relative truth in Gandhian thought.

Firstly, all the existents of the universe, not to speak of men, are sparks of fragments of the absolute truth or God. And owing to inherent imperfection he falls short of the absolute truth.

Secondly, his belief in *syadvad* in the epistemological field is no less responsible for this. Like the Jainas he admitted that a particular piece of knowledge is true from a particular angle of vision (*naya*) at a particular time and situation. A statement made by an individual who is a spark of truth can never be absolutely false for our imperfection obstructs us from giving the final verdict on anything. In his words, "What appears to be truth to the one may appear to be error to the other."[30]

Thirdly, his pragmatic insight inspired him to adopt relative truth in the experiment of absolute truth. He surmised that the observance of absolute truth on the part of ordinary beings is impossible. So in order to serve the problems of everyday life relative truth should be the medium of struggle. Of course, this relative truth must attain social recognition. Relative truth is adopted initially, and never finally, to iron out our practical purposes. But we should never treat whims of individuals as a piece of relative truth for that would lead us astray. So the relative truth must have social recognition, i.e., in a loose sense must be universal.

Fourthly, the preceding one clearly tells us that relative truth is not a whim of the individual on whom it solely depends. An extract from his testimony before the Hunter Committee in 1919 establishes the point that in the pursuit of truth the opinions of individuals may differ. In that moment of crisis the individual himself would determine the nature of truth. Experience tells us that although individual opinions differ still the individuals who have undergone proper training of vows will not lead to confusion and chaos. It leads us to non-violence as a 'necessary corollary.'[31]

Fifthly, it is evident from the above that the acceptance of relative truth leads us to non-violence as a necessary corollary. Since our view on truth by its very nature is fragmentary, and consequently we can never claim finality and infallibility of our knowledge, it is a moral obligation on our parts to admit the possibility of truth of other's opinions from their angle of vision. This patience, sympathy, tolerance and respect for others' viewpoint leads to non-violence. That is to say, to Gandhi absolute truth was undoubtedly the ultimate goal of life but his burning humanism, boundless tolerance and superhuman self-suffering for other's cause urged him to admit relative truth. To put it in other words, patience, sympathy, tolerance, self-suffering, etc., which are salient features of non-violence, directly or indirectly, compelled him to concede the possibility of relative truth that plays a prominent role in the different phases of his lifelong non-violent movement.

(2) *Non-violence (Ahimsa):* Non-violence or *ahimsa* is an another cardinal virtue of Gandhian moral philosophy. It is a basic tenet not only of his ethics but also of his thought in its entirety. In Gandhian thought truth and non-violence both are twin concepts that go together. If truth should be regarded as the soul of Gandhism, non-violence or *ahimsa* can be aptly declared as its elan vital. Because truth can never get manifested, according to Gandhi, in its absence. I.C. Sharma observes, "If the philosophy of M.K. Gandhi were to be summed up in one word, that word would be 'non-violence'. But this term, as used by Gandhi, has very wide connotation, and stands for the love born of the universal element of spirit in man. The concept of non- violence (*ahimsa*) is very old so far as Indian philosophy is concerned."[32] Indeed, non-violence has been prescribed and practised in India for thousands of years before Gandhi's emergence. And since Gandhi was deeply influenced by the traditional views of ancient India, a proper and precise appreciation

of his view on non-violence demands an elaboration of the traditional views on this. It may be noted here that it is an almost impossible task to discuss the systems of Indian philosophical thought in chronological order with certainty. Although chronological order is not indispensable for intellectual discourse it is undoubtedly helpful for a clear understanding of the evolution of thought. In the following paragraphs we shall discuss the various aspects of non-violence.

The concept of non-violence or *ahimsa* during the Vedic period (1500 Bc to 600 Bc): The popular preaching of the Vedas goes, "Do not kill any living being (*Ma himsyat sarva bhutani*). "In the *Rg-Veda* the etymological meaning of *ahimsa* is given as physical non-injury roughly. In it the god Indra is invoked to chant hymns in such a manner that it may not do any harm (*hims*) to him.[33] The forefathers (*pitr*) are prayed not to do harm (*hims*) to devotees, and forgive their offences."[34] It is evident from the above that the verb *hims* is here used in the sense of physical injury. Another verb *han* is also frequently used there to express the sense of killing or slaying physically.[35] *Himsa* is, more precisely, derived from the root *hins* (killing, injuring, etc.,) which again is a desiderative of the root *han* (killing, slaying, etc.,). In the Vedic literature *ahimsa* is also used as a noun meaning non-injury."[36] "The womb does not injure the child and the womb remains uninjured (*ahimsa*)."[37] The first reference to *ahimsa* in the ethical sense of the term occurs in the *Katha-Samhita* (31.11). Thus the virtue of *ahimsa* or non-violence was preached and practised during the Vedic period (6000 Bc to 600s Bc), the early dawn of Indian civilization.

The epic period (600 Bc to 200 Ad) which belongs to the early *Upanisadas*, the epics of *Ramayana* and the *Mahabharata*, the religious systems of Buddhism, Jainism, Saivism, Vaisnavism, etc. This period has a value of its own because most of the systems of *darsana* or schools of Indian philosophy had an early beginning in this period. In this era the development of abstract thought of ancient India attained a glorious peak, and the concept of *ahimsa* or non-violence its maturity. In the *Chandogya Upanisad* "meditation, charity, right-dealing, non-injury to life and truthfulness are laid down as right forms of conduct." (3.17).

But a critical analysis of the history and cultural heritage of ancient India will show that the comments of Rhys Davids[38], Louis Renou[39] and Bondurant[40] are unhistorical and hence not sound. The Vedic literature, frequently deals with *ahimsa*; and is undoubtedly pre-Upanisadic.

An echo of this view regarding the origin of non-violence is heard in T.K. Unnithan and Yogendra Singh who comment, "The norms of non-violence began to emerge only in the latter stages of the Vedic tradition as a reaction against the inhuman practice of ritual sacrifices sanctioned in the early Vedic texts which is evident from the Upanishads."[41] Indeed, we cannot expect a well-knit and properly categorized system of moral philosophy in the early Vedic period although it marks to some extent the beginning of a stable Vedic society, and an end to their nomadic life. An analytical probe into the matter will bring out the following facts:

Firstly, an overall victory over the non-Aryans brought them affluence in the field of their materials (especially in the procurement of food). They found out and adopted efficacious methods to procure food from agricultural and animal world. And the technique of preservation of food brought immense benefit and relief in that regard. D.D. Kosambi describes this very nicely.[42]

Secondly, the social and political factors might have contributed to that end. The settlement of nomadic Aryans opened avenues to their ownership of land, herds of cattle, etc. Trespass into others' land was dangerous; and hence collection of animals, especially of herds of cattle, became a risky and difficult task. So through the long course of evolution the early Vedic people became primarily dependent on the animals for food, agriculture, transport, etc.; and consequently the restriction of killing animals in the guise of non-violence automatically got enforced to save these invaluable assets.

Thirdly, possession of basic necessities of life often blesses man with contentment, both physical and mental; affording him leisure to ponder supramundane questions. Metaphysical discourse and philosophical speculation are inherent in human beings. The early Vedic people raised questions as to the efficacy, moral and spiritual justification of the sacrifice of valuable animals. In the course of this discourse a highly ethical doctrine like non-violence gradually came into existence. Thus the concept of non-violence is Vedic, and it got widespread publicity in the Upanisadic era which achieved distinction in the development of abstract thought.

The epics of the *Ramayana* and *Mahabharata* have been generally accepted as the eulogies glorifying heroism and war. But in them, especially in the *Mahabharata*, we come across a highly developed concept of non-violence. The *Gita* is a part of this great epic of *Mahabharata* and its predominant influence on the mind of Gandhi is beyond question. It is a *Kamadhenu*, a veritable treasure house which offered consolation and relief whenever he faced any trouble.

Buddhism preached the basic tenets of the eight-fold path and laid emphasis on non-violence, non-hatred, friendliness to all, etc., *Dhammapada* brings out the non-violent character of buddhism explicitly.

In Jainism, we have seen above, non-violence is prescribed as the cardinal virtue. A further elaboration seems to be unnecessary. S. Radhakrishnan observes, " The chief feature of Jainism is *ahimsa*, or respect for the abstinence from everything that has life...."[43] S.N. Dasgupta concludes, "*Ahimsa* may thus be generalised as the fundamental ethical virtue of Jainism...."[44]

C.D.S. Devanesen observes, "Gandhi could not escape the influence of Jainism since the atmosphere of Kathiawada was impregnated with its teachings and spirit. Gandhi's own conscious interest in Jain ethics and philosophy dates from his days in South Africa...."[45] The above opinions of different scholars point to the pivotal role of *ahimsa* in Jaina thought; and its deep-rooted influence on Gandhi's life and works.

The Vedic idea of non-violence is also brought forward by the *Dharmasastras* and the *Puranas*. In the *Baudhayana Dharmasutra ahimsa* is described as doing non-sufference to all living beings by speech, mind or body.[46] The Jaina, Buddha and Yoga views of *ahimsa* are characterized as ascetic because they admit no form of violence into the concept of *ahimsa*; no piece of *himsa* or violence as morally good. On the other hand, in the Vedic concept *himsa* or violence is bracketed within non-violence although the meaning and connotations of it remains unhurt. In this context Tahtinen comments, "The ascetic conception of *ahimsa* differs from the Vedic conception by not including any form of justified violence into the idea of *ahimsa*. Nor does it imply that any type of *himsa* is morally good. The ascetic criticism of the Vedic *ahimsa* is directed against the approval of exceptions to the universal principle of non-violence."[47]

The *Sutra* period and the scholastic period also date from the second century Ad. To them belong the six systems (Samkhya, Yoga, Nyaya, Vaisesika, Mimamsa and Vedanta) of Indian philosophy, and a galaxy of great thinkers like Kumarila, Samkara, Sridhara, Ramanuja, Madhava, Jayanta, Raghunatha, etc. The ethical concepts, especially the views on the virtues of Prasastapada (the Vaisesika thinker); Patanjali of *Yogasutra* whom Gandhi followed faithfully in the formulation of vows for the *satyagrahis*; and the virtues required for the realization of

Brahman as prescribed by the Vedanta school have been discussed above. There also, we have seen, non-violence occupies an important place. The references and discussions as regards the nature of non-violence are very few in number in Samkhya and Yoga philosophy. The few references to non-violence that are found in the Mimamsa school of thought and in Samkara's Advaita Vedanta (Samkara on *Vedanta Sutra*, 3.1.25 and 3.4.28) subscribe to the Vedic concept of non-violence. In other schools of thought there is practically no philosophy of non-violence except some casual references.

Yet another trend of thought which seems to have influenced Gandhi, demands a brief elaboration here. The *Bhakti* movement which flourished throughout India, since its inception in the tenth century till today, has cast a deep influence of non-violence on the people of India. Gandhi is not an exception to it. In the twelfth century Basava founded Virasaivism (Lingayatism) in the South which laid emphasis on the ethics of non-violence. The chief tenets of this sect are compassion to all creatures, non-killing of animals, opposition to animal sacrifice, etc.

Kabir (1440-1518), the Muslim saintly poet of North India, was an exponent of non-violence. He raised his voice against ritualism; and pleaded for brotherhood and universal love for all creatures. He was a champion of humanism, secularism and Hindu-Muslim unity.

Nanak (1469-1539) followed the humanistic trend of Kabir and emphasized non-violence as an overall ethical value. He preached non-violence not merely as a norm of self-restraint but as a positive cardinal virtue. He called upon people to practise it in thought, speech and deed; and to cultivate physical, mental and spiritual endurance for all creatures. He preaches that "when the individual soul co-mingles with universal soul inhering in all creations, all violence, doubt and sorrow vanishes away."[48]

As discussed above, Gandhi is not an exception to it. He derived mental nourishment from the tradition of ancient India to a great extent. The influence of the pioneers of non-violent movement of ancient India on Gandhi's life and works is, our later analysis will show, immeasurable. In this context Louis Renou comments, "On the whole, we must look for Gandhi's forerunners in the leaders of sects, the countless men who 'cleared paths' and 'open up ways'. In the middle ages and up to the present, there are examples of such men....Such are Basava in the twelfth century with the Lingayats; Ramananda and Kabir in the fifteenth century; Nanak, the founder of the Sikhs, in the fifteenth and sixteenth centuries. But what these great personalities viewed in terms of the locality and of the needs of the sect, Gandhi conceived of India as a whole.[49] Indeed, Gandhi often quoted the mystics like Tukaram, Chaitanya, Ramakrishna, Thiruvalluvar, etc., and his admiration for them knew no bounds. The poems of Tulsidas were his favourites. The devotional songs of Narasinha Mehta, the saintly-poet of Gujarat; those of Suradas and Mira Bai created an atmosphere of universal love, an alias of non-violence. Their importance in the making of Gandhi's mind is unmistakable and he remembered and quoted them in public times without number.

From the above discussion it is clear that the concept of non-violence that Gandhi introduced into contemporary Indian life was already in it. It was intermingled in the soil, in the air and in the environment. He was in a sense a twentieth century 'Columbus' dedicated to discover and reorient India with nothing but truth and non-violence as his only resources. In his words, "I am in the same predicament as Columbus when he started on his voyage to discover India. Perhaps I am in a worse plight in that I have no chart and no compass which Columbus had."[50] "The prophets, seers, *avatars,* etc., have preached *ahimsa* or non-violence for thousands of years for *himsa* or violence is suicidal and rushes to doom while all noble attributes—truth, harmony, brotherhood, justice, etc.,—lead us to *ahimsa* or non-violence.[51] Indeed, the ancient thinkers with their spiritual outlooks were almost confined within their self-created ethico-religious enclosure. They preferred liberation of the individual self as the ultimate goal to social and mass reformation. It is the great genius of Gandhi which seized the spirit of traditional virtues, and released it as the strongest weapon to the people of the modern world. H.N. Brailsford concurs, "When Gandhi spoke, India for the first time heard itself thinking aloud. His dominating idea (*ahimsa*) had been hers for thousands of years...."[52] So, the claims that Gandhi's concept of *ahimsa* was not derived from Hinduism but from his study of the Sermon on the Mount or from the ideals of Christianity[53] seems to be due to exaggeration of the influence of Christianity on Gandhi, on the one hand, and misapprehension of the Gandhian standpoint on the other. As Gandhi writes, "I must tell you in humility that Hinduism, as I know it, entirely satisfies my soul, fills my whole being, and I find a solace in the *Bhagavad Gita* and the *Upanishads* that I miss even in the Sermon on the Mount."[54] "The fundamental principles of Hinduism are absolute belief in truth and non-violence. Therefore, use truth as your anvil, non-violence as your hammer; and anything that does not stand with *ahimsa*, reject as non-

Hindu."[55] Gandhi's eclectic mind absorbed all noble ideas that he came across in his long experiments with truth. In spite of the Western impact on his mind he stuck to the spiritual and cultural heritage of ancient India, especially that of Hinduism. His concept of non-violence was deeply rooted in Indian tradition; and the resemblance, if any, that it seems to have to Christianity is, accidental and superficial, and never a real one. As was his nature, he accepted the tradition yet went beyond it. He released it from the ethico-religious enclosure and applied this age-old traditional virtue to all problems of life—social, economic, political, domestic, public, etc.

A relevant question may be asked: Which form of the traditional concept of non-violence did Gandhi adopt? The traditional concept of non-violence assumes two forms, namely, Vedic and non-Vedic or ascetic concept. The Vedic concept admits exceptions, i.e., permits the practice of violence at the demand of situations. For example, offering of heifers at sacrifices. On the other hand, the ascetic or *sramanic* concept rules out all exceptions in the application of non-violence. The general trend of Hinduism, Buddhism, Jainism and the Yogins is of this type. It should be noted that neither Hinduism nor Buddhism nor Jainism did prevent kings from waging warfare, punishing the criminals violently.

Which of these forms did Gandhi follow? Gandhi adopted the vow of non-violence in his life as an essential aid to perfection towards which he conducted a lifelong search and experiment. Any deviation of it will degrade the individual concerned, and fall short of perfection. He tells us that the ideal of non-violence is perfect and hence allows no exceptions whatsoever. If injury in some specific cases cannot be avoided, it is clearly *himsa* (violence).[56] This universal principle is to be followed by all in action. One has to apply the same principle to a wrongdoer as to one's father or son.[57] In this context Unto Tahtinen comments, "Gandhi's idea of *ahimsa* was not based on the Vedic concept of *ahimsa*. He ruled out all exceptions in the application of *ahimsa*. He derived his *ahimsa* from the ascetic sources, and it was this ascetic or *sramanic* concept which he applied, for the first time, to politics and economics."[58] Crooked is the course of life. During his lifelong experiment with truth he had to deviate from this ideal on some occasions at the demand of circumstances. As discussed above (see section, Means and Ends; Nature of Punishment) the world is not filled with Buddhas, Christs and Chaitanyas only. There are evilmongers too. Gandhi had to encounter men and women of lust and greed, meanness and selfishness in everyday life. The dynamic and ever-changing happenings of the world presented problems of numerous varieties in different phases of his life. The road to perfect non-violence is like the edge of a razor. Louis Renou[59] and C.G. Shah[60] have described the role of non-violence in his eventful life.

Gandhi admits that non-violence as a perfect state is an ideal, a goal towards which mankind moves. And as an ideal non-violence is a perfect principle that admits of no exceptions whatsoever.[61] To him, perfect non-violence is a theory like Euclid's point or straight line which is practically impossible to draw on a blackboard.[62] He saw his doctrine of non-violence fail but he knew and believed from the core of his heart that the doctrine was not at fault but human nature. As a staunch follower of the *Gita* he had, perhaps, in mind the *Gita* ideal that "all creatures follow their nature; what then will constraint avail?" (3/33). Further, physical existence of human beings are hindrance to attainment of perfect non-violence. Each and every living being occupies at least some space for its existence which in some way or other involves violence. To quote him, "Strictly speaking, no activity and no industry is possible without a certain amount of violence, no matter how little. Even the very process of living is impossible without a certain amount of violence. What we have to do is to minimise it to the greatest extent possible."[63] Indeed, in Gandhian thought, truth and non-violence are two sides of the same coin, of the same reality. Like absolute truth absolute non-violence too is unknown and unknowable. We can only make vain attempts to grasp it but like distant horizon it recedes as we proceed. We can increase our capacities step by step, bit by bit to practise non-violence perfectly but owing to our inherent imperfections we are destined to be rewarded with universal futility, i.e., non-realization of perfect non-violence. In this context I.C. Sharma aptly comments, "...absolute non-violence is the highest ideal, the attainment of which would convert a man to God."[64] But a man, an imperfect being can never become God although he may attain through rigorous training some godly attributes. We should not remain idle and inactive for victory lies not in achievement but in full effort.

The futility of violence as a means of universal and ultimate victory is the root cause of Gandhi's preference for non-violence. He repeatedly tells us that violence is the force and weapon of the brutes while non-violence enriches the tradition of manliness and humanity. After Gandhi we can draw the following distinctions, more specifically, marks of superiority of non-violence to violence.

Firstly, "non-violence is without exception superior to violence, i.e., the power at the disposal of a non-violent person is always greater than he would have if he was violent."[65] A protagonist of violence invariably seeks the help of a shield, a rifle, a sword, a fortress, etc., while a votary of non-violence is sufficiently equipped to face any problem with his intrinsic and inner power, i.e., love, tolerance, service, non-infliction, etc. To quote Gandhi, "The force of arms is powerless when matched against the force of love or the soul."[66]

Secondly, "Training in non-violence is diametrically opposite to training in violence. Violence is needed for the protection of things external, non-violence is needed for the protection of the *atman*, for the protection of one's honour."[67] A champion of violence can fight and oppress the external form, the visible part of our beings, while the vast part, our mental and spiritual lives, remains beyond its scope. Non-violence works subtly and invisibly; and penetrates into our mental and spiritual lives.

Thirdly, the apparent benefit that violence seems to bring to mankind is only temporary; and narrow in scope because it fails to command a universal assent. To quote Gandhi, "I object to violence because, when it appears to do good, the good is only temporary; the evil it does is permanent."[68] Further, violence fails to attain permanence or remarkable stability in history because of its inherent contradiction. It often loses the vital flow in self-created vicious circle. The offshoots of violence are often violent which multiply endlessly. Gandhi says, "Violence must beget violence."[69] Violence by its very nature increases in breadth and depth. It brings no good to mankind, rather proliferates further ominous problems endlessly.

Fourthly, to him, "there is no such thing as defeat in non-violence. The end of violence is surest defeat...the ultimate end of non-violence is surest victory—if such a term may be used of non-violence. In reality, where there is no sense of defeat, there is no sense of victory."[70] Indeed, in non-violence egoism, the root of all conflicts, and thereby of the sense of victory and defeat, is abolished. A votary of non-violence who has dedicated everything, in a sense his being in its entirety, at the feet of God is virtually reduced to non-entity, a zero. This is the reason why the terms victory and defeat lose significance in non-violence while these are the mainsprings of violence. Here the influence of the *Gita* concept of steadfast (*sthitaprajna*) is noteworthy.

Fifthly, non-violence is a universal power that can be wielded and applied by all at any time in any place. Since it is a spiritual force—not physical—it is easily applied by both the weak and the strong, the child and the old.

Sixthly, the advocates of violence, in case of conflicts, often overlook the subtle interrelation amongst human beings, and urged by egoism and sense of victory are often driven to the extreme point which presents a polar difference from the prevailing way of life, and code of conduct. In their eagerness to achieve victory they often treat the opponent as a means and never as an end in himself. On the contrary, a votary of non-violence renounces egoism and treats each and every person as an end and never as a means. This is a salient feature of Gandhian thought.[71]

Seventhly, since violence is more inherent and natural to man than non-violence, the advocates of violence are numerous while the votaries of non-violence are few. Gandhi on several occasions emphasized the importance of quality to quantity. Indeed, the strength of violence depends upon the quantity of its champions. The more the number or quantity the more is the accumulation of power and force while the strength of non-violence depends upon its quality, i.e., purity, sincerity, etc. H. Horsburgh observes it in a lovely way[72]. Gandhi's life and activities both are the burning examples of this conviction.

Eighthly, "...non-violence is an ascent, while violence is the opposite. Therefore, it is easier to throw a people into violence than to take them out of it."[73] Our experience tells us that the path to violence is easier than non-violence. When a dispute reaches its peak, a champion of violence often loses the sense of proportion and temper; and turns to violence. On the contrary, Gandhi holds that non-violence "is an intense process though it might often seem weary and long-drawn process, it is the straightest way to liberation, the surest and quickest and no effort can be too great for it. What it requires is faith—an unshakable mountain-like faith that flinches from nothing."[74]

It is evident from the above that the failure of violence as a way of life is the reason behind Gandhi's preference for non-violence. It is undoubtedly a noble, humanistic norm and hence claims high appreciation. But the harsh realities of life tell us that non-violent method is not the only one that can guarantee order and discipline in society. This world of conflicts and selfishness necessiate violence to play an important role in social relations. The failure to assert the right in critical moments cause immeasurable damage and sufference to society. In spite of his unflinching, unshakeable, faith in non-violence, Gandhi too admitted the necessity of violence, in our lives at the demand of circumstances. He adopted it as a last resort, and appealed to minimize it 'to the greatest possible extent.' The truth is that the victory and consequences that violence begets may not be long-lasting and long-paying still its mission is not a futile one. It is quite significant in its scope.

In his prescription of non-violence as a cardinal virtue Gandhi derived inspiration from the movement of history too. To him history seems to move from violence to non-violence. It is diminishing slowly and steadily.

Man, a spark of the divine, is non-violent by birth because divinity has nothing to do with blunt, crude and cruel violent force. Violence not only overshadows our divinity, and causes spiritual degradation but also sometimes leads us to physical extinction. Gandhi says, "History teaches one that those who have, no doubt with honest motives, ousted the greedy by using brute force against them have in their turn become a prey to the disease of the conquered."[75] It is here noteworthy that this historical movement of mankind is dynamic and hence it goes on endlessly. It is a ceaseless effort of mankind to free itself from violence, from the bondage of senses; and to attain freedom of the spirit in which non-violence as a divine law prevails. The supreme end of life is to identify oneself with Truth or God. But due to imperfection every man falls short of it. He may, by dint of prayer and service, go nearer Him bit by bit, but will never attain Truth or God. And since there is no question of going back to primitive cannibalism every man should get rid of violence and regain divinity latent in him through non-violence.

It is now evident that to Gandhi a man is inherently non-violent although he becomes violent owing to surroundings and circumstances. Non-violence was no doubt the tradition still violence occupies no less an important role in the history of ancient India. The eulogies of heroship and war in the *Mahabharata* and the *Ramayana* glorify the majesty of violence in the restoration of justice in our lives. The scriptures and literatures are no exceptions to this.[76] Of the two trends—violent and non-violent—why did the people of India prefer non-violent technique to the violent one which is so easily and instinctively followed by man since the beginning of recorded human history? They could have turned a deaf ear to the call of non-violent technique advocated by Gandhi and followed the reverse tradition, i.e., violent one. This demands a probe into the historico-political situation—the objective conditions—of the time in which Gandhi prescribed non-violence as a cardinal virtue for the *satyagrahis* for the liberation of the country. Our analysis will reveal explicitly Gandhi's farsight as a leader of the masses. We have discussed the traditional conditions contributing to this end. We propose to take up the objective conditions, i.e., the situation prevailing at that time in India for the prescription of non-violence as a cardinal virtue in the following passages.

Gandhi knew that in order to attain freedom he had to launch movement on mass-scale. But the people of India, the dumb millions, were not only spiritually and morally degraded but also were deprived of the opportunity of self-defence. They were tactfully kept ignorant of violent self-defence. The spirit or ideals of military science, i.e., militancy were reserved for some privileged persons. And the rest were kept far off this privilege. Gandhi explains, "I and, with me, the millions are untouched by the military spirit. From ages past India has had a military caste in numbers wholly insignificant. The caste has had little to do with the millions. This, however, is not the occasion for examining its contribution to the making of India. All I want to state, with the utmost emphasis at any command, is that the description of India as a military country is wrong. Of all the countries in the world India is the least military.[77] As a pragmatist and practical idealist Gandhi mastered a rich and keen knowledge of human psychology. This mentality of general military disability, more specifically militant or violent crippleness, is the resultant partly of temperamental traits and partly of the policy of British Government. The British Government, while depriving Indians of armaments allowed the Europeans living in India to have in their "possession any arms of any description." A handful of Indians whose loyalty was beyond any doubt were permitted to enjoy this privilege to a limited extent. Later on the British judges interpreted arms as "any implement which is capable of being used for attack or defence and is not intended for ordinary domestic purposes. "They even prohibited the possession of a large clasp-knife with a pointed end fitted to a long handle."[78]

It is evident from the above that the Indians in spite of their glorious tradition of heroism were turned into unarmed ciphers. They were victims of the network of British administrative policy. Import of arms and ammunition was almost impossible owing to the strict security measures adopted by the British Government. And the few stray attempts that were made by a very small group of patriots, especially of Bengal and Punjab, to import arms and ammunitions from foreign sources embraced disastrous ends. During the First World War some patriotic

Sikhs living in Canada and California sailed on board the ship Komagatamaru with armament but were caught near Calcutta and massacred. Amongst innumerable attempts another one was engineered by a group of Bengali patriots under the leadership of Jatin Mukerjee alias Bagha Jatin. Being detected they embraced death in a fierce battle on the bank of river Buri Balam of Orissa. Above all, the violent methods adopted by the national revolutionaries in different parts of the country created panic-stricken popularity with temporary effects. It is an irony of fate that the violent movements in general not only failed to achieve mass support and popularity but also faced criticism, condemnation and active opposition from the very people it planned to benefit. That is to say the people of India of that time were strangled by the historico-political conditions, social surroundings and other objective factors. They were children of the tradition and victims of the political interest. As a result no other means to attain freedom except a non-violent movement was left to them. In fact, the wretchedness and helplessness of the masses springing from the objective conditions in general infused a kind of indifference, more realistically disgust, to violence in the minds of majority of people. And the temperamental traits nurtured by the tradition and spiritual surroundings gave birth to a sort of belief in the efficacy of non-violence as a means to any end, here liberation, in their minds. The credit goes to the genius of Gandhi that he felt aptly, and perhaps accurately, this pulse, i.e., the spring of action of most Indians; and turned them into a mighty force.

A relevant question may be raised: What is the relation between truth and non-violence in Gandhian thought? At a glance these two terms are inseparable, and in a sense, identical. To quote him, "Non-violence is embedded in truth and *vice-versa*..."[79] "...without *ahimsa* it is not possible to seek and find Truth. *Ahimsa* and Truth are so interwined that it is practically impossible to disentangle and separate them..."[80] Gandhian standpoint is here clear. Truth and non-violence, these two terms, are two phases of the same reality. None can get preference or priority to the other owing to the fact that any decoration and ornamentation of one will mean ascription to the other also. To a critical mind these two terms as means and ends may appear as signs of succession in temporal relations. And consequent, relevant queries will lead to further complications. But in Gandhian thought, as discussed above, ends-means is a dynamic concept. They are synonymous in the sense that they are convertible terms. Further the differences that may appear to a critical mind between the two are apparent, and not real.

Like the other concepts (rights and duty, ends and means, etc.,) he conceived them as interwoven into a single concept, i.e., Truth-non-violence concept.

The truth is that Gandhi had no training in scholastic discipline. And his pragmatic mind, as discussed above, paid little heed to dry, scholastic disciplinary system. His primary concern was service to humanity which meant to him the sole path towards the realization of God too. So to demand critical accuracy in his thought is to expect too much of him. The question of the relation between truth and non-violence that is raised and explained, here and there, in his thought is made with the objective of rendering it plausible and easily understandable to the people in general. The core point that the two terms, truth and non-violence, are synonymous, convertible in the sense of being interwoven into a single truth-non-violence concept seems to be cogent and sound in the greater perspective of Gandhian thought. And any controversy of relation in this context appears as a redundant one.

Another relevant question may be asked: Is faith in God an indispensable condition of non-violence? Cannot an atheist be a votary of non-violence? Gandhi is sanguine in this context. He says, "Non-violence is impossible without a living faith in God. A non-violent man can do nothing save by the power and grace of God...."[81] If belief in God is indispensable for non-violence then how could Gandhi accommodate Buddha, Nirmal K. Bose and Gora alias G. Ram Chandra?[82] Gandhi defends that they either believe in truth or in some supreme power. But to an analytical mind this would be a *homoacopathic solution* of the problem. Belief in God as an essential condition of non-violence remains on open problem to the scholars of Gandhian thought.

We have discussed the concept of non-violence from all possible perspectives. We can lay down, after Gandhi, the following axioms of non-violence. "(1) Non-violence implies as complete self-purification as is humanly possible. (2) Man for man the strength of non-violence is in exact proportion to the ability, not the will, of the non-violent person to inflict violence. (3) Non-violence is without exception superior to violence, i.e., the power at the disposal of a non-violent person is always greater than he would have if he was violent. (4) There is no such thing as defeat in non-violence. The end of violence is surest defeat. (5) The ultimate end of non-violence is surest victory if such a term may be used of non-violence. In reality where there is no sense of defeat, there is no sense of victory."[83] Elsewhere Gandhi mentions the following prerequisites in addition to the above discussed axioms of non-violence. (a) "Non-violence is the law of the human race and is infinitely greater than and superior to brute force; (b) In the last resort it does not avail to those who do not possess a living faith in the God of Love; (c) Non-violence affords the fullest protection to one's self-respect and sense of honour, but not always to possession of land or movable property, though its habitual practice does prove a better bulwark than the possession of armed men to defend them. Non-violence in the very nature of things is of no assistance in the defence of ill-gotten gains and immoral acts; (d) Individuals and nations who would practise non-violence must be prepared to sacrifice (nations to the last man) their all except honour. It is therefore inconsistent with the possession of other people's countries, i.e., modern imperialism which is frankly based on force for its defence; (e) Non-violence is a power which can be wielded equally by all—children, young men and women or grown up people, provided they have a living faith in the God of Love and have therefore equal love for all mankind. When non-violence is accepted as the law of life it must pervade the whole being and not be applied to isolated acts. (6) It is a profound error to suppose that whilst the law is good enough for individuals it is not for masses of mankind."[84] Non-violence is overt. In it there is no place for secrecy which is an epiphenomenon of violence. Secrecy is designed to attain deception and ensure protection that a bonafide votary of non-violence has nothing to fear. He fostered an open abhorrence of secrecy throughout his life. To quote him, "My life has been an open book. I have no secrets and I encourage no secrets."[85] Theoretically, as discussed above, non-violence admits of no exception, no compromise. Exceptions and compromises are synonymous to failings which point to no blemish on the part of the supreme law of non-violence but to our flaws and faults. It is universal love and compassion. It is love in the Pauline sense, and yet something more than the 'love' defined by St. Paul.[86] In a word, non-violence is a universal love for all beings. The creed of non-violence also conveys universal compassion. It bestows upon us the blessings of infinite patience, boundless inner calm, right insight, true knowledge and self-sacrifice.[87] It is pure, unselfishness, motivelessness, and activist force in the world. A votary of non-violence can never feel helpless and miserable because it covers the whole range of human activity. In his words, "I devote my energy to the propagation of non-violence as the law of our life,—individual, social, political, national and international."[88] In short, everything human falls within its scope.

To sum up: Non-violence is an absolute concept that comprehends everything, possible and actual, in its infinite bosom; and is unlimited in scope. It covers up all spheres—the mundane, extra-mundane, physical, mental, emotional and spiritual—into which an individual may wander. Physically it means non-injury of any kind; mentally it conveys not only non-wishing of evil but also well wishing to even evildoers; emotionally, it demands complete extirpation of emotional excitement, revealed or concealed, and of coercion of all types; spiritually it points to an underlying unity behind all beings the realization of which will mean, of course step by step, identification with God, with Truth. All roads lead to Rome. Likewise, the relations that emerge from non-violence do converge into a single point, i.e., the realization of Truth or God which is of the nature of humanity, of love, of dedication, of social service and self-devotion. Since no man can attain perfect knowledge it is impossible to bring out a complete exposition of the virtue of non-violence. This is the viewpoint of Gandhi too.[89] Our summation also faces the same fate. Non-violence in its perfection is indefinable and indescribable, and hence beyond our reach.

(3) *Chastity or Celibacy or Continence (Brahmacharya):* The third vow is *brahmacharya* which is directly derived from *charya* meaning course of conduct and *Brahman*, i.e., Truth. Thus the etymological meaning of *brahmacharya* stands for the course of conduct adopted to the search of *Brahma*, i.e., Truth. In fact, all the vows are deducible from Truth as corollaries, and are meant to subserve its purpose. Realization of *Brahman* demands perfect selflessness because a selfish man will have no time to search after *Brahman*. Thus realization of Truth through selfishness or self-gratification seems to be an exercise in contradictions. Again, non-violence means universal love, i.e., love for mankind in gereral. But a married or selfish man can never rise to the height of universal love because his love is limited to some particular persons only. That is to say, *brahmacharya* is an integral part of Truth, and of other vows at the same time. And though Truth forms the nucleus of the vows still the value lies in the whole. Because they are coherent, and organically related to one another. To quote Gandhi, "All these (vows) can be derived from Truth. But life is complex. It is not possible to enunciate one grand principle and leave the rest to follow of itself.... It is well to bear in mind that all the disciplines are of equal importance. If one is broken all are.... Therefore, it is essential that all the disciplines

should be taken as one. This enables one to realize the full meaning and significance of *brahmacharya*.[90]

How did the idea of *brahmacharya* occur in his mind? Although his mind derived nourishment from the Indian traditional concept, Gandhi admits that he did not borrow it from any book, Eastern or Western. He says, "My *brahmacharya* was not derived from books. I evolved my own rules for my guidance and that of those who, at my invitation, had joined me in the experiment.[91] Indeed, Gandhi came across Patanjali along with other scriptures in 1903 long before which the ideal of *brahmacharya* was sprouting in his mind. He recollects that "the predominant factor was the influence of Raychandbhai.[92] An ardent humanism and burning spirit of social service led him to take this great vow in South Africa. The religious implication of it as an aid for the attainment of liberation or *moksa* was still unknown to him. In his *Autobiography*, he narrates it clearly.[93] During the last phase of his life he narrates elsewhere the same motto of social service behind the observance of *brahmacharya*. He preferred the life of universal brotherhood and universal love to the soft comforts of family life based on selfish bond. In short, he did not owe the concept of *brahmacharya* to any source other than his experience. And the steering force behind it was an earthly object, the service to humanity and not any spiritual goal, *moksa* or liberation. With this end in view he took the vow: "Thus *brahmacharya*, which I had been observing willy-nilly since 1900, was sealed with a vow in the middle of 1906."[94]

What is the nature of *brahmacharya* in Gandhian thought? Gandhi defines it as "correct way of life which leads to *Brahma*, i.e., God."[95] The first feature of *brahmacharya* is self-restraint, i.e., control of all the senses at all places in all times. That is to say, we are to control the senses under all circumstances. The five sense organs of eye, ear, nose, tongue and skin are often delusive and misleading. Hence control of the senses is the first feature of *brahmacharya*.

Secondly, "*Brahmacharya* is a mental condition. The outward behaviour of a man is at once the sign and proof of the inner state."[96] "*Brahmacharya* thus means control in thought, word and action, of all the senses at all times and in all places."[97] Gandhi here follows the trend of traditional observance of vows in thought, word and action. The mind steers the body and hence "an impure thought is a breach of *brahmacharya*; so is anger."[98] It is not possible to observe *brahmacharya* if one harbours evil thoughts in mind because "where the mind wanders, the body must follow sooner or later."[99] In the perfect stage of *brahmacharya* even unexpected dreams of evil thoughts never occur. A healthy soul inhabits a healthy body. To the extent the soul attains purity the body also grows into that state. Gandhi thinks, he would not have suffered from the diseases of pleurisy, dysentery and appendicitis if he had complete mastery over thoughts. In short, complete mastery over all the senses at all times, in all places in thought, word and action is the second characteristic of *brahmacharya*.

Thirdly, *brahmacharya* is indispensable not only for the attainment of inner freedom but also for the attainment of Swaraj or external freedom. If we are fully and perfectly equipped from within we shall attain efficiency to face the problems of the external world. To quote him, "The conquest of lust is the highest endeavour of a man's or woman's existence without overcoming lust man cannot hope to rule overself. And without rule over self there can be no Swaraj or *Ramraj*. Rule of all without rule of oneself would prove to be as deceptive and disappointing as a painted toy mango, charming to look at outwardly but hollow and empty within...."[100] Here Gandhi treats *brahmacharya* as an aid for the attainment of external freedom as manifested in social, political and other walks of life.

Fourthly, the religious implication of *brahmacharya* is that it ascribes godliness to the *brahmachari*, and without it none can see God. That is to say, *brahmacharya* is indispensable for realization of self or God or Truth. Gandhi says, "Observing *brahmacharya* is one of the means to the end which is seeing *Brahma*. Without *brahmacharya* no one may expect to see Him, and without seeing Him one cannot observe *brahmacharya* to perfection."[101] It ascribes "something unearthly", something "exceptionally fresh and wiry" to the *brahmachari*. It is here noteworthy that initially he had no religious implication in mind. It was fervent humanism and burning urge to render service to humanity that inspired him to take this vow.

Fifthly, *brahmacharya* confers some physical or bodily blessings on us. Perfect *brahmacharya* means complete control over all the senses, thought, speech and action. This complete mastery over everything of his being enhances the physical, mental and spiritual potency of an individual; and endows him with the creative energy of the highest order; with an indomitable spirit and unlimited power. Gandhi says, "The *brahmachari* of my conception will be healthy and will easily live long. He will not even suffer from so much as a headache. Mental and physical work will not cause fatigue. He is ever bright, never slothful. Outward neatness will be an exact reflection of the inner. He will exhibit all the attributes of the steadfast one described in the *Gita*."[102] Thus, to Gandhi, perfect *brahmacharya* is a godly attribute that transforms an individual into a steadfast one, a superman in Sri Aurobindo's sense. A similar idea appears in the golden words of Sri Ramakrishna Paramhamsa, who says, "If a man remains absolutely continent for twelve years, he achieves superhuman power. A new nerve develops in him, 'called the nerve of intelligence'."[103] In this context Romain Rolland observes, "All great mystics and the majority of great idealists, the giants among the creators of the spirit, have clearly and instinctively realised what formidable power of concentrated soul, of accumulated creative energy, is generated by a renunciation of the organic and psychic expenditure of sexuality."[104]

But this concept of absolute continence or perfect *brahmacharya* faces some difficulties. An individual by birth inherits a bundle of instincts and emotions, the complete extirpation of which is an almost impossible task. Further, a stringent treatment of the demands of sensuous life often tells heavily upon health and personality. It fosters irritation, disease, and various types of abnormalcy in an individual. Hence in medical science absolute continence fails to attain universal assent. The truth, perhaps, lies in Gandhi's unconscious mind. The peril of sexual excess was deeply rooted in his being. He looks at it even in old age as an evil, a sin. He clearly confesses in his *Autobiography*, "...I was passionately fond of her...with this devouring passion...I should either have fallen a prey to disease and premature death, or have sunk into a burdensome existence....At the age of eighteen I went to England, and this meant a long and healthy spell of separation."[105] Sex appeared to him as horror, disaster, shame, lust and disgust. Lust compelled him to perform coition but it is interesting to note that he never tells us that he enjoyed it. The pleasure that arises out of reciprocal participation of partners in the artful act of copulation is absent in Gandhi's life. The terms 'devouring passion' and 'lustful love' signify his guilt consciousness which held him responsible for the illiteracy of wife and for the absence at the critical hour of father's death. Not only this, somehow an evil idea got fixed into his mind that coition was not wholesome at all. It causes disease, premature death and invalidity. That is why he welcomes his wife's going to her parents house and his stay in England as "a long and healthy spell of separation." This is something abnormal in a boy in his teens, the period in which most of the adults in India remain almost innocent. Perhaps, coldness of Kasturba, a light apathy for the sensuous father, and his precocious sexual exhaustion formed an aversion towards sex life. While he was thus tortured in his unconscious, the dawning of the idea of *brahmacharya* was a relief, a God-send to him.

Sixthly, his idea of *brahmacharya* changes the traditional status of women and establishes them as mother, sister and daughter. In the Hindu code composed by Manu a woman is described as the "door-keeper of hell," later on an idea developed amongst the masses, including the womenfolk, that a woman is inferior to a man in various walks of life. But Gandhi as a leader realized the potentiality latent in Indian womenfolk, and gave a clarion call to them for active participation in every sphere of life. To quote him, "....the wife is not the husband's bondslave, but his companion and his helpmate, and an equal partner in all his joys and sorrows—as free as the husband to choose her own path."[106] Thus a *brahmachari*, according to Gandhi, will rise above the consciousness of sex, and infuse the purity of sexlessness into a woman sharing the same bed, if occasion demands. During the last years of his life, Gandhi conducted some experiments in this direction, and was misunderstood widely. In short, the concept of *brahmacharya* altered the status of womenfolk in his mind and opened a new horizon before his eyes, namely the liberation of women in general.

Seventhly, married *brahmacharya* may sound contradictory to the Western ear. In Western sociology marriage has been generally accepted as the social recognition of sex-relationship between a man and a woman. That is why a marital bond without sex-relation may seem to be inconceivable to them. But in India it has been prescribed long before the birth of Gandhi. In *Ramayana* we are told of Laxmana observing *brahmacharya* for fourteen years while in exile. Manu prescribed four stages of life. During the first quarter (*brahmacharya*) of life celibacy was regarded essential for all—both for students studying the Vedas and also for one who would devote himself exclusively to the realization of God. In the second stage of householders (*garhasthya*) every healthy man should marry and rear up a family. At this stage too an individual has to exercise sex-control by being loyal to his partner, and through observance of some other restrictions. Manu writes of married *brahmacharya*: "Let the husband approach his wife in due season, being constantly satisfied with her (alone); he may also, being intent on pleasing her, approach her with a desire for conjugal union on a day excepting the *Parvans*" (3/45). "He who avoids women on the six forbidden nights and eight others, is a *Brahmacharin* in whichever

Ashrama he may live" (3/50). In ancient Greece, as in ancient India, we can trace out at least one example of this self-restraint. "The most illustrious example of this in European history is perhaps afforded by Ezenobia, the queen of Palmyra, equally renowned for her beauty and valour about whom Gibbon has observed, 'She never admitted her husband's embrace but for the sake of posterity. If her hopes were baffled, in the ensuing month she reiterated the experiment'."[107]

Let us consider the Gandhian concept of married *brahmacharya*. In the strict sense of the term absolute *brahmacharya* rules out marriage as it obstructs, it is held, the way to self-realization. Gandhi also considered it in this light and said that "marriage is a 'fall' even as birth is a fall."[108] But at the same time he realized that it is not possible for an ordinary man to attain absolute *brahmacharya*; and if it were at all possible, the order of the society will stand still. So as a practical idealist he suggests gradual self-control for people of different moral grades without underrating the majesty of the ideal. He tells us that "the ideal that marriage aims at is that of spiritual union through the physical. The human love that it incarnates is intended to serve as a stepping stone to the divine or universal love."[109] He treats the marital bond purely from a socio-religious angle of vision. The steps, prescribed by him, to be observed by a married couple are meant to serve the social purpose, and at the same time to attain Truth or God through self-realization. The couple should perform sexual union not for sensual pleasure but for procreation of child so that the social order may run smoothly. Furthermore, following *Manusmriti* Gandhi calls one child as *dharmaja* (born out of righteousness) and any one after that as *kamaja* (born out of carnal desire). This being the social implication of married *brahmacharya* he brings forth the spiritual object of it. A married man with lust and selfishness can never attain non-violence or universal love; and consequently fails to realize Truth or God. Gandhi suggests, "There is a way out for them. They can behave as if they were not married....If the married couple can think of each other as brother and sister, they are freed for universal service. The very thought that all the women in the world are his sisters, mothers or daughters will at once ennoble a man and snap his chains."[110] That is to say, freedom from marital bond endows an individual with spiritual power which is a stepping stone towards self-realization or God. Moreover, in a monogamous family the husband and wife observe, "a limited *brahmacharya*" because they "renounce gratification outside the marital bond."[111]

One more point. Gandhi's staunch moralism strongly emphasized on self-control, and vehemently opposed the artificial or mechanical devices (contraceptives) adopted for birth control. Because these are highly immoral, mechanical, and sometimes unhealthy. He says, "If contraceptives are resorted to, frightful results will follow. Men and women will be living for sex alone. They will become soft-brained, unhinged, in fact mental and moral wrecks."[112] He foresaw the frightful consequences together with moral and spiritual degradation. As a way out Gandhi suggests hip-bath, a whole-hearted prayer to Rama, walk in the open air, control of the palate, etc.

To sum up: Gandhi's prescription of *brahmacharya* as a cardinal virtue was a necessity of the age. He foresaw, and perhaps aptly, that the movement of liberation would be impossible unless the *satyagrahis* were free from the chains of lust and family bondage. As discussed above, according to Gandhi, *brahmacharya* bestows unlimited physical and spiritual power on the individual. It transforms an individual into a superman, a steadfast one whom Gandhi sought fervently for the movement of liberation and thereby for the service of humanity. But to an analytic mind this seems to be a bit utopian, if not unscientific. The experimental findings of modern psychology and medical science denounce it as mere bodily repression.[113] Gandhi expects too much from an individual of flesh and blood. Spiritual taming of sex instincts may not always attain success. Our experience reveals that it often tells upon the body and mind of the individual heavily. On the contrary, history of mankind speaks of many a man of eminence who attained remarkable success in various walks of life, and enjoyed a sound longevity without observance of *brahmacharya*. Further, Gandhi is candid enough to admit that *brahmacharya* in its perfection is beyond human reach. Perhaps, here lies the truth. 'To much of everything is bad.' Neither sexual excess nor total abstinence is good for man. The sound development of our personality lies in the harmonious manifestation of all the qualities of our being. As the crown of creation our duty should be to minimize sexual opportunity; to regulate and tame sexual instinct as far as practicable. To say so is not to underrate the virtue of *brahmacharya*. It is just an admission of fact. The virtue of *brahmacharya* as an ideal will be an evershinning light, and an infallible aid towards realization of God or Truth.

(4) *Control of the Palate:* The fourth vow is the control of the palate. Though it is not included amongst the cardial virtues of Hindu code still it forms an integral part of *brahmacharya*. In Buddhistic

prescription of eight-fold path emphasis has been laid on right-conduct (*Samyag-karmanta*) which consists in abstention from killing, stealing, illegal sex-indulgence, lying and drinking liquor for ordinary citizens; and along with the above it includes abstention from eating between meals, attending social feasts, etc., for the monks. Long before taking control of the palate as a vow, the ideal was sprouting in Gandhi's mind during his stay in London as a student (1888-91). The experiments on dietetics that he conducted there were directly influenced by acquaintance with some vegetarians (e.g. Sir Edwin Arnold, Dr. Oldfield, Dr. Allinson, Mr. Hills, Mr. Howard, etc.,) and by the study of some literature on dietetics (Salt's *Plea for Vegetarianism*, Howard William's *The Ethics of Diet*, Dr. Anna Kingsford's *The Perfect Way in Diet*, Dr. Allinson's writings on health and hygiene, etc.,). During this phase of the evolution of his thought he was indirectly influenced by Indian literature on dietetics. At that time "he contributed nine articles on Hindu customs and diet to the magazine, *Vegetarian*."[114] Regarding Gandhi's life-long experiments on dietetics and the Indian influence on it. D.M. Datta's comments are valuable.[115] Thus the Indian and Western ideals got blended in his mind; and later experiences in life taught him to adopt it as an independent vow.

From the Western literature on diet he learnt that "all philosophers and prophets from Pythagoras and Jesus down to those of the present age were vegetarians."[116] Elsewhere he narrates, "My co-workers and I have seen by experience that there is much truth in the Indian proverb that as a man eats, so shall he become."[117] In this way through study and experience a deep-rooted conviction came into his mind that diet was indispensably connected with the mental and physical maturity of an individual. For the self-realization of an individual diet should contribute favourably. An individual should abstain from all irritating condiments, alcohol which excites the nerves, and narcotics which deaden the sense of right and wrong. That is to say, throughout his long life he searched after the innocent and nutritious foods that would be conducive to the physical and spiritual uplift of an individual. We have seen above that *brahmacharya* is an essential condition for the realization of Truth or God. And control of the palate is a part and parcel of *brahmacharya*. To quote Gandhi, "There is an indissoluble connection between self-control and the control of the palate. The man who observes *brahmacharya* will be controlled in everyone of his acts and will be humble."[118] "Control of the palate is very closely connected with the observance of *brahmacharya*. I have found from experience that the observance of celibacy becomes comparatively easy, if one acquires mastery over the palate."[119] He tells us that "the *brahmachari's* food should be limited, simple, spiceless and if possible, uncooked."[120] Indeed, stimulating food nourishes lower senses, the carnal mind, and thereby converts the self into a bond-slave of passion. As mentioned above, *brahmacharya* means control of all senses in all directions. So we should lead a life in such a manner that all the senses are compelled to subserve the spiritual and moral uplift of ourselves, both physical and mental.

A critical analysis will reveal the following implications of the above vow, i.e., control of the palate. Firstly, while this ideal was germinating in his mind during his stay in London the economic consideration, i.e., frugality was among the predominating considerations.[121]

Secondly, the hygienic value of it was significant. Gandhi says, "Health was the principal consideration of these experiments to begin with."[122] The truth is that Gandhi was always conscious of the evil consequences of over eating. It got deeply rooted in his unconscious mind, and ever haunted him. He tells us that parents often offer their tender ones a variety of foods... which invariably damage 'their constitution'; rear up a diseased body with a perverted taste. So we should take food as we take medicine.[123] Thus Gandhi preached a hygienic and scientific truth in the guise of a vow.

Thirdly, like other vows it is mental in the sense that it should be observed in word, thought and action. Gandhi writes, "I know that the mental attitude is everything. Just as a prayer may be merely a mechanical intonation as of a bird, so may a fast be mere mechanical torture of the flesh."[124] Without the mental control a mere mechanical and external control of the palate is useless; and this show-off Gandhi condemns from the core of his heart. He wanted a harmonious development, and a sound co-ordination of our word, thought and action for the realization of Truth or God.

Fourthly, it has a moral implication in the sense that its violation is a sin, an evil. In his words, "If we practise simultaneous self-control in all directions, the attempt will be scientific and possible of success. Perhaps, the palate is the chief sinner. That is why in the Ashram we have assigned to control of the palate a separate place among our observances."[125] Here Gandhi treats it from the ethical standpoint and takes any breach of it as a sin against self-realization or truth, an evil committed against the majesty of morality.

Fifthly, like all other vows it conveys a religious implication in Gandhian ethics. Let us listen to him: "Health was the principal consideration of these experiments to begin with. But later on religion became the supreme motive."[126] "My experiments in England were conducted from the point of view of economy and hygiene. The religious aspect of the question was not considered until I went to South Africa where I undertook strenuous experiments...."[127] What was that religious motive that became supreme in his later life, and urged him to relinquish the relish of tongue altogether? Of course that 'supreme motive' is the realization of the Supreme or God. Gandhi explains, "For the seeker who would live in fear of God, and who would see Him face to face, restraint in diet both as to quantity and quality is as essential as restraint in thought and speech."[128] Moreover, an individual cannot expect to get rid of the palate completely all on a sudden. Gandhi was clearly influenced by the *Gita* ideal which he admits elsewhere. The *Gita* ideal is: "The sense-objects turn away from an abstemious soul, leaving the relish behind. The relish also disappears with the realization of the Highest" (2/59).[129]

Sixthly, it serves a social purpose and fosters brotherhood amongst the *satyagrahis*. A common kitchen, a common menu, removes all discrepancies that may arise in taking food. A *satyagrahi* having no security of food and shelter, especially during freedom movement, can take a limited quantity of simplest food as the situation provides with a contented and thankful mind. Moreover, it lightens the burden of the host or authority who makes this provision.

Seventhly, like all other vows it involves non-attachment or *anasakti* to earthly objects. In case of *brahmacharya* coitus is permitted only for procreation, and never for sensuous pleasure. Similarly, control of the palate means taking food not for relish but for bare sustenance of the body. This undoubtedly demands a highly developed mental power of non-attachment or *anasakti*.

To sum up: Gandhi's prescription of vows has roots in his eagerness to attain freedom, both inner and outer. He foresaw that outer freedom, in the Indian context, liberation from the British Government, would be futile if inner freedom, at least restraint of the senses, was not realized. And since all the vows do form an integrated and coherent system, control of the palate is undoubtedly a stepping-stone towards that end. It was initiated at the demand of the age. Gandhi gave a clarion call to all, especially to the *satyagrahis* and ashramites, to observe this vow both for the individual self and the country. Control of the palate undoubtedly demands selflessness to a great extent. Still it is appreciable owing to the fact that it is, hygienic, economic and practical. The medical science too prescribes a limited quantity of spiceless simple food as wholesome for all. What better and cheaper food could Gandhi prescribe in those days for the destitutes, the dumb, starving millions; and for the *satyagrahis* who had taken the vows of non-possession and non-stealing?

(5) *Non-stealing (Asteya):* Let us take up the fifth vow, non-stealing (*asteya*). It is one of the five great vows (*mahavratas*) of ancient India; and Gandhi prescribes it as necessary for the realization of self or Truth. It advises us not to take away the property of anyone unless he permits us. Right to private property is a recognized custom, and hence to steal the property of somebody else is to deprive him of the possession, the source of his livelihood. That is to say, thieving means committing injury or harm to somebody else. This goes outright against the principle of Truth and non-violence which, being two sides of the same coin, form the nucleus of Gandhi's thought. Thus Gandhi, following the ancient trend, comments the vow of non-stealing in his own way.

The implications of the vow of non-stealing in Gandhian thought are as follows: Firstly, non-thieving or non-stealing is an integral part of Truth and Non-violence. Truth or God, is the supreme goal which everybody should strive to realize heart and soul. And the realization of Truth or God would be impossible without perfect observance of non-violence. If we love an individual we cannot rob him of property because thereby we shall be doing injury to him. To quote Gandhi, "It is impossible that a person should steal, and simultaneously claim to know Truth or cherish Love."[130] Thus a *satyagrahi* must not steal since it goes against the first two of the great vows.

Secondly, it has a wider range than what is commonly ascribed to it. By stealing we generally mean robbing others of their property. But Gandhi gives it a meaning and expands its scope. An individual who eats or enjoys something secretly ignoring the other members of his family (say a father eats something secretly and keeps his children in the dark about it); takes away for self-gratification something from common-property (for example, a singly crystal of sugar from the Ashram kitchen store); takes anything belonging to another without his permission although he knows it; appropriates something that appears to be nobody's property (e.g., an article lying uncared for on the roadside or elsewhere) is a thief in Gandhi's eyes. Here it is noteworthy that an accrual of property, if legitimate, does not fall within its purview.

Thirdly, to consume a commodity of any value that is unnecessary for simple and natural life is thieving, not to speak of extravagance and immoderate or wasteful luxury. To quote Gandhi, "It is theft to take something from another even with his permission if we have no real need of it. We should not receive any single thing that we do not need."[131]

Fourthly, it is an infallible redress for the present miserable poverty of the world. One of the impacts of civilization on us is constant multiplication of our wants, proper or improper. If, by utmost effort, we can at all fulfil some of the present wants, the rest proliferate into some more wants and so on *ad infinitum*. In this way the stream of happiness gets lost in the desert of ever-increasing wants. The observance of vows helps us to reduce innumerable needs, and consequently saves us from committing such theft, conscious or unconscious. Most of the dissatisfactions that modern people suffer have their roots in the ever increasing wants which are not indispensable for simple and natural life. In this way the conquest of happiness for modern man turns into a chase after wild goose. Perhaps, true happiness lies in the curtailment of unnecessary wants, in the appropriation of that which is indispensable for simple and natural life. Here Gandhi's standpoint seems to be humanistic, practical and sound, and hence deserves appreciation.

Fifthly, this vow of non-stealing has a mental implication too. Its non-observance stand as an obstruction towards self-realization. Here Gandhi picks up one of the salient features of ancient cardinal virtues which lay stress on word, thought (*manasa*) and action. Perfectly controlled thought can attain highest potency and become self-acting. So thought plays a very important role in the observance of vows. A subtle mental desire for possession of things belonging to others; to cast even a greedy look on them; a mental contemplation on relishing of delicious dishes while fasting is, to Gandhi, stealing. So we should observe non-stealing both externally and internally, mentally and physically.

Sixthly, non-anxiety for future is another characteristic of it. Our anxiety for future security—in all directions—knows no bounds. It baffles us, and mars the tranquillity of our minds. It often induces us to adopt crooked and unfair measures for the acquisition of future provisions and leads us go astray.

Seventhly, it is not only material, but also ideal. We have discussed so far the visible objects that we find in the external world. But stolen objects may be ideal also. The history of mankind records of plagiarism committed by men of letters. And even today it is not uncommon that people boastfully claim to originate some new ideas or principle which are practically some other's invention. This is evidently a case of theft. And the introduction of a new thing, say a wheel which I came across elsewhere, even with orientation without acknowledgement of gratitude is to be condemned as stealing. Gandhi explains it very nicely.[132] Indeed, plagiarism of any kind should be shunned by an observer of vows since it directly violates the first and primary one, Truth.

Eighthly, the observance of non-stealing requires an individual "to be humble, thoughtful, vigilant and in habits simple."[133] This is a universal code for all *satyagrahis*.

To sum up: Like all other vows Gandhi's prescription of non-stealing has its source in his philosophical outlook, i.e., a conscious and voluntary indifference towards earthly objects, both ideal and real. Although derived from ancient Indian tradition he reoriented and enriched it. This ascetic ideal was turned by him into one for observance by common man. In fact, an attitude of non-stealing fosters tranquillity both physical and mental in an individual. In these days of conflict and selfishness, competition and greed, it offers, however small, solace and relief; and awakens a value sense in us.

(6) *Non-possession or Poverty (Aparigraha)*: The sixth vow is non-possession or poverty. The habit of possession is inherent in man. An earthly being, a bundle of habits, instincts and feelings, spontaneously hankers after security for the future, i.e., security for the maintenance of livelihood in future. This is the psychological element, the spring of action that urges him to possess something, to make provision for the future. As discussed above all the vows are organically woven into an integrated whole. Still the present one is a direct corollary of the preceding one. And with this we enter into the core of Gandhian economy. The allied vows of non-stealing and non-possession along with the vows of bread labour and *swadeshi* constitute the salient features of Gandhian economy. A *satyagrahi* who observes non-stealing must also observe non-possession since possession often induces him to violate the former vow. Indeed, our later analysis will show that the observance of non-stealing in all its implications becomes impossible without the observance of non-possession. Let us bring out its various implications one by one.

Non-possession is a divine mandate, and is observed by God

Himself. God is the sole proprietor of all existents of the universe which we, the ordinary people, boastfully claim to be our property out of sheer ignorance. Man is a tiny speck in the infinite bosom of space and time; and consequently any claim of possession on his part seems to be ridiculous. Nothing belongs to man, not even his body. That is to say, any claim to anything as our own property, according to Gandhi, is a violation of the divine law. So we should renounce everything at the feet of God and dedicate ourselves to the service of humanity which is only another form of His service. On His part God takes the complete responsibility of the non-possessor as is manifested in the experiences of saints and prophets of India who adopted voluntary poverty along with unflinching faith in the kindness of God.[134]

Any unnecessary possession is a breach of divine law, and proves lack of faith in the goodness and kindness of God. This is the religious implication of non-possession.

It has a political implication too. It is a stepping stone towards national integrity. The evils of possession are many a time at the root of conflicts amongst us. It often breeds selfishness and non-cooperation which is undoubtedly harmful to national solidarity, and thereby for the attainment of liberation. That is why Gandhi prescribes the vow of non-possession for the restoration of brotherhood and co-operation amongst us.

Here one point is remarkable. Possession of property is not always and everywhere a bone of contention. The history of Indian freedom struggle speaks of many a man of riches who participated in it unhesitatingly without paying the least attention to his property. The fact is that the activities of human mind do not follow a uni-axial course. Crooked is the course of life. Temperamental traits often influence the activities of an individual. Hence possession is not always and everywhere an obstruction to national solidarity. It is on the individual the gravity of national integrity primarily depends.

From the economic standpoint the vow of non-possession is the matrix of the theory of trusteeship which expresses his views on accumulated wealth, talents of people, and their earnings exceeding immediate wants. Gandhi prescribes non-violent dispossession of all private property or change of attitude of the possessors. Although they possess wealth they should act as trustees not as proprietors, and utilize them for the benefit of the society. And those who have no accumulated wealth but are blessed with heavenly talents, and earn more than others, should adopt an attitude of trustee and utilize the excess of their immediate needs for the welfare of society.

Its legal implication is as follows. Possession is often a bone of contention amongst us. We often amass wealth at the cost of others. This accumulation of wealth breeds disaffection in the minds of those who are deprived. Consequently, feeling of this deprivation leads them astray, Gandhi says, "...if I kept anything as my own, I had to defend it against the whole world... and I would have to seek police assistance also if hungry, famine-stricken people, finding me in a lonely place, wanted not merely to divide the thing with me but to dispossess me."[135]

Possession of property, according to Gandhi, breeds jealousy and animosity; and ugly consequences such as burglary, dacoity in society. So we should possess only those things that are indispensable for natural and simple life. Here Gandhi's legal interpretation of non-possession seems to be sound from the sociological standpoint.

Its material implication is easily perceptible to us. It is the effect of material possession that is visible in the external world. The rich go on greedily accumulating superfluous store of wealth which for want of proper distribution is often wasted while the 'dumb millions' starve to death for want of sustenance. In fact if everybody possesses only that which was indispensably necessary for the fulfilment of immediate needs all would have lived in contentment. On the contrary, continuous accumulation of wealth might drive the 'dumb millions' to dispossess the rich at any cost to satisfy their bare human needs. Gandhi treats the problem from the spiritual standpoint, but the truth lies somewhere else. A well-organized network for the proper distribution of material necessities of life is essential for the smooth running of the social order. An equilibrium of production and distribution is a basic assumption of economics. The contention that "the only thing that can be possessed by all is non-possession" cannot be, although a good precept, a solution to that end.

Non-possession is a necessary step towards spiritual uplift. According to Gandhi, spiritual force always transcends material force; and spiritual freedom would remain an impossibility unless we crucify our material wants at its altar. It is not possible, as our experience shows us, for an ordinary man to serve both God and Mammon, and enjoy material and spiritual blessings at the same time. Ready money or material possession has very little role to play in spiritual progress. And material affluence often leads to spiritual bankruptcy. Gandhi boldly declares, "It is my certain conviction based on experience that money plays the least part in matters of spirit."[136]

Let us consider its physical (bodily) implication. Here the body is compared to a case which temporarily confines the omnipresent, eternal and everfree soul. The eternity and transmigration of the soul, and its temporary association with the organic structure is an ancient and popular belief in India. This temporary confinement of the soul which is pure in itself is due to desire for enjoyment. But when the ideal of total renunciation is attained, desire for enjoyment together with the necessity of confinement vanishes. So the being of the body is highly temporary and for the sake of soul only. Moreover, God is the creator and sole proprietor of all existents of the universe. This body which we out of ignorance claim to be ours practically belongs to God. In his words, "...even the body is not yours. It has been given to you as a temporary possession, and it can also be taken from you by Him who has given it to you."[137] So we should repay our debt to our creator through service to humanity which also means service to God. Here one point is remarkable. The treatment of the body as a possession, and distinct from the soul is a resultant of abstract and transcendental meditation which is practically beyond the reach of ordinary man. And it fosters a kind of stoic indifference, more specifically an escapistic attitude, towards physical existents, the very root of all actions, progress and prosperity. This, though it sounds harsh, is morbid, and not wholesome for the smooth running of the social order.

Violation of this divine law of non-possession is followed by divine punishment. Possession has given rise to inequalities in society; and brought all sorts of miseries as its consequences. The rich out of boundless greed hanker after more riches which ultimately leads them to corruptions and spiritual bankruptcy. In ancient times discontentment with earthly blessings brought Siddhartha, out of the royal palace and converted him through attainment of *nirvana* into Buddha. In recent years the Western youths, especially the hippies from America, are searching for spiritual emancipation in different parts of India out of discontentment. In the *Holy Bible* too a similar idea of divine punishment and non-possession appears; and perhaps, Gandhi was aware of it. We are advised to practise non-possession, "provide neither gold, nor silver, nor brass in your purses; nor scrip for your journey, neither two coats, neither shoes, nor yet staves: for the workman is worthy of his meat.[138] And the divine punishment is "...Verily I say unto you that rich man shall hardly enter into the Kingdom of heaven. And again I say unto you, it is easier for a camel to go through the eye of a needle, than for a rich man to enter into the Kingdom of heaven."[139] Thus, to Gandhi, non-possession is preferable to discontentment, spiritual bankruptcy and divine punishment.

Perfect observance of this vow brings absolute contentment and fulfilment. In order to observe non-possession precisely an individual has to live the life of a bird. A bird has no possession, no stock of provisions; still it maintains livelihood by the grace of God whose eulogies it sings with thanks and contentment. An almost similar idea appears in the *Bible* : "Behold the fowls of the air.... Your heavenly Father feedeth them."[140] Likewise, according to Gandhi, a *satyagrahi* will have no possession, no stock of food as future provisions. His food and shelter will be provided by God without fail. Gandhi throws light on this point and clears his idea in a very simple way.[141] The fact is that in this world of spiritual discontentment a *satyagrahi* seems to the public a monk, a 'godly man' who exerts spiritual influence on them; and consequently as the tradition goes they pay homage to him so earnestly that the *satyagrahi* never suffers from scarcity of necessities. This means that total renunciation or absolute non-possession may seem an impossibility to an ordinary man. But we should strive to realize this ideal constantly. We can thoroughly scrutinize our necessities and reduce them, bit by bit, to the least possible number. It may take days, months and years but progress towards the goal will relieve us of all troublesome burdens and bless us with a positive joy.

Non-possession is the only way to Truth, true knowledge. Here Gandhi had in mind the nature of knowledge as elucidated in chapter thirteen of the *Gita* in which humility (*amanitvam*), non-pride (*adamvitva*), etc., are mentioned as constituents of true knowledge. The observance of non-possession urges us to possess true knowledge in the mind; and the thoughts that never contribute to self-realization, on the contrary, obstruct it, are to be shunned. That is to say, Gandhi here dips into the depth of human psychology. Thoughts are very potential and are often converted into action. In other words, our world of actions is often steered by the trend of thought that occurs in our minds. Hence thoughts should not be possessed by ignorance which offers hindrance to God-realization.

Non-possession fosters not only thought but also actions promoting truth (*sattvika* type). The realization of true knowledge tends to actions arising from pure psychical tendencies, i.e., a psychical state devoid of sentient life naturally aims at spiritual uplift. A perfect observer of non-possession will dedicate the whole of his working hours to the service of humanity. He cannot remain idle even for a moment. Gandhi says, "Every moment of our life should be filled with mental or physical activity, but that activity should be *sattvika*, tending to Truth."[142] In this way non-possession determines the course of our actions, and thereby the welfare of the society.

So far as our present analysis discloses, is that non-possession is a symbol of dignity amongst the people, and a sign of friendship with God. He writes, "...God is the friend of the poor..."[143] Gandhi narrates the way of life of a recluse, Bhansali, who adopted absolute non-possession."[144] Here Gandhi refers to some saintly personalities who used to wander from one corner of the country to the other without any provision, and who were entertained by householders everywhere as 'godly guests' (*Atithi Narayan*). An observer of non-possession possesses a rare treasure, contentment which is rarely enjoyed by the rich. And a poor takes pride in poverty which is free from, as mentioned above, all the evils of riches. Here Gandhi glorifies poverty as a sign of social dignity, and blessing of God. We can do justice to this viewpoint only if we treat it in the above perspective.

To sum up: Non-possession as a cardinal virtue was prescribed by Gandhi for the *satyagrahis* who dedicated themselves specifically to the liberation of the motherland, and generally to the welfare of humanity. It was a necessity of the day and an integral part of the eleven vows. Its key role in the spiritual uplift of an individual is well accepted. Anyone acquainted with the history and cultural heritage of India will admit that the saints, recluses, i.e., spiritual personalities in general had, and still have, no want of basic necessities which are spontaneously and respectfully supplied by the masses. During those days of freedom movement the *satyagrahis* too commanded a similar position amongst the people and enjoyed the privileges. In this light the Gandhian prescription of non-possession is apt so far as the *satyagrahis* are concerned. But saints, recluses, *satyagrahis* (in perfection) etc. are exceptional and supranormal persons. The common man for whom and by whom the social order is running is an earthly being who possesses merits and demerits, a feeling of 'give and take', a yearning for accumulation and charity, possession and non-possession simultaneously. The craving for security, i.e., future provision to a limited extent is quite natural, and perhaps, not inapt for an ordinary man. The lifestyle (perfect non-possession) adopted by the birds, saints, recluses, etc., may be regarded as an ideal but none would deny that some sort of possession is necessary for the smooth maintenance of livelihood of any man. The question relates to the degree, the quality and quantity of possession. We should minimize our necessities and possessions (not ascetic curtailment and suppression) so that it may suit a normal, natural and simple life; and may not become an eye sore to the neighbours. This is lively humanism, and perhaps, a sound one.

(7) *Physical Labour or Bread Labour:* It is a corollary of the above mentioned virtue of non-stealing and non-possession, especially a means for the attainment of the latter. In it the spiritual, political and social outlook of Gandhi is blended. Our later analysis will reveal that the attainment of the total manifestation of all the traits of an individual together with economic self-sufficiency was the primary motive behind his prescription of this vow. According to Gandhi, "God can only appear as bread and butter" to the hungry and dumb millions of India. The provision of food to them was urgent and important. Hence he prescribed physical labour or bread labour to that end. Let us bring forth the salient features latent in it.

(a) It conveys a wider implication than what is commonly meant by the term 'bread'. The term 'bread' is here used as a symbol to cover all the unavoidable primary necessities of life. Of course, in the Gandhian sense, it includes spinning, weaving, carpentry, smithery, watering, splitting firewood, cooking, sweeping, washing clothes, sanitary service, farming, dairying, tanning, etc. It means every productive labour necessary for simple and plain living of a *satyagrahi*, i.e., self-reliance in every walk of life.

(b) His eclectic mind derived nourishment both from the East and the West in the formation of this noble ideal. The term 'bread-labour' was first coined by a Russian writer T.M. Bondaref and was later widely publicised by Tolstoy and Ruskin. After reading Ruskin's *Unto This Last* in 1904 Gandhi was unconsciously observing this great vow to a great extent. But it was the later reading of Tolstoy's works that made him actively conscious of the urgency and importance of this noble ideal."[145] This divine commandment is also mentioned in the *Bible* which preaches, "In the sweat of thy face shalt thou eat bread, till thou return into the ground; for out of it wast thou taken : for dust thou *art*, and unto dust shalt thou return."[146]

Not only the *Bible*, Gandhi acknowledges his debt to *Gita*, the mother *Kamdhenu* (especially Chapter 3) too.[147] The prescription of bread labour was undoubtedly a bold and revolutionary one because during the first quarter of this century the rich, *Rajas* and *Nawabs* of the then India, were living idle life, and indulging in all sorts of dandyism and orgies in the name of fashion while the dumb millions were starving to death. In the midst of these political and social adversities Gandhi launched this movement of physical labour which was dimly and less audibly preached more than two thousand years ago in Indian scriptures. In the *Dharmashastras* Manu laid emphasis on the dignity of labour and the ideal that an individual should take the minimum from the society and give the maximum in return. Thus the influence of both Eastern and Western thought in Gandhi's prescription of bread labour is beyond question.

(c) To Gandhi bread labour is divine and mandatory for all irrespective of caste and creed, riches and poverty. It has the sanction, both of the *Gita* and the *Bible*. Gandhi followed this tradition and enriched it with divinity."[148] It is universally applicable to each and everybody; and none can evade it. More than nine-tenths of humanity live by physical labour, and the rest should follow their footprints so that there may be enough food for all. The traditional division of labour and its modern practice could not satisfy him fully. The neglect of the toiling mass (*Shudras*) by the lazy intellectuals, middle men, and aristrocrats of India pained him. The hatred of the so-called men of upper strata of the toiling masses—the bottom dogs of society—automatically gave rise to inertia, lethargy, and a dislike for physical labour.[149] Observance of bread labour as a vow by all, irrespective of caste and creed, will abolish the social barrier between the toiling masses and the intellectuals. In this way the social distance between the bottom dogs who are entrusted with the duty of physical labour and the people of upper strata who usually claim a monopoly of intellectual and spiritual labour may be shortened. According to Gandhi, God tells man to perform some productive labour of any kind so that 'invidious distinctions of rank' along with incidental inertia and aversion to labour may die out.

(d) This implies division of labour or work or duty. Those who perform duties according to their respective stations in life are also bread-labourers. But their duties must include some sort of productive physical labour so that the *Varnashrama* may retain its character. That is to say Gandhi wanted to retain *Varnashrama* (division of labour) in the sense of performing imposed duties by birth, and not casteism, along with some sort of productive physical or bread labour."[150] Gandhi retains traditional division of labour with a condemnation of casteism, and supplements it with physical labour. Physical labour is in no way an obstruction rather an aid in the performance of all kinds of labour, i.e., intellectual, military, commercial, agricultural, etc.

(e) Bread labour has a very close relation to other virtues. Gandhi says, "Bread labour is a veritable blessing to one who would observe Non-violence, worship Truth, and make the observance of *brahmacharya* a natural act."[151] A votary of truth and non-violence must observe also non-stealing and non-possession not in the absolute but in the relative sense of possession, i.e., unavoidable and immediate primary needs. It is conducive to observance of *brahmacharya* too. He admits the fruitful effect of physical labour on it. The whole day's hard labour resulting in complete physical exhaustion contribute much to this effect. Gandhi concludes this from his experience.[152]

(f) The virtue of bread labour is a voluntary and not a compulsory one, because compulsion breeds slavery while voluntary bread labour is a blessing. From the ethical standpoint a man under compulsion cannot be held responsible for an action. Further it has an oppressive effect on the mind of the agent because it often deadens the finer feelings, the subtle psychical qualities of our minds. As a result our physical labour becomes a drudgery, a burden, a troublesome job ultimately giving rise to economic poverty, physical and mental disease, and spiritual discontentment. Gandhi describes this point also.[153] Voluntary bread labour infuses joy and happiness, sound health and perfect peace, engender energy and capacity for service to humanity.

(g) Intellectual labour is compatible with bread labour and hence the former must be supplemented by the latter. Intellectual work and physical labour are of equal importance, and one cannot supersede the other. Gandhi makes a sharp distinction between physical labour and intellectual labour although, to him, they compensate one another. It is the duty of the body to meet its needs by physical labour while the soul contemplates plans, and performs some creative works for its own satisfaction. Intellectual labour may create some invaluable piece of (work which may claim highest oppreciation and worldwide form but it no) way it can serve the purpose of physical labour. The sonnets of Shakespeare and Rabindranath Tagore, the masterpieces of Da Vinci and Picaso, the single heavenly symphony of Beethoven and Tansen are undoubtedly assets of humankind, but they in no way, singly or collectively, can produce a grain of foodstuff which is indispensable for living beings. In other words, intellectual labour can never be a substitute for physical labour. While the latter can stand by itself, the former would be an impossibility without it. Gandhi surmised some objections from the intellectual corner, and in anticipation commented, perhaps rightly, "Let me not be misunderstood. I do not discount the value of intellectual labour, but no amount of it is any compensation for bodily labour which everyone of us is born to give for the common good of all. It may be, often is, infinitely superior to bodily labour, but it never is or can be a substitute for it, even as intellectual food, though far superior to the grains we eat, never can be a substitute for them. Indeed, without the products of the earth those of the intellect would be an impossibility."[154]

Gandhi's anticipation of misunderstanding was not at all baseless. Some people argued that those who served society through brain work ought to be exempted from manual labour. Because their physical labour is a sheer wastage of time during which they might have rendered some service to the society more valuable and more productive than the output of physical labour. The intellectual giants like Rabindranath, Raman and others who were performing useful social work in some way or other were to be exempted from it. To these objections Gandhi emphatically answers, "Intellectual work is important and has an undoubted place in the scheme of life. But what I insist on is the necessity of physical labour. No man, I claim, ought to be free from that obligation. It will serve to improve even the quality of his intellectual output. I venture to say that in ancient times Brahmins worked with their bodies as with their minds. But even if they did not, body labour was a proved necessity at the present time. In this connection I would refer to the life of Tolstoy... "[155] Gandhi's clarion call to mankind in general, whether intellectual or physical labourer, was to perform some sort of physical labour for the welfare of society. Otherwise, they would be eating stolen goods and living in a way somehow ungodly. This is true of all people irrespective of caste and creed, status and vocation. The *munis*, *sannyasis*, *yogins*, recluse and others who live on alms and charity of the people are no exceptions to it. Because offering sacrifice is 'a vital condition of our very existence' and it is with this bond that we are born. Mere stoppage of work is not renunciation but inertia. After a long discussion on various aspects of bread labour with Prof. Bhansali, a recluse, Gandhi concludes, "You know that the *Gita* says that he who eats without offering the daily sacrifice steals his food. To beg one's food is a good thing, but only after one has offered one's sacrifice ...e.g., Jain *munis* and *sannyasis*. They live on alms, but they do so because they persuade themselves that they are offering sufficient sacrifice in the shape of the teaching they impart. Here they are somewhat mistaken, as I think. It is their duty to impart spiritual teaching, but all the same they must offer some sacrifice in the shape of bread-labour, and rather than expect their food as a reward of their sacrifice... To do no work is no renunciation. It is inertia."[156] The same principle is applicable to persons, who due to some unavoidable circumstances, live on doles and rations. As a matter of principle Gandhi was against giving any kind of alms and charity. But he admitted a concession to those who, due to some unavoidable circumstances, say earthquake, cyclone, flood, famine, etc., were compelled to live on doles temporarily. And these people would enjoy doles for a limited period within which they must find out some means for maintenance of livelihood. In his words, "It was wrong for any citizen to expect rations without doing some physical work."[157] In short, Gandhi prescribed physical labour for all—householders, *satyagrahis*, recluses, *sannyasis*, refugees—without any exception.

Some critics may still argue that physical labour cannot go with intellectual work since the former obstructs the development of the latter, and consequently, leads to intellectual bankruptcy. By intellectual development they generally mean abstract contemplative knowledge concerning the universe. But Gandhi refutes this objection by saying, "People often say that in an institution like the *Ashram* where body labour is given pride of place there is no scope for intellectual development, but my experience is just the reverse. Everyone who has been to the *Ashram* has made intellectual progress as well,..."[158] In support of this above argument he cites the life of Tolstoy, the burning example that he had in mind while propounding this ideal of bread labour.[159] Indeed, a sound body possesses a sound mind. Physical labour builds our bodies fairly well, and at the same time enhances the potentiality of inner being which is the main spring of intellectual work. This point was readily seized by Gandhi who preached bread labour for all men of the intelligentsia. Above all, "educational psychology has for long recognized that the use of hands profoundly helps mental growth."[160]

Here the contribution of some great thinkers to this end will, perhaps, be conducive towards a proper assessment of Gandhian standpoint. Karl Marx in his monumental work, *Das Capital* asserts that physical labour refreshes our minds, and improves on intellectual ability."[161] Lenin too stressed the eradication of the distinction between intellectual and manual labour for the unified, integrated and harmonious development of humanity.[162]

The Chinese communists have implemented the principle of

'learning through doing' with the same objective. Their 'half work, half-study'curriculum has made remarkable advancement in the field of education. It offers a full-time formal school curriculum for a particular period followed by various practical studies in the factories and in the fields."[163]

The Zakir Hussain Committee in India investigated the problems of education; and found out a healthy and wholesome influence of manual labour upon the overall development of intelligence and personality.[164]

We have so far discussed the views of great thinkers on bread labour and its wholesome effect on the intellectual development of an individual. This is exactly the standpoint of Gandhi. The moot point behind his prescription of the vow of bread labour was to make people self-sufficient, productive; and thereby to attain manifestation of their being in its entirety. He assumed and believed that "the principal means of stipulating the intellect was manual training"; and manual and intellectual labour were indispensable necessities of life. They are complementary to each other, and their reciprocal influence brings immense benefit to mankind.

(h) It has an economic implication which forms an integral part of his social philosophy. Quite early in his struggle for India's independence Gandhi realized that political freedom could not be fully realized unless economic solvency was achieved. Bread labour was aimed at the solution of food and clothing problem of poverty stricken India. If people spin and weave their clothings, produce food-stuff necessary for sustenance, they would automatically attain self-sufficiency, and the bond of dependence would automatically loosened. This means the loss of chain of dependence on others.[165] Moreover, bread labour together with non-possession, if sincerely and honestly observed by all, will lead to economic equality which is the nucleus of *sarvodaya* or universal eudaemonism. Above all, it places the intellectual labour on the same level with physical labour from the economic standpoint too, i.e., in an ideal society the intelligentsia would get remuneration equal to that of manual workers. It would remove the disparity between man and man.

(i) From the utilitarian standpoint it serves various purposes of society. It will solve food and clothing problems. The cry of over population, disease and misery would be heard no more. It improves general health, engenders energy for the attainment of self-sufficiency. It simplifies our way of life, promotes the observance of non-violent values. It inaugurates a new horizon by initiating insight into our inner being, and co-ordinates it with physical labour. As a result of which there shall be an end to inertia and lethargy of our semi-comatic life. It will introduce a revolutionary change in our traditional trade and commerce. Large-scale mechanical productions, ever-increasing profit-motive of greedy businessmen, dehumanization of human beings by oppression and exploitation, will be no more. In social life, everybody will be his own master and consequently the class-distinction between rich and poor, high and low, touchable and untouchable will be abolished.

(j) It conveys a message of closest co-operation and universal brotherhood. The two establishments that he founded in South Africa taught him that non-violence and truth without common physical labour would turn into futility. Physical labour places some constructive programme before it without which it takes to violence. In order to execute the constructive programme physical labour engenders fellow-feeling and brotherhood amongst the co-workers who feel like free birds in the air and rise above the artificial barriers of religion, caste, nationality, profession, etc.'[166] Verily, in those days of harsh and rigid conservatism when the status of an individual was determined by religion, profession, caste, etc. Gandhi performed an almost impossible task by assembling them together under the symbol of bread labour and wove them into a nexus of co-operation.

(k) According to Gandhi, bread labour conveys the message of service to humanity, the highest mission of human life.[167] Gandhi brings forth the nature of servitude latent in bread labour. In the above paragraphs we have also seen that sacrifice and bread labour were synonymous to Gandhi. Its ideal is that so long as we live we should render service to others. Gandhi went a step further and conferred the right of voting to those only who performed physical labour. In an ideal state although all members are equal, and are entitled to enjoy facilities without any discrimination, he would not grant voting right to non-physical labourers simply on the ground that bread labour is a part of our being. And hence non-performers being devoid of beinghood and divinity should be deprived of voting right."[168]

(l) Although Gandhi brought forth the various social features of bread labour yet one aspect of it—the mode of production and distribution—remains untouched here. Gandhian standpoint of the retention of old *varna* system together with the observance of bread labour seems to have failed to yield a scientific and correct solution of the problem. A sound social order would demand a revolutionary change of the present mode of production and distribution. In this context

Buddhadeva Bhattacharyya comments, "Gandhi did not approach the problem from this sociological point of view. He would have replied that one need not wait for the distant future, but start from the immediate present."[169]

To sum up: Bread labour is voluntary, divine and an obligation for all. It serves various social purposes, and engenders co-operation and brotherhood amongst co-workers. It is a key to social service and statutory power. Without it an individual would lose the very essence of his being. In those days of rigid conservatism and political hypocrisy the introduction of bread labour as a moral discipline for all was undoubtedly a bold step. It was characteristically progressive and humanitarian in outlook, and a vehement revolt against the traditional division of labour and caste system of India of that era. He viewed this virtue from all quarters—social, moral, spiritual, economic, intellectual, political, etc.—and strove to infuse energy and valour into the life of a semi-comatic nation.

Swadeshi

The eighth vow is *swadeshi* which plays a pivotal role in the development of Gandhian philosophy in all its aspects—metaphysical, social, ethical, political, economic, educational, cultural, religious, etc. The vows of bread labour and *swadeshi* jointly aim primarily at economic self-sufficiency, especially in respect of food and clothing of the nation. The problem of starving, miserably clad dumb millions deeply moved him. At that time the British merchants used to buy raw materials from India at very low prices and brought back from England the finished goods to sell in Indian market at a high profit. And with this end of exploitation in mind they tactfully destroyed the excellent indigenous industries, and caused unemployment and starvation to millions of workers in India. While launching *swadeshi* programme, Gandhi optimistically hoped to provide employment to starving millions so that they may attain self-sufficiency, a stepping stone towards freedom or *swaraj*. By propagating *swadeshi*, in a nutshell, Gandhi intended an individual to identify himself with the dumb millions in every sphere of life. Its implications are as follows:

(a) It has generally been interpreted both in broad and narrow senses. Gandhi says, "The broad definition of *swadeshi* is the use of all home-made things to the exclusion of foreign things, in so far as such use is necessary for the protection of home industry, more especially those industries without which India will become pauperized.

In my opinion, therefore, *swadeshi* which excludes the use of everything foreign, because it is foreign, no matter how beneficial it may be, and irrespective of the fact that it impoverishes nobody, is a narrow interpretation of *swadeshi*."[170] Here Gandhi's motif behind *swadeshi* programme is to foster the interest and development of home industry. And in that venture he would take foreign help in so far as it does not hamper the above interest. Everything foreign is not bad and, in fact, the eclectic mind of Gandhi got nourishment, as discussed above, from various Western sources. His farsight warned, "To reject foreign manufactures merely because they are foreign, and to go on wasting national time and money in the promotion in one's country of manufactures for which it is not suited would be criminal folly, and a negation of the *swadeshi* spirit..."[171]

(b) Apart from the above broad and narrow senses, it is a dynamic principle which underwent an evolutionary process of modification during Gandhi's lifetime as circumstances changed. In his words, "I swear by *swadeshi* because it is an evolutionary process gaining strength as it goes forward."[172] This dynamism is the life of Gandhian thought. His pragmatism and practical idealism taught him as he moved. He abandoned an earlier position, whatever its value might be, if it failed to subserve the dumb millions and thereby to attain truth. In 1916, his original standpoint regarding *swadeshi* was to attain complete self-sufficiency for the pauperized nation and hence to some extent economic isolation of autarchy from the rest of the world was in his mind.[173] But his pragmatic mind surmised the evil consequences of boycotting everything foreign. At that time India was miserably poor in scientific and technological field. The West was attaining progress and prosperity by dint of its newly achieved experiments. Gandhi's farsight did not overlook it. He fervently intented to take this technological assistance from the foreign countries. That is why later on in 1926 he amended his earlier position and condemned the rejection of "foreign manufactures merely because they are foreign as a criminal folly." (see the preceding paragraph). In 1939, while discussing the same issue he made a similar statement, "Any article is *swadeshi* if it subserves the interest of the millions, even though the capital and talent are foreign but under effective Indian control... I would love to secure the engineering talent of the West to give me a village wheel which will beat the existing wheels."[174] Thus *swadeshi* is a dynamic principle which underwent modifications during Gandhi's lifetime. It, in spite of strict adherence to its true spirit, welcomes foreign assistance whatever might be its nature, if it promotes the interest of the nation.

(c) It is a universal law in the sense that its observance means service to mankind in general. Gandhi here takes the world as a family; and its members as organically related to one another in such a manner that the service to one's next door neighbour means the same to an individual living at a distant place with a different nationality. This feature of universal service enriches the glory of Gandhian humanism.[175] Its true spirit fosters nationalism and internationalism at the same time. It advises us to serve the motherland in preference to others; and to serve the nearest surroundings in preference to remoter ones; to prefer indigenous mores and customs, ideals and institutions to foreign ones. Of course, all sorts of prejudice and dogmatism should be abandoned in this context because irrationality and unhealthy nationalism obstruct the way to progress and development. Moreover, some persons, in the immediate surroundings, say relations, dependents and neighbours do require my service as much as I require theirs. If I leave them they will be "out of gear" and my "Knight-errantry", i.e., servitude to foreigners will create disturbance in the new place. Here his categorical advice is, "...a culpable neglect of my immediate neighbours, and an unintended disservice to the people whom I wish to serve, would be the first fruits of my violation of the principle of Swadeshi."[176] But from this we should not conclude that swadeshi is confinement within one's own narrow surroundings. It also is a clarion call to internationalism, to service towards the whole of humanity. It is through pure service of the neighbourhood that we extend our service to humanity in general. It is the purity of service i.e., selfless, legitimate, liberal, non-injurious quality of actions, that constitutes the very essence of swadeshi. Thus swadeshi fosters nationalism and internationalism at the same time if we can sacrifice our narrow, self-interests at the altar of national and international service[177]. Thus observance of swadeshi is, in guise, service to mankind in general.

(d) Swadeshi is directly based on the *Gita* ideal of *svadharma*.[178] But this *svadharma* is quite compatible with internationalism. It teaches us not to harbour ill-will against anybody on earth. It is a cult of universal love and self-less service to humanity in general.[179] Moreover, this virtue of swadeshi provides for the observance of culture and customs of foreigners while staying in foreign countries without impairing its spirit. The idea is that through the observance of mores and customs of foreigners, while living amongst them, the visitor will earn their selfless love that promotes universal brotherhood. Gandhi says, " 'In Rome do as the Romans do', is not a meaningless saying. We must observe the manners and the customs of the country whose salt we eat. When I was in South Africa I tried to use as many things as I could made by African hands."[180] Thus swadeshi urges us to love indigenous mores and customs, ideals and institutions; and at the same time not to hate but to love other's manners and mores, cult and customs while having intercourse with them.

(e) It implies service to non-neighbours as co-extensive with *svadharma*. It is both exclusive and inclusive. That is to say, although swadeshi instructs us to serve the next-door neighbours and immediate surroundings, still those who dedicate themselves to the whole humanity are not to be condemned. All men are not born with equal potentiality and capacity. Those who are God-gifted, and possess unlimited energy are to be encouraged in their mission of service to humanity. Their confinement within the narrow limitation of village or district or province or nation is a sheer wastage of their invaluable service which, if extended to humanity in general, will bring heavenly blessing on earth.[181] It gathers strength as it extends, and indicates the limitation of human capacity for service. Indeed, the true spirit of swadeshi urges an individual to sacrifice himself at the altar of universal service. In its purest form swadeshi is the zenith of altruism.

(f) The spiritual implication of swadeshi is that it is a stepping stone towards the emancipation of the soul. It is generally accepted by the systems of Indian philosophy that the soul in itself is pure but it becomes subject to pleasure and pain of the body with which it is associated for the time being. Gandhi shares this view and tells us to seek freedom from earthly bondage through service to humanity with which God stands identical.[182]

(g) Its religious implication is as follows. In a preceding paragraph we have seen that the physical body is an obstruction to liberation of the soul, and consequently a hindrance to service to humanity and God. Hence swadeshi should be observed as a religious discipline regardless of physical discomfort. In his words, "(it is) a religious discipline to be undergone in utter disregard of the physical discomfort it may cause to the individual."[183] Gandhi was a *sanàtani* Hindu though his eclectic mind absorbed the noble ideas of various religions of the world. He did not accept the prejudice (untouchability, corruptions, pomp and glitter) of his ancestral religion. However, he rectified it and remained absolutely faithful to it.

(h) In the political field the spirit of swadeshi shows him the right path through the maze of crazy violence dominating the world. The techniques of political movement that he applied against the opponent party were in some form or other in keeping with the traditional thought of India. The non-violent techniques of non-co-operation, civil disobedience, boycott, fasting, picketing, etc. are to some extent refined modernized forms of political protest launched in ancient India[184]. Gandhi confesses his debt to ancient India. A reader of Gandhi's life and works knows it well that he observed and applied these institutions of ancient India in his own style and rectified them as circumstances demanded.

(i) His educational ideas too are dominated by the swadeshi spirit. Throughout his life he insisted on a national scheme of education based on the ancient tradition and appropriate to the present surroundings. He ardently intended our education to have its roots in the soil of our country. His suggestion of education to be imparted through the mother tongue is scientific, realistic and sound. He condemns the foreign medium of instruction which causes brain-fag, turns our students into crammers, imitators and unfit for original work and thought. Above all, foreign medium is totally unsuitable for mass communication.[185] Hence he warns us[186]. This swadeshi spirit is manifested at every step of his educational scheme which aimed solely at the service of dumb millions in all respects.

(j) In social philosophy his ideas on family, marriage, caste, *varnashrama*, communal peace, etc. bear testimony to his swadeshi outlook. He condemned the existing caste-system as a blemish on society; and highly appreciated the system of *varnashrama dharma*, division of labour for its beneficial effect on the toiling masses. His ceaseless effort to establish communal harmony was prompted by the swadeshi ideal which in its spiritual aspect means realization of divine unity amongst all earthly creatures. The same spirit of swadeshi plays a pivotal role in his campaign for intermarriage, interdining, removal of untouchability, etc.

(k) This swadeshi spirit is also predominant in his metaphysical and ethical concepts. In the preceding chapters we have seen that he derived nourishment from the Indian traditional thought; and reoriented and applied it to solve modern problems at the demand of circumstances. As we have discussed them above no further elaboration seems necessary here.

(l) The nucleus of the vow of swadeshi is its economic implication. Gandhi explains his standpoint by saying, "In that of economics, I should use only things that are produced by my immediate neighbours and serve those industries by making them efficient and complete where they might be found wanting."[187] His primary aim, as discussed above, in preaching this vow was to utilize the whole manpower of poverty-stricken India, and thereby achieve self-sufficiency for all in every walk of life. He would permit import of those essential commodities which India could not produce herself. He forbids us to use machine or mill products which often incur deception of workers. This leads us to his programme of Khadi (home spinning and weaving industry), the main-spring of his economic movement. In this context K. Ramakrishna Rao observes, "The swadeshi concept has political and moral as well as economic implications. But Gandhi worked out more fully its economic implications by his emphasis on Khadi.....When applied to economics, swadeshi takes the form of encouraging and propagating Indian-made goods, particularly the minor, small-scale home industries like Khadi."[188] Let us explain it.

Regarding the nature of Khadi Gandhi says, "...I hit upon Khadi as the necessary and the most important corollary of the principle of swadeshi in its application to society."[189] The above excerpt illustrates the simple truth that apart from Khadi programme the vow of swadeshi is useless. It is 'the first indispensable step towards the discharge of swadeshi *dharma*, towards society.' The idea of Khadi first dawned on his mind in 1908 and took its concrete shape in 1915 while he was prescribing observances for the ashramites. Later on it absorbed his mind so deeply that it became the primary sacrifice and principal physical activity or bread labour for the ashramites.[190] In his later life, enriched with a variety of experiences, he emphasized Khadi to fight against concentration of power and capital; to bring forth amongst the masses an equitable distribution of wealth. Khadi appeared to him as the most powerful non-violent weapon, "the nearest moral equivalent of the infantryman's rifle,"[191] to wipe out the evil forces that paralyzed the economic life of a semi-comatic nation. Through the introduction of Khadi and spinning wheel he strove to regenerate a new economic era, to regain the lost paradise that the imperialist ruling party tactfully destroyed by gradual unjust tyrannical methods. An elaborate discussion of Gandhian economics is not the objective of this treatise. Not only that a detailed discussion of Khadi movement also would be irrelevant here since at present we are concerned with swadeshi as a vow. However, some points are to be noted here in order to understand properly the exact nature of swadeshi. Khadi and the spinning wheel stand for a symbol which is widely popular amongst the Indian masses; and promotes national solidarity. B. Kumarappa, an eminent Gandhian scholar, observes, "The most outstanding and the most popular of all the symbols associated with Gandhi is undoubtedly the spinning wheel."[192] Moreover, it provided the dumb millions with a political weapon of defence giving rise to nationwide united action in concrete form. And lastly, Khadi is constructive and purposeful in the sense that it, keeping with the tradition, introduced a new economic trend which like a banyan tree exerted a far-reaching influence in British India.

Gandhi's emphasis on Khadi and other indigenous small-scale industries has often been a target of criticism. His strong propaganda for using India-made goods; and advocacy for imposition of protective duties upon foreign goods so that national interests may be nurtured gave birth to some rumour that he had secret understanding with the Indian capitalist class. Gunnar Myrdal, for example, criticises, "Ironically, *swadeshi* later lent ideological support to national economic planning."[193] But this criticism overlooks the true spirit of Gandhian swadeshi movement. Gandhi who dedicated his life to the service of the dumb millions, and lived the life of a *fakir* had in no sense the interest of the Indian capitalist class in mind while preaching swadeshi. Buddhadeva Bhattacharyya aptly observes "...a correct reading will be that he was not guided by any such definite interest, though objectively the Indian capitalists benefited by this demand."[194] Philip Spratt also holds a similar opinion, saying "His support is no doubt likely to benefit the capitalists rather than anybody else, but he does not advocate with that intention. His protection is a villager's protection, designed to help the effort for self-sufficiency, not that for profits."[195] Gandhi himself says, "The person who has taken the vow of swadeshi will never use articles which conceivably involve violation of truth in their manufacture or on the part of their manufacturers. It follows, for instance, that a votary of truth will not use articles manufactured in the mills of Manchester, Germany or India, for he cannot be sure that they involve no such violation of truth. Moreover, labourers suffer much in the mills.....Further reflection will show that the use of foreign cloth can be held to involve a breach of the vows of non-stealing and non-possession."[196] Thus Gandhi's clarion call was to nurture indigenous small-scale industries, and avert mill products in general whether it was of Manchester or India.

To sum up: The vow of swadeshi represents in a nutshell the

salient features of Gandhian thought. As discussed above it implies his cultural, educational, spiritual, religious, metaphysical, ethical, social, political, economic and other ideas. His aim was to provide basic necessities, especially food and clothing without which a social man cannot live, freely available to all like God's air and water. With this end in view he planned an economic system in which everybody would get sufficient work to make both ends meet. This means that the basic necessities of life should be produced and distributed under the efficient control of dumb millions. This objective necessarily led him to the propagation of swadeshi which in course of time stood as a symbol of minor, small-scale home industries. And consequently, it caused his aversion to mechanical civilization which centralized wealth in the hands of a few, and dehumanized human beings. Of course, his fervent humanism and burning passion for service to humanity was the matrix of all these.

Fearlessness

The ninth in the series of vows is fearlessness. It is one of the essential qualities of a good man, and is included in the list of virtues of ancient India. In the *Upanisads*, the *Vedanta* and the *Gita* fearlessness has been appraised as one of the cardinal virtues. Gandhi recognizes the importance of fearlessness by saying, "In my opinion, however, fearlessness richly deserves the first rank assigned to it. For it is indispensable for the growth of the other noble qualities. How can one seek Truth, or cherish Love, without fearlessness?"[197] Gandhi prescribed it in response to political situation of his time. Like other virtues, we should remember, it is prescribed as a code of discipline for the *satyagrahis* who were trained to suffer inhuman oppression, and in exceptional cases, even death in their non-violent techniques. In those turbulent days of movement for independence the satyagrah is observed and carried out these vows as divine commandments and faced valiantly the ruling imperialist power whose oppression knew no bounds.

A question may be raised: What, according to Gandhi, is the nature of fearlessness? Gandhi brings out its nature by saying, "Fearlessness connotes freedom from all external fear,—fear of disease, bodily injury and death, of dispossession, of losing one's nearest and dearest, of losing reputation or giving offence, and so on."[198] It implies absence of all kinds of fear—fear of death, molestation, hunger, humiliation, criticism, ghosts, evil spirits, etc. The above mentioned causes of fear are earthly, delusive, deceptive and hence fall short of perfection. Perfect fearlessness is heavenly, and can be attained only through gradual combat of the causes of fear bit by bit; through the realization of God. It is God's grace that can bestow perfect fearlessness on us. Like perfection of other concepts of Gandhian thought perfect fearlessness also remains beyond the reach of imperfect human beings.

Fearlessness is the backbone of all other virtues. It fosters their interest and promotes development. But its absence breeds panic which often goes into the depth of man's constitution, mental and physical, and destroys the morale of an individual in such a way that it turns him into a cripple, impotent and comatic.

Fearlessness assumes two aspects—external and internal. In its external form fearlessness takes into account all the causes of fear that are visible in the external world. It includes fear of disease, death of one'self and nearest one's, physical injury, ill-name, etc. There are some self-styled heroes who pretend to be dauntless and fearless but at the moment of crisis, say the minor ills of life or separation from loved ones, they simply show a clean pair of heels. Some misers save their possessions even at the cost of their lives. Some will commit any number of mischiefs and go up to any extent only to save the self created ivory tower of prestige. It is our everyday experience that some people are so afraid of incurring the world's odium that they never raise their heads and wander in the narrow crooked paths. So to realize Truth we must conquer all these external fears without fail.

Fearlessness has an internal form too. It demands the conquest of our inner being in its entirety. The animal passions are enemies to self-realization. The mental activities like anger, greed, etc., give rise to a variety of fear. So we should cultivate the virtue of non-attachment for which a complete victory over the animal passions, the internal enemies, is a *sine qua non*. Gandhi insists on the achievement of mental balance through which the internal adversary can be easily overcome. And once the inner passions are conquered, the external fear will vanish like mists. In fact, our soul is pure in itself, and has no room for impurity in it. Hence in order to get rid of fear—both internal and external—we must know the *Atman* that transcends the body.

The knowledge of the *Atman* and the cultivation of non-attachment leads to the problem of God whom alone we should fear. Let us see what Gandhi says in this context, "You will find that God is always by the side of the fearless. Therefore, we should fear Him alone and seek His protection. All other fear, will then by itself disappear."[199]

"...there is only one Being,—if Being is the proper term to be used,—whom we have to fear, and that is God. When we fear God, we shall fear no man, no matter how highly placed he may be."[200] In this way we may multiply instances of Gandhi's views expressed at different times of his life to prove God as the acme of fearlessness. The inmost truth of fearlessness seems to lie in the fact that the habit of non-attachment and truth-realization removes our illusion regarding earthly objects including this body. So we should fear none except God who is the creator and destroyer of the order of the universe. He is the only Almighty being at whose mercy all beings—living and non-living—do exist. This is the reason why Gandhi advises us to fear God alone. It is here noteworthy that the Gandhian virtue of fearlessness is apparently an absolute and unconditional concept. It is absolute and unconditional as regards earthly beings. But when applied to God it becomes conditional and relative because it is Him, the only Almighty one, whom we should fear, i.e., fearlessness falls short of God.

A relevant question may be asked: How can we know God, the acme of fearlessness? Gandhi's emphatic answer is: through self-purificatory sacrifice we can know Him. Regarding the efficacy of self-purification through prayer.[201] In fact, an individual who prays honestly and sincerely to God can never have any improper desire because true prayer demands self-purification through relinquishment of the two roots of fear—death and material possessions. It has been experienced that a man of prayer and self-purification attains gradually that enlightened state of mind which readily embraces death as a godly blessing and gets rid of possessions as of no worth. He relinquishes wealth in the spirit that he has no moral right to possess it while millions are prey to miserable pauperism and starvation. In this way an individual through self-purificatory sacrifice of the two roots of fear, death and possession, becomes a purified being and achieves that rare state of mind—perfect fearlessness—by the grace of God.

In this connection the relation between fearlessness and cowardice demands a special discussion because Gandhi highly esteemed fearlessness, and hated cowardice from the core of his heart. His hatred of cowardice was so deep that in spite of his firm faith in non-violence he would prefer violence to cowardice. He says, "Cowardice and *ahimsa* do not go together any more than water and fire."[202] "Cowardice is impotence worse than violence."[203] The above excerpts point to one truth that cowardice arises from fear and lack of absolute faith in Almighty God. Gandhi, a man of indomitable courage and valour, liked valorous and lively personalities who, given proper opportunities, can create a new era in history, can reorient the surroundings. That is to say, the world can expect service some day or other from them. On the other hand, the cowards are escapists who fly from each and every problem of life. They render no service to society rather seek help from others. So Gandhi calls them impotent, unmanly, unnatural, and unfit for human society. Moreover, cowards are denied divine blessings owing to their lack of faith in God. Their activities lack moral worth inasmuch as they depend on others for maintenance of livelihood. In his words, "Fearlessness is the first requisite of spirituality. Cowards can never be moral."[204] In fine, the actions of cowards can never have moral worth in that they are motivated not by voluntary will but by panic and fear.

And lastly, his concept of fearlessness implies a political motive too."[205] His prescription of vows was motivated by a political end. While launching movement for the freedom of India he foresaw the necessity of millions of superman who would be truthful, non-violent, fearless. They would be ready to sacrifice everything including their lives at the altar of motherland. They would be a symbol of infinite courage and fearlessness. His farsight warned him that a nation-wide network of non-violent movement could turn into a farce unless it observed perfect fearlessness. So this vow of fearlessness is a pivotal point of the other vows, and of his political thought.

To sum up: On Gandhian vow of fearlessness Jawaharlal Nehru comments, "Fearlessness was his greatest git ..."[206] John S. Hoyland observes, "...the greatest single gift which Mr. Gandhi has conferred upon his fellow-countrymen is the power of conquering this fear complex...."[207] Buddhadeva Bhattacharyya opines, "Gandhi considered weakness, cowardice and fear as signs against the human spirit. *Abhaya* or fearlessness was the greatest legacy that Gandhi bestowed upon us."[208] Indeed, before the emergence of Gandhi *abhaya* or fearlessness was a mere scriptural preaching, a religious dogma without any relevant rituals, i.e., without any significant role in practical life of the masses. The virtues of valour, fearlessness, etc. were ornaments of the warrior class (Kshatriyas) to whom primarily the security of the society was entrusted. And the other classes, as discussed above, were almost inert owing partly to the religious and cultural heritage, and partly to the prevailing conditions of the surroundings. Gandhi's astute pragmatic and practical common sense felt the pulse of the masses deeply; and restored the spirit of self-respect amongst them. He translated the scriptual precept of fearlessness into action, and gave it a concrete shape."[209] The people regained, in a sense, their essence, their lost paradise, self-dignity and became free from all fear, both external and internal. In other words, Gandhi turned the cripple, semi-comatic dumb millions into dauntless supermen with the slogan, 'Do or Die.' This achievement, this infusion of fearlessness, was undoubtedly an outstanding and revolutionary one; and hence deserves the highest praise. But to welcome it as the 'greatest gift' is to underrate the other virtues since all virtues are integrally and organically related to one another. To ascribe importance to any one of them is to convey the same to other virtues also.

Removal of Untouchability

The tenth in the series of vows is removal of untouchability. To Gandhi, it is not merely a vow that is to be observed, rather it is the mission of his life. A vow, although a mental state, refers to some external agency. It is to be initiated first, and solemnized later on. But in the case of Gandhi, removal of untouchability, although preached by him, was not a vow to be solemnized in the form of oath-taking. It was a mental attitude, an inherent propensity for him.

The fact that the root of anti-untouchability movement was an innate disposition, an inherent element of his being, will be evident from the following excerpt which he made in the form of reminiscence at a mature age. He writes, "A variety of incidents in my life have conspired to bring me in close contact with people of many creeds and many communities, and my experience with all of them warrants the statement that I have known no distinction between relatives and strangers, countrymen and foreigners, white and coloured, Hindus and Indians of other faiths, whether Musalmans, Parsis, Christians or Jews. I may say that my heart has been incapable of making any such distinctions. I cannot claim this as a special virtue, as it is in my very nature, rather than a result of any effort on my part, whereas in the case of *ahimsa* (non-violence), *brahmacharya* (celibacy), *aparigraha* (non-possession) and other cardinal virtues, I am fully conscious of a continuous striving for their cultivation."[210] The very term "as it is in my very nature" proves undoubtedly the depth of the anti-untouchability feeling in Gandhi's mind. He had to, according to his confessions, undergo a continuous process of observance for the cultivation of other cardinal virtues but for anti-untouchability he had to perform nothing as it automatically bloomed in his life.

The earliest manifestation of this feeling can be traced back to his teens; in juvenile-delinquent Moniya, the pet-name of Gandhi in his early boyhood. Even in those turbulent days of juvenile delinquency—he recollects in mature age—he had amongst others two distinct concepts in mind. One is that of morality as the basis of all, and the other is an inherent aversion to and active protest against the traditional custom of untouchability. The idea of mere touch of Uka, the house scavenger, and that of 'untouchables' constituting a sin, revolted the sensitive mind of young Gandhi. He narrates, "I was hardly yet twelve when this idea had dawned on me. A scavenger named Uka, an untouchable, used to attend our house for cleaning latrines. Often I would ask my mother why it was wrong to touch him, why I was forbidden to touch him. If I accidentally touched Uka, I was asked to perform the ablutions, and though I naturally obeyed, it was not without smilingly protesting that untouchability was not sanctioned by religion, that it was impossible that it should be so. I was a very dutiful and obedient child and so far as it was consistent with respect for parents, I often had tussles with them on this matter."[211] The above excerpt clearly shows that the movement for the uplift of the 'untouchables' was not at all a political stunt. It was characteristically a movement launched purely from the humanitarian standpoint. It was in 1916 that he prescribed eradication of untouchability as a vow, but long before that while practising in Durban in 1898 he observed anti-untouchability movement in his domestic life. As a host he entertained guests belonging to various castes, creeds, and religions. Once Kasturba declined to clean off the chamber-pot of a Christian clerk born of Panchama parents. Gandhi treated her cruelly and compelled her to do the same with pearl drops streaming down her cheeks."[212] Thus he started his anti-untouchability movement even before his affiliation, of any kind, to political field. In course of time it got blended with political issues and turned into a vehement force in the nationwide movement for independence.

In 1915 while establishing the Ashram near Ahmedabad, he faced obstructions, both internal and external, in preaching removal of untouchability as a vow. The internal turmoil commenced with admission of Dudabhai and his family into the Ashram. Kasturba, Maganlal Gandhi and his wife proposed to leave the Ashram. Later on, after a long persuasion, Kasturba quieted down; and Maganlal Gandhi with his wife went to Madras for a better training in weaving for six months after which they returned to Ashram with their hearts clean of untouchability.

At the same time, external pressure came. Financial assistance from the external source was discontinued. But unexpectedly a stranger donated rupees thirteen thousand in cash to the Ashram fund. The anonymous donor was Ambalal Sarabhai, an industrialist of Ahmedabad. The problem of drawing water from the common well was also solved through a non-violent technique. The above is in a nutshell the story of the origin of anti-untouchability movement. His dedication to the uplift of untouchables is immeasurable and hence beyond our competence. The use of the term *Harijan*, in stead of the traditional usage *Pariah* (the victims of untouchability) or *Bhangi* (untouchable) or *Antyaja* (the last born), etc. indicates his progressive and religious outlook. Regarding the significance of the word *Harijan* Gandhi explains, "Only the other day a friend suggested to me that the word '*Harijana*' (man of God) be substituted for the word 'Antyaja' (the 'last born') that is being used for 'untouchables'. It was a word used by the great saint Narasinha Mehta, who belonged to the Nagar Brahmin community and who defied the whole community by claiming the 'untouchables' as his own. I am delighted to adopt that word which is sanctified by having been used by such a great saint, but it has for me a deeper meaning than you may imagine. The 'untouchables', to me, is, compared to us, really a '*Harijana*'—a man of God, and we are '*Durjana*' (man of evil)."[213] A detailed account of this movement[214] will take us off the principal objective, i.e., the history of the removal of untouchability as a vow. Since these vows, prescribed by him, are closely and integrally related to one another, it is our primary aim to bring out its various implications and to show its role in various fields of his thought.

Its spiritual significance arises out of the absolutistic elements of his idealism. It is the Absolute, God or Truth that manifests itself in innumerable beings of the universe. That is to say, all creatures and beings of the universe are living incarnations of God. He believes in the spiritual oneness of all existents. In a metaphorical expression, the Supreme Being, the creater, is the ever-shining fire and all existents are sparks coming out of Him. To quote Gandhi, "None can be born untouchable, as all are sparks of one and the same Fire."[215] And to carry the comparison a step further, as all sparks are not equal in length, breadth, lustre and longevity, so also all beings, in this context human beings, are not equal to one another in all respects, i.e., they differ according to their heredity, environment, property, opportunity, natural gifts liks talents, mental dispositions, etc. Since natural endowments are beyond our competence to change we can break down the artificial barriers amongst beings, especially among human beings. The removal of untouchability is one of those barriers, and a step, if cultivated properly, that leads towards *ahimsa* or universal love.

A corollary of this custom of untouchability is the distinction of high and low among human beings. If this evil distinction of highness and lowness can be removed, the ugly system of untouchability will automatically vanish."[216] Gandhi tells us that mere birth cannot determine highness or lowness, superiority or inferiority of an individual. In the *Vanaparva* of *Mahabharata*, *Vishnu-Bhagavata* and *Manusmriti* we are told that if a Shudra manifests *sattva* or good qualities he may become a Brahman while a Brahman who fails to cultivate them becomes a Shudra."[217] There is no reality in the distinction between high and low, high-class and low-class, high-born and low-born. Because they are mere creations of our ignorant minds, sometimes of vested interests. The differences of natural endowments, i.e., of heredity, environment, mental dispositions, abilities, etc., have nothing to do with the so-called distinction of high and low leading to the sin of untouchability.

Moreover, Gandhi's movement for removal of untouchability bears a universal appeal in its spiritual implication. Since all beings are creatures of God, and all creatures are interwoven into a spiritual unity, Gandhi fervently intended to remove all sorts of untouchability from the surface of the earth. The inhuman torture by the Christians of the Jews, the barbarous oppression by the so-called whites of the coloured people, the various divisions amongst the Musalmans are all offshoots of untouchability. His sensitive mind rebelled against the oppression of humanity in general—Hindus, Musalmans, Jews, coloured people—and endeavoured to end it. His agony is well expressed in the sayings, "Even the Musalmans caught the sinful contagion from us; and in South Africa, in East Africa and in Canada, the Musalmans no less than Hindus came to be regarded as Pariahs. All this evil has resulted from the sin of untouchability."[218] In short, urged by burning humanism he vehemently protested against the outrage of human personality and dignity of any kind, against the denial of equality of all human beings irrespective of caste and creed, race and religion, colour and nationality. He believed that Hinduism purged of the sin of untouchability will display a shining example before the world and promote brotherhood amongst human beings. He optimistically hopes, "It is my certain conviction that, if the Hindu heart is completely purged of the taint of untouchability, the event will have its inevitable influence not only upon all the communities in India but on the whole world."[219] Thus he intended Hinduism to be the pioneer in this tough and long march. And the students of modern history know it well that his efforts did not go in vain. The black movement under the leadership of late Martin Luther King in America is one of the shining examples of modern times.

Let us now illustrate the religious implication of this vow. The caste Hindus who invented this sinister design to keep the so-called untouchables under subjection achieved their goal under cover of religion. They proclaimed the sanction of Hindu religion for it, and the religious minded people of ancient India accepted it as a divine command. Gandhi challenged this interpretation of Hinduism and struck at the root. He expresses his viewpoint by saying, "Even on untouchability, my method of approach is perhaps different from that of many, if not of most Congressmen. For me, this is a deeply religious and moral issue."[220] The canker of untouchability was eating into the vitals of Hinduism. In its truest form Hinduism prescribes the same status for all—a Brahman, a dog-eater (*shva-pacha*), an ant, an elephant—all are equal. There is one all-embracing fundamental unity behind the outward diversity of the universe. Though the forms are many, the underlying spirit is one; and it pervades all life. To put it in another way, in the eyes of the creator, God who is also the inherent unity behind all lives, all are equal. The outward forms of an elephant and an ant are undoubtedly dissimilar but this sort of diversity in the universe in no way indicates inequality or untouchability. Indeed, the basic tenets of Hinduism emphasize the brotherhood not only of all human beings but also of all that live. He claims no authority on the Hindu scriptures although he had a fair knowledge of them. He does not find a statement in the *sastras* in support of untouchability. He recollects the texts—*Jale Vishnuh sthale Vishnuh* (there is the Lord present in water, there is the Lord present on land)—of the scriptures of *Ramaraksha* and *Vishnu Puja* which he read in boyhood deeply influenced him. These scriptures nowhere mention contact of untouchables as sin.[221] Gandhi assumes, "....untouchability could be no part of the Hindu religion, that our remote ancestors through whom we received the inspiration of the Vedas and who gave us the rich heritage of the Upanishads, never believed in untouchability, even as I don't, and that it is merely a vicious excrescence upon Hinduism."[222] Gandhi finds no text in the scriptures supporting untouchability as a divine sanction. It is an artificial barrier between man and man erected by people of vested interests for the exploitation of the outcastes. Elsewhere Gandhi writes, "I have failed to find a single warrant for the existence of untouchability as we believe and practise it today in all those books which we call Hindu Shastras."[223] In this context P.M. Modi shares the same opinion with Gandhi.[224]

Apart from the above reference to scriptures in defence of removal of untouchability he makes an appeal to our good sense also. Gandhi claims to have realized the true spirit of Hinduism which does never admit the sin of untouchability. He explains, "God did not create men with the badge of superiority or of inferiority and no scripture which labels a human being as inferior or untouchable..."[225] Gandhi advises us to take into account the privileges that we enjoy at the cost of the sufferings of the so-called untouchables. In this sense we may be condemned as untouchables because we rear up evil passions like anger, lust, hatred, greed, etc., which directly or indirectly foster various divisions amongst human beings.

Having shown that untouchability has no sanction of Hindu *sastras* and that our good sense also cannot defend it, he sounds clarion call to the nation to remove it at any cost.[226] He often describes it as 'a serious blot on Hinduism', an ulcer, a monster, a cancer, etc. which has turned it astray. Hence he cries, "If this is Hinduism, O Lord, my fervent prayer is that the soonest it is destroyed, the best."[227] But, in fact, he loves Hinduism dearer than life itself. So what he wants is not the destruction of Hinduism but the eradication of the cancer, the blot, the excrescence of Hinduism, that is untouchability.

This vow has also an important political implication. Gandhi, however, denies outright any political end in this movement. He tells us with an open mind that the ultimate goal of this anti-untouchability movement is the purification of Hinduism.[228] But in course of its long journey the movement could not maintain religious purity. It gradually got blended with the nation-wide movement for independence. Gandhi's speeches and activities made after the commencement of this movement contradict his earlier statements to which we shall return very shortly. In this context the observation of Buddhadeva Bhattacharyya seems to be a relevant and correct one. He comments, "...it was not with any ulterior political purpose or any other end in view that he had organized the movement. The aim of the anti-untouchability campaign was primarily and essentially humanitarian. But this does not mean that the problem of emancipation of about one-fifth of the total Hindu population (1931 census) was less important in any scheme of national freedom and social reconstruction in India. Indeed, how could the freedom movement at all march forward keeping such a vast mass of the toiling people beyond the pale of society? In that sense it had a bearing on the political movement, though not in any narrow sense."[229] Thus although initially it was purely a religious movement, and since the workers were striving heart and soul to attain independence, the movement got a political tinge as time rolled on.

As a pragmatist and a practical idealist Gandhi realized that the unity of the nation would face a setback if one-fifth of its population is compelled to lag behind. The 'Divide and Rule' policy of the imperialist power weakened our solidarity. He fervently intended the nation as a whole to participate actively in this long march of freedom-movement. Hence comes his clarion call to the nation, "....we can never reach swaraj, with the poison of untouchability corroding the Hindu part of the national body....."[230] On various occasions Gandhi expressed his views on untouchability. The inhuman oppressions that were inflicted on the untouchables by the so-called *varna* Hindus in India are more painful and cruel than those by the British ruler. We have compelled them to crawl on their bellies, rub their noses on the ground, in some extreme cases burnt them to death. In this way the non-scriptual, fiendish or satanic practice of untouchability has turned our fellow men into animals. Not only this, the boundless inhuman torture has sometimes compelled the so-called untouchable brothers and sisters into the arms of Islam and Christianity.

Its social implication has many roots going to the very core of Hindu society. It is like a many-headed hydra which exhibits various shapes and forms; visible or subtle institutions, customs, mores of a society. It cripples the thought, speech and actions of the so-called untouchables at every step of social life. To quote Gandhi, "Socially they are lepers. Economically they are worse. Religiously they are denied entrances to places we miscall houses of God. They are denied the use, on the same terms as the caste Hindus, of public roads, public schools, public hospitals, public wells, public taps, public parks and the like. And in some cases their approach within a measured distance is a social crime, and in some other rare cases their very sight is an offence...."[231] The above excerpt, and also our experience, confirms the above picture of social boycott of the so-called 'untouchables', 'unapproachables', 'invisibles'. The caste Hindus have deprived them of the fundamental necessities of life; of the facilities of education and health by dint of which they could manifest their potentialities and save their lives. In order to share their sorrow and sufferings he ardently intends to be "an untouchable by choice" and an untouchable by birth if rebirth occurs at all. And if this plague, blot of Hindu society is removed, the artificial barriers amongst men and men will vanish like mists. It means perfect order, harmony and hearty co-operation amongst all people living in a society irrespective of caste, creed, race and religion, as a result of which all men and women living in a society will be free from superiority-inferiority complex; from social exploitation and oppression. In his words, "when untouchability is rooted out, these distinctions will vanish and no one will consider himself superior to any other. Naturally, exploitation too will cease and co-operation will be the order of the day."[232] In short, Gandhi, through his efforts for removal of untouchability, strove to establish social equality and justice for all, a social order free from exploitation and oppression based on full harmony and co-operation.

Apart from the above social implications, it is a stepping stone to communal peace; in a more concrete usage, Hindu-Muslim unity. To the *varna* or caste Hindus not only the Hindus of the lower strata are untouchables but so also are the Muslims and Christians. In his childhood, we have seen above, as per mother's instruction he used to touch a Muslim, an untouchable, only to purify himself from the sin of touching an untouchable Hindu. Gandhi thinks that hatred, disbelief and superiority complex are at the root of untouchability. So he optimistically hopes that if the sin of untouchability is removed from Hinduism, communal harmony among the Hindus and Muslims will be automatically established.[233] Thus the vow of the removal of untouchability was a stepping-stone to peaceful co-existence of all kinds of communities, towards universal brotherhood.

The economic implication of the movement is also not less important. We have seen above that the thought, speech and actions of the so-called untouchables were chained by the traditional social order in such a manner that they were hardly left with any ostensible means for their economic development. Since they were 'invisible,' 'unapproachable', 'untouchable' they were entrusted with filthy and obnoxious duties such as cremation of dead bodies, scavenging the nightsoil, etc. They were not allowed by the caste Hindus, due to vested interests, to participate in the various occupations of social life through which they could earn prosperity and progress for themselves and the community.[234] Thus the economic backwardness of the so-called untouchables was due to this many-headed monster of untouchability. If they are freely and fairly admitted to participate in every occupation of life all the sources of economic uplift will be opened to them, and bring them solvency. To put it in other words, the so-called untouchables are sturdy and industrious who, given proper chance in every walk of life, will undoubtedly attain prosperity.[235] Gandhi suggests the revival of weaving and tanning amongst the *Harijans*. At that time the industry of weaving among the *Harijans*, especially in Gujarat, was almost on the verge of destruction owing to the conspiracy of caste Hindus. And consequently, since there were no ostensible means left for their livelihood, most of the Harijan weavers were compelled to take up scavenging for a living.[236] Above all, in an ideal society of Gandhi, "the emoluments of all crafts and professions should be equal and amount to a living wage."[237] The village *vaidya* (physician) and the carpenter will earn an equal amount, i.e., a living wage. In this age of mechanical civilization the social status of an individual is often determined by monetary power. The richer the man, as the practice goes, the higher his position is. That is why Gandhi optimistically hopes that in an ideal society there should be no distinction of high and low, caste and outcaste, touchable and untouchable. And everyone will get a living wage for one's sustenance so that no financial discrepancy, no pecuniary barrier may grow up, and thereby disturb the smooth running of a well-ordered ideal society. It is here noteworthy that in the ultimate analysis the removal of untouchability is a religious and not an economic problem. Hence Gandhi warns, "The ulcer of untouchability has gone so deep down that it seems to pervade our life. Hence the unreal differences: Brahman and Non-Brahman, provinces and provinces, religion and religion...When untouchability is rooted out.... exploitation too will cease....."[238]

To sum up: Untouchability, a blot and cancer of Hinduism, existed with all the associated evils of oppression centuries after centuries. The inhuman deprivation of the so-called untouchables in every sphere of life has no parallel in the history of mankind although inequalities of rights, status, privileges, etc., are recorded in different societies in the past as well as in the present. Though this sin of Hinduism had the blessings of religion and much old tradition, still Gandhi, a religious-minded champion of humanism, vehemently opposed it and sought its removal with a view to reforming Hindu society. The value of this vow of removal of untouchability is that it has initiated a new pattern in the basic socio-economic structure of society. It awakened a nation-wide consciousness of solidarity which in course of time contributed remarkably to freedom movement. From the scholastic viewpoint one may or may not rank him high as a social reformer but it is undeniable that the movements launched by him, of which removal of untouchability is a constituent, created a tremendous commotion in the bosom of the semi-comatic lenation, and initiated a democratic consciousness based on equality, justice, brotherhood and other noble qualities.

Tolerance or Equality of Religions

The eleventh and last one in the series of vows is tolerance, otherwise termed equality, of religions. The term tolerance is chosen here for want of a more suitable word. To Gandhi, "Tolerance may imply a gratuitous assumption of the inferiority of other faiths to one's own...."[239] The term tolerance usually conveys a feeling of compassion, a feeling of superiority and domination over others. But a true votary of non-violence should not entertain such ill-feelings in mind. He uses this word, in spite of its implication of superiority-complex, only to express his mind for want of a better and more appropriate term. It means a due respect to each and every religion of the world without leaving one's own faith.

This vow of tolerance has its origin in his epistemological, relative ideas; and in the equimindedness of religious outlook. He tells us that an individual can never attain perfect or absolute knowledge. Everything on earth may be viewed from various angles of vision. This is the reason why our knowledge is always relative, and never an absolute one which means identity with God (*supra: a syadvadi* in chapter III). Indeed, our imperfect nature leads to imperfect knowledge of God, and is the fountain of all errors and conflicts. To put it in other words, the epistemological implication is that since we can attain only relative knowledge, all our knowledge, thus acquired, is equally or more or less imperfect. In his words, "Everybody is right from his own standpoint, but it is not impossible that everybody is wrong.[240] Similar is the case with religion too. To know God in His perfection is quite impossible on the part of an imperfect being like man. The various religious ideas regarding God are also liable to errors, i.e., partially perfect and partially imperfect.[241] The history of religious consciousness unfolds an evolutionary process of religious faiths from animism, tree-worship, totem and taboo, etc., up to present modern stage, man's religious consciousness has passed through many phases of evolution. It rectifies errors and purges off imperfections as it passes. The various interpretations, commentaries and revelations expressed through human medium are also by nature imperfect and erroneous. In short, imperfect knowledge of religious ideas leads us to tolerance or equality of religions as a vow.

Here Gandhi warns us against ill-feeling towards any other faith or conversion into other faith. His deep reverence for other religions of the world is the same as that for his own faith, i.e., Hinduism. Hence the question of conversion does not arise. We should help a Hindu to become 'a better Hindu, a Muslim a better Muslim and a Christian a better Christian.'[242] The principal faiths of the world, according to him, are all basically one and conducive to one another. Their ultimate goal is to provide moral, spiritual and religious uplift for each and every individual; and thereby to promote material prosperity in everybody's life. But their evolution for thousands of years at different stages of history; and their various reformations through numerous interpretations and commentaries in the light of contemporary trend have given rise to diverse opinions. These apparent differences and conflicts of various faiths of the world which are fundamentally one, are due to our imperfection and ignorance. So the question of comparative appreciation and condemnation of their merits and demerits respectively does not arise at all. We should reverentially study all faiths of the world, absorb their noble ideas into our own. This study and appreciation of other religions will not weaken, will rather strengthen, our own religious conviction, and extend tolerance and regard to other faiths. This equal regard for all religions of the world is a unique feature of Gandhian thought, and has been highly appreciated by different thinkers. Here it is noteworthy that reverence and regard here in no sense mean blind and irrational faith. One should ceaselessly strive to remove the defects of one's faith in stead of relinquishing it. Gandhi did not give up Hinduism in spite of its various blots. He rather endeavoured to purge it of those blots. This conservative outlook of 'no-conversion' is deeply rooted in his social, psychological, religious and historical convictions. We are products of heredity and environment. The hereditary tendencies, physical environment, cultural, social and religious heritage make us what we are. Our own religious conviction efficiently awakens spiritual consciousness which no alien faith can infuse in us. The teachings of the scripture especially the *Gita* and the *Upanisad* nurtured his personality both physically and mentally. And the history of mankind narrates the broadness of Hinduism which advises us to remain loyal to our own faith and at the same time enjoy the noble ideas of other faiths. In ancient times Hinduism, urged by this broadness and tolerance, "gave shelter to the early Christians who had fled from persecution, also to the Jews known as Beni-Israel as also to the Parsis (Zoroastrians)."[243] In this connection it is quite relevant that though he does not object to any one choosing his own faith, he vehemently opposes any forcible or organized attempt at conversion.

Gandhi distinguishes between religion and irreligion for a better understanding of the question at issue. He appreciates the noble ideas of every religion, and condemns the malpractices that pass as rituals. With a heavy heart he declares, "I should be ashamed to think that dedication of girls to virtual prostitution was a part of Hinduism. Yet it is practised by Hindus in many parts of India. I consider it positive irreligion to sacrifice goats to Kali and do not consider it a part of Hinduism."[244] He not only condemned, as discussed above, but also launched a movement against untouchability, the cancer of Hinduism. Malpractices like these mar the spirit of religion and degrades its status. They obstruct manifestation of universal love and tolerance of other faiths. So we should condemn irreligion, and observe tolerance and equal regard to other faiths.

This leads us to the necessity of tolerance. The imperfection of human knowledge is universally admitted. The opinions of different faiths on different matters may not coincide in all respects, may also differ. But this does not mean that either opinion is wrong. The partial truth of diverse faiths demands the necessity of tolerance which infuses a spiritual insight, a true understanding in us. It removes the barriers and resolves conflicts amongst faiths. It is the golden rule not to be impatient with others' faiths which may be erroneous, and even injurious to us. The vow of tolerance advises us to be tolerant to other faiths even if it causes great suffering to us. Because "decency and toleration to be of any value, must be capable of standing the severest strain."[245] "I am striving to become the best cement between the two communities. My longing is to be able to cement the two with my blood, if necessary. But, before I can do so, I must prove to the Musalmans that I love them as well as I love the Hindus. My religion teaches me to love all equally."[246] To put it in other words, tolerance follows as a natural conclusion from Gandhi's conviction that '(a) all religions are true; (b) all religions have some error in them; (c) all religions are almost as dear as our own faith.'[247] Only tolerance can do justice to other faiths. An almost similar treatment towards other faiths has been prescribed by Asoka, the great emperor of ancient India. In the twelfth rock edict he prescribes, "(I) promotion of basic tenets which are common to all religions; (II) cultivation of a sense of unity of all religions and sects;

(III) coming together of exponents of different religions in religious assemblies; (IV) learning the texts of other religions so as to become proficient in the scriptures of different religions."[248] Both Gandhi and Asoka prescribed tolerance in order to lessen tension between people of different religions and communities.

A corollary of the vow of tolerance is egalitarian attitude towards all religions. Shriman Narayan observes, "Mahatma Gandhi entertained equal respect for all religions and stressed the need for developing *Sarvadharma Samabhava* in national life with a view to establishing a secular democracy in India."[249] Equimindedness or equal regard for all faiths bestows a kind of broadness on our mind. While dealing with the scriptures of Christianity, Islam, Zoroastrianism, Judaism and Hinduism he was equalitarian towards all these faiths. A reverential study of scriptures of various faiths from the point of view of followers of those faiths reveals the fact that all religions are God-given, at bottom one, and helpful towards one another. It helps us to cultivate restraint bear out criticisms and flaws of other faiths."[250] Indeed, equimindedness is the golden means of pointing out each other's error with patience and tolerating the difference of opinion between without any hatred and malice. Elsewhere he says, "The key to the solution of the tangle lay in everyone following the best in his own religion and entertaining equal regard for the other religions and their followers."[251] Thus equimindedness is the key to solve the various conflicts and problems of our lives.

Our discussion of the vow of tolerance will remain incomplete without the mention of universal or perfect religion in this context. Because equal regard for all faiths of the world, and tolerance towards their errors culminate in something that transcends them, i.e., perfect or universal religion. What is the nature of this perfect and true or universal religion that Gandhi had in his mind? He explains, "It is not the Hindu religion, which I certainly prize above all other religions, but the religion which transcends Hinduism, which changes one's very nature, which binds one indissolubly to the truth within and whichever purifies. It is the permanent element in human nature which counts no cost too great in order to find full expression and which leaves the soul utterly restless until it has found itself, known its Maker and appreciated the true correspondence between the Maker and itself."[252] "It means a belief in ordered moral government of the universe.... This religion transcends Hinduism, Islam, Christianity, etc. It does not supersede them. It harmonizes them and gives them reality."[253] The true and perfect religion is beyond the reach of our understanding. Like God it ever remains beyond our reach. It is so deeply rooted in the very nature of man that without its manifestation manhood loses significance and worth. In other words, it is the basic element because of which a man is called man. That is why S.K. George brands it as a basic religion which is unlimited in scope, all pervasive and "unreserved acceptance of the validity of all religions."[254] Vincent Sheean calls it "essential religion" for its universal appeal.[255] It is variously called basic or essential or universal or perfect or true or ethical religion because of its dynamic open mindedness. It is not limited by 'geographical areas' (village, district, province, and state); social barriers (caste, creed, cult and community); historical phases (past, present and future). In short, it is unlimited by space and time; natural and human activities. And the disagreements between the various faiths of the world, as we have seen above, are due to our imperfect knowledge of the nature of universal religion. In the ultimate analysis they are all one and interwoven with one another. To quote Gandhi, "why should there be so many different faiths? The Soul is one, but the bodies which she animates are many. We cannot reduce the number of bodies; yet we recognize the unity of the Soul. Even as a tree has a single trunk, but many branches and leaves, so is there one true and perfect Religion ..."[256] But the realization of this fundamental unity of the different faiths is not an easy task. It requires a reverential study of the scriptures of different faiths together with equimindedness, love, humility, courtesy and other noble qualities. And consequently, this reverential study will bestow on us a progressive insight, "a grasp of the rock-bottom unity of all religions and afford a glimpse also of that universal and absolute truth which lies beyond the 'dust of creeds and faiths'."[257] An almost similar type of universal religion has been preached by King Asoka. He engraved moral instructions containing cardinal virtues, and tolerance of every faith of the country in rock edicts acceptable to every citizen irrespective of caste, creed and cult."[258]

And lastly, this vow of tolerance has some political significance too. It is the plinth of democracy. Gandhi says, "If we want to cultivate a true spirit of democracy, we cannot afford to be intolerant. Intolerance betrays want of faith in one's cause."[259] Indeed, tolerance is the basis, the very nucleus of democratic set-up. In those days of nation-wide movement for independence Gandhi in prescribing the vow of tolerance or equal regard of all faiths fervently solicited the active co-operation of all countrymen irrespective of caste and creed, religion and race. His practical idealism blessed him with a pragmatic farsight that inspired him to prescribe equal regard to all faiths so that all fellow fighters may assemble at the altar of motherland without any hesitation and obstruction. And it is undeniable that in those days of communal orgies his appeal to the nation was heard like a heavenly voice.

To conclude: We have discussed above in detail the nature, origin and end of the eleven vows together with their role in social, religious, political, economic, etc., fields of our lives. Of the eleven vows the first five already formed an integral part of moral discipline of ancient India. Gandhi says, "Patanjali has described five disciplines.... And for this age the five have been expanded into eleven."[260] In the preceding sections we have already discussed the ancient concept of these five great vows and of the remaining six vows which Gandhi claims to have added to the ancient list, two (control of the palate and fearlessness) had already formed part, in one form or another, of the discipline and training of the spiritual aspirants of ancient India. It is, therefore, the remaining four (bread labour, *swadeshi*, abolition of untouchability, and tolerance or equality of religions) that seem to be new additions by Gandhi. But a close scrutiny will reveal the fact that the vow of bread labour is not at all a new invention of Gandhi. It was, as discussed above, introduced by a Russian writer, T.M. Bondaref; and widely publicized by Tolstoy and Ruskin. Of course, it is a credit to the genius of Gandhi that he seized this invaluable virtue essential for mankind, and implemented it in the semi-comatic life of Indian people. Thus, virtually only three vows (*swadeshi*, removal of untouchability and tolerance or equality of religions) are new additions by Gandhi which he prescribed to fulfil the necessities of the age. In other words, Gandhi accepted from the tradition, Indian and Western, eight virtues and prescribed three new additions to meet the needs of the age although he interpreted and remodelled them in the light of his experience. His motive was to awaken and inspire the inner being so that an ordinary individual may achieve the feats of a superman. In an ultimate analysis these vows point to a goal, the control and sublimation of sensuous appetites and emotions leading to self-realization. And lastly, one more point demands special clarification. Are these vows mere theoretical abstractions? Does not Gandhi expect too much of human nature? As Margaret Sanger asks, "Mr. Gandhi, there are thousands, millions, who regard your word as that of a saint. How can you ask them who are so humble, so weak, to follow, when you who are so much stronger and wiser, have taken years to bring about that self-control in your life? Mr. Gandhi just smiled."[261] The proof of their efficacy and practicability is written in red letters in the history of freedom movement of India under Gandhi's leadership. He asked people to do what he thought, did and observed. He demanded nothing that may be impossible on the part of a human being. Mortification of flesh is undoubtedly a difficult task. But this is indispensable as demanded by these vows for spiritual uplift and self-realization. And who does not know that the path to self or God-realization is paved with sufferings?

References

1. Aristotle, *Ethica Nicomachea*, BK. IV, trans. *Aristotle*, David Ross, p. 194.
2. S.K. Maitra, *The Ethics of the Hindus*, p. 8.
3. *Ibid.*, p. 10.
4. Patanjali, *Yogasutra*, Bhasya, 2.31, in Surama Dasgupta, *Development of Moral Philosophy in India*, p. 129; S.K. Maitra, *op. cit.*, pp. 211-17.
5. Umasvami, *Tattavarthadhigama-Sutra*, 1.1.
6. S. Radhakrishnan, *Indian Philosophy*, vol. I, p. 325.
7. S.K. Maitra, *op. cit.*, pp. 220-21.
8. *Ibid.*, pp. 221-25; Surama Dasgupta, *op. cit.*, pp. 151-88.
9. Surama Dasgupta, *Development of Moral Philosophy in India*, p. 188.
10. *Ibid.*, p. 111.
11. S.C. Chatterjee and D.M. Datta, *An Introduction to Indian Philosophy*, p. 106.
12. *Rg Veda*, 7.31.11.
13. *Brhadaranyaka-Upanisad*, 1.5.21.
14. John Mackenzie, *A Manual of Ethics*, p. 332.
15. *From Yeravda Mandir*, p. 32.
16. *CWMG*, vol. XLI, p. 273.
17. D.G. Tendulkar, *Mahatma*, vol. II, p. 154.
18. *From Yeravda Mandir*, p. 32.
19. *Ibid.*, p. 33.
20. *Ibid.*
21. *CWMG*, vol. XLI, p. 273.
22. *Ibid.*, p. 274.
23. *Harijan*, 6 April 1940, p. 74.
24. *Ashram Observances in Action*, pp. 110-16; also *From Yeravda Mandir*, pp. 1-43.
25. *An Autobiography*, p. 49.
26. *Op. cit.*, p. 6; also *CWMG*, vol. XVIII, p. 402, *CWMG*, vol. XVII, pp. 488, 493, *CWMG*, vol. XXI, p. 472; *From Yeravda Mandir*, p. 3.
27. *Harijan*, 18 July 1948, p. 170.
28. *CWMG*, vol. XXI, p. 457.
29. *Harijan*, 14 August 1937, p. 212.

30. *Satyagraha*, p. 6; also *From Yeravda Mandir*, p. 2.
31. *Young India 1919-22*, pp. 33-36.
32. I.C. Sharma, *Ethical Philosophies of India*, p. 300.
33. *Rg Veda*, 10.22.13.
34. *Ibid.*, 10.15.6.
35. *Ibid.*, 7.104.1; 1.114.7; 2.33.5.
36. *Taittiriya-Samhita*, 5.2.8.7.
37. *Satapatha-Brahmana*, 6.3.1.26.
38. T.W. Rhys Davids, *Ahimsa* in James Hastings (ed.), *Encyclopaedia of Religion and Ethics*, vol. I, p. 231.
39. Louis Renou, 'Gandhi and Indian Civilization,' in Kshitis Roy (ed.), *Gandhi Memorial Peace Number*, p. 235.
40. Joan V. Bondurant, *op. cit.*, p. 111; for further references of Upanishadic period see T.K.N. Unnithan & Yogendra Singh, *Traditions of Non-Violence*, pp. 75-82.
41. T.K.N. Unnithan & Yogendra Singh, *Traditions of Non-Violence*, pp. 31-32.
42. D.D. Kosambi, *The Culture and Civilization of Ancient India in Historical Outline*, p. 34.
43. S. Radhakrishnan, *Indian Philosophy*, vol. I, p. 327.
44. S.N. Dasgupta, *A History of Indian Philosophy*, vol. I, p. 200.
45. C.D.S. Devanesen, *The Making of the Mahatma*, p. 30.
46. Govindasvami's commentary to *Baudhayana-Dharmasutra*, 3.1.24.
47. Unto Tahtinen, *Ahimsa (Non-Violence) in Indian Tradition*, pp. 8-9.
48. Nanak, *Selections from the Sacred Writings of Sikhs*, p. 67.
49. Louis Renou, *op. cit.*, p. 233.
50. *Harijan*, 29 September 1940, p. 301.
51. *Non-Violence in Peace and War*, vol. I, p. 328.
52. H.N. Brailsford, in E.R.A. Seligman (ed.), *Encyclopaedia of the Social Sciences*, vol. VII, pp. 667-68.
53. A.C. Underwood, *Contemporary Thought of India*, p. 185.
54. *Young India*, 6 August 1925. p. 274.
55. Cited in R.S. Betai, *Gita and Gandhiji*, p. 221.
56. M.K. Gandhi, in Ananda T. Hingorani (ed.), *My Philosophy of Life*, p. 43.
57. *Speeches and Writings of Mahatma Gandhi*, (4th edn.), p. 345.
58. Unto Tahtinen, *op. cit.*, p. 121.
59. Louis Renou, *op. cit.*, pp. 231-32.
60. C.G. Shah, *Marxism, Gandhism, Stalinism*, p. 283.
61. M.K. Gandhi, *My Philosophy of Life*, pp. 39-43.
62. *Harijan*, 21 July 1940, p. 211.
63. *Ibid.*, 1 September 1940, p. 271; 5 May 1946, p. 123.
64. I.C. Sharma, *op. cit.*, p. 326.
65. *Harijan*, 12 October 1935, p. 276.
66. *Satyagraha*, p. 14.

67. M.K. Gandhi, *For Pacifists*, p. 20.
68. *CWMG*, vol. XXVII, pp. 133-34.
69. *Harijan*, 20 March 1937, p. 43; 31 August 1947, p. 301; 30 March 1947, p. 86; 7 July 1946, p. 212.
70. *Ibid.*, 12 October 1935, p. 276.
71. Supra (section ends and means in ch. V).
72. H. Horsburgh, *Non-violence and Aggression*, p. 157.
73. K.G. Mashruwala, 'Satyagraha Against War', in Kshitis Roy (ed.), *op. cit.*, p. 124.
74. *Young India*, 30 April 1925, p. 153.
75. *CWMG*, vol. XXX, p. 414.
76. For militarism of ancient India, see Nirad C. Chaudhuri, *The Continent of Circe*, pp. 97-101.
77. *Harijan*, 30 September 1939. p. 285.
78. *Encyclopaedia of the General Acts and Codes of India*, Calcutta, 1935, pp. 126-29.
79. *My Socialism*, p. 5.
80. *From Yeravda Mandir*, p. 6.
81. *Communal Unity*, p. 24.
82. *Harijan* (An Atheist in ch. IV).
83. *Ibid.*, 12 October 1935, p. 276.
84. *Ibid.*, 5 September 1936, pp. 236-37.
85. *Communal Unity*, p. 167.
86. *Harijan*, 14 March 1936, p. 39.
87. *Hindu Dharma*, pp. 312-13.
88. *Harijan*, 11 February 1929, p. 8.
89. *Ibid.*, 3 March 1946, pp. 28-29.
90. *Ibid.*, 8 June 1947, p. 180.
91. *Ibid.*, 23 July 1938, p. 193; *Harijan*, 4 November 1939, p. 326.
92. *An Autobiography*, p. 149.
93. *Ibid.*, p. 233; also *Harijan*, 3 October 1936, p. 268.
94. *Ibid.*, p. 234.
95. *Harijan*, 22 June 1947, p. 200.
96. *Ibid.*, 15 June 1947, p. 192.
97. *Young India*, 5 June 1924, p. 186; also *CWMG*, vol. XXIV, p. 116.
98. *Harijan*, 23 July 1938, p. 192.
99. *From Yeravda Mandir*, p. 8.
100. *Harijan*, 21 November 1936, pp. 321-22.
101. *Ashram Observances in Action*, p. 55.
102. *Harijan*, 8 June 1947, p. 180.
103. Cited in Romain Rolland, *The Life of Ramkrishna*, p. 199.
104. *Ibid.*, p. 198.
105. *An Autobiography*, p. 10.
106. *Ibid.*, p. 18.

107. *In Search of the Supreme*, vol. II, p. 84 fn.
108. *Speeches and Writings of Mahatma Gandhi*, (4th edn.) p. 829.
109. *Young India*, 21 May 1931, p. 115.
110. *From Yeravda Mandir*, pp. 7-8; also Sri Ramakrishna who says, "After the birth of one or two children a married couple should live as brother and sister. They should then constantly pray to God that their minds may not run after sense pleasures any more and that they may not have any more children." *The Gospel of Sri Ramakrishna*, p. 854.
111. *Ashram Observances in Action*, p. 51.
112. *Amrita Bazar Patrika*, 12 January 1935. Cited in Nirmal Kumar Bose, *Selections From Gandhi*, p. 281.
113. See C.F. Andrews, *Mahatma Gandhi's Ideas*, p. 101; P. Spratt, 'Gandhiji as a psychologist', in *The Indian Review*, July, 1938, vol. XXXIX, pp. 449-53. *The Aryan Path*, Sept., 1938, p. 452; S. Radhakrishnan (ed.), *Mahatma Gandhi*, pp. 18, 48, 105, 191, etc.
114. Tendulkar, *op. cit.*, vol. I, p. 31.
115. D.M. Datta, *The Philosophy of Mahatma Gandhi*, pp. 112-13.
116. *An Autobiography*, p. 35.
117. *Ibid.*, p. 200.
118. *Harijan*, 7 September 1935, p. 234.
119. *From Yeravda Mandir*, p. 10; also *An Autobiography*, p. 152.
120. *An Autobiography*, p. 152.
121. *Ibid.*, pp. 40-41.
122. *Ibid.*, p. 35.
123. *Young India*, 5 June 1924, p. 187.
124. *CWMG*, vol. XXII, p. 419.
125. *From Yeravda Mandir*, pp. 9-10.
126. *An Autobiography*, p. 35.
127. *Ibid.*, p. 42.
128. Cited in Nirmal Kumar Bose, *Selections From Gandhi*, p. 247.
129. *An Autobiography*, p. 154.
130. *From Yeravda Mandir*, p. 13.
131. *Ibid.*, p. 14.
132. *Ibid.*, p. 15.
133. *Ibid.*
134. *Ibid.*, pp. 15-16; and also *Speeches and Writings of Mahatma Gandhi*, (4th ed.) 10.1066.
135. *Speeches and Writings of Mahatma Gandhi*, p. 1066.
136. *Harijan*, 26 December 1936, p. 368.
137. *Speeches and Writings of Mahatma Gandhi*, p. 1066.
138. *The Holy Bible*, St. Mathew, Ch. X, 9-10.
139. *Ibid.*, St. Mathew, Ch. XIX, 23-4.
140. *Ibid.*, St. Mathew, Ch. VI, 26.
141. *From Yeravda Mandir*, p. 16; also *Speeches and Writings of Mahatma Gandhi*, p. 1066.

142. *From Yeravda Mandir*, p. 18.
143. *Harijan*, 21 July 1946, p. 232.
144. *Ibid.*, 13 April 1935, pp. 66-67; also *Harijan*, 20 April 1935, pp. 74-75.
145. *Ashram Observances in Action*, pp. 60-61.
146. *The Holy Bible*, Genesis, Ch. III : 19.
147. *Ashram Observances in Action*, pp. 61-62.
148. *From Yeravda Mandir*, p. 23; also *Harijan*, 29 June 1935, p. 156.
149. *Harijan*, 1 August 1936, p. 195; 8 March 1935, p. 32; *From Yeravda Mandir*, p. 24, D.P. Mukerji, *Diversities*, pp. 224-25.
150. *Ashram Observances in Action*, p. 62; *CWMG*, vol. XXI, p. 247.
151. *From Yeravda Mandir*, p. 24.
152. *An Autobiography*, p. 150.
153. *Harijan*, 29 June 1935, p. 156.
154. *CWMG*, vol. XXVIII, p. 339.
155. *Harijan*, 23 February 1947, p. 36; 2 March 1947, p. 47.
156. *Ibid.*, 20 April 1935, p. 75.
157. *Ibid.*, 2 March 1947, p. 47.
158. *Ashram Observances in Action*, pp. 64-66.
159. D.G. Tendulkar, *Mahatma*, vol. II, p. 319; *CWMG*, vol. XXXVII, p. 266.
160. Gopinath Dhawan, *The Political Philosophy of Mahatma Gandhi*, p. 92.
161. Karl Marx, *Capital*, vol. I, pp. 482-84.
162. Beatrice King, *An Outline of Education in the U.S.S.R.*, pp. 9-13.
163. *Peking Review*, No. 51, 17 December 1965, p. 5 cited in Stuart Fraser (ed.), *Education and Communism in China*, p. 237.
164. Cited in T.S. Avinashilingam, *Gandhi's Experiments in Education*, pp. 63-64; Buddhadeva Bhattacharyya, 'The Principle of Labour in Education' in O.P. Shah and D. Mukherjee (eds.), *Education in India Today*, pp. 147-68.
165. *Harijan*, 7 September 1947, p. 316.
166. D.G. Tendulkar, *op. cit.*, vol. V, pp. 225-26.
167. *Harijan*, 1 June 1935, p. 125; *From Yeravda Mandir*, p. 34; *CWMG*, vol. XXXIV, p. 410.
168. *Ibid.*, vol. VII, p. 329.
169. Buddhadeva Bhattacharyya, *Evolution of the Political Philosophy of Gandhi*, pp. 272-77.
170. *CWMG*, vol. XXXI, p. 12.
171. *From Yeravda Mandir*, p. 43.
172. *CWMG*, vol. XVI, p. 482.
173. *Speeches and Writings of Mahatma Gandhi*, p. 278.
174. *Harijan*, 25 February 1939, p. 25.
175. *Ashram Observances in Action*, pp. 67-68.
176. *From Yeravda Mandir*, p. 40.
177. *Speeches and Writings of Mahatma Gandhi*, p. 281.
178. *Ibid.*, *CWMG*, vol. XXIII, p. 340.

179. *Ibid.*, p. 41; *Ibid.*
180. D.G. Tendulkar, *op. cit.*, vol. IV, p. 20.
181. *Ashram Observances in Action*, p. 69.
182. *From Yeravda Mandir*, p. 39.
183. *CWMG*, vol. XIII, p. 223.
184. *Ibid.*, p. 219.
185. *Ibid.*, vol. XXI, pp. 39-40.
186. *Ibid.* 170; vol. XXI, p. 38.
187. *Ibid.*, vol. XIII, p. 219.
188. K. Ramakrishna Rao, *Gandhi and Pragmatism*, pp. 179-80.
189. *From Yeravda Mandir*, p. 41.
190. *Ashram Observances in Action*, p. 73.
191. Philip Zealey, 'Comments on Khadi,' in *Gandhi Marg*, vol. II, no. 4, p. 295.
192. Bharatan Kumarappa, 'Gandhian Symbols', in Kshitis Roy (ed.) *Gandhi Memorial Peace Number*, p. 33.
193. Gunnar Myrdal, *Asian Drama*, vol. II, p. 1209.
194. Buddhadeva Bhattacharyya, *op. cit.*, p. 276.
195. Philip Spratt, *Gandhism: An Analysis*, p. 223.
196. *CWMG*, vol. XIII, p. 93.
197. *From Yeravda Mandir*, p. 18.
198. *Ibid.*
199. *Harijan*, 8 December 1946, p. 442.
200. *Ashram Observances in Action*, p. 139; *Harijan*, 1 September 1940, p. 268.
201. *Young India*, 7 January 1932, p. 8; *In Search of the Supreme*, vol. II, pp. 63-64.
202. *Harijan*, 4 November 1939, p. 331.
203. *Harijan*, 15 September 1946, p. 312.
204. *CWMG*, vol. XXI, p. 286.
205. *Ashram Observances in Action*, p. 140.
206. Jawaharlal Nehru in Francis Watson and Mourice Brown, *Talking of Gandhiji*, p. 37.
207. John S. Hoyland in S. Radhakrishnan (ed.), *Mahatma Gandhi : Essays and Reflections*, p. 116.
208. Buddhadeva Bhattacharyya, *op. cit.*, p. 387.
209. Humayun Kabir brings forth the Gandhian steps for initiation of this sense of *abhaya* as follows: "Gandhiji's first task was to revive the spirit of self-respect of the Indian people.... The first task he set his followers was the comparatively easy one of overcoming the fear of arrest and imprisonment..... Once the fear of jail had disappeared, Gandhiji felt the time had come for a second step. His aim this time was to free the people from the fear of loss of property... The third and final step in this process of strengthening the nation's fibre was ....to risk one's life... Gandhiji knew that this supreme test be imposed only when the conditions

promised victory. These conditions were created after the outbreak of the war in 1939... It was then and then alone that Gandhiji gave the call of 'Do or Die'... Gandhiji taught the common man in India to overcome the fear of death." Humayun Kabir, 'Gandhiji and the Indian Revolution' in Kshitis Roy (ed.), *op. cit.*, pp. 220-27.

210. *An Autobiography*, p. 204.
211. *CWMG*, vol. XIX, pp. 570-71.
212. *An Autobiography*, p. 204; D.G. Tendulkar, *op. cit.*, vol. IV, p. 158.
213. *CWMG*, vol. XLVII, pp. 245, 248.
214. The Vykom Temple Road Satyagraha against untouchability was launched in 1925 and became successful. For details, see M.K. Gandhi, *Satyagraha*; D.G. Tendulkar, *Mahatma*, Vol. II; R.R. Diwakar, *Satyagraha : Its Technique and History*; J.V. Bondurant, *Conquest of Violence*; K. Shridharani, *War Without Violence*; Om Prakash Jaggi, *Religion, Practice and Science of Non-Violence*; C.F. Andrews, *Mahatma Gandhi's Ideas*. For other Satyagraha campaigns see above mentioned books; Gene Sharp, *Gandhi Weilds the Weapon of Moral Power*; Simone Panter-Brick, *Gandhi against Machiavellism*; Richard B. Gregg, *The Power of Non-Violence*; Nirmal Kumar Bose, *Studies in Gandhism*; M.K. Gandhi, *An Autobiography*; *Satyagraha in South Africa*; Rajendra Prasad, *Satyagraha in Champaran*; *Mahatma Gandhi and Bihar : Some Reminiscences*; P.C. Roy Choudhury, *Gandhi's First Struggle in India*; D.G. Tendulkar, *Gandhi in Champaran*; B.N. Ganguli, *Gandhi's Social Philosophy*; J.M. Brown, *Gandhi's Rise to Power*; Erik H. Erikson, *Gandhi's Truth*; Mahadev Desai, *A Righteous Struggle*; V.P. Gaur, *Mahatma Gandhi*.
215. *From Yeravda Mandir*, p. 20.
216. *CWMG*, vol. LIII, p. 261; *Harijan*, 30 January 1937, p. 408.
217. *CWMG*, vol. LIV, pp. 410-11.
218. *Ibid.*, vol. XIX, p. 571.
219. *Ibid.*, vol. LVI, p. 196.
220. D.G. Tendulkar, *op. cit.*, vol. III, p. 297.
221. *CWMG*, vol. XIX, p. 570.
222. D.G. Tendulkar, *op, cit.*, vol. II, p. 272.
223. *CWMG*, vol. XXXV, p. 102; pp. 98 and 107.
224. P.M. Modi, 'Foreword' in R. S. Betai, *Gita and Gandhiji*, p. v.
225. D.G. Tendulkar, *op. cit.*, vol. III, p. 280.
226. *From Yeravda Mandir*, p. 21.
227. D.G. Tendulkar, *op. cit.*, vol. II, p. 211.
228. *CWMG*, vol. LI, p. 368; *My Souls Agony*, pp. 19-20; D.G. Tendulkar, *op. cit.*, vol. III, p. 128.
229. Buddhadeva Bhattacharyya, *op cit.*, p. 184.
230. *CWMG*, vol. XX, p. 136; also *Young India*, 27 April 1921, pp. 135, 269; D.G. Tendulkar, *op. cit.*, vol. IV, p. 163.
231. D.G. Tendulkar, *op. cit.*, Vol. III, p. 182.
232. *Ibid.*, vol. VII, p. 50.
233. *Ibid.*, vol. IV, p. 239; *Ibid.*, vol. VII, p. 161.

234. *Harijan*, 27 April 1934, p. 85.
235. *CWMG*, vol. LVII, p. 286.
236. *Ashram Observances in Action*, p. 79.
237. *Ibid.*, p. 88.
238. *Harijan*, 10 February 1946, p. 4.
239. *From Yeravda Mandir*, p. 25.
240. *Ibid.*, p. 26.
241. *Ibid.*, p. 25.
242. *CWMG*, vol. XXXV, pp. 46-52.
243. M.K. Gandhi, *Hindu Dharma*, p. 229.
244. *CWMG*, vol. XXI, p. 250.
245. D.G. Tendulkar, *op. cit.*, vol. VIII, p. 132.
246. *CWMG*, vol. XXV, p. 202.
247. *Ibid.*, vol. XXXV, p. 461.
248. O.P. Jaggi, *Religion, Practice and Science of Non-Violence*, p. 20.
249. Shriman Narayan, *Mahatma Gandhi: The Atomic Man*, p. 6.
250. *From Yeravda Mandir*, p. 28.
251. *Harijan*, 4 January 1948, p. 497.
252. *CWMG*, vol. XVII, p. 406.
253. *Harijan*, 10 February 1940, p. 445.
254. S.K. George, 'Basic Religion: A Study in Gandhi's Religion', in Kshitis Roy (ed.), *Gandhi Memorial Peace Number*, p. 96.
255. Vincent Sheean, *Lead, Kindly Light*, p. 253.
256. *From Yeravda Mandir*, p. 26.
257. *Young India*, 6 December 1928, p. 406.
258. R.K. Mukherjee, 'The Greatness of Asoka's Conquest', in *Prabuddha Bharat*, Dec., 1939, p. 585.
259. *CWMG*, Vol. XIX, p. 313.
260. *Harijan*, 8 June 1947, p. 180.
261. Margaret Sanger in *Asia*, November, 1936, pp. 698-702. Cited in Nirmal Kumar Bose, *Selections From Gandhi*, p. 283.

8

HUMANISM OF GANDHI

Know then thyself, presume not God to Scan;
The proper study of mankind is man.[1]

Concept of Humanism

"Man is an old and eternally philosophical problem. From times of old, man, his essence, his existence, aims, his past and future have been a subject of philosophical research. In recognizing the world about him, man has meditated upon his place in this world. When changing the surrounding reality, he has pondered his role in the world, his strength and possibilities."[2] Indeed, man is an eternal problem to man. As the 'prime mover' of the world process he raises problems and solves them too. The most favourite and popular topic is 'he' to himself. Even to the average man, not to speak of intellectuals and rare personalities, it is a favourite topic. And consequently, 'know thyself' or *Atmanam Biddhi* has been, as we shall see, the pivotal theme of both Occidental and Oriental thought. To put it more specifically, each and every social science (e.g. history, political science, etc.,) begins with asking, explicitly or implicitly, questions concerning man, such as, what is man? What is human nature? What is his role; function and end in the world process? Gandhian thought is no exception to this trend. Before we take it into account some rudimentary concepts demand brief elucidation.

Opinions of various types as regards human nature and humanism has arisen during the long course of civilization. Because of the abundance of opinion and critique; argument and reargument, it has become a difficult task to define properly the word 'humanism'.[3] As far as our knowledge goes the word 'humanist' was first used in the fifteenth century in Italy to designate some scholars who were not only proficient in Greek and Latin, but also committed to human values as opposed to the life-denying trend of medievalism.[4] And from the historical standpoint the philosophic usage of the word 'Humanism' is of very recent origin. A. Seth Pringle-Pattison incidentally used it as a synonym for 'anthropocentric', and opposed to naturalistic in his *Man's Place in the Cosmos*,[5] F.C.S. Schiller[6] and Marvin Farbiner[7] two great thinkers treat humanism from a positivistic angle of vision which, we shall see, is partial and incomprehensive.

Erich Fromm defines humanism as "belief in the unity of the human race and man's potential to perfect himself by his own efforts."[8] Paul Kurtz opines, "...Humanism is an ethical philosophy in which man is central."[9] These thinkers go beyond mere human experience, and point to a normative interpretation of the topic. The traits of self-transcendence and self-manifestation are duly emphasized.

According to Radha Kamal Mukherjee, "Humanism may be defined as an integrated system of human meanings, goals and values and harmonious programme of human fulfilment, individual and collective...."[10] Indeed, humanism is that branch of knowledge that takes into account the human meanings and their relation to the rest of the universe in its entirety. In this light the definition offered by Radha Kamal Mukherjee seems to be a sound and satisfactory one.

We can bring out the following features of humanism after Schiller.[11] Firstly, Humanism is confessedly a relativism, and as such a denial of all sorts of transcendentalism and absolutism which ignore their relation to man. Secondly, pragmatism and humanism are closely related to each other. Thirdly, humanism like pragmatism is primarily the name for a method, and not for a system of philosophy. Fourthly, it tenders vehement protest against dehumanization in every field. Fifthly, it provides grand scope for toleration and other virtues. Sixthly, dynamism is its another feature. It establishes common truth on the basis of social agreement which undergoes continuous modification, elaboration and improvement. Seventhly and lastly, it promotes common sense, and diminishes the philosophic importance of dialectical subtleties which fail to appeal to the mass.

Historical Development of the Concept of Humanism : Occidental and Oriental

Humanism in the West has its roots in Hellenic thought. Thinkers from Thales to Democritus primarily busied themselves with cosmological and ontological problems. It was the Sophists, the earliest known humanists, who declared for the first time the importance of man in every sphere of life. Protagoras, the pioneer of Sophists, proclaims the magnificent role of man in the universe by saying, "Man is the measure of all things; of those that are that they are, of those that are not that they are not."[12] He applied anthropocentric criterion of humanism in every walk of life.

Socrates, the greatest of the Sophist philosophers, preached theocentric humanism that linked man with the transcendental and the formal. Man's role is pivotal in the world process; and all other existents, natural or artificial, are subservient to human personality. To him man's fundamental reality and central place amongst the existents are quite harmonious with their objectivity. Plato carried this Socratic message to great lengths, and constructed a theocentric humanism that linked man's rational faculty with the guiding principle of the universe. Humanism is the underlying note of his works, especially that of ethics and politics. The writings of Aristotle are most warmly and genuinely humanistic. He treated man as man, and not as angel or devil. Man who is by nature a political animal attains highest fulfilment in communal life. In contrast to theocentric humanism of his two predecessors Aristotlean humanism is out and out anthropocentric. In this context Herschel Barker observes, "Humanism has never been argued more soundly, or stated more appealingly."[13] Indeed, this humanistic ideal of Hellenic civilization and culture reached its zenith in every sphere of life—art, drama, politics, ethics, etc.—during this period. The later Hellenistic systems contributed very little in this respect. The humanistic tendency—anthropocentric or theocentric—disappears in the rigorism of Stoics and Cynics (Zeno, Cicero, etc.); sensuousness of hedonists (Aristippus, Epicurus, etc.); nihilism of sceptics (Pyrrho, Xenophanes, etc.); mysticism of Neo-Platonics (Plotinus). Man was no longer treated as the crown of nature, *facile princeps* of all things. He is reduced to a mere sensitive organism or a part of divinity, i.e., no longer in himself.

Jesus is another glittering star in the galaxy of humanistic movement. He laid utmost emphasis on the greatness of human personality. His life and works converge on a single point: service to humanity. All human institutions—social, political, religious, etc.—are meant for service to human beings. Jesus boldly proclaims, "Sabbath is intended for man and not man for Sabbath."[14] A close scrutiny reveals Christianity as a religion of humanism; and Jesus as one of the greatest champions of mankind. Amiya Chakravorty says, "Christ, one of the greatest of Humanists in the world, proclaimed the noble truth that son of man is the son of God, and that all institutions should subserve his development and that his nature should not be crushed and crumbled to fit in a worn-out shell."[15] It is here noteworthy that Christianity although theocentric theoretically, is anthropocentric in practice. These two aspects of humanism are curiously blended in it which, we shall see later, adorn Gandhian humanism too.

The later Christian exponents (Paul, Augustine, Ambrose, Jerome, etc.,) substituted reason for faith, suspended individualism for the enhancement of God's glory, and let philosophy cross the boundary of religion, of mysticism. The Church fathers offered morbid ideals to suppress the lively and humanitarian traits of mankind. Life was treated as something wretched, a sin, a shame. No scope for intellectual freedom, human aspiration and self-development was provided. In fine, five centuries following Augustine was generally unproductive of original thought. This Slough of Despond and depravity of medieval era was branded as the dark ages, perhaps aptly, in the history of European thought. Mark Mitin observes, "Medieval thinkers, as a rule, ignored the human aspect of man, his living, sensuous, transcient nature."[16]

Now, let us turn to the humanistic thought of the Renaissance era. H.J. Blackham comments, "The characteristic philosophy of the Renaissance was Platonism, of which there were many representatives from Cusa to Campanella, religious Philosophies, universalist, drawing all humanity into immortal participation in the divine life, expressing the accented sense of the grandeur of man and the awakened thirst for all knowledge, and for fame."[17] From the fourteenth to the seventeenth century we find a grand revival of humanistic tradition in European countries. Petrarch declared an open war against the logicians and materialists of his time for their failure to appeal to masses. Erasmus was the most eminent exponent of the movement. He rejected all dogmas and judged the contemporary opinions with an open mind. He initiated in man a new wave of self-esteem and self-fulfilment; and encouraged them to free themselves from all barriers of theological despotism and medieval orthodoxy. S. Dresden observes: "To Erasmus—and this is where he is a typical humanist—the Gospel was primarily a philosophy of life in that it gave the divine message telling men how to lead their lives, and what is implied by true *humanitas*."[18] Montaigne, another exponent, laid great emphasis on the mutability of man and the world. He preached that a man can attain perfection through proper enjoyment of his being or life. In short, the Renaissance movement was characteristically anthropocentric. The man was once again proclaimed an end in himself, as the centre and creater of all values. It opened a new humanistic horizon for the modern world. Amiya Chakravarty aptly comments, "The great humanistic revival during the European Renaissance may be taken to be the foundation of modern culture and civilization in the world...."[19]

In modern times the humanistic tradition was carried on by Bacon, Emerson, Tolstoy, Kierkegaard, Berdyaev, Maritain, Martin Buber, Tillich, Schweitzer, Dostoevsky, Comte, Spencer, Durkheim, Hobhouse, Max Scheler, Bougle, Giddings, Ross, the existentialists and Marxian thinkers. Of them we shall take up, for obvious reason, the account of existentialists and Marxian humanism very briefly.

Of the existentialist thinkers Kierkegaard,. Nietzsche, Jaspers, Marcel, Heidegger, Sartre demand our attention for the novelty and profundity of their thought. The anti-humanistic note of Nietzschean thought is proverbial.[20] The others primarily busied themselves with the meaning and problems of existence, especially man's own inner existence. Karl Jaspers and Gabriel Marcel followed to a great extent the theocentric path while the approach of Heidegger and Sartre is, beyond question, atheistic, Jaspers' condemnation of modern mechanical civilization as a 'social disease' on account of its dehumanizing effect reminds us of Gandhi.[21] Sartre strives to find an existentialist type of humanism on the metaphysical foundations of *Being and Nothingness*.[22] Elsewhere he preaches existentialist humanism by laying emphasis on truth and action. An individual should seek truth and find fulfilment through action since "he is nothing else but the sum of his actions."[23] Self-transcendence and selfless action are predominating notes of Sartre's existentialist humanism which bears a close resemblance to the meaning-systems of Gandhi.[24] He declares, "...I am obliged to will the liberty of others at the same time as mine."[25] In this context H.J. Blackham concludes on Sartre, "Sartre proposes to clear the ruins and re-construct a dogmatic humanism which understands and assumes the eternal human situation, offering a liberation of mankind which starts with a total knowledge of man by himself."[26] In short, the concept of man's alienation is the pivotal point not only of existentialist humanism but also the nucleus of other systems of humanism. Existentialist humanism presents man as a solitary, abandoned creature; and brings his complex psyche—his finitude and insignificance, sense of life and death, fear and anxiety—to light. It separates man from himself and from everything else. It is primarily "concerned with the manoeuvre of existing individuals whose being is ambiguous (both bound and free, separated and joined) in a total existence which is ambiguous (finite and infinite, end and means, a plenitude and nothing)."[27] That is to say, the existentialist's contribution to humanistic tradition is not at all positive and praiseworthy. Its pessimistic and fragmentary outlook leads, to a great extent, to the denial of man's ideal, scope and possibility.

Let us turn to Marxian humanism. The co-founders of Marxism did not compose any treatise dealing specifically with the problem of humanism. Still in their hard task to set up a socialist society they propounded some prepositions as regards the nature and welfare of mankind that throw light on humanism from different angles. The Marxian works, especially the *Economic and Philosophic Manuscripts of 1844* and *Capital* play significant role in the formation of Marxist theory of humanism. Marx writes, "He that would criticise all human acts, movements, relations, etc., by the principles of utility must first deal with human nature in general and then with human nature as modified in each historical epoch."[28] Indeed, man is the pivotal point of his thought; man is his first and foremost concern.

In his early writings Marx expresses his mind concerning human problems through various expressions such as 'real humanism', 'practical humanism', 'positive humanism', etc., (1) Marx's life and works are basically humanistic in the sense that he was a champion of human dignity and personality, a bold resister and critic of injustice and oppression. There was a fiery passion in his fight for justice and righteousness. (2) "Socialism aims at the emancipation of the individual; it desires to set him free from the crippling and degrading forces of modern capitalism, to open to him, for the first time in history, the fullest opportunity for the development of his personality. It desires to rescue men from the pitiable, fragmentary, self-divided society in which they find themselves."[29] Emancipation of man from all sorts of enslavement, bondage, oppression, alienation, etc., was the mission of his life. The highest value that an individual can attain in life is disalienation, i.e., a thorough going emancipation in every sense of the term, external and internal, possible and actual, material and spiritual. In this context M. Markovic aptly comments, "The key concept in a normative ethical theory in the tradition of Marx's humanism is the concept of disalienation."[30] John Lewis observes, "Behind the whole philosophy of Marxism then is passionate opposition to all relations, all conditions in which man is a humiliated, enslaved, despised creature. That is why Marxism is a humanism."[31] (3) Marx's concept of history is out and out humanistic. He makes history a creation, an output of human activities. He presents man as the acme of existents; and put him at the zenith of values.[32] (4) Humanism is the nucleus of his teachings and preachings as manifested in epistemology, ethics, sociology, economics, politics, etc., (a) Since man draws his knowledge from sensation, and thereby from the world of senses, we should arrange the empirical world fit for him, i.e., a truly human world. (b) The fundamental rules of morality should not go against the interest of humanity. Criminals are to be reformed and the anti-social sources of crime are to be abolished. (c) Since man is shaped by environment, his environment must be made human. Since man is social by nature, and that he can develop his physical and mental faculties best in society only, the rules and regulations of society should be based on humanistic principles."[33] The humanistic character of his economic and political thought requires no further elucidation. (5) The communism that Marx preaches is 'the real appropriation of the human essence by and for man. It is the complete return of man to himself. Therefore communism equals to humanism."[34] The above is a very brief account of Marxian humanism—a complete exposition of which, perhaps, cannot be expressed in a single volume, and it is not our objective too. The whole life and work of Marx is a burning example of humanism. With Mark Mitin we can conclude, "Marxism has never ignored the problem of man either in the period of the preparation and formation of Marxism, or in the period of the maturity of Marxist theory, or throughout its entire tremendous history; it has never lost sight of this problem, never dismissed it."[35]

Thus the Occidental tradition of humanistic thought presents both theocentric and anthropocentric trends. Similar is the case, we shall see very shortly, with Indian tradition too. The difference is that while the Indian thinkers lay emphasis on the former the Western thinkers emphasize the latter.

Now, we shall take up very briefly the humanistic tradition of Indian thought for a sound understanding of the Gandhian standpoint. The earliest record of the humanistic ideal in Indian thought is found in the Rig Vedic hymns which centre round man as an earthly being.

Their way of life, offerings to Gods, etc., are based openly on utilitarian and humanistic of interests. The universal appeal of the humanistic tradition is well expressed in the verse "He is my own, he is a stranger; this is the way light-minded people reckon; but for the high-minded, the world is their family-home."[36] These concepts of world-home and universal kinship that bind mankind in a single nexus is something unique in the history of thought, both Eastern and Western.

The period of Upanishads is, perhaps, the most glorious era of Indian humanism. The Upanishads proclaim the existence of spiritual unity behind all physical existents. The *Atman* is the fundamental, and single active principle that steers the sense-organs. Just as sparks come out of fire so also from the *Atman* come forth all organs, all worlds, all gods, all beings, etc. In this sense the whole world is its own creation. *Atman* declares, "I, indeed, am this whole world."[37] "This *Atman* is the same in the ant, the same in the gnat, the same in the elephant, the same in these three worlds ... the same in the whole universe."[38] Thus the *Atman* or self-comprehends in its infinite bosom every existent of the universe. Amiya Chakravarty observes, "If Humanism means candid recognition of the greatness of the human personality as such in spite of man-made limitations due either to birth or wealth, then we must admit that the Upanishadic period of Indian thought is a glorious period of Humanism."[39]

The epic period (*Mahabharata* and *Ramayana*) contributes to this end. The humanistic element of *Mahabharata* is brought forth in the saying, "I tell you this, the secret of the *brahman*: there is nothing superior to man." Here the focus of attention is not anything transcendent or supernatural. It is the earthly man that is put at the zenith of creation.

In contrast with the above spiritualistic trend the Charvakas adopted an atheistic and materialistic outlook. They denounced the law of *Karma*, the soul, the rebirth, God, everything supernatural and confined themselves to this mundane world to make the best use of it. They proclaimed self-assertion, and challenge the authority, especially to the authority of the Vedas. In a sense it was a revolt against all sorts of alienation of man, against priestly exploitations carried on in the guise of rituals. S. Radhakrishnan opines a similar view.[40]

Both Buddhism and Jainism arose as a reaction to Vedic authority. They preached the message of liberation from bondage and sufferings. Buddha advised his disciples to go to the people and work tirelessly for their welfare since there was nothing higher and nobler than man. In Buddhism we are told, "It is the longing for renunciation; the hope to live in love with all; the aspiration of true humanity."[41] "I must bear the burden of all creatures."[42] Not only this, Buddha countered off the spiritual tradition by saying that in order to attain Nirvana or liberation an individual need not bother about pleasing gods and ancestors. To a liberated man gods themselves pay homage, as they did to Buddha. Together with the human personality the human body is also given a unique place of importance because it is through this physical body that an individual performs penance, and thereby attains liberation from suffering. It is here noteworthy that both these schools share the anthropocentric tradition of humanistic thought.

The Sankhya-Yoga schools carry the same humanistic message to mankind. According to Sankhya, *purusa*, the human personality, is eternally free. Its contamination with the *prakrti* gets it entangled in *samsaric* cycle of births and deaths, sorrows and sufferings. An individual can get rid of this cycle by realizing his true self through self-knowledge and self-development. The allied system, Yoga, prescribes eightfold discipline to get rid of this pollution both physical and mental. The humanistic note underlying these twin systems is that they centre round the man. They are intended for man and are possible only with man.

The realistic schools of Nyaya and Vaisesika too lay emphasis on the true knowledge of self for the attainment of liberation. The Purvamimamsa school although preoccupied with the importance of rituals and sacrifices as a path to salvation did stop with man as the highest being, and followed the humanistic trend of the Upanisads. Vedantism or Uttarmimamsa holds Brahman to be the only reality, and all other existents of the world are mere manifestations, mere appearances of it. Here Indian humanism faces a set-back, and becomes out and out spiritualistic and theocentric. This trend was carried on by *Bhakti* (devotion) campaigners such as Chandi Das,[43] Chaitanya, etc., in medieval times; and in modern times in the nineteenth and twentieth centuries by Rammohun Roy, Dayananda Saraswati, Vivekananda,[44] Tagore, Aurobindo and Gandhi.

To conclude, despite their scholastic differences the Indian thinkers to a great extent agree on a vital issue, namely, the primary and practical importance of human personality, the perfection of which depends on self-discipline and true knowledge. A progressive manifestation, with trifiling variation, of human personality and freedom is observed throughout its development. It requires no further elucidation that these are the postulates of humanistic thought. Since human nature is primarily assumed to be spiritualistic in nature; and liberation, the ultimate goal of life, is thought to be non-sensuous, the anthropocentric spirit of Indian humanism gives way to theocentric speculation. To put it otherwise, the history and development of Indian humanistic tradition exhibit a leaning towards spiritualism.

Human Nature in Gandhian Thought

Now we shall take up the main problem: the humanism of Gandhi. This vital problem demands a precise enunciation of human nature. An analytical mind will find out the following characteristics of human nature in Gandhian thought. (1) An individual's inherent nature is distinct and different from his deeds creations and institutions. He is untainted and beyond his creations. Irrespective of merits and demerits of his creations his inner being deserves respect. To quote him, "Man and his deed are two distinct things. Whereas a good deed should call forth approbation and a wicked deed disapprobation, the doer of the deed, whether good or wicked, always deserves respect, or pity as the case may be. 'Hate the sin and not the sinner' is a precept."[45] "I have discovered, that man is superior to the system he propounds."[46] (2) The above is a corollary of his belief that a man is divine by nature. He says, "We are all sparks of Truth. The sum total of these sparks is indescribable, as yet unknown Truth, which is God."[47] "He often spoke of man as the part (*amsa*) of God, as an incarnation of God, (*Jiv-matra ishvarke avatar hai*). As man is not God; but neither is he different from the light (or spark) of God (*adam Khuda nahin: lekin Khuda ke noor se adam juda nahin*)."[48] Gandhi's belief in Vedantic Brahman is responsible for his concept of divinity in human nature. (3) Another offshoot is his belief in the oneness and essential unity of all human beings. In his words, "I believe in absolute oneness of God and therefore also of humanity. What though we have many bodies? We have but one soul."[49] "...I believe in the essential unity of man and for that matter of all that lives."[50] The above characteristics of human nature play a key role in his concept of non-violence. (4) Man is not only a divine being but also a brute; an irrational, sensual, cruel, passionate animal. Brutality and divinity go together in human being. Gandhi says, "We were perhaps all originally brutes, and I am prepared to believe that we have become men by a slow process of evolution from the brute."[51]

But this brutality is not an inelastic element of human nature. Man's mission on earth is to overcome this brutal force, by love, self-sacrifice, self-renunciation; and thereby realize the true man, the divinity that dwells in him. In his words, "We were thus born with brute strength, but we were born men in order to realise God who dwells in us...."[52] The fundamental difference between man and the brute is that man can tame the brutality through self-discipline, and realize divinity inherent in him while animals cannot. Here Gandhi derives the concept of human nature from the fundamental tenets of Hinduism.[53] (5) Gandhi had a never-failing faith in the infinite possibilities and goodness of man. This boundless faith in the goodness of man is the plinth of satyagraha, his way of fighting evils. Gandhi says, "Never lose faith in humanity. A few dirty drops can't soil the ocean which humanity is."[54] "My belief in the capacity of non-violence rejects the theory of permanent inelasticity of human nature."[55] He is an 'irrepressible optimist' who believes that an individual, however depraved and rotten he may be, can be overcome by noble and friendly actions, by ceaseless service and sufferings. (6) Imperfection is an important characteristic of human nature in Gandhian thought. He says, "No one can attain perfection while he is in the body..."[56] "Man will ever remain imperfect, and it will always be his part to try to be perfect."[57] "Since no man is free from error, an individual may strive to attain perfection which he may achieve by degrees, and not in its entirety. Imperfection is inherent in his nature."[58] This concept of human imperfection forms an integral part of Gandhi's metaphysical outlook. (7) Human nature is elastic, and hence can be changed. In his words, "Man is the maker of that line (course of life) and he can therefore unmake it."[59] "We can mend or mar the present and on that will depend the future."[60] Although much too engressed in divinity Gandhi was a champion of human freedom. He also admitted that though an individual can bring a revolutionary change in his constitution or basic nature through self-discipline, his *samskaras* (tendencies caused by previous births) can be erased either with great difficulty or never."[61] In this context R.N. Iyer aptly observes, "Gandhi believed that the goodness of man is grounded not in some instinctive inclination of sympathy, but in man's capacity for self-determination...."[62] (8) The concept of human nature in Gandhian thought is concrete, and not an abstract one. Louis Fischer narrates it beautifully in his study.[63] This idea has its roots in his concept of practical idealism. (9) To him an individual is an end in himself. A man is a man, an individual is an individual beneath all external influences as maintained by Marx.[64] Like Marx he does not seek human nature in social relations. To Gandhi the roots of human motivations are embedded in human nature itself. Hence comes his vehement emphasis on self-discipline. (10) That does not mean Gandhi does not take into account environmental factors altogether. Indeed, environment like heredity plays an important role in the formation of human personality.[65] And since environment contributes to the growth of human nature, change of environmental factors is necessary for an effective change of human nature.[66]

The above is a very brief account of the salient features of human nature in Gandhian thought. A close scrutiny will reveal that Gandhi laid much emphasis on the inner being, and thereby on the spiritual or non-sensuous aspects of human nature. The sentient self in spite of his practical idealism is reduced to a secondary role. In this context F.R. Moraes comments, "few will deny that Gandhi by elevating his fellow men to his own moral plane tends to take a far too optimistic view of human nature."[67]

Humanism of Gandhi

Now, we shall take up the main problem: the humanism of Gandhi. We have seen that though Gandhi inherited the spiritualistic tradition of ancient India, his concept of human nature is real, concrete, and deeply rooted in the soul of this empirical world. His whole life and work was dedicated to one goal: To bring down the Kingdom of God on earth and thereby elevate human beings to the level of celestial ones. Gandhi anthropomorphized God and divinized man. He preached his philosophy of man and life in the traditional background revised and remodelled in the light of modern noble ideas. It is in this sense that the humanism of Gandhi is to be understood.

Gandhi had multidimensional approach to human problems. But a close scrutiny reveals that the word 'humanism' does not come within the terminology of Gandhi. Olivier Lacombe correctly observes, "We are quite right in speaking of the humanism of Gandhi. But let us not forget that he never used this term himself. He spoke of a human fraternity, but he never spoke of humanism."[68] To us it matters little whether Gandhi used the tenn humanism or not since naming is not an essential element of it. "What's in a name? That which we call a rose/By any other name would smell as sweet."[69] Like rose the humanism of Gandhi is a self-illuminating lustre, a self-fragrant musk. It does not wait for scholastic baptizement.

The multidimensional ways to approach Gandhi's humanism are as follows: (1) With an apology to scholastic discourse, we can present the nucleus of Gandhian thought in two words: Truth and Non-violence. As shown above he not only conducted a life-long experiment in them but sacrificed life at their altar. He even identified them with God whose being constantly he felt, breathed and lived for. On some occasions he made exceptions to these cardinal virtues, in a sense the elements of his being. The killing of some animals (monkey, etc.) which devoured and destroyed foodstuff; the suicide of a leper; the civil disobedience by Gharwali soldiers; some comments on war, etc., may be cited in this regard. But these exceptions are initial, and not final. They are not deviations rather admission of fact on humanitarian ground. His ardent humanism inspired him, compelled him to respond to the suffering humanity."[70] If any inconsistency, real or apparent, is observed in his preaching and practice of these two concepts, it was unhesitatingly done only for the sake of humanity, not for want of his honesty and sincerity. If a piece of work brought redress to dumb millions he cared little for dry syllogistic concepts. Because it is in the masses that he found the concrete, living incarnations of truth and non-violence. Prem Kripal correctly comments, "With truth and non-violence as his guiding stars, man was Gandhi's recurring theme."[71]

(2) Gandhi's concept of history is quite humanistic in nature. Truth and non-violence is the 'ceaseless growth' of the human race. When there is, "an interference with nature" it is recorded and becomes history."[72] That is to say, to Gandhi history is essentially ethical and spiritual in character. It shows man's steady progress towards truth and non-violence. To an analytical mind the above interpretation may appear as mystical and metaphysical approach to history. But in 1937 he spoke of history purely from earthly and humanistic standpoint. Gandhi says, "Whereas generally history is a chronicle of Kings and their wars, the future history is the history of man."[73] Here Gandhi refers to the important role that man is playing in making and remaking the modern world. Here certainly he had in mind the nationwide freedom movement through which the people of India was trying to create a new historic era under his leadership. In this context, Buddhadeva Bhattacharyya observes, "The role of the individual was central to Gandhi's view of history."[74]

(3) "...Gandhiji as a profoundly religious man was the supreme humanist in the modern crisis."—observes Amiya Chakravarty on the humanistic elements of Gandhi's religious ideas.[75] We have seen that he was out and out a theist, more particularly an ethico-religious personality. But his was not a transcendent rather an immanent, an anthropomorphized God to be found amongst the dumb millions. To quote him, " Man's ultimate aim is the realization of God.... If I could persuade myself that I should find Him in a Himalayan cave I would proceed there immediately. But I know that I cannot find Him apart from humanity."[76] "My creed is service of God and therefore of humanity."[77] "... Rama whom I see face to face in the starving millions of India."[78] Gandhi's burning humanism inspired him to anthropomorphize God and divinize man. On some occasions he made atheistic remarks, and wanted to relinquish God in whom he lived and breathed only for the sake of humanity. During a serious communal riot in Bombay, Gandhi with a heavy heart exclaimed that if God is the cause of Hindu-Muslim riot we should go without Him.[79] His conversion of the term 'God is Truth' to 'Truth is God' and *Ram Raj* to *Khudai Raj* is based on the same humanistic theme, the welfare of mankind. Gora, the atheist, brings out this note very nicely: "His primary concern was humanity. On account of this deep concern, he could proclaim boldly: 'I can neither say my theism is right, nor atheism is wrong."[80] Joan V. Bondurant observes, "God was, in Gandhi's definition, even the atheism of the atheist. There was no insistence upon an objective absolute."[81] Moreover, his ardent humanism urged him to remove, in spite of his highest regard to Hinduism, untouchability, the age-old human custom. S. Radhakrishnan observes, "The success he has achieved in removing this blot on Hinduism will stand out as one of his greatest contributions to the progress of humanity."[82] Thus Gandhi's religion leads to humanism, and in a sense, presupposes it.

(4) His political ideas too necessarily follow as corollaries from indomitable humanism. As Rene Fulop-Miller observes, "...all the ideas which Gandhi made the basis of his political system are rooted in his humanity."[83] We have already explained that Gandhi was primarily an ethico-religious personality. The motto of service to humanity inspired him to enter into politics. To quote him, "Hence my passion for the service of the suppressed classes. And as I cannot render this service without entering politics, I find myself in them."[84] "I do not care whether Marxism is right or wrong. All I know is that the poor

are being crushed. Something has got to be done for them. To me this is axiomatic."[85] Thus politics to Gandhi; is not a lip-service, a stepping-stone to attainment of power. It is rather a weapon to fight against evils of the suffering humanity.

(5) Gandhi's aesthetic concepts too contribute to his humanism. Gandhi's opinions on art, music, literature, beauty, etc., arose out of his deep concern for mankind. He did not lose sight of man even in this field. To quote him, "Whatever can be useful to these starving millions is beautiful to my mind."[86] "The hungry millions ask for one poem—invigorating food."[87] The *charka* or spinning wheel which employed and provided food and clothings to starving millions was a symbol of 'sweet song,' purity and beauty to him. The handspun piece of cloth or Khadi in spite of its coarseness is lovely and graceful on account of "the delicate touch of the hands of men and women," while the most expensive superfine mill cloth appears to him "a dead polish."

The clay, metal and horn products of hunger-stricken craftsmen from Orissa charmed him. A musical conference in which Hindu and Muslim singers sit side by side appeals to him not for artistic note but for anti-communal and humanistic characteristics. On literary works his opinion manifests the same trend. He tells us to compose "a literature that can speak to the millions."[88] Thus his opinions on the numerous facets of aesthetics converge at a single point: humanism. Mulk Raj Anand observes, "The essence of his teachings, however, seems to be the struggle for human decency. And, it is in this sense, that I call him an humanist."[89]

(6) Let us take up his economic policy. It is not a scholastic theory. It arose from his naive mind, from innate feelings, i.e., from humanistic urge. Gandhi says, "According to me the economic constitution of India and for the matter of that of the world should be such that no one under it should suffer from want of food and clothing."[90] To him human beings are the most valuable wealth of a country; and hence upon them the prosperity of a country depends. He preached economic programmes for the best utilization of manpower. His concepts of khadi, swadeshi, bread labour, small-scale and cottage industries; apathy for large-scale and mechanical industries, etc. do enhance the significance of his humanistic outlook."[91] On the humanistic elements of his economic thought F.R. Moraes observes, "To him the basic fact of economics is that man must eat. Freedom from want is the first article of his creed, and throughout his public

life he has worked passionately to free his countrymen from the degradation of poverty."[92]

(7) Gandhi's sociology assumes the following humanistic forms: (a) His dislike for machineries which deprive the starving millions of bread has its root in humanism. To quote him, "The supreme consideration is man. The machine should not tend to make atrophied the limbs of man."[93] The centre of his sociology is man. Machinery exist for man, and not man for machinery. The so-called labour saving machinery ride on human beings and cause starvation to dumb millions. This is something inhuman and hence Gandhi's apathy for machines. (b) His concept of man, as discussed above, and his relation to society is living, concrete and quite humanistic. He says, "The individual is the one supreme consideration."[94] "Ultimately, it is the individual who is the unit."[95] He emphasized the role of the individual in a social system. The individual is the ultimate authority, the prime mover of all social changes. His humanistic mind did not submit the individual to any institution or organization like society. Buddhadeva Bhattacharyya aptly comments, "Gandhi's individual is a social individual. He did not want to subordinate the individual to an abstraction like the society or the State...."[96] (c) The humanistic element of his theory of education is manifested in the following excerpt: "Real education consists in drawing the best out of yourself. What better book can there be than the book of humanity."[97] Indeed, the object of *Nai Talim* (vocational training) was to give light and food to the starving millions. (d) His antipathy to modern civilization is also the result of his humanism. He condemns it as 'Satanic', a symbol of 'Black Age', irreligious, immoral, etc. Gandhi dedicates his *Hind Swaraj* or *Indian Home Rule* to the service of the common man. Although his preachings faced severe criticism from several quarters the humanistic note of his critique is undeniable. M.D. Jouvenal appraises that "his was essentially a humanistic critique of industrial civilization."[98] (e) His concept of socialism is based on humanistic outlook. Although he disliked the Marxian materialistic approach he appreciated the dictums, "All for each and each for all," "From each according to his ability to each according to his needs." These Marxian principles impressed Gandhi owing to their humanistic appeal. In this light he wanted to organize and construct the socio-economic structure of society in his own style, the non-violent way. Thus his concept of socialism was essentially ethical and humanistic in outlook. (f) Gandhi's concept of non-possession, protest against dehumanization, abolition

of private property, emancipation of women, etc., arose from his ardent humanism to free mankind from exploitation in any form. For obvious reasons it is not possible to take into account the other facets of his sociology that stemmed from humanistic urge. Nevertheless, we can unhesitatingly conclude that his sociological concepts arose out of boundless love for humanity.

(8) The whole work and life of Gandhi is based on a fundamental assumption that man is inherently moral and spiritual in nature. This is the reason why he dedicated his life to the moral recovery of mankind. Since there is no division of the works into watertight compartments Gandhi emphasized the point of moral recovery in every sphere—i.e., political, social, economic, etc. The virtues and vows that he prescribed were directed towards one goal—the removal of dehumanization, elimination of alienation, recovery of the true moral self. The means adopted by him for the purpose is also out and out moral in character. The theory of conversion or change of heart of the opponent, the technique of satyagraha for fighting evils, the moral purity of the ends and means, the reformative concept of punishment, etc., are all actuated by the noble zeal that neither the campaigner nor the opponent should be injured either physically or morally hurt or debased. This is certainly an eternal note of humanism. Joan V. Bondurant observes, "Truth in satyagraha leads to an ethical humanism."[99]

(9) The method he adopted towards the world lies embedded in the matrix of humanism. His method was an experiment with truth through the service of humanity. Gandhi writes, "I will give you a talisman. Whenever you are in doubt or when the self becomes too much with you, try the following expedient. Recall the face of the poorest and the most helpless man whom you may have seen and ask yourself: if the step you contemplate is going to be of any use to him. Will he be able to gain anything by it? Will it restore him to control over his own life and destiny?"[100] A close scrutiny will reveal the truth that at every step of his interpretation of the world men was at the centre of his study. His method assumes the following humanistic forms: (a) A logic or argument that renders no service to humanity is dry and barren. A piece of reasoning should be subservient to mass-welfare and not the converse. As a man of action he reacted to the given situation intuitively; and obviously for the interest of the dumb millions. Not logic but humanism was his medium towards them owing to the fact that the spirit of human welfare often loses its

elan vital in the vicious circle of intellectual reasonings and dialectical subtleties. Indeed, dry syllogism often ignores human interests and becomes fatal to mankind."[101] (b) As discussed above, humanism and pragmatism are closely related to each other. For the sake of humanity the humanists often adopt pragmatic measures to achieve their end. Gandhi is no exception to that trend. Throughout his life he applied pragmatic measures on numerous occasions. But he disliked utilitarianism or the principle of utility from the core of heart. Nevertheless, he employed, rather indulged in pragmatic method, in every walk of life for the welfare of mankind."[102] (c) Dynamism is a characteristic of humanism, and it enriches Gandhian thought too. Gandhi was an ever-growing, ever-making, ever-developing personality. His fervent responsiveness to the call of the hour, to the concrete and everchanging demands of mankind compelled him to modify his stand on numerous occasions. These 'contradictions' in his thought are apparent, and not final. Since absolute truth is beyond the grasp of human beings, Gandhi apprehended it bit by bit; and was coming nearer to it day by day. Hence he claimed no finality for his preachings. His sole objective was to elevate the suffering humanity to human lever. And on account of this burning humanism he cared very little for being systematic, consistent, coherent, logical and integrated."[103] When Gandhi, an absolutist, adopts his ideas to the ever-changing surroundings in the aforesaid manner, the key lies with his humanism. It is, in Nietzschean phrase, 'human, all too human'.

(10) "Gandhi was humanist, shall we say, from the very first moment of his self-consciousness."[104] Even in early youth the elements of humanism were manifested in his passion for nursing others. In those odd days of juvenile delinquency Gandhi performed all sorts of nursing to his ailing father as a duty. He did never neglect it rather "loved to do this service."[105] Since then "aptitude for nursing gradually developed into a passion"[106] for him. We find him nursing various types of persons under various circumstances. On some occasions he nursed wife, son, brother-in-law, a leper; while elsewhere we find him serving in hospitals, ambulance, corps in wars (Boer war and Zulu rebellion), in Black Plague (in Bombay and Johannesburg), in matters of public sanitation and cleanliness, etc. His life and writings (especially *An Autobiography*) reveal openly that nursing, nay service to humanity, became one of his elements.

(11) Gandhi's utopianism too contains humanism. He was both a realist and an idealist. He dreamt as well as acted. He used to call

himself a 'practical idealist'. His eager search for truth and non-violence in every sphere of life in the highest degree, i.e., perfection led him to a great extent to transcend his realistic surroundings. Indeed, true humanism is transcendent in character. As Radha Kamal Mukherjee opines, "True human existence is transcendence. True humanism is transcendent or cosmic."[107] Kingsley Martin contends that the charge of utopianism against humanists is often recorded in history, but it is untenable because the humanists with their utopian vision open a new horizon to mankind and "point the way to a better society and better human beings."[108] Gandhi too was a utopian, a dreamer who strove to set-up the kingdom of God on earth, to establish a new social order, *Ram Rajya* where truth and non-violence would be the guiding stars, and people would enjoy freedom in every sense of the term. In order to prepare the blueprint of the future society Gandhi consciously transcended the prevailing structure. But his love for humanity blended with his practical sense, and his pragmatic outlook planted him on the ground. In brief, Gandhi's utopianism too arose out of his love for humanity.

(12) His respect for healthy tradition, and as also his reformative zeal, have the same root, i.e., humanism. From the core of his heart Gandhi knew that the dumb millions whose leader he was and whom he was addressing were mostly naive and illiterate. The modern linguistic usages, although scientific and universal, would be unintelligible to them. That is to say, his deep insight of mass-psychology foretold him that modern scientific phraseology would seem to the masses of India to be a mysterious utterings, 'full of sound and fury but signifying nothing'. Hence he picked up for mass communication the traditional idioms and concepts that were intermingled with their blood, with the soil of the country. The idioms like *ahimsa*, Gopal, *satya*, Brahma, *brahmacharyya*, *charkha*, *daridranarayan*, *hartal*, *harijan*, karma, *maya*, *swaraj*, *swadeshi,* etc., are household words in India. Gandhi innovated them in the modern perspective; and infused life into their mode of intercourse for the attainment of a greater objective, the independence of India.[109] Thus Gandhi infused life into the traditional ideas, idioms and concepts; and adopted them as a technique of mass communication only to identify himself with the masses, to be one of them. In this context Louis Massignon comments, "He was a genius in investing common words with unique meanings...."[110] The urge for identification with the people of India was so deep in him that it became an element of

his being. He could not help living amongst the dumb-millions. William Miller observes, "Gandhi expresses this solidarity in his very way of life: this solidarity was not only verbal but existential."[111] This identification with the people is a salient feature of humanism.

(13) Gandhi was an anti-communalist, and thereby a humanist par excellence. It is for communal harmony that he lived, and breathed his last. Since his early youth an equal regard for all religions grew in him; and in later life he became a votary of amity amongst people of different faiths. During pre-independence days communal riots, under the direct or indirect instigation of British rulers, often broke throughout India, and caused havoc. Gandhi appealed to his countrymen, "I write in the name and for the sake of heart unity which I want to see established among the people of this land professing different faiths."[112] "The key to the solution of the tangle (communalism) lay in everyone following the best in his own religion and entertaining equal regard for the other religions and their followers."[113] "I am striving to become the best cement between the two communities. My longing is to be able to cement the two with my blood, if necessary."[114] The world knows how tragic and true was this prophecy. During those days of communal frenzy he became a symbol of human brotherhood amongst people of all religions. He wandered from one corner of the country to another for the restoration of communal peace and harmony. This humanitarian role of Gandhi has been appreciated by a galaxy of scholars. Buddhadeva Bhattacharyya says, "...the posterity shall certainly acclaim him as one of the noblest spirits that walked upon this earth."[115] Carl Heath claims, "His humanity to men and to all living things has given him multitudes of friends in every place and nation under the sun..."[116] C.G. Shah comments, "By assassinating Gandhi, political Hindu communal reaction has destroyed the life of one who was a living embodiment of rich and profound humanism, one whose heart was resonant with deep emotion of love for entire humanity, and whose outlook transcended the mere local or national."[117] The above appraisals from different perspectives sufficiently exhibit the magnitude of the vastness of Gandhian humanism. His was not a lip-service but a demonstration in his life and works. He offered blood as living ablation to the abolition of communalism in India. He sacrificed his life at the altar of communal peace and harmony; and thereby set an example of burning humanism before the world ridden with hatred and conflict.

(14) Gandhi's humanism knew no bounds of nationalism and

internationalism. In him nationalism got fairly married with internationalism, and formed an integrated whole of his being. We shall take up the nationalism and internationalism of Gandhi one by one. (a) C.G. Shah comments on Gandhi's nationalism, "To portray Gandhi and evaluate his great and significant role in the life of the Indian people *as objectively as possible* is the highest homage that we can tender to this human Titan. Gandhi was a nationalist *par excellence*."[118] As discussed above a wave of reformation and nationalism, although confined within a limited circle (the progressive and educated sections) was flowing throughout India since the early days of Gandhi's life. His acquaintance with Western ideology during his stay in London as a student kindled a burning inspiration of nationalism in him which became a fierce force through his bitter experiences of South Africa. Later as a public leader the spirit of nationalism got infused into his being; and steered him throughout life to attain freedom for the suffering millions of India. Here regarding the nationalistic character of his thought the following points are remarkable. Firstly, his metaphysical outlook dominates here. Since all men are sparks of truth, and all land belongs to God our nationalism should transcend all barriers, geographical—(a Gujrati, a Bengali, an American, etc.,) religious (a Hindu, a Muslim, a Christian, etc.), social (racial, caste, etc.), political (sectional, partisan, provincial, etc.) on the ground that "God never made those frontiers."[119] Elsewhere Gandhi says, "I live for India's freedom and would die for it, because it is part of Truth."[120] "Indian nationalism is not exclusive, nor aggressive, nor destructive. It is health-giving, religious and therefore humanitarian."[121] The pivotal point is that his nationalism was open and broad, without any limitation and barrier like the blue sky. C.G. Shah correctly estimates Gandhi's nationalism when he observed, "Gandhi was the highest expression of nationalism.... The consciousness of Gandhi, the nationalist of the classical type, was also completely free from even the faintest trace of provincial particularism or communalism. He was not a Gujrati, or a Hindu but an Indian, a nationalist *par excellence*."[122] Secondly, the movement for independence of India before the emergence of Gandhi was to a great extent sectional, theoretical, limited and speech-based. The people were kept outside the arena. In a sense it was a favourite pastime of the pre-Gandhian intelligentsia. But Gandhi's profound insight of human psychology prompted him to find out genuine struggling spirit amongst the suffering millions. Accordingly he organized and turned them into roaring lions. It was for the first time that a massconsciousness of nationalism was incited, and successfully awakened throughout India. He made heroes out of semi-comatic people; and assembled them under the banner of nationalism. Here C.G. Shah's observation is sound and invaluable, "Gandhi's supreme contribution to the Indian nationalist movement lay in the fact that he created a mass basis for that movement. He was the author of the first mass national liberation struggle of the Indian people...."[123] Thirdly, Gandhi's nationalism is coterminus with humanity. To quote him, "For me patriotism is the same as humanity. I am patriotic because I am human and humane."[124] "My patriotism includes... the service of humanity."[125] "I am a humble servant of India, and in trying to serve India, I serve humanity at large."[126] His fervent humanism supersedes intense nationalism. He would stake nationalism if necessary, at the altar of humanism so that human races might live. Fourthly, Gandhi's nationalism is continuous with his internationalism. Like the concepts of ends-means, rights-duties, truth-non-violence, etc., his concepts of nationalism and internationalism too are two faces of the same reality, i.e., humanism. In his words, "My nationalism is intense internationalism."[127] This point will be discussed. (b) Broadly speaking his internationalism too has its roots in humanism. Gandhi says, "I want India's rise so that the whole world may benefit. I do not want India to rise on the ruin of other nations."[128] "Our nationalism can be no peril to other nations, inasmuch as we will exploit none, just as we will allow none to exploit us. Through Swaraj we would serve the whole world."[129] Multiplication of citations is unnecessary. Gandhi admitted no antithesis between nationalism and internationalism. His concept was not an abstract internationalism. He found it in nationalism; and endeavoured to realize it in and through nationalism because internationalism presupposes nationalism. The clash that occurs between them is apparent, and not in themselves. The narrow, selfish and crooked nature of man is responsible for this."[130] It is in this light that Gandhi dreamt of 'world federation', 'World-State' and 'one world.'[131] All these dreams were inspired by one spirit, humanism. D.M. Datta observes, "Love of man impelled Gandhi to be both a nationalist and an internationalist."[132] Fuad Bustany comments, "...this great man was, at one and the same time, an Asian, and an Indian and also a man of the world; a philosopher, a practical politician, a humanist and a humanitarian."[133] C.G. Shah says, "As a humanist Gandhi was a passionate internationalist."[134] Indeed, by its very nature humanism 'transcends all national, sectional and provincial limitations. It is a supranational, panhuman philosophy of universal appeal'."[135]

(15) Gandhi was a champion of human freedom, one of the postulates of humanism. His belief in divinity does not hamper his worship of human freedom. He says, "Man is the maker of that line and he can therefore unmake it."[136] He treated human being as the crown of creation; and hence fought for human freedom in every walk of life. During his public life for more than fifty years he continuously fought for it. In this context Amiya Chakravarty observes, "Mahatma Gandhi's work for peace is unique in world history. Few, in the whole chronicle of mankind, have so effectively harnessed spiritual resources to the task of winning freedom for man. Freedom from war and freedom from hunger and disease and servitude, freedom from fear."[137] G. Ramachandran contributes, "The first element in the humanism of Gandhi is the freedom of man. No man unfree was part of the great humanity of his dreams. Freedom and free men alone can make a just and human society."[138] Thus Gandhi's concept of freedom arose out of his humanism.

(16) The key to the attainment of India's independence through non-violent means is Gandhi's humanism. The twentieth century world saw a wonderful event after the second world war, the peaceful and non-violent achievement of independence by the people of India under Gandhi's leadership. Gandhi had a profound insight into mass-psychology. He keenly studied the prevailing conditions. The tradition loving mass-populace were dumb, hungry, disarmed, and mostly non-violent by nature. The sporadic violent uprisings flashed and died like sparks. Above all, Gandhi's path was different since he was a votary of truth and non-violence."[139] With the magic spell of humanism he instilled life, self-confidence, dignity and patriotism in the semi-comatic nation. With the touchstone of humanism he awakened the dumb millions from torpor, lethargy, and age-old slumber. In a sense, it was the humanism of Gandhi that made the masses of India men in the proper sense of the term. Mulk Raj Anand observes, "The pain borne by some of Gandhi's weak soldiers made them into morally strong human beings. And I believe that this was his greatest contribution as a humanist."[140]

(17) Gandhi was a man of speech, deed and thought. What he preached, he practised. He assumed no multiple personality, no duplicity in life which was as pure and clear as a crystal. His mode of life (food, cloth, dwelling, etc.,) became a symbol of the dumb

millions of India. In Champaran he found the peasants as living incarnations of God, Non-violence and Truth[141] S. Radhakrishnan describes him as "the representative of the peasant."[142] Jawaharlal Nehru picturized him "a symbolic expression of the confused desires of the people"[143] Indeed, Gandhi saw the world with the eyes of a peasant."[144] In this context Jawaharlal Nehru comments, "He does represent the peasant masses of India... he is the greatest peasant, with a peasant's outlook on affairs, and with a peasant's blindness to some aspects of life. But India is peasant India, and so he knows his India well..."[145] He was a peasant, and yet transcended him by dint of his keen intellect, wide outlook, sound farsight, magnetic and gigantic personality. He represented not only the peasants, but also the outcastes, the untouchables, the weavers, the workers, the oppressed or suffering humanity in general. As G.S. Spinks comments, "In a sense Mr. Gandhi was the vicarious conscience of earth's dumb, depressed millions."[146] He became, and identified himself, with the suffering humanity; and vehemently opposed anything and everything that dominated or subjugated or underminded it. The welfare of the suffering humanity ceaselessly absorbed his mind, and possessed it so to say, entirely. In this sense the suffering humanity got infused into his being and became one of its elements.

To conclude: The above discussion is a very brief account of the multidimensional facets of Gandhian humanism a complete exposition of which is, perhaps, beyond human reach. "Humanism was inherent in every spoken word and thought of Gandhi."[147] No word in his writings, no moment of his thinking, no phase of his colourful active life can be detected that does not contribute, directly or indirectly, to humanistic objective. He lived and breathed his last for it. So a patient and painstaking investigation solely dedicated to it, his humanism, may unearth more treasure that lay hidden or latent there. The posterity will take note of this. However, what is remarkable is his boundless love for humanity, especially for the oppressed and poor ones. His universal appeal to mankind in general is something unique in the history of humanistic tradition. His ever responsive mind was always ready to suffer to any extent, even to sacrifice life for the sake of humanity. This lively spirit of self-sacrifice and self-suffering out of limitless love for humanity formed the plinth of Gandhian humanism "which made Gandhi the leader of suffering humanity for all time."[148] It is because of this that Gandhi hoped his humanistic spirit to glitter bright even after death. And wished to be alive even in the grave only to serve humanity.[149] This is the eternal mission of each and every humanist.

References

1. Alexander Pope, 'An Essay on Man', in John Butt (ed.) *The Poems of Alexander Pope*, p. 516.
2. Mark Mitin, 'The Concept of Man in Marxist Thought, 'in S. Radhakrishnan and P.T. Raju (eds.), *The Concept of Man*, p. 476.
3. S. Dresden, *Humanism in the Renaissance*, p. 9.
4. Donald Clark Hodges, 'Marx's Contribution to Humanism', in *Science and Society*, vol. XXIX, 1965, p. 174.
5. F.C.S. Schiller, 'Humanism,' in James Hastings (ed.), *Encyclopaedia of Religion and Ethics*, vol. VI, p. 831.
6. *Ibid.*, p. 830.
7. Marvin Farber, 'Humanistic Ethics and the Conflict of Interests', in Paul Kurtz (ed.), *Moral Problems in Contemporary Society*, p. 255.
8. Erich Fromm, 'Introduction', in Erich Fromm (ed.), *Socialist Humanism*, p. ix.
9. Paul Kurtz, 'What is Humanism?', in Paul Kurtz (ed.), *op. cit.*, p. 2.
10. Radha Kamal Mukherjee, *The Way of Humanism: East and West*, p. 1.
11. F.C.S. Schiller, *op. cit.*, pp. 830-31.
12. F. Copleston, *A History of Philosophy*, vol. I, p. 87.
13. Herschel Barker, *The Image of Man*, p. 65.
14. *The Holy Bible*, St. Mathew, 12.
15. Amiya Chakravarty, *Humanism and Indian Thought*, p. 4.
16. Mark Mitin, *op. cit.*, p. 487.
17. H.J. Blackham, *The Human Tradition*, p. 26.
18. S. Dresden, *op. cit.*, p. 129.
19. Amiya Chakravarty, *Humanism and Indian Thought*, p. 5.
20. F. Nietzsche, *Beyond Good and Evil*, passim.
21. Karl Jaspers, *Man in the Modern Age*, pp. 37-67; also his *The Perennial Scope of Philosophy*, passim.
22. J.P. Sartre, *Being and Nothingness*, pp. 432, 440, 461, 476, 495, 554, passim. H.E. Barnes comments on this work, "Sartre seems to have reduced all of this to purely human data." Introductory note, p. xxvi.
23. J.P. Sartre, *Existentialism and Humanism*, p. 41.
24. *Ibid.*, pp. 55-56.
25. *Ibid.*, p. 52.
26. H.J. Blackham, *Six Existentialist Thinkers*, p. 148; also Margaret Chatterjee, *The Existentialist Outlook*, pp. 57-63; B.N. Ganguli, *op. cit.*, pp. 137-42.
27. H.J. Blackham, *op. cit.*, p. 153; For Gandhi's relation to existentialism, see G. Srinivasan, 'Gandhi: A Practical Existentialist', in *Gandhi Marg*, vol. II, 1980, pp. 181-85.

28. *Capital*, vol. I, p. 668.
29. John Lewis, *Socialism and the Individual*, p. 12.
30. M. Markovic, 'Marxist Humanism and Ethics,' in *Science and Society*, vol. XXVII, 1963, p. 18.
31. John Lewis, *Marxism and the Open Mind*, p. 146.
32. *The Holy Family*, p. 110.
33. *Ibid.*, p. 154.
34. *Economic and Philosophic Manuscripts of 1844*, p. 90.
35. Mark Mitin, *op. cit.*, pp. 534-35.
36. *ayani nijah paro veti ganana laghucetsam under charitanamtu vasudhaiva kutumbakam-trans.* Sylvain Levis *Eastern Humanism*, p. 5.
37. *Chhandogya Upanisad*, 7.25.1.2.
38. *Brahadaranyaka Upanisad*, 1.3.22; also S. Radhakrishnan, *Indian Philosophy*, vol. I, p. 158.
39. Amiya Chakravarty, *Humanism and Indian Thought*, p. 13.
40. S. Radhakrishnan, *op. cit.*, p. 283.
41. *Suttavibhanga* cited in S. Radhakrishnan, *op. cit.*, p. 420.
42. *Ibid.*
43. Chandi Das proclaims, "Listen, O brother man! Above all is the truth of man; there is none higher than this."
44. Vivekananda, the monk and social reformer, preaches: "After so much austerity, I have understood this as the real truth—God is present in every Jiva; there is no other God besides that. 'Who serves Jiva, serves God indeed'." *The Complete Works of Swami Vivekananda*, vol. VII, p. 247.
45. *An Autobiography*, p. 203.
46. *Young India*, 13 July 1921, p. 221.
47. Answer to three questions put by S. Radhakrishnan in S. Radhakrishnan and J.H. Muirhead (eds.), *Contemporary Indian Philosophy*, p. 21.
48. *Young India*, 11 October 1928, p. 340; also D.M. Datta, *The Philosophy of Mahatma Gandhi*, p. 70; *Harijan*, 29 August 1936, p. 226.
49. *Young India*, 25 September 1924, p. 313.
50. *Ibid.*, 4 December 1924, p. 398; also *Gandhiji's Correspondence with the Government 1942-44*, p. 88; *Young India*, 29 October 1931, p. 325.
51. *Harijan*, 2 April 1938, p. 65.
52. *Ibid.*
53. *The Amrita Bazar Patrika*, 2 August 1934, in Nirmal Kumar Bose, *Selections from Gandhi*, p. 92.
54. Gandhi's letter to Amrit Kaur in a conversation entitled 'The Last Phase,' in Francis Watson and Maurice Brown *Talking of Gandhiji*, p. 111.
55. *Harijan*, 7 June 1942, p. 177.
56. *Young India*, 20 September 1928, p. 319.
57. Cited in Nirmal Kumar Bose, *op. cit.*, p. 9.
58. For details, see *syadvad* in ch. III.

59. *Harijan*, 2 January 1937, p. 375.
60. Pyarelal, *The Last Phase*, vol. II, p. 202.
61. *An Autobiography*, pp. 194-96.
62. R.N. Iyer, *The Moral and Political Thought of Mahatma Gandhi*, pp. 106-7.
63. Louis Fischer, *The Life of Mahatma Gandhi*, pt. I, p. 191.
64. Karl Marx, *Economic and Philosophic Manuscripts of 1844*, pp. 104-5
65. *An Autobiography*, p. 230.
66. *Harijan*, 21 September 1934, p. 250.
67. F.R. Moraes, 'Gandhi: The Humanist,' in D.G. Tendulkar (ed.), *Gandhiji: His Life and Work*, p. 23.
68. Oliver Lacombe, 'The relations of truth and non-violence in Gandhi's thinking,' in T.K. Mahadevan (ed.), *Truth and Non-violence*, p. 74.
69. William Shakespeare, *Romeo and Juliet*, Act II, Scene II, in *William Shakespeare: The Complete Works*, p. 912.
70. For details, see chapters four (sect., End and Means); six (sec. Nature of Punishment); seven (sec. Truth and Non-violence), etc.
71. Prem Kripal, *op. cit.*, p. 31; also B.B. Majumder who observes that 'man is the sun in his solar system.' *Gandhian Concept of State*, p. 5.
72. *Hind Swaraj*, p. 45; also *Young India*, 16 September 1926, pp. 324-25.
73. Cited in B.N. Ganguli, *op. cit.*, p. 114.
74. Buddhadeva Bhattacharyya, *Evolution of the Political Philosophy of Gandhi*, p. 120.
75. Amiya Chakravarty, *Modern Humanism: An Indian Perspective*, p. 78.
76. *Harijan*, 29 August 1936, p. 226.
77. *Young India*, 23 October 1924, p. 350.
78. *Ibid.*, 24 March 1927, p. 93; also *Young India*, 15 October 1931, p. 310. Elsewhere he says, "I could not be leading a religious life unless I identified myself with the whole of mankind ... I do not know any religion apart from human activity." *Harijan*, 24 December 1938, p. 393.
79. Cited in Gora alias Ramchandra Rao, *An Atheist with Gandhi*, pp. 46, 54.
80. *Op. cit.*, p. 52. Elsewhere Gora observes, "He was moving humanity and he was moving with humanity." *op. cit.*, pp. 55.
81. Joan V. Bondurant, *op. cit.*, p. 193.
82. S. Radhakrishnan, 'Gandhi's Religion and Politics,' in S. Radhakrishnan (ed.), *Mahatma Gandhi: Essays and Reflections on His Life and Work*, p. 21.
83. Rene Fulop-Miller, *Gandhi: The Holy Man*, p. 57.
84. *Young India*, 11 September 1924, p. 298; also see *Harijan*, 2 March 1934, p. 24; F.R. Moraes, *op. cit.*, p. 23; S. Chakravarti, 'Truth and Non-violence in Gandhi's Humanism,' in T.K. Mahadevan (ed.), *op. cit.*, p. 40; *supra* (ch. V, sec. from Morality to Politics).
85. D.G. Tendulkar, *Mahatma*, vol. VI, p. 293.
86. Cited in B.N. Ganguli, *op. cit.*, p. 125.

87. *Young India*, 23 October 1921, p. 326; 15 October 1931, p. 310.
88. D.G. Tendulkar, *op. cit.*, vol. IV, p. 93.
89. Mulk Raj Anand, *The Humanism of M.K. Gandhi*, p. 24.
90. *Young India*, 15 November 1928, p. 381; also *Harijan*, 9 October 1937, p. 292.
91. For details, see supra (Ch. VII, sec. Bread labour, *Swadeshi*, etc.).
92. F.R. Moraes, *op. cit.*, p. 24; also Gandhi's saying to P.C. Ghosh in Francis Watson and Maurice Brown, *op. cit.*, p. 95.
93. *Young India*, 13 November 1924, p. 378.
94. *Ibid.*
95. *Harijan*, 28 July 1946, p. 236.
96. Buddhadeva Bhattacharyya, *op. cit.*, p. 493.
97. *Harijan*, 30 March 1934, p. 55.
98. Cited in Buddhadeva Bhattacharyya, *op. cit.*, p. 172.
99. Joan V. Bondurant, *op. cit.*, p. 32.
100. Cited in Mulk Raj Anand, *op. cit.*, p. 30.
101. See Pyarelal, *Mahatma Gandhi: The Last Phase*, vol. I, p. 120; *Harijan*, 14 August 1937, p. 212; F.C.S. Schiller, *op. cit.*, p. 831; *supra* (Ch. IV, sec. God as Truth: Truth as God).
102. For details, see *supra* (Ch. III, sec. Pragmatism).
103. *Harijan*, 30 September 1939, p. 288; also *Harijan*, 28 January 1939, p. 445; 24 September 1938, p. 266.
104. Romesh Thapar, 'The relations of truth and non-violence in Gandhi's thinking,' in T.K. Mahadevan (ed.), *op. cit.*, p. 66.
105. *An Autobiography*, p. 21.
106. *Ibid.*, p. 126.
107. Radha Kamal Mukherjee, *op. cit.*, p. 2.
108. Kingsley Martin, 'Is Humanism Utopian?' in H.J. Blackham (ed.), *Objection to Humanism*, p. 89.
109. *Young India*, 14 April 1927, p. 120.
110. Louis Massignon in *Gandhian Outlook and Techniques*, p. 37; also Nirmal Kumar Bose, *Cultural Anthropology*, p. 84.
111. William Miller, 'The Dilemma of Middle Class Pacifism' in *Gandhi Marg*, vol. IV, no. 4, 1960, p. 303.
112. *Young India*, 20 August 1925, p. 292.
113. *Harijan*, 4 January 1948, p. 497.
114. *Young India*, 25 September 1924, in *Young India 1924-26*, p. 83.
115. Buddhadeva Bhattacharyya, *op. cit.*, p. 196.
116. Carl Heath, M.K. Gandhi: 'Apostle of Light and Truth-force,' in S. Radhakrishnan (ed.), *op. cit.*, p. 85.
117. C.G. Shah, *Marxism, Gandhism, Stalinism*, p. 290.
118. *Ibid.*
119. *Young India*, 31 December 1931, p. 427.

120. *Young India*, 3 April 1924, p. 109.
121. *Ibid.*, 13 October 1921, in *Young India 1919-22*, p. 673.
122. C.G. Shah, *op. cit.*, p. 292.
123. *Ibid.*, p. 291; also Clare Sheridan who says that Gandhi's message "has enabled the humble to raise their heads, and recognize their place in the sun." Clare Sheridan, 'The Great Little Mahatma,' in S. Radhakrishnan (ed.), *Mahatma Gandhi: Essays and Reflections*, p. 248.
124. *Young India*, 16 March 1921, in *Young India 1919-22*, pp. 646-47.
125. *Ibid.*, 17 September 1925, p. 320.
126. *Harijan*, 17 November 1933, p. 5; also Mahadev Desai, *Gandhiji in Indian Villages*, p. 170; *Young India*, 12 March 1925, p. 88.
127. *Gandhian Outlook and Techniques*, p. 123.
128. *Young India*, 12 March 1925, p. 88.
129. *Ibid.*, 16 April 1931, p. 79.
130. *Ibid.*, 18 June 1925, p. 211.
131. D.G. Tendulkar, *op. cit.*, vol. VI, p. 158; *Gandhian Outlook and Techniques*, *op. cit.*, p. 274; George Catlin, *In the Path of Mahatma Gandhi*, p. 281.
132. D.M. Datta, *The Philosophy of Mahatma Gandhi*, p. 159.
133. Fuad Bustany, 'The relations of truth and non-violence in Gandhi's thinking' in T.K. Mahadevan (ed.), *op. cit.*, pp. 81-82.
134. C.G. Shah, *op. cit.*, p. 297.
135. Corliss Lamont, *op. cit.*, p. 282.
136. *Harijan*, 2 January 1937, p. 375.
137. Amiya Chakravarty, *Modern Humanism : An Indian Perspective*, p. 164.
138. G. Ramachandran, 'The relations of truth and non-violence in Gandhi's thinking,' in T.K. Mahadevan (ed.), *op. cit.*, p. 71; An echo of the Gandhian concept of man, the maker, the mover is heard in Carl Sandburg who writes, "And man the stumbler and finder, goes on, Man the dreamer of deep dreams, Man the shaper and maker, Man the answerer." in Carl Sandburg, *The People, Yes*, p. 241.
139. For details see *supra* (ch. VII).
140. Mulk Raj Anand, *op. cit.*, p. 23.
141. M.K. Gandhi: *An Autobiography*, p. 304.
142. S. Radhakrishnan in *Mahatma Gandhi: Essays and Reflections*, p. 23.
143. Jawaharlal Nehru, *An Autobiography*, p. 75.
144. Horace Alexander, 'Mahatma Gandhi: An Estimate,' in S. Radhakrishnan (ed.), *op. cit.*, p. 39.
145. Jawaharlal Nehru, *An Autobiography*, pp. 69-70.
146. G. Stephens Spinks, 'Politics and Morality,' in Kshitish Roy (ed.). *Gandhi Memorial Peace Number*, p. 209; also Edward Thompson, 'Gandhi: A Character Study,' in S. Radhakrishnan (ed.), *op. cit.*, p. 268; Mulk Raj Anand, *op. cit.*, p. 27; S. Radhakrishnan, 'Gandhi's Religion and Politics,' in S. Radhakrishnan (ed.), *op. cit.*, p. 39; Mare Edmund Jones, *Gandhi Lives*, p. 49; Victor Hugo, cited in *Young India*, 21 July 1921, p. 232

147. G. Ramachandran, 'The relations of truth and non-violence in Gandhi's thinking,' in T.K. Mahadevan (ed.), *op. cit.*, p. 83; also George S. Arundale who observes, "Of course no volume can commemorate his great and unique services to India." 'The Essence of Gandhiji,' in S. Radhakrishnan (ed.), *op. cit.*, p. 49.
148. Tridib Kumar Chaudhuri, 'Gandhiji and the Revolutionary Socialist Party,' in *Gandhi Marg*, vol. III, no. 3, July 1959, p. 184.
149. Pyarelal, *Mahatma Gandhi : The Last Phase*, vol. II, p. 649.

9

CONCLUSION

His life was gentle; and the elements
So mix'd in him that Nature might stand up
And say to all the world 'This was a man!'[1]

In the preceding chapters we have travelled much in space and time. Different ideas of different parts of the world, especially India and Europe, came within our purview. Similarly we have taken into account the various occurrences, their relevant concepts and temporal relations. The ancient and modern ideas and ideals of Oriental and Occidental civilizations do form, sometimes singly, sometimes jointly, the subject-matter of this work. But this long journey, was not, as mentioned above, an aimless one. It was done to fulfil some design, i.e., proper and precise assessment of the colossal personality of Gandhi in the wide perspective of human civilization. The correct judgement of a great man like Gandhi is a difficult, and perhaps an impossible task. Still the spirit of man refuses to bow to difficulties. We strove to appraise Gandhian thought, in a synoptic form, in its entirety although special emphasis was laid on his contribution to moral science, the object of this work. The other topics, discussed here, have relevance, directly or indirectly to the main topic.

A scholastic study of any creative thinker, especially of a social reformer like Gandhi, should transcend personal relations in order to be sound and precise. Because personal attachment, emotion, etc., often delude free thinking; and obstruct rational judgement. Hence personal relations are not wholesome in this context. Moreover, in a scholastic discourse both blind adoration and nihilistic criticism are condemnable for their dogmatic and unhealthy contribution. That is why we have tried to the best of knowledge to be objective, critical and comparative so that Gandhi may be appraised and understood correctly. We have offered criticism and expressed appreciation as objectively as possible. This is the predominating note of this work.

In the second chapter (The Roots) we took into account the factors (hereditary and environmental, religious, social, political, cultural, geographical, etc.,) that contributed towards the growth and development of Gandhi's mind. The moral convictions that he inherited from family members (grandfather, father, mother, Kasturba—his wife, Rambha—the housemaid) were sharpened and enriched through his acquaintance with the spiritual and moral thinkers like Raychand Bhai, Emerson, Thoreau, Tolstoy, Ruskin and others. Here we observe the initiation of the concept of truth and non-violence in him in the family circle. Raychand Bhai acted as a 'friend, philosopher and guide' for sometime in the beginning of his public life from whom he received religious and moral guidance many a time. Gandhi's political, social, economic ideas were to a large extent influenced and moulded by those of Ruskin, Tolstoy, Thoreau, Emerson, Gokhale, etc. High regard and tolerance for all religions was awakened in him by contemporary conditions prevailing in the religious circle of his native land. His later acquaintance with Christianity, Islam, Buddhism, Jainism, and Zoroastrianism reinforced his belief in toleration and formed the plinth of universal religion, more precisely humanism. Morning shows the day. Gandhi's attitude towards Uka, the scavenger, marks in his early childhood the beginning of the movement of untouchability in a very rudimentary form. He learnt the first lesson of *ahimsa* or non-violence from his ailing father to whom he confessed his guilt. While staying in South Africa as a householder, and a host of office assistants Kasturba's boundless patience amidst heart-pricking humiliation taught him the elementary knowledge of *satyagraha*, his moral weapon to fight against opponents, both internal and external. In a sense, we trace here some of the fundamental roots of Gandhian thought.

An objective study of Gandhi must include both the psychograph and the sociograph of him.[2] That is to say, his inner world—willing, thinking, feeling—together with the external conditions should be considered with equal attention. Gandhi himself admits, "My words and deeds are dictated by prevailing conditions."[3] Indeed, the inner and outer world of Gandhi acted and reacted upon one another reciprocally. His firm convictions created tremendous commotion in the surroundings which, in turn, moved and deeply affected his mind too. Objectivity demands an unbiased analysis of the two. Chapters three and four (His Philosophical Outlook) are devoted to that end. In our attempt to find out the salient features of Gandhian thought we found him: epistemologically a self-styled *syadvadi*, a pragmatist, a conscientious ethicist, a mystic, a rationalist, an empiricist, an eclectic, a defender of faith, etc.; metaphysically, a critic of materialism, an absolute idealist, a practical idealist, an idealistic realist, a monist, a pluralist, a relativist, an agnostic, an *advaitist*, a dualist; ethically an ascetic, a rational intuitionist, an altruist, an eudaemonist, an advocate of human freedom and divine domination at the same time; psychologically, a masochist, a defender of inner voice, an abnormal, a sadist, a mother with femininity, i.e., a personality riddled with contrary and contradictory traits; in aesthetics an eternal worshipper of truth and beauty yet pragmatic and utilitarian on humanitarian ground; religiously, a theist, a pantheist, an *advaitist*, a sanatani Hindu, a genuine Christian, an atheist on humanistic cause; sociologically a conservative, a radical; politically, a shrewd politician, a utopian, a reformist, a revolutionary, an anarchist, a socialist, a democrat—to speak in the language of exaggeration, anything and everything that may be ascribed to him. He is an anigma that transcends human expression. Erik H. Erikson observes, "There is nothing more consistent in the views of Gandhi's critics than the accusation of inconsistency: at one time he is accused of sounding like a socialist, and at another a dreamy conservative; or again, a pacifist and a frantic militarist; a nationalist and a communalist; an anarchist and a devotee of tradition; a Western activist, and an Eastern mysticist; a total religionist and yet so liberal that he could say, "He saw God even in the Atheist's atheism."[4] Jawaharlal Nehru comments, "Again I think of the paradox that is Gandhiji."[5]

These inconsistencies or contradictions are often found in Gandhi's speech and writings. He was conscious of it. Gandhi admits "At the time of writing I never think of what I have said before. My aim is not to be consistent with my previous statements on a given question, but to be consistent with truth as it may present itself to me at a given moment...."[6] Thus Gandhi was conscious of 'inconsistencies', and advises us to look for, if any, "an underlying and abiding consistency between the two seeming inconsistencies." Here lies the truth of the problem of inconsistency or contradiction in Gandhian thought. Our analytical discussion has revealed that these inconsistencies are not real but apparent which arose out of his response to the varying circumstances of humanity. This is neither intentional nor deliberate but an admission of fact, a humanitarian response to the call of mankind which Gandhi could never avert. Moreover, these contradictions were embedded in the objective conditions, in the socio-political movements of the time. Hence he could not avert it in public life. Subhash C. Kashyap made an amazing comment on Nietzsche, "His name has been the centre of veritable controversies almost from the very beginning of his reputation. Perhaps, no two writers on Nietzsche entirely agree with each other in regard to 'what Nietzsche means'. Many interpretations, often contradictory, are, in fact, possible. Some critics go as far as to assert that there are *as many Nietzsches* as there are readers of his works and that his works are like a mirror in which everyone finds and sees himself."[7] The same, of course with necessary changes, may be said of Gandhi. Since he neither founded a system nor thought systematically each and every system of thought that till now mankind has preached will find, in a broad sense, directly or indirectly, its elements, small or huge, in Gandhi's thought, a product of his eclectic mind. We do find a humanistic note underlying these inconsistencies and contradictions which, in fact, belong not to the psychograph but to the sociograph of Gandhi. To put it in other words, these riddles are not in Gandhi himself but in the objective conditions, in the concrete demands of humanity. So Gandhi's boundless love for humanity is the root cause of the discrepancies, riddles, inconsistencies, contradictions, and sporadic views that we encounter in his spoken and written word.

In the succeeding chapters (five and six) we have discussed the bona fide ethical problems of Gandhian thought in the wide perspective of the history of the moral science. The problems like moral judgement, standard of moral action, elements of morality, the nature or characteristics of moral law, the object of moral judgement; the relations between means and ends, rights and duties, morality and religion, morality and politics, morality and economics, morality and aesthetics, morality and social philosophy; the concept of evil, the nature of crime and punishment, the problem of the freedom of the will, etc., do constitute the subject-matter of any standard treatise on moral science. Since Gandhi had no systematic training in moral discipline and was not ambitious to compose a book on it, the harvest of our endeavour may not appear strictly integrated, coherent and conclusive one. Perhaps, this is due to the eclectic and prolific nature of Gandhi's mind. His treatment of natural calamities as human sin;

disease as punishment of the patient concerned for some sin or offence, visible or invisible; prayer, self-purification, fasting, etc., as reformative measures for crime is something unique in the history of moral science. With this he initiates a new trend in ethics, and brings the inner being of man, the pivotal point of moral science into limelight. The moral efficacy of prayer is admitted by all faiths of the world. Psychologically, it exerts tremendous impact on the person concerned. It is through prayer that an individual cleanses off his offences, seen or unseen, detected or undetected in public life; and gets reformed. Gandhi's view on crime and punishment is quite in parity with the modern humanistic outlook. On the relation of means and ends his treatment of man as an end in himself is sound, noble, and hence promotes humanism. The concept of rights accruing from duty, from service to humanity is exemplified in Gandhi's life. The postulate of the freedom of the will is the nucleus of moral science. Unless an individual exercises his will freely he cannot be held responsible for actions. In spite of his firm belief in divine determinism Gandhi did not take the inexorable law of *Karma* and freedom of the will as antithetical. His boundless love for humanity inspired him to prescribe *purusakar* or personal endeavour through which an individual can come out of *Karmic* puzzle and become the architect of his fate. In short, our analysis reveals that these topics are primarily concerned with man, and hence these are "human, all to human."

The following chapter (seven) elucidates cardinal virtues in the perspective of traditional views, both Oriental and Occidental. The concept of the truth that Gandhi preached is not alien to human nature. Each and every individual is a spark of truth which, in its totality, an individual can never grasp due to imperfection but can realize it, come nearer it bit by bit. The prescription of relative truth as a beacon, a shield and buckler so long as absolute truth remains beyond grasp exhibits Gandhi's deep concern for human interest. Moreover, the bold proclamation that he would not find Truth or God in the cave of the Himalayas apart from humanity is an incontrovertible evidence of his burning humanism. The same conclusion follows from his concept of non-violence or *ahimsa*. The dumb millions of India were non-violent by nature, i.e., traditionally, psychologically and physically. And it was Gandhi's firm conviction that the history of mankind is a ceaseless progress towards non-violence. Moreover, truth and non-violence are two phases of the same reality. The few deviations from absolute non-violence that we observe here, as discussed above, like that of truth are apparent and not real, initial and not final. These apparent deviations arose out of his response to the various necessities, to the numerous demands of humanity. So these basic tenets of Gandhian thought, these two cardinal virtues of Gandhian ethics have roots in his humanism.

The same note predominates, as discussed above, in our elucidation of other cardinal virtues also. To avoid repetition we can roughly, and perhaps safely, say that the cardinal virtues that he prescribed and practised were solely aimed at the restoration of man to his true nature. It is man's return to himself, nay to his true self by dint of some self-imposed regulations independent of any extraneous conditions, i.e., through potentially inherent in himself. It is through the observance of fearlessness that Gandhi helped the people of India to regain their self-dignity, their lost paradise. The motive underlying the vow of *swadeshi* was to make the countrymen, especially the dumb millions, self-sufficient financially, and thereby to restore stability in Indian economy. To put it in other words, the *swadeshi* and *khadi* campaigns were launched to make the starving millions self-sufficient in every walk of life, i.e., fooding, clothing, housing, etc. In short, in his prescription of the cardinal vows, eleven in number, he fervently intended the people to attain freedom, both internally and externally. Man was the fundamental category, the only postulate of Gandhian thought.

The concluding discussion is on the humanism of Gandhi. All discussions on Gandhi have an inevitable end, i.e., they converge on his humanism. He never lost sight of man throughout life. His sole aim was to disalienate man in every sphere of life. His objective was to rehabilitate man—spiritually, morally, politically, socially, economically—in every field of life. He vehemently opposed everything that enslaved, degraded and humiliated man. Gandhi was the one who not only preached but practised and lived with the downtrodden, outcastes and untouchables. In stead of ruling the people, although he had the right, power and opportunity, he turned himself into one of them, nay into a servant of them. "Who else, I wonder, is a greater humanist than the one who tried to help, through his own suffering, the single largest group of human beings—the 60 million untouchables of India—to achieve equal citizenship rights with all other people."[8] Louis Fischer comments, "If man is to survive, if civilization is to survive and flower in freedom, truth, and decency, the remainder of the twentieth century and what lies beyond must belong not to Lenin or Trotsky, not to Marx or Mao or Ho or Che, but to Mahatma Gandhi."[9] Verily, because of his boundless love and service for humanity "he will be remembered as one of the very few who have set the stamp of an *idea* on an epoch."[10] Even a committed Marxist like C.G. Shah appraises, "We, socialists, treasure what was most precious in Gandhi's psyche, his deep humanism, his limitless love for fellow-men, his readiness to even squander away his life for their liberation *as he conceived it*.... We socialists are direct heirs of bourgeois humanist among whom Gandhi was one of the best."[11]

To sum up: In this treatise we have travelled a long distance, and covered the thoughts, both Oriental and Occidental. We have taken into account the views from Thales, the earliest Greek thinker, to existentialism, the contemporary trend of Western thought; from the Vedic concepts to up-to-date views of Indian thought. The motive is to study objectively; and examine and evaluate Gandhi's contribution to mankind, especially to moral science, in a wide perspective, in the background of human civilization. That is to say, we have tried to understand the moral concepts of Gandhi in the background of his mental development as well as in the context of his objective situation. This is a long, difficult, and perhaps an inconclusive, if not an impossible task. This is the reason why we do not claim, like Gandhi, to have the last word on the subject. Gandhian thought should be studied from the Gandhian standpoint, both in theory and practice. This idea is well expressed in the words of T.S. Eliot,

"These are only hints and guesses,
Hints followed by guesses; and the rest
Is prayer, observance, discipline, thought and action,"[12]

Still man does not yield. Man's success lies in his meliorism. In spite of riddles and 'contradictions' if Gandhi's method and outlook can ever be expressed in a word: it is humanistic. If the subject-matter that all the volumes of his *Collected Works* deal with can ever be expressed in a word: it is humanism. In this sense Gandhism is a synonym of humanism. With humanity Gandhi *was*. With humanity Gandhi *is*. And with humanity Gandhi *shall be*.

References

1. William Shakespeare, Julius Caesar, Act 5, Scene 5, in *William Shakespeare: The Complete Works*, p. 998.
2. H.T. Mazumdar, *Mahatma Gandhi: A Prophetic Voice*, p. 8.

3. *Harijan*, 28 January 1939, p. 445.
4. Erik H. Erikson, *Gandhi's Truth*, p. 396.
5. Jawaharlal Nehru, *An Autobiography*, p. 528.
6. *Harijan*, 30 September 1939, p. 288.
7. Subhash C. Kashyap, *The Unknown Nietzsche*, p. 1.
8. N.G. Ranga, 'The significance and implications of truth and non-violence in the world today,' in T.K. Mahadevan (ed.), *Truth and Non-Violence*, p. 252.
9. Louis Fischer cited in Shriman Narayan, *Mahatma Gandhi: The Atomic Man*, p. 186.
10. Edward Thompson, 'Gandhi: A Character Study,' in S. Radhakrishnan (ed.), *Mahatma Gandhi: Essays and Reflections on His Life and Works*, p. 269.
11. C.G. Shah, *Marxism, Gandhism, Stalinism*, p. 299.
12. T.S. Eliot, 'The Dry Salvages,' in *Four Quarters*, p. 44.

BIBLIOGRAPHY

Alexander, Horace : *Gandhi Through Western Eyes*, Asia Publishing House, Calcutta, 1969.

Amarji, Ranchodji : *Tarik-i-Sorath*, (trans. James Burgess) Trubner and Co., London, 1882.

Anand, Mulk Raj : *The Humanism of M.K. Gandhi*, University of Punjab, Chandigarh, 1967.

Andrews, C.F. : *Mahatma Gandhi's Ideas*, George Allen and Unwin Ltd., London, 1949.

Aristotle : *The Nicomachean Ethics*, (trans. J.A.K. Thomson, *The Ethics of Aristotle*), George Allen and Unwin Ltd., London, 1963.

Avinashilingam, T.S. : *Gandhi's Experiments in Education*, Ministry of Education, Govt. of India, New Delhi, 1960.

Barker, Ernest : *Greek Political Theory*, Methuen, London, 1967.

Barker, Herschel : *The Image of Man*, Harper and Brothers, New York, 1961.

Barr, F. Marry : *Conversations and Correspondence with Mahatma Gandhi*, International Book House, Bombay, 1949.

Basava : *Sayings of Basava*, (trans. P.G. Halakatti), Indian Antiquary, Vol. LI, 1922.

Bedekar, D.K. : *Towards Understanding Gandhi*, (ed. Rajabhau Gawande), Popular Prakashan, Bombay, 1975.

Bergson, Henry : *The Two Sources of Morality and Religion*, (trans. Audra and Others), Macmillan and Co., London, 1935.

Betai, Ramesh S. : *Gita and Gandhiji*, Gujrat Vidyapith, Ahmedabad, 1970.

Bhattacharyya Buddhadeva : *Evolution of the Political Philosophy of Gandhi*, Calcutta Book House, Calcutta, 1969.

The Holy Bible : Trinitarian Bible Society, London,1970.

Blackham, H.J. : *The Human Tradition*, Routledge and Kegan Paul Ltd., London, 1953.

— : *Six Existentialist Thinkers*, Routledge, London, 1961.

— (ed.) : *Objection to Humanism*, Constable, London, 1963.

Blanshard, Brand : *The Nature of Thought*, George Allen and Unwin Ltd., London, 2 Vols., 1964.

Bondurant, Joan V. : *Conquest of Violence: The Gandhian Philosophy of Conflict*, OUP (London), 1959.

Bose, Nirmal Kumar : *Cultural Anthropology*, Asia Publishing House, London, 1961.

— : *My Days with Gandhi*, Orient Longman, Calcutta, 1974.

— : *Selections from Gandhi*, NPH (Navajivan Publishing House, Ahmedabad), 1972.

— : *Studies in Gandhism*, Merit Publishers, Calcutta, 1962.

Both, R.B. : *Life and Work in India 1865-1899*, J.G. Hammond and Co., London, 1912.

Bradley, F.H. : *Appearance and Reality*, OUP, 1962.

— : *Ethical Studies*, OUP, 1962.

Brahmachari, S. Goverdhandas : *Mahatma Gandhi and Kavi Rajchandraji: Questions-Answers*, Srimad Rajchandra Gyan Pracharak Trust, Ahmedabad, n.d.

Brick-Panter, Simone : *Gandhi against Machiavellism*, Asia Publishing House, Bombay, 1966.

Brown, J.M. : *Gandhi's Rise to Power: Indian Politics 1915-1922*, Cambridge University Press, 1972.

Brown, Maurice and Francis Watson : *Talking of Gandhi*, Orient Longman, Calcutta, 1957.

Browning, Robert : *Poems of Robert Browning*, (ed. H. Milford), OUP, 1972.

Burnet, John : *Greek Philosophy*, Macmillan and Co., London, 1962.

Caird, John : *An Introduction to the Philosophy of Religion*, Chuckervertty, Chatterjee and Co., Calcutta, 1956.

Carus, Paul : *The Gospel of Buddha*, The Publications Division, Govt. of India, 1961.

Catlin, George : *In the Path of Mahatma Gandhi*, Macdonald and Co., London, 1948.

Chakravarty, Amiya : *Humanism and Indian Thought*, University of Madras, 1937.

— : *Modern Humanism: An Indian Perspective*, University of Madras, Madras, 1968.

Chatterjee, Margaret : *The Existentialist Outlook*, Orient Longman, Calcutta, 1973.

Chatterjee, S.C. : *The Problems of Philosophy*, University of Calcutta, Calcutta, 1964.

Chaucer, Geoffrey : *The Complete Works of Geoffrey Chaucer*, (ed. F.N. Robinson), OUP, 1974.

Chaudhuri, Nirad C. : *The Continent of Circe*, Chatto and Windus, London, 1965.

Chaudhury, P.C. Roy : *Gandhi's First Struggle in India*, NPH, 1955.

Condry, William : *Thoreau*, S. Chand and Co., Delhi, 1962.

Copleston, F. : *A History of Philosophy*, Vol. I, Burns Oates and Washbourne Ltd., London, 1951.

Damodaran, K. : *Man and Society in Indian Philosophy*, People's Publishing House, New Delhi, 1970.

Dandavate, Madhu : *Marx and Gandhi*, Popular Prakashan, Bombay, 1977.

Das, Rishi : *Gandhi-Charit*, (a Bengali Publication), Orient Book Company, Calcutta.

Dasgupta, Surama : *Development of Moral Philosophy in India*, Orient Longman, Calcutta, 1961.

Dasgupta, Surendra N. : *A History of Indian Philosophy*, Cambridge University Press, 1951.

Datta, D.M. and S.C. Chatterjee : *An Introduction to Indian Philosophy*, University of Calcutta, Calcutta, 1960.

— : *The Philosophy of Mahatma Gandhi*, University of Calcutta, Calcutta, 1968.

Davids, Rhys : *Dialogues of the Buddha* (Potthapada Sutta, Dialogues, I), Sacred Books of the Buddhists Series, OUP.

Davidson, William, L. : *Political Thought in England—The Utilitarians from Bentham to Mill*, OUP, 1947.

Desai, Mahadev : *Gandhiji in Indian Villages*, S. Ganesan, Madras, 1927.

— : *The Gospel of Selfless Action or the Gita According to Gandhi*, NPH, 1977.

— : *A Righteous Struggle*, NPH, 1951.

Devanesen, C.D.S. : *The Making of the Mahatma*, Orient Longman, Madras, 1969.

Dewey, John : *Human Nature and Conduct*, The Modern Library, New York, 1957.

— : *Logic, The Theory of Inquiry*, Henry Holt and Co., New York, 1938.

Dhawan, Gopinath : *The Political Philosophy of Mahatma Gandhi*, NPH, 1962.

Diwakar, R.R. : *Satyagraha: Its Technique and History*, Hind Kitabs, Bombay, 1946.

— : *Satyagraha: The Power of Truth*, Henry Regency Co., 1948.

Doke, J.J. : *M.K. Gandhi: An Indian Patriot in*

South Africa, The London Indian Chronicle, 1909.

Dresden, S. : *Humanism in the Renaissance*, World University Library, London, 1968.

Edman, Irwin (ed.) : *The Works of Plato* (trans. Benjamin Jowett), The Modern Library, New York, 1956.

Eliot, T.S. : *Four Quartets*, OUP, Delhi, 1977.

Engels, F. : *Anti-Duhring*, (trans. Emile Burns), Progress Publishers, Moscow, 1977.

Erikson, Erik H. : *Gandhi's Truth*, Fabar and Fabar Ltd., London, 1970.

Falckenberg, R. : *History of Modern Philosophy* (trans. A.C. Armstrong), Progressive Publishers, Calcutta, 1960.

Farquhar, J.N. : *Modern Religious Movements in India*, The Macmillan Co., New York, 1915.

Fischer, Louis : *The Life of Mahatma Gandhi*, Bharatiya Vidya Bhavan, Bombay, 1965, pts. I and II.

Fischer, Frederick, B. : *That Strange Little Brown Man*, Orient Longman, Calcutta, 1970.

Frankena, William and John T. Granrose (eds.) : *Introductory Readings in Ethics*, Prentice-Hall, Inc., New Jersey, 1974.

Fraser, Stuart (ed.) : *Education and Communism in China*, International Studies Group, Hong Kong, 1969.

Fromm, Erich : *Man For Himself*, Rinohart, New York, 1947.

— (ed.) : *Socialist Humanism*, Allen Lane The Penguin Press, London, 1967.

Gandhi, Madan G. : *Gandhian Aesthetics*, Vikas Bharati, Delhi, 1969.

— : *Gandhi and Marx*, Vikas Bharti, Chandigarh, 1969.

Gandhi, M.K. : *All Men are Brothers*, (comp. and ed. Krishna Kripalani), NPH, 1960.

— : *Ashram Observances in Action*, (trans. V.G. Desai), NPH, 1955.

Gandhi, M.K. : *An Autobiography*, NPH, 1959.

— : *Bapu's Letters to Mira*, NPH, 1949.

— : *The Collected Works of Mahatma Gandhi*, (*CWMG*), vols. I (1896-1897), 1959; II (1896-1897), 1959; III (1898-1903), 1960; IV (1903-1905), 1960; V (1905-1906) 1961; VI (1906-1907), 1961; VII (June-Dec. 1907), 1962; VIII (Jan.-Aug. 1908), 1962; IX (Sept. 1908-Nov. 1909), 1963; X (Nov. 1909-March 1911), 1963; XI (April 1911-March 1913), 1964; XII (April 1913-Dec. 1914), 1964; XIII (Jan. 1915-Oct. 1917), 1964; XIV (Oct. 1917-July 1918), 1965; XV (Oct. 1918-July 1919), 1965; XVI (Aug. 1919-Jan. 1920), 1965; XVII (Feb.-June 1920), 1965; XVIII (July-Nov. 1920), 1965; XIX (Nov. 1920-April 1921), 1966; XX (April-Aug. 1921), 1966; XXI (Aug.-Dec. 1921), 1966; XXII (Dec. 1921- March 1922), 1966; XXIII (March 1922-May 1924), 1967; XXIV (May-Aug. 1924), 1967; XXV (Aug. 1924-Jan. 1925), 1967; XXVI (Jan.-April 1925), 1967; XXVII (May-July 1925), 1968; XXVIII (Aug.-Nov. 1925), 1968; XXIX (Nov. 1925-Feb. 1926), 1968; XXX (Feb.-June 1926), 1968; XXXI (June-Nov. 1926), 1969; XXXII (Nov. 1926-Jan. 1927), 1969; XXXIII (Jan.-June 1927), 1969; XXXIV (June-Sept. 1927), 1969; XXXV (Sept. 1927-Jan. 1928), 1969; XXXVI (Feb.-June 1928), 1970; XXXVII (July-Oct. 1928), 1970; XXXVIII (Nov. 1928-Feb. 1929), 1970; XXXIX (Feb. 1929), 1970; XL (Feb.-May 1929), 1970; XLI (June-Oct. 1929), 1970; XLII (Oct. 1929-

Feb. 1930), 1970; XLIII (March-June 1939), 1971; XLIV (July-Dec. 1930), 1971; XLV (Dec. 1930-April 1931), 1971; XLVI (April 16-June 17, 1931), 1971; XLVII (June-Sept. 1931), 1971; XLVIII (Sept. 1931-Jan. 1932), 1971; XLIX (Jan.-May 1932), 1972; L (June-Aug. 1932), 1972; LI (Sept. 1-Nov. 15, 1932), 1972; LII (Nov. 1932-Jan. 1933), 1972; LIII (Jan.-March 1933), 1972; LIV (March 6-April 22, 1973), 1973; LV(April 23-Sept. 15, 1933), 1973; LVI (Sept. 16, 1933-Jan. 15, 1934), 1973; LVII (Jan. 16-May 17, 1934), 1974; LX (Dec. 16, 1934-April 24, 1935), 1974; LXV (March 15-July 31, 1937), 1976, The Publications Division, Govt. of India, New Delhi.

Gandhi, M.K. : *Communal Unity*, (ed. B. Kumarappa), NPH, 1949.

— : *Constructive Programme*, NPH, 1961.

— : *Ethical Religion*, NPH, 1968.

— : *For Pacifists*, NPH, 1949.

— : *From Yeravda Mandir*, (trans. from the original Gujarati by V.G. Desai), NPH, 1968.

— : *Gandhiji's Correspondence with the Government 1942-44*, NPH, 1945, (2nd edn.).

— : *Gandhiji's Correspondence with the Government 1944-47*, NPH, 1959.

— : *Hind Swaraj or Indian Home Rule*, NPH, 1946.

— : *Hindu Dharma*, NPH, 1950.

— : *In Search of the Supreme*, (ed. V.B. Kher), 3 Vols., NPH, 1961.

— : *The Moral Basis of Vegetarianism*, (comp. R.K. Prabhu), NPH, 1959.

Gandhi, M.K. : *My Philosophy of Life*, (ed. A.T. Hingorani), Pearl Publications Pvt. Ltd., Bombay, 1961.

— : *My Socialism*, (comp. R.K. Prabhu), NPH, 1969.

— : *The Nature Cure*, (ed. Ananda T. Hingorani), Pearl Publications Pvt. Ltd., Bombay, 1965.

Gandhi, M.K. : *Non-Violence in Peace and War*, (ed. B. Kumarappa), 2 Vols., NPH, 1962.

— : *Ruskin's Unto This Last: A Paraphrase*, NPH, 1968.

— : *Satyagraha*, (ed. B. Kumarappa), NPH, 1959.

— : *Satyagraha in South Africa*, (trans. from the Gujarati by V. G. Desai), NPH, 1928.

— : *Speeches and Writings of Mahatma Gandhi*, G.A. Natesan and Co., Madras, 1933 (4th edn.).

— : *Young India 1919-22*, S. Ganesan, Madras, 1922.

— : *Young India 1924-26*, S. Ganesan, Madras, 1927.

— : *Young India 1927-28*, S. Ganesan, Madras, 1935.

Gandhi, P. : *My Childhood with Gandhiji*, NPH, 1957.

Ganguli, B.N. : *Gandhi's Social Philosophy*, Vikas Publishing House, Delhi, 1973.

Gaur, V.P. : *Mahatma Gandhi*, Sterling Publishers Pvt. Ltd., New Delhi, 1977.

Gokhale, B.G. : *Indian Thought Through the Ages*, Asia Publishing House, Bombay, 1961.

Goldmann, Lucien : *Immanuel Kant*, (trans. Robert Black), NLB, London, 1971.

Gora (G. Ramchandra Rao) : *An Atheist with Gandhi*, NPH, 1951.

Government of India : *Gandhian Outlook and Techniques*, Ministry of Education, Govt. of India, 1953.

Hartmann, Edward Von : *Philosophy of the Unconscious*, Routledge and Kegan Paul Ltd., London, 1950.

Hastings, James (ed.) : *Encyclopaedia of Religion and Ethics*, T. and T. Clark, Edinburgh, Charles Scribners Sons., New York, 1925.

Hingorani, Ananda T. (ed.) : *The Teaching of the Gita*, Bharatiya Vidya Bhavan, Bombay, 1962.

Horsburgh, H.J.N. : *Non-Violence and Aggression*, OUP, 1968.

Hunter, W.E. (ed.) : *Imperial Gazetteer of India*, OUP, 1908.

Hutchins, R.M. (ed.) : 'An Essay Concerning Human Understanding' in *Great Books of the Western World, Locke, Berkeley, Hume*, The University of Chicago, Vol. XXXV, 1971.

— : *Great Books of the Western World*, University of Chicago, 1971.

Huxley, Aldous : *Ends and Means*, Chatto and Windus, London, 1957.

Iyer, Raghavan N. : *The Moral and Political Thought of Mahatma Gandhi*, OUP, 1973.

Jaggi, O.P. : *Religion, Practice and Science of Non-Violence*, Munshiram Manoharlal Publishers Pvt. Ltd., Delhi, 1974.

James, William : *The Varieties of Religious Experience*, Longmans, Green and Co., London, 1947.

Jaspers, Karl : *The Future of Mankind*, (trans. E.B. Ashton), The University of Chicago Press, 1961.

— : *Man in the Modern Age*, (trans. Eden and Cedar Paul), Routledge and Kegan Paul, London, 1966.

— : *The Perennial Scope of Philosophy*, (trans. Ralph Manheim), Routledge and Kegan Paul, London, 1950.

Jones, Mare Edmund : *Gandhi Lives*, Mckay Company, Philadelphia, 1948.

Joseph, H.W.B. : *An Introduction to Logic*, OUP, 1970.

Kalarthi, Mukulbhai : *Ba and Bapu*, (trans. from Gujarati by Gurdail Mallik), NPH, 1962.

Kalelkar, K. (ed.) : *To a Gandhian Capitalist*, Jamnalal Seva Trust, Wardha, 1951.

Kant : *Critique of Practical Reason*, (trans. T.K. Abbott), in R.M. Hutchins (ed.): *Great Books of the Western World*, Kant, The University of Chicago, Vol. XLII, 1952.

Kant : *Groundwork of the Metaphysics of Morals*, (trans. H.J. Paton), Hutchinson University Library; London, 1962.

Kashyap, Subhas C. : *The Unknown Nietzsche*, National Publishing House, Delhi, 1970.

King, Beatrice : *An Outline of Education in the U.S.S.R.*, International Publishing House, Calcutta, 1945.

Kipling, Rudyard : *Barrack-Room Ballads and Other Verses*, Methuen and Co. Ltd., London, 1956.

osambi, D.D. : *The Culture and Civilization of Ancient Indian Historical Outline*, Routledge and Kegan Paul, London, 1965.

K 'uran, George : *Ahimsa: Gautama to Gandhi*, Sterling Publishers Pvt. Ltd., New Delhi, 1973.

Krip lani, J.B. : *Gandhian Thought*, Orient Longman, Calcutta, 1961.

— : *The Latest Fad: Basic Education*, Hindustani Talimi Sangh, Wardha, 1954.

Kurtz, Paul (ed.) : *Moral Problems in Contemporary Society*, Prentice-Hall, New Jersey, 1969.

Lamont, Corliss : *The Philosophy of Humanism*, Pemberton Publishing Co. Ltd., London, 1965.

Levi, Sylvain : *Eastern Humanism*, University of Dacca, Dacca, 1922.

Lewis, John : *Marxism and the Open Mind*,

Routledge and Kegan Paul, London, 1957.

Lewis, John : *Science, Faith and Scepticism*, Lawrence and Wishart, London, 1959.

— : *Socialism and the Individual*, Lawrence and Wishart, London, 1961.

Lillie, William : *An Introduction to Ethics*, Allied Publishers Pvt. Ltd., Calcutta, 1967.

Lodge, R.C. : *Plato's Theory of Ethics*, Routledge and Kegan Paul Ltd., London, 1950.

Lotze, Hermann : *Outlines of a Philosophy of Religion*, Chuckerverty, Chatterjee and Co., Calcutta, 1954.

Lucas, J.R. : *The Freedom of Will*, Clarendon Press, Oxford, 1970.

Mahendranath Gupta : *The Gospel of Sri Ramkrishna*, (trans. Swami Nikhilananda), Sri Ramakrishna Math, Madras, 1974.

Macdonell, Arthur A. : *A History of Sanskrit Literature*, Munshiram Manoharlal, New Delhi, 1972.

Machiavelli N. : *The Prince*, (trans. George Bull), Penguin Books, 1970.

Mackenzie, John S. : *A Manual of Ethics*, OUP, Delhi, 1977.

Mahadevan, T.K. (ed.) : *Truth and Non-Violence: A UNESCO Symposium on Gandhi*, Gandhi Peace Foundation, New Delhi, 1970.

Maitra, S.K. : *The Ethics of the Hindus*, University of Calcutta, Calcutta, 1963.

Majumdar, B.B. (ed.) : *Gandhian Concept of State*, M.C. Sarkar and Sons, Calcutta, 1957.

Maritain, Jacques : *Man and the State*, Phoenix, 1961.

Marx, Karl : *Capital*, Foreign Languages Publishing House, Moscow, 1954.

— : *Economic and Philosophic Manuscripts of 1844*, Progress Publishers, Moscow, 1977.

— : *The Holy Family*, Progress Publishers, Moscow, 1977.

Marx, Karl : *On Religion*, Progress Publishers, Moscow, 1977.

Marx, Karl and F. Engels : *Manifesto of the Communist Party*, Progress Publishers, 1966.

Mashruwala, K.G. : *Gandhi and Marx*, NPH, 1960.

Mazumdar, H.T. : *Mahatma Gandhi: A Prophetic Voice*, NPH, 1963.

Menon, V. Lakshmi : *Ruskin and Gandhi*, Sarva Seva Sangh Prakashan, Varanasi, 1965.

Mill, J.S. : *Utilitarianism* in R.M. Hutchins (ed.), *Great Books of the Western World, J.S. Mill*, University of Chicago, Vol. XLIII, 1971.

Mill, J.S. : *Utilitarianism* (ed. K.C. Banerji), Ram Narain Lal, Allahabad, 1928.

Miller, Rene-Fulop : *Gandhi : The Holy Man*, (trans. F.S. Flint and D.F. Tait), G.P. Putnams Sons, London, 1931.

Milton, John : *Paradise Lost, Book III*, (ed. M. Macmillan), Macmillan and Co. Ltd., London, 1953.

Muirhead, J.H. and S. Radhakrishnan : *Contemporary Indian Philosophy*, George Allen and Unwin Ltd., London, 1966.

Mukherjee, D.P. : *Diversities*, People's Publishing House, New Delhi, 1958.

Mukherjee, Radha Kamal : *The Way of Humanism: East and West*, Academic Books, New Delhi, 1968.

Mure, G.R.G. : *The Philosophy of Hegel*, OUP, 1965.

Murthi, V.V. Ramana : *Non-Violence in Politics: A Study of Gandhian Techniques and Thinking*, Frank Bros. and Co., Delhi, 1958.

Myrdal, Gunnar : *Asian Drama: An Inquiry into the Poverty of Nations*, Penguin Books, 1968.

Nanak : *Selections from the Sacred Writings of Sikhs*, UNESCO, George Allen and Unwin Ltd., London, 1960.

Narasimhaiah, C.D. (ed.) : *Gandhi and the West*, University of Mysore, Mysore, 1964.

Narayan, Shriman : *Gandhi: The Man and His Thought*, Publications Division, Govt. of India, 1969.

— : *Mahatma Gandhi: The Atomic Man*, Somaiya Publications Pvt. Ltd., Bombay, 1971.

Nehru, Jawaharlal : *An Autobiography*, Allied Publishers Pvt. Ltd., Bombay, 1962.

— : *Independence and After*, The Publications Division, Govt. of India, 1949.

Nehru, Jawaharlal : *Mahatma Gandhi*, The Signet Press, Calcutta, 1949.

Nietzsche, F. : *Beyond Good and Evil*, (trans. Helen Zimmern), George Allen and Unwin Ltd., London, 1923.

Palgrave, F.T. (ed.) : *The Golden Treasury*, Collins Clear Type Press, London, 1861.

Parvate, T.V. : *Bal Gangadhar Tilak*, NPH, 1972.

Petrosyan, M. : *Humanism*, Progress Publishers, Moscow, 1972.

Pillai, G.P. : *Representative Indians*, George Routledge and Sons Ltd., London, 1897.

Plato : *Great Books of the Western World*, Plato, (ed. R.M. Hutchins), University of Chicago, Vol. VII, 1971.

Pope, Alexander : *The Poems of Alexander Pope*, (ed. John Butt), Methuen, London, 1963.

Power, Paul F. : *Gandhi on the World Affairs*, Allen and Unwin, London, 1961.

Prasad, Rajendra : *Mahatma Gandhi and Bihar: Some Reminiscences*, Hind Kitabs, Bombay, 1949.

— : *Satyagraha in Champaran*, NPH, 1949.

Pyarelal : *The Epic Fast*, Mohanlal Maganlal Bhatt, Ahmedabad, 1932.

Pyarelal : *Mahatma Gandhi: The Last Phase*, NPH, 2 Vols., 1958.

— : *A Nation Builder at Work*, NPH, 1952.

Radhakrishnan, S. : *Indian Philosophy*, George Allen and Unwin Ltd., London, 2 Vols., 1962.

— : *The Reign of Religion in Contemporary Philosophy*, Macmillan and Co., London, 1920.

— (ed.) : *Mahatma Gandhi: Essays and Reflections on His Life and Works*, Jaico Publishing House, Bombay, 1956.

— (ed.) : *Mahatma Gandhi: 100 Years*, Gandhi Peace Foundation, New Delhi, 1968.

Radhakrishnan, S. and Raju P.T. (eds.) : *The Concept of Man*, George Allen and Unwin Ltd., London, 1966.

Raju, P.T. : *Idealistic Thought of India*, George Allen and Unwin Ltd., London, 1953.

Ramakantha : *Commentary on Bhagabad Gita*, Nirnaya Sagar Press, Bombay, 1943.

Rao, K. Ramakrishna : *Gandhi and Pragmatism*, Oxford and IBH Publishing Co., Calcutta, 1968.

Ray, Benoy Gopal : *Gandhian Ethics*, NPH, 1950.

Rogers, R.A.P. : *A Short History of Ethics*, Macmillan and Co. Ltd., London, 1948.

Rolland, Romain : *The Life of Ramakrishna*, (trans. E.F. Malcolm-Smith), Advaita Ashram, Calcutta, 1974.

— : *Mahatma Gandhi: The Man Who Became One With the Universal Being*, (trans. Catherine D. Groth), The Swarthmore Press Ltd., London, 1924.

Ross, David : *Aristotle*, Methuen, London, 1964.

— *Kant's Ethical Theory*, Oxford, the Clarendon Press, 1962.

Roy, Kshitis (ed.) : *Gandhi Memorial Peace Number*, The Visva-Bharati Quarterly, Santiniketan, 1949.

Ruskin, John : *Unto This Last*, (ed. J.D.C. Monfries and G.E. Hollingworth), OUP, Calcutta, 1978.

Sandburg, Carl : *The People, Yes*, Harcourt Brace, New York, 1936.

Sartre, J.P. : *Being and Nothingness*, (trans. H.E. Barnes), Methuen and Co., London, 1957.

Existentialism and Humanism, (trans. Philip Mairet), Methuen, London, 1963.

Sastri, K.S. Ramaswami : *The Evolution of Indian Mysticism*, International Book House Ltd., Bombay, n.d.

Seligman, E.R.A. (ed.) : *Encyclopaedia of the Social Sciences*, The Macmillan Co., New York, Vols. II, IV, V, VII.

Sethi, J.D. : *Gandhi Today*, Vikas, New Delhi, 1978.

Shah, C.G. : *Ends and Means*, Popular Prakashan, Bombay, 1972.

— : *Marxism, Gandhism, Stalinism*, Popular Prakashan, Bombay, 1963.

Shah, O.P. and Mukherjee, D. (eds.) : *Education in India Today*, Firma KLM Pvt. Ltd., Calcutta, 1980.

Sahani, Ranjee : *Mr. Gandhi*, The Macmillan Co., New York, 1961.

Shakespeare, William : *William Shakespeare: The Complete Works*, (ed. Peter Alexander), Collins, London, 1964.

Sharma, B.S. : *Gandhi as a Political Thinker*, Indian Press Pvt. Ltd., Allahabad, 1956.

Sharma, I.C. : *Ethical Philosophies of India*, George Allen and Unwin Ltd., London, 1965.

Sharp, Gene : *Gandhi Wields the Weapon of Moral Power*, NPH, 1960.

Sheean, Vincent : *Lead, Kindly Light*, Random House, New York, 1949.

Shelvankar, K.S. : *Ends are Means*, Lindsay Drummond Ltd., London, 1938.

Shridharani, Krishnalal : *War Without Violence*, Harcourt Brace, New York, 1939.

Shukla, C. : *Gandhi's Views of Life*, Bharatiya Vidya Bhavan, Bombay, 1956.

Sitaramayya, B.P. : *The History of the Indian National Congress*, The Working Committee of the Congress, Allahabad, 1935.

Snow, Edgar : *Red China Today: The Other Side of the River*, Penguin Books, London, 1970.

Spratt, Philip : *Gandhism: An Analysis*, The Huxley Press, Madras, 1939.

Stace, W.T. : *The Philosophy of Hegel*, Dover Publications, New York, 1955.

Sub-Committee for celebration of Gandhi Centenary Abroad, New Delhi : *Gandhiji and the Emancipation of Man*, New Delhi, 1970.

Suda, J.P. : *Manu, Marx and Gandhi*, Jai Prakash Nath, Meerut, 1967.

Sunavala, A.J. : *Vijaya Dharma Suri, His Life and Work*, Cambridge University Press, 1922.

Tahtinen, Unto : *Ahimsa (Non-Violence) in Indian Tradition*, Rider and Harper, London, 1976.

Tendulkar, D.G. : *Gandhi in Champaran*, The Publications Division, Govt. of India, 1957.

— : *Mahatma: Life of Mohandas Karamchand Gandhi*, Publications Division, Govt. of India, 8 Vols., 1969.

— (ed.) : *Gandhiji: His Life and Work*, Karnatak Publishing House, Bombay, 1949.

Tennyson, A.L. : *Poems of Alfred Lord Tennyson*, (ed. Charles Tennyson), Collins, London, 1970.

Thoreau, H. D. : *Collected Poems of Henry Thoreau*,

(ed. Carl Bode), Packard and Co., Chicago, 1943.

Thoreau, H.D. : *Henry D. Thoreau: Selected Writings on Nature and Liberty*, (ed. Oscar Cargill), The Liberal Arts Press, New York, 1952.

Tod, James : *Travels in Western India*, W.H. Allen and Co., London, 1839.

Tolstoy, Leo : *The Kingdom of God and Peace Essays*, (trans. A. Maude), OUP, 1936.

Topa, Ishwara : *Ethos of Non-Violence*, NPH, 1964.

Trotsky, Dewey Novack : *Their Morals and Ours*, Merit Publishers, New York, 1966.

Umasvami : *Tattavarthadhigama-Sutra*, (trans. J.L. Jaini), The Central Jaina Publishing House, Arrah, India, n.d.

Underhill, Evelyn : *Mysticism*, George Allen and Unwin Ltd., London, 1952.

Underwood, A.C. : *Contemporary Thought of India*, Williams Norgate Ltd., London, 1930.

Unnithan, T.K.N. and Yogendra Singh : *Traditions of Non-Violence,* Arnold-Heinemann India, New Delhi, 1973.

Varma, Viswanath Prasad : *The Political Philosophy of Mahatma Gandhi and Sarvodaya*, Lakshmi Narain Agarwal, Agra, 1959.

Verma, Surendra : *Metaphysical Foundation of Mahatma Gandhi's Thought*, Orient Longman, Calcutta, 1970.

Vivekananda Swami : *The Complete Works of Swami Vivekananda*, Advaita Ashram, Calcutta, 1972.

Wadiyar, J.C. : *The Gita and Indian Culture*, Orient Longman, Calcutta, 1968.

Warren, H.C. : *Buddhism in Translations*, Harvard University Press, 1922.

Watson, J.S. : *Plato and Xenophen-Socratic Discourses*, J.M. Dent and Sons Ltd., London, n.d.

Wayper, C.L. : *Political Thought*, The English University Press, London, 1964.

Wilcox, John T. : *Truth and Value in Nietzsche*, the University of Michigan Press, 1974.

Wolfson, H.A. : *The Philosophy of Spinoza*, Meridian Books, New York, 1958.

Woodcock. George : *Anarchism*, Penguin Books, 1963.

Wordsworth, William : *William Wordsworth: Selected Poems*, (ed. H.M. Margoliouth) Collins, London, 1970.

Young India (Selections), pt. I (1919-1932), II (1924-1926), 1927; and III (1927-1928), 1935, Madras.

PERIODICALS

Gandhi Marg, New Delhi
Harijan, Ahmedabad
The Indian Review, Madras
The Modern Review, Calcutta
Science and Society, London
Young India, Ahmedabad
The Times of India, Delhi

Index